# Praise for
## *Software Build Systems*

"This book represents a thorough and extensive treatment of the software build process including the choices, benefits, and challenges of a well designed build process. I recommend it not only to all software build engineers but to all software developers since a well designed build process is key to an effective software development process."

— **Kevin Bodie**, Director Software Development, Pitney Bowes Inc.

"An excellent and detailed explanation of build systems, an important but often overlooked part of software development projects. The discussion of productivity as related to build systems is, alone, well worth the time spent reading this book."

— **John M. Pantone**, Objectech Corporation, VP,
IT Educator and Course Developer

"Peter Smith provides an interesting and accessible look into the world of software build systems, distilling years of experience and covering virtually every type of tool in the build engineer's toolbox. Well organized, well written, and very thorough; I would recommend this book to anyone with a build system under their responsibility."

— **Jeff Overbey**, Project Co-Lead, Photran

"*Software Build Systems* teaches how to think about building software. It surveys the tools and techniques for building software products and the ways things go wrong. This book will appeal to those new to build systems as well as experienced build system engineers."

— **Monte Davidoff**, Software Development Consultant,
Alluvial Software, Inc.

# Software Build Systems

# Software Build Systems

*Principles and Experience*

Peter Smith

✦ Addison-Wesley

Upper Saddle River, NJ • Boston • Indianapolis • San Francisco
New York • Toronto • Montreal • London • Munich • Paris • Madrid
Cape Town • Sydney • Tokyo • Singapore • Mexico City

Many of the designations used by manufacturers and sellers to distinguish their products are claimed as trademarks. Where those designations appear in this book, and the publisher was aware of a trademark claim, the designations have been printed with initial capital letters or in all capitals.

Electric Cloud, ElectricAccelerator, and SparkBuild are registered trademarks of Electric Cloud, Inc.

The author and publisher have taken care in the preparation of this book, but make no expressed or implied warranty of any kind and assume no responsibility for errors or omissions. No liability is assumed for incidental or consequential damages in connection with or arising out of the use of the information or programs contained herein.

The publisher offers excellent discounts on this book when ordered in quantity for bulk purchases or special sales, which may include electronic versions and/or custom covers and content particular to your business, training goals, marketing focus, and branding interests. For more information, please contact:

> U.S. Corporate and Government Sales
> (800) 382-3419
> corpsales@pearsontechgroup.com

For sales outside the United States, please contact:

> International Sales
> international@pearson.com

Visit us on the Web: informit.com/aw

*Library of Congress Cataloging-in-Publication Data:*

Smith, Peter, 1970-

   Software build systems : principles and experience / Peter Smith.
      p. cm.
   Includes bibliographical references and index.
   ISBN-13: 978-0-321-71728-3 (hardback : alk. paper)
   ISBN-10: 0-321-71728-7 (hardback : alk. paper)  1.  Compilers (Computer programs)
2.  Programming software. 3.  Self-adaptive software. 4.  Application software--Development--Computer programs.  I. Title.
   QA76.76.C65S65 2011
   005.4'53--dc22
                          2010051013

> Pearson Education, Inc.
> Rights and Contracts Department
> 501 Boylston Street, Suite 900
> Boston, MA 02116
> Fax (617) 671-3447

ISBN-13: 978-0-321-71728-3
ISBN-10: 0-321-71728-7

Text printed in the United States on recycled paper at Courier in Westford, Massachusetts.

First printing March 2011

**Editor-in-Chief**
Mark Taub

**Executive Editor**
Chris Guzikowski

**Senior Development Editor**
Chris Zahn

**Managing Editor**
Kristy Hart

**Project Editor**
Anne Goebel

**Copy Editor**
Krista Hansing
Editorial Services

**Indexer**
WordWise Publishing
Services, LLC

**Proofreader**
Apostrophe Editing
Services

**Editorial Assistant**
Raina Chrobak

**Interior Designer**
Gary Adair

**Cover Designer**
Anne Jones

**Compositor**
Gloria Schurick

*To Grace and Stan*

# Contents

# Preface

Are you a software developer? Are you interested in how build systems work? You're reading this book; so there's a good chance you answered "Yes" to both questions. On the other hand, many software developers aren't interested in how their program is compiled. Most people just want to press a button and have their source code turned into an executable program. If they need to fix a bug, they change the source code and press the same button again. Their joy is in seeing their program do all the exciting things it's supposed to do. The build system is just something that needs to be there in the background.

Anything more than a small collection of source files requires some type of automated build system. This may be a shell script that you run after each source code change, a makefile that knows the relationship between the source and object files, or a more complex build framework that scales to thousands of source files.

If you've developed code in a UNIX or Windows command-line environment, the following command should look familiar:

```
cc -o sorter main.c sort.c files.c tree.c merge.c
```

In this example, five C-language files are being compiled and linked to create a single executable program, named sorter. This may be unfamiliar to those who use an integrated development environment (IDE), but it's essentially the same as creating an IDE project with five source files and then pressing the build button on the toolbar.

After you've compiled your program a few times, you'll probably decide to store this command in a shell script and rerun it any time you make a code change. Alternatively, you can retrieve the command from your command-line history and replay the sequence each time you modify the code.

If you have some basic knowledge of the Make tool, you can create yourself a makefile and type make each time you need to rebuild. The advantage of Make is that it rebuilds the program only if any of the source files changed since the last compilation. Here's a simple makefile for compiling the sorter example:

```
sorter: main.c sort.c files.c tree.c merge.c
        cc -o sorter main.c sort.c files.c tree.c merge.c
```

If you're familiar with Make, you'll immediately realize that this isn't a good way to write a makefile. The first mistake is that the source files are listed twice, once for the dependency relationship and a second time in the compilation command. Next, all source files are compiled each time you rebuild the program, even if they haven't all been modified. Finally, there's no mention of dependencies that a C file may have on header files.

A better solution is to break up the compilation steps so that each source file is compiled, and recompiled, independently of the others. Additionally, there should be dependency files (with a suffix of .d) to track header file usage. The list goes on, so rather than go into all the technical details, take a look at the final makefile that does everything you need:

```
SOURCES = main.c sort.c files.c tree.c merge.c

OBJECTS = $(SOURCES:.c=.o)

sorter: $(OBJECTS)
        $(CC) -o $@ $^
-include $(SOURCES:.c=.d)

%.d: %.c
        @$(CC) -MM $(CPPFLAGS) $< | sed 's#\(.*\)\.o: #\1.o
 \1.d: #g' > $@
```

That's all there is to it—a simple makefile that does the bare-minimum amount of work, with the least amount of repetition. Easy, right?

If you're a developer and not a build expert, though, do you really understand what's going on in the previous example? A seasoned Make expert certainly understands the syntax and would probably suggest a more efficient way of achieving the same result. However, most of us who just want a push-button build are destined to waste a lot of time getting the makefile correct in the first place.

Build systems tend to be complex to implement and maintain. A badly designed build system can waste many hours if a file isn't recompiled when it should have been. When scaled to thousands of source files, a developer can literally waste half a day tracking down a problem, only to find that starting the build from scratch (removing all the object files) is the only way to make things work. So much for a push-button build!

# Why Do Build Systems Become Complex?

You might be surprised to read that build systems can be complex and hard to maintain. With graphical user interfaces so common these days, you'd expect build tools to be equally simple to use. Unfortunately, many see creating a build system as a black art. Only a few knowledgeable gurus understand the full syntax of the build tool or the subtleties in the dependency system. Although IDE-based build tools go part of the way toward solving this problem, they can't support the complexities of a large-scale build system.

In most cases, a software product starts with a small number of source files that are compiled and linked into a program. A simple makefile is sufficient in this case, and these can be thrown together in a couple hours by copying the makefile template from a user manual. For several months, nobody needs to change this build system, aside from adding new source files or libraries.

After a while, people start to see problems in the build process. They notice that files aren't recompiled when they should be, or perhaps that files are incorrectly being recompiled when none of the data they depend on has changed. In other cases, files may be compiled multiple times in the same build, leading to slower build times. It quickly becomes part of the engineering culture to always do a "clean build" (removing all object files first) or to modify files for the sole purpose of making them recompile.

When this simple build system becomes painful to use, a makefile expert needs to rethink the design. They might create a framework that solves all the build problems, while keeping the implementation detail away from the end users. For example, software developers want to have visibility into the list of source files, libraries, and compilation flags being used, but they aren't interested in how the dependencies are managed. For example:

```
SOURCES := main.c sort.c files.c tree.c merge.c

PROGRAM := sorter
LIBRARIES := libc libz

include framework.mk
```

The end goal is to have a correct and easy-to-use build system, while hiding all the complexity inside the framework.mk file. This is an ideal solution for the software developer who just wants a push-button build.

This framework approach works efficiently for a while, although growing pains start some time in the future. This is particularly true for a successful product whose software grows over a number of years. The build system that worked for a small-to-medium product no longer works when the product scales.

Consider how you'd integrate a new code module purchased from a third-party vendor. The new code already has its own build system and uses a different build framework than your original product. When developers modify the code, they create interdependencies between this newly acquired code and your existing code base, requiring the build system to understand the more complex file relationships. The end result is that one or both of the build frameworks requires significant rework—and possibly a complete rewrite.

As frameworks grow over time, maintaining them properly becomes challenging. In some cases, the original author of the framework is no longer available to make changes, so a nonguru steps in to perform the work. Developers who lack sufficient build experience often use quick-and-dirty techniques to get the software to build. As discussed later, these techniques include badly written shell scripts, copious use of symbolic links, and, worst of all, duplicate copies of source files. The build process becomes a rat's nest of complexity that nobody is comfortable maintaining.

It's sad that many organizations don't feel compelled to fix their build system. If they're experts in some other field (such as computer gaming, telecommunications, or business applications), their enthusiasm is directed toward creating their product and adding new features to entice and excite their end customer. The build system is viewed as a necessary part of the product life cycle, but people don't see it as their job to fix. The task certainly never appears in a company's corporate objectives or quarterly feature plan.

As you'll see throughout this book, plenty of issues must be considered when designing a build system. It's not just a matter of having a makefile guru on call to help with problems. You should also keep the development environment in a maintainable state. The time and money spent cleaning up a build system can pay off many times when you consider a software team's overall productivity.

## The True Cost of a Build System

If you don't already believe that a reliable build system is important, think about the true cost. That is, what costs will you incur if you don't have a good build system? These aren't numbers that appear on any accountant's balance sheet; they're hidden inside the day-to-day productivity of software developers.

One industry survey [1] found that developers perceived an average productivity loss of 12% due to build problems, although some of the respondents felt that 20%–30% was not uncommon. It's worth noting that this survey focused on smaller development groups (with less than 20 people), who likely didn't suffer from the scalability problems encountered with much larger software.

Let's start by assuming that all software developers in your team lose 10% of their time to problems with the build system. Your reaction to this figure will vary, based on your previous experience with software projects. For some people, 10% may seem like an exaggerated figure, but for many groups, this is on the low side.

What are the reasons for this 10% loss of productivity? Consider some typical problems your team has almost certainly experienced in the past:

- **Bad dependencies causing false compile errors:** The build system has somehow acquired incorrect dependency information and is failing to recompile parts of the source code correctly. When this happens, the developers focus all their time on trying to complete a successful build. They're faced with cryptic error messages completely unrelated to the area of code they've been changing. Until these are fixed, they're unable to proceed with productive work.

- **Bad dependencies that create failed software images:** As in the previous case, bad dependencies cause parts of the build to compile incorrectly. However, instead of giving a compilation error, the program no longer generates the correct output. This simply gives the developer and software testers the impression that the code is buggy, and they often blame themselves instead of the build system. Developers waste a day or two trying to debug a test failure, only to discover that their private code changes aren't causing the problem. Starting with a fresh build tree makes the problem go away.

- **Slow compilation:** This is more of a problem for larger software systems, because smaller software can be built in a matter of minutes. If your software code base requires many hours to compile, developers waste time while they wait for the compilation to complete. This is particularly troublesome for incremental builds in which changing a single source file can result in a delay of 5–10 minutes before the program is ready to execute again.

You may feel that people can productively do other work while they wait for their compilation, but this isn't always the case. Developers have many types of "waiting" activities, such as reading the latest news headlines, updating social networking sites, getting more coffee, or going off to chat with a friend. Even if a developer can multitask while the build completes, the cost of context switching between the different tasks is a productivity loss. Developers can get distracted and completely forget about one of the tasks they were working on.

- **Time spent updating build description files:** If the software build framework isn't trivial to understand, developers may need to ask an expert to make modifications. For example, if they need to add a new type of source file or a new compilation tool, they must first engage in a discussion with a build guru. This can take days of waiting while the build guru finds time to help. After that, the build guru might need a few weeks to complete the job.

If you now believe that a 10% productivity loss is a realistic number, what's the financial cost of this loss? The best way to evaluate this is to determine 10% of your organization's salary payment. This clearly doesn't apply if you're volunteering to write the software (as is commonly the case in the open-source world), but the numbers are interesting all the same.

Assume that you have ten software engineers, each of which is paid $75,000 per year. This is high for some cities and low for others, so it's worth evaluating the numbers from your own perspective. An accountant would likely double this estimate when considering the additional costs of employee medical benefits, electricity, rent, parking, and other perks a developer enjoys. Assume, therefore, that each developer costs $150,000 per year.

> Thus, the total cost of paying your developers to deal with build problems is
> *10% x US$150,000 per year x 10 developers = $150,000 per year*

That's equivalent to having a full-time developer sitting around for a whole year without doing any productive work! If you assume 250 working days per year, your company is paying $600 every day simply because of build problems!

If you were a software manager, what would you consider to be more profitable? Continuing to pay $600 per day for your team to waste time, or paying $600 per day for a few months to hire a new build guru to fix your problems? It's definitely worth considering what your own organization is doing. Remember, a company can make a profit in two ways: either by increasing revenue by selling more of the product, or by reducing the cost associated with creating the product in the first place.

## The Focus of This Book

You should spend time reading this book for two reasons:

- **To understand the basic principles underlying a build system:** This book provides an end-to-end survey of build system features and usage scenarios, giving you an understanding of how a build tool performs its work.

- **To gather more experience about build systems:** This book encapsulates years of experience in creating and maintaining build systems, using many different build tools. After reading this book, you can avoid making the same trial-and-error mistakes that previous build system developers have made.

Armed with such knowledge, you can make well-informed choices on which build tool to use, how to construct a reliable build system, and how to foresee traps and pitfalls before they impact your productivity. The outcome is that building software should get faster, easier, and more reliable.

It's also important to note what this book does not attempt to address:

- **Not a hands-on tutorial:** Except for a few small examples (such as those in Chapter 2, "A Make-Based Build System"), this book doesn't provide a hands-on tutorial on any particular build tool or technology. Popular build tools already have web sites and books devoted to teaching you every syntactic and semantic detail you'll ever need. Refer to those books for the finer details of each tool.

- **Doesn't show a fully functional build system:** Although this book contains a number of examples on how to use each build tool, and many supporting tools, it doesn't demonstrate the end-to-end creation of a full build system. Again, you should refer to each build tool's documentation to see fully worked-out examples.

Of course, read this book first so that you understand the pros and cons of each build tool and can judge for yourself which features your build system should use.

Instead of staying specific to a single development environment or programming language, this book offers examples and concepts from a variety of different angles:

- **C/C++ builds:** This is perhaps the most traditional type of build process. This style of building originated in the 1970s and hasn't changed much since then. The only recent challenge is the growth in the number of files and third-party libraries that are now used in a typical software product.

- **Java builds:** The Java language became popular in the late 1990s and has had a considerable impact on the design of build systems. As one example, Java source files must be stored in a directory hierarchy that matches the software package structure.

- **C# builds:** Whereas C, C++, and Java are platform-neutral programming languages and can thus be used on any operating system (such as Linux, Solaris, Mac OS X, and Windows), the C# build environment is more tailored toward the Microsoft way of doing things.

In addition to covering multiple programming languages, this book discusses two different approaches to constructing large software products:

- **Monolithic builds:** In this approach, the entire code base is compiled from source code into an executable program in a single build process. This is a common approach for small programs, but it doesn't scale well because it leads to large source trees and long compilation times.

- **Component builds:** In contrast to monolithic builds, this approach breaks the source code into multiple stages, each compiled separately. The final step is to integrate the various prebuilt components, to produce the final executable program.

Finally, this book goes beyond the common assumptions that Make is the primary tool of choice for C/C++ development and that all Java and C# software should be built inside an IDE.

## Who Should Read This Book?

This book was written with several audiences in mind, although the primary focus is software developers:

- **Developers:** If you're a software developer with years of experience writing source code but only minimal experience with build systems, you can learn about the issues involved in constructing and maintaining a build system. You can also study the different tools that describe the build process.

- **Managers:** From this book, you can learn the concepts and tricks-of-the-trade at a fairly high level instead of seeing too much of the complex detail. This enables you to evaluate the work your team is doing, and ask the appropriate "direction-setting" questions.

- **Build gurus:** Even with years of experience in constructing build systems, you can expect to learn new things. Not only will you be exposed to modern build tools that you may never have used, but the discussions on scalability and performance of large build systems will make you think twice when you start to write your next build framework.

---

## How This Book Is Organized

This book is divided into four main parts, each looking at build systems from a slightly different angle. Depending on your experience and level of interest, you might choose to focus on different parts of the book. Novice developers should focus on Parts I and II, whereas more experienced users should skim through Part I but focus their attention on Parts II, III, and IV.

### Part I: The Basics

This first part provides a gentle introduction to build systems, for software developers who haven't had much exposure to the topic. Even advanced users should skim these chapters to ensure that they have a complete picture of the basic concepts. For example, C/C++ developers can learn new things about the C# language.

Chapter 1, "Build System Overview," provides an introduction to high-level build system concepts such as source and object trees, build tools, and compilation tools. Chapter 2, "A Make-Based Build System," provides a quick tutorial on writing a makefile, for those who have never done so. Chapter 3, "The Runtime View of a Program," describes the structure of a program as it executes on a computer, with the goal of describing what a build system needs to construct. Chapter 4, "File Types and Compilation Tools," goes into detail on the different types of input and output file used in the build process and uses examples in the C/C++, Java, and C# languages. Chapter 5, "Subtargets and Build Variants," describes the basic idea behind build variants, which later chapters cover in more detail.

After reading Part I, you'll have a good understanding of the basic concepts surrounding the design of build systems.

## Part II: The Build Tools

The second part of this book compares five build tools. Each tool was selected both because of its popularity and because it demonstrates a particular way of building software. Each chapter starts with an introduction to the syntax of the build tool and then describes the tool's main usage scenarios. To provide a meaningful comparison, a standard set of examples is used across all chapters.

Chapter 6, "Make," discusses the GNU Make tool, which is the most common tool for C/C++ development. Chapter 7, "Ant," examines the Ant build tool, which is the de facto standard for compiling Java. Chapter 8, "SCons," investigates the more recent SCons build tool, which uses the Python language to describe the build process. Chapter 9, "CMake," shows the CMake tool, which generates a native build system (such as a Make-based system) from a high-level description of the build process. Finally, Chapter 10, "Eclipse," describes the build-related features of the Eclipse IDE.

After reading Part II, you'll have an appreciation for the state of the art in build tools and will understand the pros and cons of using each.

## Part III: Advanced Concepts

The third part discusses more advanced build system concepts, such as dependency analysis, software packaging and installation, version management, and the management of build machines and compilation tools. These chapters assume that you've had experience working on nontrivial software projects and can therefore relate to the issues discussed.

Chapter 11, "Dependencies," goes into detail on various dependency-checking techniques that discover whether a file must be recompiled. Chapter 12, "Building with Metadata," shows how a build system can generate metadata to aid with debugging, profiling, and source code documentation. Chapter 13, "Software Packaging and Installation," provides simple examples of packaging the software and getting ready to install it on the target machine. Chapter 14, "Version Management," surveys version-control issues as they relate to build systems. Chapter 15, "Build Machines," provides best practices for managing the build machine on which the software is compiled. Chapter 16, "Tool Management," provides a similar discussion for compilation tools.

After reading Part III, you'll understand many of the advanced topics involved in constructing a build system and a number of best practices.

## Part IV: Scaling Up

The final part of this book discusses the design of build systems for large software products. As a software product grows in size, it faces scalability problems, such as an increase in complexity, a dramatic increase in disk usage, and an increase in build times. All these problems tend to make software development less productive.

Chapter 17, "Reducing Complexity for End Users," provides approaches for reducing the complexity of a build system, as perceived by the end user. Chapter 18, "Managing Build Size," describes how a large software product can be divided into multiple components to make development more efficient. Finally, Chapter 19, "Faster Builds," discusses techniques for measuring and improving the time taken to perform a software build.

After reading Part IV, you'll have a better appreciation of how you should design your small-scale build system, in case it ends up becoming much larger.

## Summary

A good-quality build system isn't easy to construct, and failure to do so causes significant problems for your software team. If source code isn't recompiled when it should be, your team members will face longer build times or random build failures. They may also waste days debugging an invalid software image. It's worth putting in the time to make sure your build system is doing the correct thing.

The true cost of using a poor quality build system can be measured in monetary terms. A typical software organization might find that developers waste 10% of their time with build problems, which translates into large sums of money wasted each year.

This book explains a number of build system concepts, introduces you to a range of commonly available build tools, provides a number of best practices, and discusses the issues surrounding the construction and maintenance of large build systems.

# Acknowledgments

This book wouldn't be complete without a big thanks to my wife, Grace. I spent many evenings and weekends in my "man cave," tapping away at the keyboard. Grace understood the value I placed on writing this book (it was on my bucket list), and her patience and support made it all possible. Thanks also to Stan (our Bichon Maltese), who learned that sitting on the floor is often better than on my lap or keyboard.

Thanks go to my parents, Sally and Smithy, for allowing me to author several chapters from their dining room table. I also thank them for years of correcting my spelling and grammar, making it easier to write something the size of this book.

I appreciate the support of the team at Pearson Education who accepted this book for publication. Thanks to Raina Chrobak, Chris Zahn, and Chris Guzikowski for their guidance through the writing and editing process. Thanks also to the manuscript reviewers who provided feedback either from a practitioner's perspective or from the eyes of a build system expert. The reviewers include Monte Davidoff, Jeffrey Overbey, J. T. Conklin, Kevin Bodie, Brad Appleton, John Pantone, and Usman Muzaffar.

Next, I appreciate the support of Kevin Cheek and Bob McLaren, along with others on the team at Ericsson who allowed me to renegotiate my ongoing contract. This provided me with enough time to write a book. Thanks also to the many friends and colleagues who relayed experiences of their past and present build systems. I hope that I've given each of their experiences a suitable place in this book.

Finally, acknowledgment must be given to everybody who has contributed to the design or construction of a build tool. Most software projects use some type of build tool, making the build system a critical piece of technology. The people who create these tools don't always get the credit they deserve.

# About the Author

**Peter Smith** is a freelance consultant for Arapiki Solutions, Inc. (www.arapiki. com), based in Vancouver, Canada. He obtained a Ph.D. in computer science from the University of British Columbia in 1998, focusing on compilers and language design. He spent several years teaching undergraduate courses in compiler design, programming language design, software engineering, and computer networks. He also served on the Object-Oriented Programming, Systems, Languages & Applications (OOPSLA) conference committee for three years. Peter has worked primarily in the telecommunications industry, as a software engineer, a project manager, and the manager of a tools support team. Recent consulting jobs included the adoption and development of new software tools to improve end-user productivity.

# PART I

## The Basics

Part I provides a gentle introduction to the concepts used in software build systems. This part starts with a high-level view of the various stages of the build process, describes what a build system aims to create, shows the various input and output files used during compilation, and introduces the concepts of build targets and variants. You'll explore these topics:

- **Chapter 1, "Build System Overview":** A brief tour of the major components of a build system, including a number of important definitions that you need for later chapters.

- **Chapter 2, "A Make-Based Build System":** A short tutorial on using the GNU Make build tool, for those who've never been exposed to a text-based build system.

- **Chapter 3, "The Runtime View of a Program":** The many ways in which a program can be loaded into a computer and executed. A software build system must create the executable programs, libraries, and data files that are loaded into memory.

- **Chapter 4, "File Types and Compilation Tools":** The tools used to compile C/C++, Java, and C# source code. These compilation tools are the building blocks of a complete build system.

- **Chapter 5, "Subtargets and Build Variants":** The approach taken when building software for multiple target CPUs or creating multiple editions of the product.

Although Part I provides an introduction to build systems and their purpose, this book doesn't discuss build tools until Part II; there you more deeply immerse yourself in studying GNU Make, Ant, SCons, CMake, and the Eclipse builders. By the time you finish reading Part I, you'll be in a good position to evaluate each of these build tools.

# Chapter 1

# Build System Overview

This first chapter provides a complete overview of software build systems. Before diving into the details of how a build system works, it's important to understand the high-level process of building software. This chapter also acts as a roadmap for the rest of the book.

The most common goal of a build system is to translate human-readable source code into an executable program. In addition, build systems support the packaging of web-based applications, the generation of documentation, the automatic analysis of source code, and many related activities. Although the exact details of this process vary for each programming language and for each operating system, the basic concepts are universal.

This chapter starts with an end-to-end view of a few common build system scenarios. You then get an introduction to some of the high-level concepts involved; later chapters cover the finer details of each topic. By the end of this chapter, you'll understand each of the main steps in the build process, along with the common build-related concepts and terminology.

## What Is a Build System?

With such a wide range of programming languages and development environments, no single model can represent all possible build systems. A build system can manage any type of activity that involves translating one form of data (the input) into another form of data (the output). This discussion focuses on constructing software, hence the emphasis on *software* build systems.

In any software development environment, you're likely to encounter the following build-related scenarios:

- The compilation of software written in traditional compiled languages, such as C and C++. This can be extended to include newer languages such as Java and C#.

- The packaging and testing of software written in interpreted languages such as Perl and Python.

- The compilation and packaging of web-based applications. These include static HTML pages, source code written in Java or C#, hybrid files written using JSP (JavaServer Pages), ASP (Active Server Pages), or PHP (PHP: Hypertext Preprocessor) syntax, along with numerous types of configuration file.

- The execution of unit tests to validate small portions of the software in isolation from the rest of the code.

- The execution of static analysis tools to identify bugs in a program's source code. The output from this build system is a bug report document rather than an executable program.

- The generation of PDF or HTML documentation. This type of build system consumes input files in a range of different formats but generates human-readable documentation as the output.

Of course, this list isn't exhaustive, and you can probably think of many other uses for a build system. To simplify the discussion, this book focuses primarily on the traditional model of compiled languages. It's important to note that many of the build system concepts are the same, no matter what you're building.

## Compiled Languages

Figure 1.1 depicts the high-level view of a traditional build system for compiled languages such as C, C++, Java, and C#. In this model, source files are compiled into object files, which are then linked into code libraries or executable programs. The resulting files are collected into a release package that can be installed on a target machine. This model should be quite familiar to software developers.

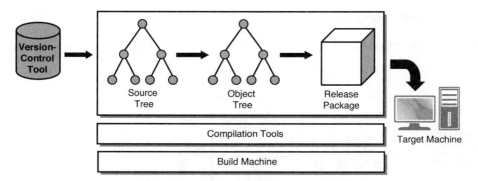

**Figure 1.1** *Overview of a traditional build system for compiled languages.*

The key components of Figure 1.1 are listed here:

- **Version-control tool:** A tool that stores the program's source code and enables multiple developers to make concurrent changes to the code base. It also facilitates the retrieval of historical versions of the code. Common examples of a version-control tool include CVS [2], Subversion [3], Git [4], and ClearCase [5].

- **Source trees and object trees:** The set of source files and compiled object files that a particular developer works with. Developers can make their own private changes in these trees, without impacting other people.

- **Compilation tools:** The tools that take input files and generate output files (for example, converting source code files into object code and executable programs). Common examples of compilation tools include a C or Java compiler, but they also include documentation and unit test generators.

- **Build machines:** The computing equipment on which the compilation tools are executed.

- **Release packaging and target machines:** The method by which the software is packaged, distributed to end users, and then installed on the target machine.

Each of these topics is discussed in more detail, both later in this chapter and later in this book. Many of these topics are so detailed that they warrant a full chapter of their own.

## Interpreted Languages

For interpreted languages, the build system model is slightly different (see Figure 1.2).

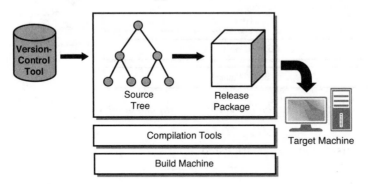

**Figure 1.2** *Overview of a build system for interpreted languages.*

Interpreted source code isn't compiled into object code, so there's no need for an object tree. Instead, the source files themselves are collected into a release package, ready to be installed on the target machine. If compilation tools are required in this type of build system, which they often are, their focus is on transforming source files and storing them in the release package. Compilation into machine code is not performed at build time, even though it may happen at runtime.

## Web-Based Applications

The build system for a web-based application is a mix of compiled code, interpreted code, and configuration or data files. As Figure 1.3 shows, some files (such as HTML files) are copied directly from the source tree to the release package, whereas others (such as Java source files) are first compiled into object code. In addition, both the web application server and the end user's web browser play a role in interpreting or compiling code, but that's beyond the scope of this build system.

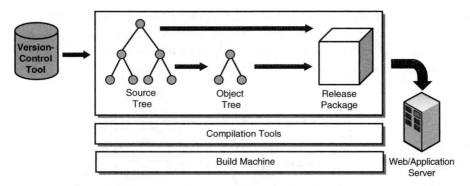

**Figure 1.3** *Overview of a build system for web-based software.*

A typical web application deals with many of the following file types:

- Static HTML files, containing nothing more than marked-up data to be displayed in a web browser. These files are copied directly to the release package.

- JavaScript files containing code to be interpreted by an end user's web browser. These files are also copied directly to the release package.

- JSP, ASP, or PHP pages, containing a mix of HTML and program code. These files are compiled and executed by the web application server rather than by the build system. These files are also copied to the release package, ready for installation on the web server.

- Java source files to be compiled into object code and packaged as part of the web application. The build system performs this transformation before packaging the Java class files. The Java classes are executed on the web application server or even within the web browser (using a Java applet).

Of course, there's no reason that the build system can't autogenerate some of these HTML, JavaScript, or JSP/ASP/PHP files (from other input file formats). Many compilation steps might take place before the output is finally copied to the release package.

## Unit Testing

The build system for a unit testing environment is simply an extension of the models already discussed. Instead of producing a release package to be installed on the target machine, the build system produces a number of smaller unit test suites. Each suite is executed on the target machine and produces a "pass" or "fail" result to indicate whether the software behaved as expected.

Figure 1.4 shows how the traditional compiled language build system (shown in Figure 1.1) can be extended to generate unit tests rather than a standard release package.

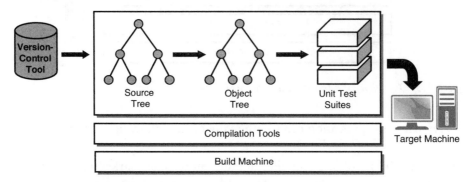

**Figure 1.4**  *Overview of a build system that generates unit tests.*

For interpreted languages (see Figure 1.2) and web-based applications (see Figure 1.3), a similar unit test build system can be created. In fact, a unit test build system is simply a variant of a standard build system. Chapter 12, "Building with Metadata," discusses unit testing in more detail.

## Static Analysis

Figure 1.5 shows a build system that performs static analysis. A static analysis tool, such as Coverity Prevent [6], Klocwork Insight [7], and FindBugs [8], examines a program's source code with the goal of identifying potential bugs. The analysis is done statically (at build time) instead of the more common approach of executing the software to see if it behaves correctly.

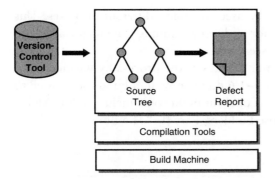

**Figure 1.5** *Overview of a build system for static analysis.*

The input to a static analysis system is the same source code used in a regular build system. However, instead of generating an object tree and release package, the output is some type of defect report document (often in text or HTML format). Chapter 12 discusses static analysis in more detail.

## Documentation Generation

The final build system scenario considers the generation of human-readable documentation, as shown in Figure 1.6.

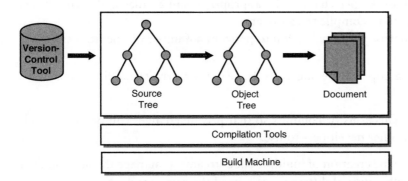

**Figure 1.6** *Overview of a build system for generating documentation.*

The output from this build system is a PDF file, a collection of HTML pages and graphic images, or anything else that could be considered documentation. Generating documentation might also include a number of intermediate data files, so the concept of an object tree still applies. No target machine is mentioned in this case, although, technically, the document would need to be viewed in some way, whether via a printer, a web browser, or a PDF viewer.

In summary, a build system can be used for many different purposes. This book focuses more on build systems for traditional compiled languages, although the concepts are the same for other scenarios.

The important point to understand for now is the process by which a build system operates. Although Figures 1.1–1.6 don't show it, a **build tool** is used to orchestrate the entire build process. Common build tools include GNU Make, Ant, SCons, CMake, and the Eclipse builders; Part II, "The Build Tools," discusses each one.

## Components of a Build System

Now that you've seen the high-level view of a software build system, you can dig deeper in each of the main sections. Later chapters cover many of these topics, so for now you'll cover only the basics.

### Version-Control Tools

Although you won't explore version-control systems until Chapter 14, "Version Management," a version-control tool is the first component of a build system. Before any software can be compiled, the developers must obtain a private copy of the source code. As part of their assigned work (fixing a bug or adding a new feature), each developer changes the appropriate source files and then triggers the build system to compile the software.

Version-control tools enable you to perform a number of operations:

- Obtain a copy of the source code, ready for private modifications to be made.

- Control **check-ins** or **commits** so that private changes can be made available for other developers to use.

- Facilitate the creation of multiple code streams to manage the development and maintenance of different versions of the same product.

- Control access to files so that only authorized developers can change certain source files.

- Enable a developer to view older (historical) versions of each source file, even if newer revisions have superseded them.

This isn't a book about version control, so it doesn't discuss specific version-control tools. However, Chapter 14 focuses extensively on the many ways in which the build system must interact with a version-control tool. There you'll consider which files should or shouldn't be kept under version control, and you explore the use and management of version numbers.

The next section focuses more on the source code stored within the version-control system.

## Source and Object Trees

As you might expect, a program's source code is stored as a number of disk files. This arrangement of the files into different directories (or folders, in Windows terminology) is known as the **source tree**. The way in which the source code is structured within the source tree has a significant impact on the design of the build system.

The structure of the source tree often reflects the architecture of the software. Figure 1.7 illustrates how the source code files for a Microsoft Windows-based accounting application can be stored, based on the various major components of the system.

Notice that each directory contains a file named Makefile. The implication here is that you use Make to build the software, which is common only for older Windows applications. The build description files (known as makefiles) are stored in the same directory as the source files they describe. This isn't the only way to store the build description, but it does make it easy to locate the parts of the build system that deal with the files in each directory.

Alongside the source tree is the **object tree** (see Figure 1.8). Although it's entirely possible to store object files in the same directory as the source files, it's often considered a messy approach (as you see in later chapters). You should instead create a separate tree hierarchy that stores any object files or executable programs constructed by the build process. Notice that Figure 1.8 contains not only object files, but also the final executable program (accounting.exe).

**Figure 1.7** *Source tree for a small Microsoft Windows application.*

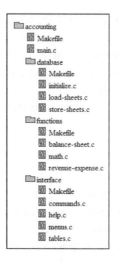

**Figure 1.8** *Corresponding object tree for a small Microsoft Windows application.*

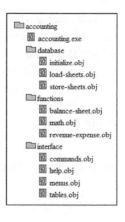

Although a small program such as this accounting application could be stored inside a single source code file, this is unrealistic for larger programs. Several important considerations call for dividing a program into multiple source files and then placing those files into different directories on the disk:

- **Comprehension:** Conceptually, people find it easier to think about programs when they're divided into logical subsections. This is the basic premise of object-oriented programming, in which people can think about the program as a collection of different classes. Each class must have both an external behavior that programmers can keep fresh in their minds and an internal implementation that hides the complexity of the class away from view. In a build system, therefore, it's best to divide the source code into multiple sections, each encapsulating a specific area of the program's functionality.

- **Source code control:** When a program's source code is spread across multiple files and directories, it becomes easier to manage them with a source code control tool. Conversely, if the entire program was stored inside a single disk file, it would be challenging for different developers to submit code changes without constantly stepping on each other's work.

- **Performance:** Development tools such as editors and compilers perform much more efficiently with smaller units of work. Although these tools are capable of dealing with source files that are megabytes in size, they do so inefficiently.

Throughout this book, you'll learn more about the design and construction of source and object trees.

## Compilation Tools and Build Tools

When developers have a source tree to work with, they must have some way to translate the human-readable source files into the machine-readable executable program. A **compilation tool** is a program that reads input files and translates them into output files. This might sound like a generic statement, but there's no limit to the type of data translation these tools could undertake.

The following are common examples of compilation tools:

- **C compiler:** Reads human-written C language source files and produces object files that contain a machine code translation of that same program. In this scenario, the output from the compilation tool should be functionally equivalent to the input, although closer to what the target machine can understand.

- **Linker:** Joins a number of different object files to produce a single executable program image. In this case, the object files are the input to the linker tool, but in the previous build step, they were the output from a compiler. In this example, it makes more sense to talk about input and output files than source and object files.

- **UML-based code generator:** Reads a UML model file as input and produces an equivalent program written in a general-purpose programming language such as Java, C++, or C#.

- **Documentation generator:** Reads a human-written file written in a markup language and generates a PDF file (or similar) as output.

- **Command-line tool for making a new directory:** Creates a new directory on the file system (for example, using the UNIX mkdir command). In this scenario, the name of the new directory is the only input data provided.

At this point, it's worth noting the distinction between a compiler and a compilation tool. A compiler typically translates high-level programming language source code into object code, which is the first of the previous examples given. However, a compilation tool is defined as any tool that translates input data to output data.

In contrast, a **build tool** is a program that functions at a level above compilation tools. That is, it must have sufficient knowledge of the relationship between source files and object files that it can orchestrate the entire build process. The build tool calls upon the necessary compilation tools to produce the final build output.

This book takes care to distinguish between compilation tools and build tools. Both play a critical role in creating a good build system, but they do so in different ways. Chapter 4, "File Types and Compilation Tools," looks at a number of compilation tools (such as gcc and javac) and explores how they manipulate the various types of files in the source and object trees. Chapter 16, "Tool Management," discusses some best practices for managing compilation tools over the lifetime of the software. Part II looks in more detail at build tools (Make, Ant, SCons, CMake, and the Eclipse builders) that orchestrate the entire build process.

## Build Machines

It may not appear so at first, but the machine on which the compilation and build tools execute plays a vital role in the management of a build system. Each of the tools must be capable of executing on the build machine, even though the underlying machine hardware and operating system might change over time. As you'll learn in Chapter 15, "Build Machines," numerous issues surround the management of build machines, particularly when you need to reproduce older versions of software or to provide a uniform environment in which different developers can compile the same source code.

You must also consider whether the software itself is being compiled and executed on the same type of machine or whether the software is destined to run in a completely different environment (CPU type and operating system). Figure 1.9 illustrates both a **native compilation** environment and a **cross-compilation** environment. In the native case, the software is executed on a **target machine** that's identical to the **build machine**; the cross-compilation case requires two different machines, with a different operating system or CPU on the target machine.

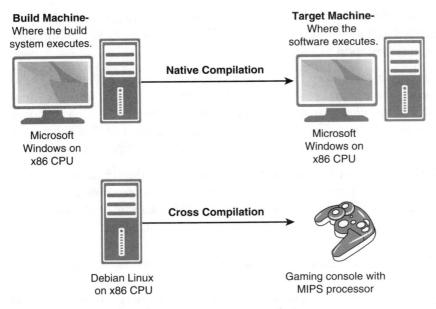

**Figure 1.9** *Native compilation versus cross-compilation.*

You'll learn more about native and cross-compilation environments in Chapter 15, which studies build machines in more detail.

## Release Packaging and Target Machines

Although much of a build tool's work focuses on generating object files and executable programs, the final packaging step produces something that you can actually install on a user's machine. It's not realistic to hand novice users a number of executable programs and data files and expect them to install and configure them by hand. Instead, you need to provide a single file that they can download, or a single CD or DVD that they can insert into their computer's CD-ROM drive. For software written for the home consumer market, the installation process should involve nothing more than double-clicking an icon and answering a few basic questions.

The final step of a build process is therefore to extract the relevant files from the source and object trees and store them in a **release package**. If at all possible, the release package should be a single disk file and should be compressed, to reduce the amount of time it takes to download or the number of DVDs required. Additionally, any nonessential debug information should be removed so that it doesn't clutter the software's installation.

Chapter 13, "Software Packaging and Installation," examines three common ways of packaging and installing software:

- **Archive files:** This is the most straightforward approach, with files compressed and joined into a single disk file. The end user must perform the reverse operation to install the software.

- **Package-management tools:** These are common in UNIX-like environments where complete software packages are downloaded from the Internet and installed as an optional part of the operating system. Installation is a one-step process, and any prerequisite packages are installed at the same time. Common examples include .rpm and .deb package files.

- **Custom-built GUI installation tools:** These are familiar to anyone who has installed software on the Microsoft Windows operating system. The installation process is started by double-clicking an icon, and the end user interacts with a custom-built GUI to install the software.

One final option, which isn't discussed in detail here, is that the software may be partially installed yet partially accessed at runtime. A portion of the software is installed on the end user's computer, but the rest of the code and data is accessed when the program is running. Common examples include video games in which graphic images, movies, and sound files are loaded off the DVD whenever they are required, but are never stored on the target machine's hard disk. Additionally, tools such as Google Earth [9] require that a client program be installed, but the rest of the data is downloaded from the Internet when required.

The generation of a release package marks the end of the software build process. The next section considers how this process is implemented within a build tool.

## The Build Process and Build Description

Now that you've covered each part of the build system at a high level, take a brief look at a couple of examples. In Figure 1.10, you can see the process by which the build tool invokes each of the compilation tools to get the job done (using the traditional compiled languages model shown in Figure 1.1). This end-to-end sequence of events is known as the **build process**.

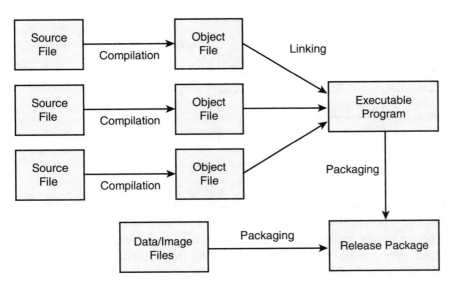

**Figure 1.10** *Overview of a build system for compiled languages.*

Although it's easy for humans to visualize this process in the form of a diagram, a build tool needs the **build description** to be written in a text-based format. For example, when using Make, the interfile dependency information is specified in the form of **rules**, which are stored in a file named Makefile. In contrast, the SCons build tool uses Python-language functions to describe the compilation steps; it keeps this information in a file named SConstruct.

To illustrate, the following SCons build description file states that the stock program should be generated by compiling the source files, `ticker.c` and `currency.c`.

```
Program("stock", ["ticker.c", "currency.c"])
```

In this case, SCons uses the default C compiler to create `ticker.o` and `currency.o`, even though the build description does not explicitly state that step. It then links those object files into the final executable program, `stock`. Figure 1.11 shows the equivalent diagram, to help you visualize the individual steps in the process:

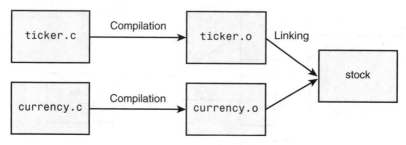

**Figure 1.11** *Overview of a SCons-based build process.*

Because the example stock program consists of only a small number of source files, the build description remains simple and fits nicely into a single text file. For larger programs (with thousands of source files in the code base), the build description may consist of hundreds of small files that work together to capture the build recipe for the entire program.

From a software developer's perspective, the text-based build description is at the heart of the whole build process. Every build tool has its own syntax for describing the build process, including file dependencies and compilation commands. You'll learn more about these build description languages in Part II.

## How a Build System Is Used

In a software development organization, three different types of software build are commonly performed. Each uses the same build system, but the end purpose of the build is different:

- **Developer (or private) build:** The developer has checked out the source code from version control and is building the software in a private workspace. The resulting release package will be used for the developer's private development instead of being shared with other people. The developer makes source code changes many times a day, incrementally recompiling the software each time.

- **Release build:** One or more people, known as **release engineers,** are assigned to perform release builds. The sole purpose is to provide a complete software package for the test group to validate. When the testers are convinced that the software is of high enough quality, that same package is made available to customers. The source tree used for a release build is compiled only once, and the source tree is never modified.

- **Sanity build:** This is similar to a release build, except that the software package isn't destined for a customer. Instead, the build process determines whether the current source code in the version-control system is "sane"—that is, whether the software build is free of errors and passes a basic set of sanity tests. This type of build can occur many times per day and tends to be fully automated. Many developers use the terms **daily build** or **nightly build** to describe this scenario.

As you can see, the key distinction among these three scenarios is how the build system is used—how often it's invoked and how the final program image is used. For the purposes of this book, the upcoming chapters don't discuss these topics in much detail, unless there's a need to distinguish how the build system accommodates each type of user.

## Build-Management Tools

The use of **build-management** tools has increased in recent years. Given the focus of this book, a build-management tool should be viewed as an extra layer of management on top of an existing build system rather than as part of the build system itself. Figure 1.12 illustrates the distinction.

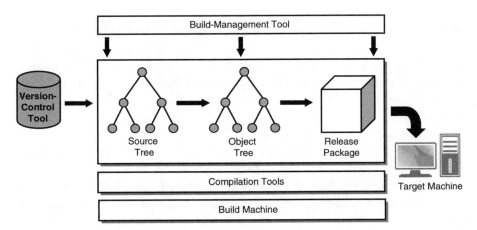

**Figure 1.12** *The use of a build-management tool, to oversee the use of a build system.*

The build-management tool communicates with the version-control tool to check out a build tree, calls upon the build system to compile the software, and then informs the developer when the build is complete. Depending on your perspective, you may view a build-management tool as just another part of the build system, but this book keeps them separate.

A good build-management tool provides the following features:

- Checks out and builds a source tree on a predetermined schedule, or simply when new code has been committed.

- Provides a queuing mechanism so that multiple build jobs can share a pool of build machines. When a sufficient number of machines are available, the next job is started.

- Sends email notification messages to various groups of users (when the build starts, completes, succeeds, or fails).

- Provides a graphical user interface to show when builds took place and whether they failed or succeeded.

- Manages version numbers, incrementing them after each successful build.

- Stores the final software package in an archive directory, ready for testers to use.

- Starts executing sanity tests on any successful build.

- Can identify which developers are on the "guilty list" of people who may have recently checked in bad code.

A build-management tool is vital for any software projects that have more than a few developers. A number of tools are available, either commercially developed and supported or from the open-source world. Some of these common tools include Build Forge [10], ElectricCommander [11], CruiseControl [12], and Hudson [13]. With the wide range of tools available, you can easily find something that meets your needs, and you won't need to implement your own build-management solution.

Aside from this brief introduction to build-management tools, this book doesn't cover the topic in any detail. Instead, it focuses on all the build system functionality below the build-management tool (see Figure 1.12). For a good overview of build management and the concepts of continuous integration, refer to [14].

# Build System Quality

As with any software-related topic, a number of system attributes define whether it's perceived as high quality, low quality, or somewhere in between. According to one build tool expert [15], a good build system should have the following characteristics:

- **Convenience:** The tool and the description files should be easy to use and should not place too much burden on the software developers who need to use them. The developer should focus on writing source code rather than dealing with the complexities of the build tool.

- **Correctness:** The build tool should always compile/link the correct files, using the correct compiler options. When it matters, the tool should compile the files in the correct order so that the final executable program always reflects the content of the source files.

- **Performance:** In an ideal world, the build process would complete without any noticeable delay. Realistically, though, it must perform as fast as possible for the computing equipment it's running on.

- **Scalability:** The build tool must be convenient, provide correct release images, and perform well, even when the tool is building a large program (for example, with thousands of source files). Part IV, "Scaling Up," discusses this topic of scalability.

The rest of this book spends a lot of time examining both good and bad ways to create a build process, and the pros and cons of using a range of different build tools. The book makes a special effort to consider these four characteristics, because they're important in the operation of a build system.

# Summary

This chapter offered a high-level overview of a complete **build system** and introduced the terminology for describing the steps in an end-to-end **build process**. Due to the wide range of build-related applications, there is no single type of build system.

The first step in a build system is usually to store and control access to the source code using a **version-control tool**. Next, you make source code changes in a **source tree** and generate the object files into the corresponding **object tree**. This depends on whether you're compiling source code or working with an interpreted language.

A **build tool** handles the end-to-end management of the build process. These build tools orchestrate the use of **compilation tools** to generate object files from source files (or whatever makes sense for the file types being used). Each of these tools must execute on the **build machine**.

The end product of the build system is called a **release package**. This is usually an archive file or an installation program that's capable of installing the software on the **target machine**. In some cases, the output of the build system is a documentation file rather than an executable file.

For the build tool to understand the details of the build process, you must create a suitable text-based file known as a **build description**. For example, with the SCons tool, the build description must be written in the Python programming language and stored in a file named `SConstruct`.

# Chapter 2

---

# A Make-Based Build System

One of this book's key assumptions is that you already have experience in developing software. However, this doesn't mean that you have experience writing your own build system, or even understanding an existing system. Many developers work on projects in which other people create and maintain the build system, or perhaps use an integrated development environment (IDE) to build at the push of a button. In either of these cases, you may not see the underlying build system.

This chapter introduces a build system for a small C-language program with only five source files. The build system is implemented using GNU Make [16] syntax, not only because it's an extremely popular tool, but also because Make syntax helps you understand the fundamental concepts underlying any build system.

If you've never written a makefile, take the time to study this example before moving to the more advanced concepts. Many of this book's examples use Make syntax, so understanding these concepts is important.

If you're already experienced with makefile syntax, feel free to skip forward to the next chapter. Chapter 6, "Make," presents more advanced details of the GNU Make tool.

---

## Calculator Example

This chapter uses a simple calculator program as its running example. You don't need to understand how the program works, other than knowing that it contains five C-language source files: Four are .c files (`add.c`, `calc.c`, `mult.c`, and `sub.c`), and the fifth is a .h file (`numbers.h`). In the C language, files with a .c suffix contain the main body of the source code, whereas files ending with .h provide type, variable, and function definitions to be shared by all .c files. Everything is then linked together into a single executable program, named `calculator`.

Here's the content of the source code directory, before anything is compiled:

```
$ ls
add.c  calc.c  mult.c  numbers.h  sub.c
```

Figure 2.1 shows a corresponding source tree diagram, with all files in the same directory. Source trees are a fundamental part of a build system, so you'll see many of these diagrams throughout this book. As you can imagine, the build system for this program is one of the simplest you can create, other than the standard "Hello World" program.

**Figure 2.1** *The source tree for a simple calculator example.*

In the C programming language, each .c file is compiled into a single object file containing the compiled machine code instructions (.o suffix in UNIX-like systems, or .obj in Window systems). With four different .c files, you can expect four different compilation commands, each producing a unique .o file. You'll use the GNU C Compiler [17], commonly known as GCC, with all examples performed in a UNIX environment.

```
$ gcc -g -c add.c
$ gcc -g -c calc.c
$ gcc -g -c mult.c
$ gcc -g -c sub.c
```

In each gcc command, the -c option requests that an object file be created, with the -g option requesting that debugging be enabled. You'll learn more about GCC in Chapter 4, "File Types and Compilation Tools."

The source code directory now contains a few more files:

```
$ ls
add.c  calc.c  mult.c  numbers.h  sub.o
add.o  calc.o  mult.o  sub.c
```

If you look carefully, you see that each .c file has a corresponding .o file. Note that numbers.h doesn't have an object file; instead, it was included (imported) by the add.c, calc.c, mult.c, and sub.c files. In build system terminology, each of the .c files is dependent on numbers.h.

To build the final calculator program, these .o files are linked together into a single executable file.

```
$ gcc -g -o calculator add.o calc.o mult.o sub.o
$ ls
add.c   calc.c   calculator   mult.o     sub.c
add.o   calc.o   mult.c       numbers.h  sub.o
```

That completes the entire process of building the calculator program. To illustrate this graphically, consider the concept of a **dependency graph**, shown in Figure 2.2.

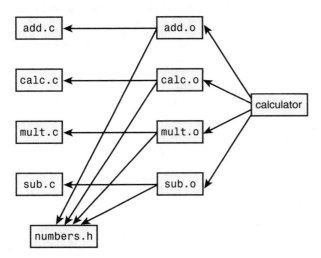

**Figure 2.2** *The dependency graph for the simple calculator example.*

For several reasons, a dependency graph is important in build systems. Not only does it list the files involved in the build process, but it also shows the dependencies between those files. A **build tool** such as GNU Make uses a dependency graph to determine which files should be compiled, and when they should be compiled.

For example, the arrows originating from add.o toward both add.c and numbers.h state that both these sources files contribute to the compilation of add.o. Additionally, if either of these files is edited, add.o must be recompiled to include any recent changes. Conversely, if neither add.c nor numbers.h has changed since the last time add.o was compiled, it doesn't need to be compiled again.

With these concepts in mind, you'll now explore how GNU Make enables you to specify the dependency graph for the example program. This book spends a lot of time looking at different build tools (such as GNU Make, Ant, SCons,

CMake, and the Eclipse builders), to show different ways of specifying a build system's dependency graph.

## Creating a Simple Makefile

This section examines how the example can be implemented using the GNU Make build tool. A dependency graph is a purely mathematical concept, so you need some way to express the graph in a source code format. This should use plain text to list the files, describe the dependencies between them, and show which compiler commands are to be used. The GNU Make tool offers a straight-forward translation.

The following text file, called Makefile, is stored in the same directory as the source and object files.

```
1   calculator: add.o calc.o mult.o sub.o
2           gcc -g -o calculator add.o calc.o mult.o sub.o
3
4   add.o: add.c numbers.h
5           gcc -g -c add.c
6
7   calc.o: calc.c numbers.h
8           gcc -g -c calc.c
9
10  mult.o: mult.c numbers.h
11          gcc -g -c mult.c
12
13  sub.o: sub.c numbers.h
14          gcc -g -c sub.c
```

As you'll see when you study GNU Make in more detail (see Chapter 6), this is an inefficient way of implementing a makefile. However, this direct translation of the dependency graph is easy to understand.

Each section of the makefile introduces a new **rule**. Line 1 of the listing states that the file named calculator is dependent on all the files, add.o, calc.o, mult.o, and sub.o. Line 2 then provides a UNIX command to generate the calculator file from all those object files.

Line 4 specifies that add.o depends on both add.c and numbers.h, and line 5 provides the UNIX command for compiling add.o. The rest of the makefile provides similar rules for the other source and object files.

One important warning is that all UNIX commands (lines 2, 5, 8, 11, 14) must be preceded by a TAB character instead of spaces. This feature is historic and confuses many new makefile developers. If you forget this rule, you see the following error:

```
Makefile:2: *** missing separator (did you mean TAB instead of
➥8 spaces?).
```

Assuming that you've created the makefile in the same directory as all the source files, you're ready to build the software. To start, perform a **full build** by executing the gmake command in the UNIX shell.

```
$ gmake
gcc -g -c add.c
gcc -g -c calc.c
gcc -g -c mult.c
gcc -g -c sub.c
gcc -g -o calculator add.o calc.o mult.o sub.o
```

The GNU Make program examines the makefile, reconstructs the dependency graph in its memory, and then determines which commands to execute. GNU Make automatically determines that all object files must exist before the calculator program can be created, hence the ordering of the commands in the output.

The next important concept in a build tool is that of **incremental builds**. Instead of blindly executing commands, GNU Make does some upfront analysis to see if files actually need to be compiled or whether they already exist. After performing the build for the first time, you can easily invoke GNU Make a second time:

```
$ gmake
gmake: 'calculator' is up to date.
```

In this case, GNU Make determines that all generated files are more recent (that is, have a later time stamp) than all the source files, so no additional work must be done. As a software developer, you should be familiar with this concept, even if you've never thought about how it was implemented.

As you might expect, if you modify a source file (such as add.c), you'll be changing the time stamp of that file. As a result, GNU Make determines that add.o is no longer up-to-date and that both add.o and calculator should be recompiled.

```
$ gmake
gcc -g -c add.c
gcc -g -o calculator add.o calc.o mult.o sub.o
```

The situation changes a little if you modify numbers.h, because every source file is dependent on that file. This causes all object files, and the final program, to be recompiled:

```
$ gmake
gcc -g -c add.c
```

```
gcc -g -c calc.c
gcc -g -c mult.c
gcc -g -c sub.c
gcc -g -o calculator add.o calc.o mult.o sub.o
```

As a final note, this type of incremental build isn't possible in GNU Make if you don't create a separate makefile rule for each object file. If you instead list all the source files on the right side of the rule, GNU Make has no choice but to recompile all source files each time one of them changes.

```
1  calculator: add.c calc.c mult.c sub.c numbers.h
2         gcc -g -o calculator add.c calc.c mult.c sub.c
numbers.h
```

Even though line 2 has only a single command to execute, it compiles all the source files each time it's invoked. Compare this with the previous example that linked the separate .o files. In this case, you're compiling all the files from source code and then linking them in one command.

Let's now consider how you can optimize the example makefile. After all, it seems wasteful to provide a separate rule for each source and object file pair.

## Simplifying the Makefile

Regardless of whether you've seen a makefile before, you should be questioning the need for so much repetition in the example. Developers know that duplication is a bad thing, and build systems are no exception. To make it easier to construct a makefile, GNU Make provides built-in rules for common operations, such as a compiling a .c file into a .o file. Therefore, this example can be rewritten in significantly fewer lines:

```
1  calculator: add.o calc.o mult.o sub.o
2         gcc -g -o calculator add.o calc.o mult.o sub.o
3
4  add.o calc.o mult.o sub.o: numbers.h
```

Lines 1 and 2 are the same as before, but the rest of the makefile has mostly been eliminated. GNU Make already knows that any file ending with .o depends on the corresponding file with a .c suffix. The only thing you need to state explicitly is that all object files depend on numbers.h.

This is a fairly good optimization, although you should probably use symbolic names to make the code more readable. GNU Make provides the familiar concept of variables, similar to other programming languages. Consider the revised example:

```
1   SRCS = add.c calc.c mult.c sub.c
2   OBJS = $(SRCS:.c=.o)
3   PROG = calculator
4   CC = gcc
5   CFLAGS = -g
6
7   $(PROG): $(OBJS)
8           $(CC) $(CFLAGS) -o $@ $^
9
10  $(OBJS): numbers.h
```

Line 1 defines the SRCS variable to include the full list of source files in the program. Line 2 is a clever piece of GNU Make syntax that replaces .c with .o in each file's name in the list of source files. OBJS is therefore defined as the complete list of object files.

Line 3 defines the name of the executable program, and line 4 defines the name of the compilation tool. If these values were referenced multiple times in the makefile, defining them in one place makes perfect sense (which is why many programming languages allow constant definitions).

Line 5 sets the CFLAGS variable to enable debugging information. Note that the previous example, which used the implicit rule for creating .o files from .c files, didn't have the CFLAGS variable defined. That example wouldn't have included the -g flag when compiling source code, which isn't what we wanted.

Lines 7 and 8 are the same as in previous examples, after having expanded the variable definitions. Note that $@ is a syntactical shortcut for the files mentioned on the left side of the rule (calculator), and $^ refers to the files listed on the right side (all the object files). These shortcuts are rather cryptic but are useful in larger build systems. Chapter 6 offers a more detailed explanation of these concepts.

Now you can consider some other activities the makefile should perform, other than simply compiling the software.

## Additional Build Targets

A build system can do more than just compile a program. As you saw in Chapter 1, "Build System Overview," you can generate web applications, create PDF documentation, perform static analysis, and run unit tests. In fact, a build system can handle any activity in which output files are created from input files. This also includes removing files and copying of files from one place to another.

In a C-language build system, two of the most common operations are to "clean" the build tree and install the executable program onto the target machine. The goal of the clean target is to remove any generated files that were created when compiling the software. For the install target, the goal is to copy the final executable program into the target machine's standard binary path.

Consider how these build targets are implemented using makefile syntax:

```
1   SRCS = add.c calc.c mult.c sub.c
2   OBJS = $(SRCS:.c=.o)
3   PROG = calculator
4   CC = gcc
5   CFLAGS = -g
6   INSTALL_ROOT = /usr/local
7
8   $(PROG): $(OBJS)
9           $(CC) $(CFLAGS) -o $@ $^
10
11  $(OBJS): numbers.h
12
13  clean:
14          rm -f $(OBJS) $(PROG)
15
16  install: $(PROG)
17          cp $(PROG) $(INSTALL_ROOT)/bin
```

The clean target has been added on lines 13 and 14. This is a standard GNU Make rule, but without any input files listed on the right side. This simply means that the target will always be executed, and there's no need to check the time stamp on the input files. The output from invoking this build target is as follows:

```
$ gmake clean
rm -f add.o calc.o mult.o sub.o calculator
```

You haven't listed any input files on the right side of the rule, so invoking the clean target a second time has the same result:

```
$ gmake clean
rm -f add.o calc.o mult.o sub.o calculator
```

In this rule, GNU Make has no way to avoid executing the rm command. The rule has no file time stamps to check that would stop it from repeating the same command each time. This contrasts with the previous rules, which compared source and object file time stamps, such as add.c and add.o. One problem arises if a file named clean already exists on the disk, but Chapter 6 discusses that.

The install target has been added on lines 16 and 17. This time the rule has the calculator file listed on the right side, so invoking the install target automatically ensures that the whole calculator program is brought up-to-date. The cp command on line 17 copies the executable program into the directory specified by the INSTALL_ROOT variable (defined on line 6).

```
$ gmake install
gcc -g   -c -o add.o add.c
gcc -g   -c -o calc.o calc.c
gcc -g   -c -o mult.o mult.c
gcc -g   -c -o sub.o sub.c
gcc -g -o calculator add.o calc.o mult.o sub.o
cp calculator /usr/local/bin
```

For the `install` target, invoking the target for a second time still performs some work, but not as much as the first time.

```
$ gmake install
cp calculator /usr/local/bin
```

GNU Make determines that the `calculator` file already has a more recent time stamp than all the `.o` files, so it doesn't attempt to recompile the `calculator` program. However, because there's no file on the disk named `install`, GNU Make invokes the `cp` command each time, just as you saw with the `clean` target.

## Using a Framework

The example build system is small here, but you can see that it's starting to get more complex. As build systems get larger and more detailed, more expert knowledge is required to read and understand the makefile. After you've read Chapter 6 in detail, you'll see that a makefile using GNU Make syntax can become challenging to understand.

A common practice in most build systems is to create a **framework**. That is, all parts of the build system that a software developer doesn't care about are kept in a separate set of files. In contrast, the interesting parts of the build system, such as the list of source files and compiler options, are more visible to the developer. Most software developers don't need to read the complex framework and, therefore, don't bother doing so.

As an example, the following makefile provides only the information that an average software developers needs to understand.

```
1   SRCS = add.c calc.c mult.c sub.c
2   PROG = calculator
3   HEADERS = numbers.h
4
5   include framework.mk
```

Lines 1–3 provide the most basic information: which source files should be compiled, the name of the executable program, and the list of header files. This is all the information required to compile a simple program and, therefore, all that a software developer typically cares about.

Line 5 proceeds to include the framework file, essentially appending `framework.mk` to the end of `Makefile`. This file encapsulates the GNU Make rules and other advanced definitions:

```
1   OBJS = $(SRCS:.c=.o)
2   CC = gcc
3   INSTALL_ROOT = /usr/local
4
5   ifdef DEBUG
6   CFLAGS = -O -g
7   else
8   CFLAGS = -O
9   endif
10
11  $(PROG): $(OBJS)
12          $(CC) $(CFLAGS) -o $@ $^
13
14  $(OBJS)  : $(HEADERS)
15
16  clean:
17          rm -f $(OBJS) $(PROG)
18
19  install: $(PROG)
20          cp $(PROG) $(INSTALL_ROOT)/bin
```

Most of `framework.mk` should look familiar, although you don't see any mention of source filenames or executable programs. These are kept out of the framework and appear only in the user-facing makefile.

One notable addition in this framework, in lines 5–9, is that you're testing for the existence of the DEBUG symbol. This can be set (or not) by the makefile that includes the framework, or even by the user on the UNIX command line.

For example, a standard build of the calculator program uses the -O (optimize) compiler flag:

```
$ gmake
gcc -O    -c -o add.o add.c
gcc -O    -c -o calc.o calc.c
gcc -O    -c -o mult.o mult.c
gcc -O    -c -o sub.o sub.c
gcc -O -o calculator add.o calc.o mult.o sub.o
```

On the other hand, setting the DEBUG variable to 1 on the gmake command line incorporates the -g (debug) flag:

```
$ gmake DEBUG=1
gcc -O -g    -c -o add.o add.c
gcc -O -g    -c -o calc.o calc.c
gcc -O -g    -c -o mult.o mult.c
gcc -O -g    -c -o sub.o sub.c
gcc -O -g -o calculator add.o calc.o mult.o sub.o
```

As you'll see many times throughout this book, using a separate framework file centralizes much of this complexity in a single place. The build system can contain a large number of `Makefile` files, each including the same common framework.

## Summary

A dependency graph is a mathematical structure that shows the relationship between files in the build tree. If one file depends on another file (that is, there's an arrow in the dependency graph), any change to the content of the source file might require the object file to be regenerated.

To invoke a software build system, the dependency graph must be encoded in a form that a build tool can understand. In the case of the GNU Make tool, the dependency graph is expressed in a text-based form known as a makefile.

As a starting point, a build tool performs a full build to generate all the object files from the corresponding source files, eventually linking them into an executable program. If object and executable files already exist, the build tool examines their time stamps to see whether any files have changed since the last time a build was invoked. This approach, known as an incremental build, ensures that the minimum number of recompilation steps is performed.

Build tools are more than just a way to represent a dependency graph. They include variables, conditional statements, and other syntax tricks to make it easier to implement a build system.

Most build systems include additional build targets, such as `clean` and `install`, beyond basic compilation of the program. Finally, a framework often is used to separate the developer-facing details of the build process (such as filenames and options) from the complexity of the underlying build tool.

# Chapter 3

## The Runtime View of a Program

Chapter 1, "Build System Overview," took a high-level view of the build process, originating with an untouched source code tree and ending with a software package installed on the target machine. Before looking at each of these build steps in detail, you should learn more about what you're actually building. That is, what does a program look like when it runs inside the target machine, and what are all the disk files that the target machine needs to load into memory?

To fully understand the sequence of steps the build system performs, you need to visualize the program's runtime view. Seeing how your program will be loaded into memory and executed makes it easier to determine which object files, executable programs, and release packages must be created. Is the program translated into pure machine code, or is it partially interpreted by the runtime system? Is it a single program, or does it consist of multiple interacting programs? The answers to these questions determine what the build system must generate.

The runtime view of the program also depends on which programming language is used and which operating system provides the runtime environment. Chapter 4, "File Types and Compilation Tools," examines the specific details of UNIX- and Windows-based programs, but for now, you can focus on the high-level concepts that are the same on most computing platforms:

- **Executable programs:** The sequence of machine-readable instructions that the CPU executes, along with associated data values. This is the fully compiled program that's ready to be loaded into the computer's memory and executed.

- **Libraries:** Collections of commonly used object code that can be reused by different programs. Most operating systems include a standard set of libraries that developers can reuse, instead of requiring each program to provide their own. A library can't be directly loaded and executed on the target machine; it must first be linked with an executable program.

- **Configuration and data files:** These are not executable files; they provide useful data and configuration information that the program can load from disk.

- **Distributed programs:** This type of software consists of multiple executable programs that communicate with each other across a network or simply as multiple processes running on the same machine. This contrasts with more traditional software that has a single monolithic program image.

The following sections examine each concept in detail, using diagrams to help illustrate the structure of the software. In each case, keep in mind that the build system must create each of the build artifacts. In most cases, these artifacts are stored in disk files.

## Executable Programs

An executable program is a sequence of instructions that's loaded in memory and executed by the central processing unit (CPU). Typically, this program is started by double-clicking an icon in a windowing environment or typing the name of the program into a command shell. In other cases, a program is loaded into memory when the computer first boots or is started at a specific time of day by a scheduling tool.

After the program is loaded, several mechanisms exist for executing the software, depending on how much compilation took place before the program was loaded and how much operating system support the program requires.

### Native Machine Code

In this scenario, the build system fully converted the executable program into the CPU's native machine code. The CPU simply "jumps" to the program's starting location, and all the execution is performed purely using the CPU's hardware. While it's executing, the program optionally makes calls into the operating system to access files and other system resources (see Figure 3.1).

In modern software systems, native machine code is most commonly used for languages such as C or C++, when execution of the program must be as fast as possible or when the program requires full access to the CPU's features. There's no faster way to execute code.

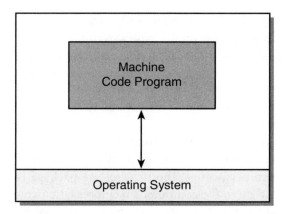

**Figure 3.1**  *A machine code program interacting with the operating system.*

In the case of a native machine code program, the build system produces an executable program file. In common terminology, you might hear these referred to as a program, an executable, or a binary.

## Monolithic System Images

Given that most desktop computers run an operating system such as Linux, Mac OS X, or Windows, computer users are familiar with using a mouse and keyboard and with viewing a program's output on their display monitor. However, for an embedded system that exists inside an automobile, a television, or a kitchen appliance, there's often a much smaller operating system, or no operating system at all (see Figure 3.2). In many cases, the computer can run only one program at a time.

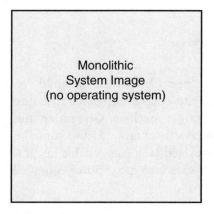

**Figure 3.2**  *A monolithic system image, with no operating controlling the machine.*

Most embedded systems are designed to be cheap and easy to make, so they have limited CPU power and memory. As you might expect, writing software for an embedded system can often be trickier than designing code that runs on a full-fledged operating system. To make things possible, the build system must run on a separate build server, running something like Linux or Windows. After the software is compiled, the final release package is transferred to the embedded device for the program to be executed.

Although interpreters are sometimes used, many embedded systems use the native machine code model of execution, with the program itself using the entire system memory. From a build system perspective, the final release package is simply a large file that's loaded directly into the computer's memory. Often you hear these programs called an image (short for "memory image" or "system image"), because they tend to be the only thing loaded into the computer.

## Full Program Interpretation

A number of programming languages are never compiled into machine code; instead, the runtime system loads the entire source code into memory and interprets it (see Figure 3.3). This was true of early versions of the BASIC language and is still the case with UNIX shell scripts.

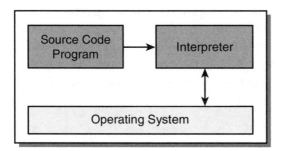

**Figure 3.3** *Source code being processed by an interpreter.*

Although no compilation of source code to object files occurs, the build system still has a lot of work to do. It's necessary to collect the source files into a release package that can be installed on the target machine. Generating unit tests, performing static analysis, and generating documentation is also common as part of the build system. Finally, some interpreted languages enable integration with compiled languages, turning the software into a hybrid of compiled and interpreted code.

## Interpreted Byte Codes

Byte codes are similar to native machine code, except that the CPU doesn't directly understand them. It first translates them into native machine code or interprets them as the program executes. A byte code environment therefore requires that an additional interpreter or compiler be loaded alongside the program.

For example, the Java language is designed to be platform-independent. This means that the build system calls upon the Java compiler to create machine-independent byte-code files instead of generating a CPU's native machine code. When the program is later executed (see Figure 3.4), it starts up within a **Java Virtual Machine (JVM)**. The virtual machine has the option of interpreting and acting upon the byte codes as the program runs, but it more likely uses **Just In Time (JIT)** compilation to translate the program into native machine code as it executes.

In common terminology, byte-code programs often are referred to as byte-code files, class files (in Java terminology), or managed code assemblies (in .NET terminology). In most cases, the build system creates a disk file to be loaded by the byte-code interpreter.

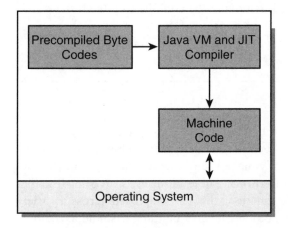

**Figure 3.4** *A Java virtual machine converting byte codes into native machine code.*

Before going any further, contrast the byte-code model with that of languages such as Perl and Python. From a build system perspective, Perl and Python languages are interpreted rather than compiled. That is, the build system collects the source files into the release package, ready to be interpreted on the target machine. The build process has no explicit compilation phase.

However, these interpreted languages use byte codes at runtime, as shown in Figure 3.5. The simple act of executing the Perl or Python script automatically triggers the generation of byte codes. In this respect, part of the traditional build system is embedded into the runtime environment.

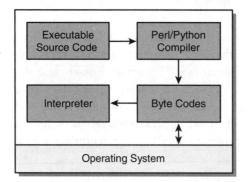

**Figure 3.5** *Runtime compilation of Perl or Python source code into byte codes.*

The advantage of this approach is that changes to source code will take effect the next time the script is executed, removing the compile step from the standard edit-compile-run cycle. One major downside of this approach is that syntax errors in the code might not be found until the program starts executing.

## Libraries

The **library** file is also an important build artifact. At first glance, you might think that a single group of developers wrote a program. This is true in some cases, although developers frequently make use of prewritten code libraries developed by other people or organizations. These libraries, stored in disk files of their own, collect a set of code functions that can be reused across a variety of programs. Therefore, developers aren't always building a single executable program file; they instead join custom-developed software and prebuilt libraries into a single program.

In many programming languages, a library function can be viewed as an extension to the standard language and is used in the same way as functions written by the developers. For example, to print a string in the C language, you use the `printf` library function:

```
printf("Hello World\n");
```

In Java, the `println` method is used:

```
System.out.println("Hello World");
```

In both examples, the developer uses a function (or method) that was written by somebody else but is conveniently linked into the executable program during the build process. Unless you're familiar with the language, you might not even know whether a function or method is from a library or whether it was custom written.

Most operating systems have a preinstalled set of libraries for operations such as file and network I/O, mathematical functions, user interface manipulation, and sometimes database access. A developer can obtain libraries from third-party sources, such as downloading them from the Internet. Developers can also publish their own libraries.

In the realm of build systems, there are two main operations on libraries:

- **Creating a new library:** If you want to create your own library, the first step is to compile all the object files you want to store. With this collection in hand, you use a special **linking** or **archiving** operation to bundle the object files into a single library file, and create a suitable index of all the functions that exist.

- **Linking with a library:** When an executable program is created, the build system must provide a list of libraries to search. If a function is referenced in the source code but the developer didn't explicitly write it, the list of libraries is searched to locate the required function. When the function is found, the appropriate object file is copied into the executable program.

In Chapter 4, you'll see exactly how a library can be created and referenced in various programming languages and operating systems. Even before then, you still need to understand the two different approaches of integrating a library into an executable program.

## Static Linking

In this first approach, a library is just a collection of individual object files. During the build process, when the linker tool determines that a function is required, it extracts the appropriate object file from the library and copies it into the executable program. In this sense, the library's object file appears identical to any of the object files the developer created on his or her own.

Note that the act of linking a library with the developer's own software happens during the build process. Therefore, you end up with a single executable program to be loaded onto the target machine (see Figure 3.6). In this sense, a static library is a build-time concept rather than anything that exists at runtime. After the final executable program has been created, it's impossible to separate the program from its libraries.

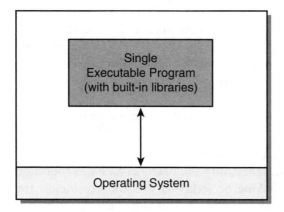

**Figure 3.6** *A program with libraries statically linked into the executable program.*

## Dynamic Linking

In contrast to static linking, the dynamic linking method doesn't copy the object file into the executable image; instead, it notes which libraries are required to successfully execute the program. When the program later starts running, the libraries are loaded into memory as separate entities and then are connected with the main program (see Figure 3.7). A special dynamic linker is required to connect the links between the functions that the program requires and the libraries that supply those functions.

From a build system perspective, a dynamic library is a disk file that is constructed by joining object files. The library is then collected into the release package and installed on the target machine. Only then can it be loaded into the machine's memory.

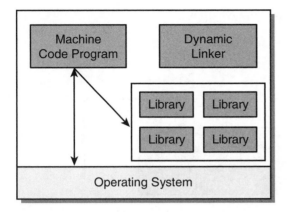

**Figure 3.7** *A program with libraries dynamically linked at runtime.*

Although this is a more complex approach than static linking, using dynamic libraries offers two significant benefits. First, it's possible to upgrade to a newer version of a library (adding features or fixing bugs), without needing to re-create the executable program. Second, many operating systems can optimize their memory usage by loading only a single copy of the library into memory, yet sharing it with other programs that require that same library. These features aren't possible when using the static linking method.

For more details on how static and dynamic linking work, refer to [18] in References.

## Configuration and Data Files

Every computer program in existence uses some type of data, even if it's just adding two numbers. In some cases, the data is directly linked into the executable program, as is the case with an initialized array of numbers. However, any program of significant size uses external data sources, such as a file on a disk. Your program makes calls into the operating system to request that data be read into memory (see Figure 3.8).

There's no limit to the ways in which data can be used. For example, all these are forms of data:

- A bitmap graphic image displayed onscreen

- A sound stored as a digitized wave form

- A configuration file that customizes the behavior of a program

- A set of documents containing online help text

- A database containing names and addresses

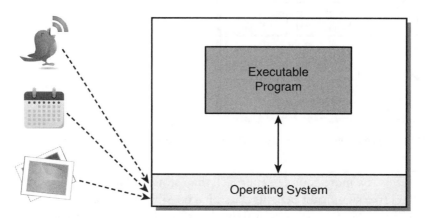

**Figure 3.8** *Various data files read into the program at runtime.*

From the perspective of a build system, you need to transfer these data files into the program's release package so that they can be installed on the target machine. The exception to this is if the data files are stored on an Internet site that could be accessed remotely.

Although data files are often copied into the release package without modification, in some scenarios data files must first be modified or created by the build process. For example, a configuration file might need to include the software's version number, such as 4.2.3. Furthermore, a database might not have any content when the software is first built, so the build process simply creates an empty set of database files.

## Distributed Programs

The final runtime concept to consider is programs distributed around multiple parts of the system. Most modern operating systems enable you to have multiple programs running at the same time, so you also have the option of multiple programs communicating together as a single piece of software. This concept can be extended to have geographically remote computers communicate across a network but still behave as if they're a single program.

In build systems, the concept of a release package now plays a more important role. No longer are you building a single executable program that's stored in a single disk file. Instead, you must build and package many different executable programs, along with the necessary configuration files and start-up scripts.

For example, a software system might use the client/server model, with a single server program running on one computer and a large number of client programs running on many other computers (see Figure 3.9). In this scenario, the build system could create two release packages, given that different people will be installing the server program versus the client program. Alternatively, the same release package could be used to install the two separate programs.

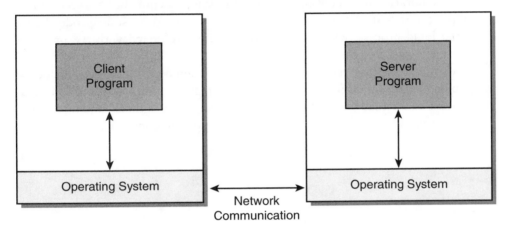

**Figure 3.9** *A single program divided across two physical machines, using a network to communicate.*

To support multiple programs, the build system also requires a few additional features. For example, developers need to specify which executable program should be built, rather than attempting to rebuild and repackage all files each time they build the software. Given that developers often work on one executable program at a time, this can lead to some important productivity improvements.

The build system must also support the concept of a shared application programming interface (API). That is, the different programs communicate with each other by sharing a number of data structures (often by sending those data structures across a network). Each program that the build system can construct must use the same set of data definitions to avoid consistency problems.

The key message here is that build systems can be detailed, especially when the software becomes larger and more complex because of the distributed runtime view.

## Summary

The way a program is loaded into memory and executed has a significant impact on the design of the software build system. An executable program is loaded into memory and executed. It can contain native machine code instructions, or perhaps byte-code instructions to be interpreted or compiled at runtime. The software's build system needs to do a different amount of work, depending on how much upfront compilation is required.

Code libraries are a convenient way of reusing functionality between different programs. Static libraries are linked with custom-written source code as part of the build process, whereas dynamic libraries are linked with the program after it's loaded into memory.

A software release package can contain any number of data files, including graphic images, sound files, and database content. In addition, a single piece of software can actually consist of multiple executable programs, communicating together via a network or as multiple processes on the same machine.

# Chapter 4

## File Types and Compilation Tools

In contrast to Chapters 1, 2, and 3, which discussed the conceptual view of a build system, this chapter takes a more hands-on view of the various files and compilation tools that can be used during a build. You'll examine the tools used with several programming languages, including C, C++, Java, and C#, and look at command-line examples on both Linux and Windows operating systems. These languages and operating systems were chosen solely because of their popularity.

In addition, this chapter briefly touches on file formats that could appear in a build system. For example, any nontrivial program contains graphical images, sound waveforms, or database content. This data is important for the successful execution of the program and, therefore, must be constructed and packaged appropriately.

In reference to the big picture, this chapter focuses on the compilation tools that convert individual files from the source tree into individual files in the object tree (see Figure 4.1). As an extension, object files can also be converted into other object files, both of which are stored in the object tree.

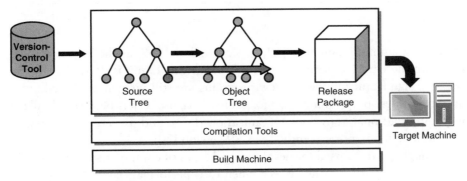

**Figure 4.1** *Big-picture diagram (for traditional compiled software), showing that source files are compiled into object files.*

Recall the distinction between **build tools** and **compilation tools**. This chapter focuses only on compilation tools, each of which translates one or more input files into an equivalent output file. On the other hand, a build tool such as Make or Ant is responsible for the higher-level orchestration of the build process, such as deciding which files need to be compiled and which compilation tools to use. Part II, "The Build Tools," focuses more on build tools.

As you might expect, anyone constructing a build system must be intimately familiar with the file types being manipulated and the tools being used. This knowledge is used on a regular basis, especially when you need to change the build process or find out whether it's working correctly. If the build tool fails to create a valid executable program, you need the skills to determine the root cause of the problem.

This chapter focuses on the following questions:

- What is the purpose of each source and object file type?

- What is their basic format?

- Which compilation tool is used to generate the object files?

- What are some important options when using the compilation tool?

- How do you examine the content of the file to see if it looks valid?

Because of the sheer number and complexity of these tools, this chapter can provide only an overview of each type. Additionally, this chapter focuses only on the aspects of the language and tools relevant to build systems. To fill in the gaps, you're encouraged to read the reference manual for each of the tools.

## C/C++

The C Programming Language [19] was created in 1969, as the language to be used with the UNIX Operating System (from which Linux is derived). Despite its age, a significant number of new programs are still written in C, making it one of the oldest programming languages in active use. C has been standardized by the International Standards Organization (ISO), and a number of versions have been defined (most recently, the C99 version [20]).

Although C can be used for developing all types of computer software, newly developed C code is most likely seen when CPU performance and "bare-metal" access to the computer's hardware is important. Compared with most other languages, programming in C is just one step above programming directly in assembly language. C doesn't provide features such as garbage collection or multithreading support, and it doesn't have any complex data types built into the language. Therefore, it's a compact and efficient language, often the choice for embedded systems.

In the early 1980s, the C++ language [21] was created as a means to add object-oriented concepts to the basic C language. C++ was designed to be a superset of C, so the two languages can be used in the same program—and even within the same source file. The language includes concepts such as classes, inheritance, and templates, and has complex data structures that aren't a standard part of C. Given the newer features, C++ is more commonly used for application programming, although it still can support embedded systems and high-performance computing.

## Compilation Tools

Many C compilers exist, although the most widely used is likely the C compiler from the GNU Compiler Collection (GCC) [17]. First released in 1987, GCC has become the de facto standard for compiling open-source software and is used extensively for commercial development. One of the major strengths of GCC is its capability to generate object code for a wide range of CPU types, including lesser-known embedded processors (such as in video game consoles and kitchen appliances).

Other popular compilers, which this book doesn't examine in detail, include the Microsoft Visual Studio C++ compiler [22], the Green Hills Compiler [23], and the Intel C++ compiler [24].

GCC uses the **toolchain** approach to compiling code. As the name suggests, it consists of a chain of tools invoked in the necessary sequence. This consists of the following components:

1. The **C preprocessor,** for expanding macro definitions

2. The **C compiler,** which translates source code into assembly language

3. The **assembler,** which translates assembly language into object files

4. The **linker,** which joins different object files into a single executable program

The upcoming examples demonstrate the compilation of C and C++ code, using the GCC compiler on Linux. Although the details vary from platform to platform, the same basic concepts apply to most modern systems, including Microsoft Windows. Note that many of the commands mentioned actually existed long before the introduction of Linux, so the book refers to them as UNIX commands.

If you plan to use GCC in your build system, spend time becoming familiar with GCC's usage and options. The GCC manual is a good starting point [25], but you can also find textbooks written on the subject [26]. Although this book covers some of the basic options, there are literally hundreds of configuration parameters.

## Source Files

The basic units of compilation in the C language are the **C source file** (with file suffix .c) and the **C header file** (with file suffix .h). By convention, a source file contains the definition of functions and global variables, and this is where most of the source code is kept. On the other hand, a header file contains such things as type, macro, and constant definitions, and function prototypes that declare which parameters and return values each function takes.

When compiling code, each C source file is compiled into a single object file (with file suffix .o in UNIX or .obj in Windows). However, each source file can include header files to obtain all the definitions it needs. When structuring software, header files are used for defining macros, constants, types, or function prototypes that must be shared between multiple source files.

In the following example are two source files (main.c and hello.c) and a single header file (hello.h). The main.c file is as follows:

```
 1   #include "hello.h"
 2
 3   int main(int argc, char *argv[])
 4   {
 5       if (MAX(1,2) == 2){
 6           hello("World");
 7       }
 8
 9       return 0;
10   }
```

Line 1 uses the #include directive to state that hello.h must also be scanned for additional definitions. As you'll see shortly, one of those definitions is the MAX macro, which returns the maximum of two numeric input values. This macro is used inside the body of the main function, on line 5.

Next, line 6 calls the hello function, which also happens to be defined in another file, hello.c. The capability to call functions defined in other source files demonstrates another way in which source files are logically linked.

The second source file, `hello.c`, includes two header files:

```
1   #include <stdio.h>
2   #include "hello.h"
3
4   void hello(const char *string)
5   {
6       printf("Hello %s\n", string);
7   }
```

The first header file is the built-in `stdio.h`, providing information about the standard `printf` function, which is used on line 6. The second header file is `hello.h`, which is the same file that was included into `main.c`. This guarantees that both `main.c` and `hello.c` have a consistent view of their shared definitions.

The final file in this example is `hello.h`, the header file that was referenced by both the source files.

```
1   extern void hello(const char *string);
2
3   #define MAX(a,b) ((a) > (b) ? (a) : (b))
```

On line 1 is a function prototype that informs the compiler which parameters and return value the `hello` function expects. By including this prototype in each of the source files, the compiler can validate that the `hello` function is defined and used consistently in all places.

Next, line 3 shows the definition of the `MAX` macro that you've used before. A macro is different from a function, in that it exists only at compile time and is textually replaced wherever it's used in the source code. You'll see an example of this shortly.

When you compile the example, you end up with two different object files: `main.o` and `hello.o`. Note that the `-c` option to GCC requests that the source files be compiled into object files.

```
$ gcc -c hello.c
$ gcc -c main.c
$ ls
hello.c   hello.h   hello.o   main.c   main.o
```

No object file is generated for `hello.h`, because header files can be used only by including them in a source file; they can't be compiled on their own.

By using the `-E` option to GCC, you can see the C preprocessor portion of the toolchain at work. This option instructs GCC to only process #include directives and macro expansions instead of actually doing any compilation work (as was the case with `-c`). Note that, in the following example, `hello.h` has essentially been merged into the same compilation unit as `main.c`, and the `MAX` macro in the body of the `main` function has been replaced by its definition.

```
$ gcc -E main.c
1 "main.c"
# 1 "hello.h" 1
extern void hello(const char *string);
# 2 "main.c" 2

int main(int argc, char *argv[])
{
    if (((1) > (2) ? (1) : (2)) == 2){
        hello("World");
    }

    return 0;
}
```

Although GCC implicitly calls the preprocessor, and the developer doesn't normally need to think about it, examining the output of the preprocessor is useful in some cases. For example, if your program appears to contain a bug that might be caused by a macro, it's often useful to expand the macro and look at the underlying C code that's being compiled. Second, if a type or constant definition appears to be missing (causing compile errors), it's useful to expand the C code to determine whether the definition is actually included.

## Assembly Language Files

With the GCC compiler, creating an object file from a source file is a multistep process. You've already explored the preprocessing step (-E option), but it's also interesting to examine the generation of assembly language code (-S option). Keep in mind that GCC uses the toolchain approach, in which the source file is first preprocessed, then compiled into assembly language, and then assembled in object files that contain machine code instructions.

The following output shows the result of asking GCC to create an assembler file (with file suffix .s). For more details of the file's format, refer to any book that describes your computer's assembly language. (In this example, it's Intel x86 code, often referred to as i386-series code.)

```
$ gcc -S hello.c
$ cat hello.s
    .file    "hello.c"
    .section        .rodata
.LC0:
    .string "Hello %s\n"
    .text
.globl hello
    .type    hello, @function
hello:
    pushl    %ebp
    movl     %esp, %ebp
```

```
subl    $8, %esp
movl    8(%ebp), %eax
movl    %eax, 4(%esp)
movl    $.LC0, (%esp)
call    printf
leave
ret
```

Although this is an intermediate step that's usually hidden from the developer, you should care about assembly language files for several reasons. Some software is written directly in assembly language, so your build system must cater to that need. This is usually in system-level programming where high-performance is required or special CPU features must be used. Assembly language programming isn't for the faint-of-heart and isn't the slightest bit portable, so try to limit yourself to high-level languages, if you can.

It's not unheard of for developers to complain that the compiler is generating bad code. Using the -s option in GCC enables you to view the exact sequence of instructions the CPU will execute. If the sequence of instructions doesn't look correct when you compare it with the C code, the compiler is probably at fault. For popular CPU types such as x86 and PowerPC (used and tested for many years), you're less likely to see this type of compiler error.

Sometimes, even when you use only C source files, you might see a compile error reported at the assembly language level. The message may be reported in some obscure temporary file that GCC created internally. In this case, either you've hit another compiler bug or somebody has inserted bad assembly language code into an asm directive in your C source file.

## Object Files

An object file is a container for machine code instructions. It's not yet capable of being executed by the computer, because it still needs to be linked with other object files and all the required libraries. As you saw earlier, to compile a source file into object code, you use the -c option for GCC:

```
$ gcc -c hello.c
$ file hello.o
hello.o: ELF 32-bit LSB relocatable, Intel 80386, version 1
(SYSV), not
stripped
```

An object file isn't human readable (it's just a series of numbers), so you use the UNIX file command to give you some high-level information on the content. In this case, file is confirming that you produced the following type of file:

- The object file uses the Executable and Linking Format (ELF) structure when storing the various components of the program. ELF [27] is a common object file format that supersedes older formats, such as a.out and COFF.

- The file is a 32-bit program, as distinct from newer 64-bit programs or older 16-bit programs.

- The data is stored in least significant byte format (**little endian**), as opposed to most significant byte format (**big endian**).

- The machine instructions are for the Intel x86 family of processors, as opposed to MIPS, PowerPC, or many other CPU types.

- The file is still relocatable and hasn't yet been stripped. This means that the file contains the information necessary to link it with other object files and libraries but doesn't contain enough information to be loaded into memory and executed.

If your build system produces programs for a single CPU type, this information will only be of passing interest. On the other hand, if you're compiling for a multiple CPU–type system, you must pay great attention to get all the file type details correct. If your build system accidentally mixed two types of object file, you'd end up with a lot of confusing errors in which the files couldn't be linked. Even trying to mix 32-bit and 64-bit object files can cause obscure compilation errors, even if the CPU family is the same.

Another way to examine an object file is to ask which symbols that file defines or requires. This is equivalent to asking which functions and variables are defined in a C source file, or which functions and variables are used by that file but defined in some other file. Recall how you used header files to define the function prototypes; now you're looking at the same mechanism from the object file's perspective.

Using the UNIX nm command, you can determine that hello.o defines the hello function (with machine code starting at position 0 within the file). It also requires that some other object file define the printf function, because it's undefined in hello.o.

```
$ nm hello.o
00000000 T hello
         U printf
```

The nm command is invaluable for resolving undefined symbol compilation errors, in which a function is required but, for some reason, isn't being linked into the executable program. By running the nm command on all your object files, you can locate where the missing symbol is referenced and where it's defined.

For power users, the UNIX `objdump` command can provide even more information about your object files. The following example shows how the `-x` option provides summary information about `hello.o`. It provides extensive information about the file's type, the list of sections it contains (such as program text, data, uninitialized data, and read-only data), where those sections are located within the file, and where they'll be loaded into memory. It also provides a superset of the information provided by both the `file` and `nm` commands.

```
$ objdump -x hello.o
hello.o:     file format elf32-i386
hello.o
architecture: i386, flags 0x00000011:
HAS_RELOC, HAS_SYMS
start address 0x00000000

Sections:
Idx Name          Size      VMA       LMA       File off  Algn
  0 .text         00000014  00000000  00000000  00000034  2**2
                  CONTENTS, ALLOC, LOAD, RELOC, READONLY, CODE
  1 .data         00000000  00000000  00000000  00000048  2**2
                  CONTENTS, ALLOC, LOAD, DATA
  2 .bss          00000000  00000000  00000000  00000048  2**2
                  ALLOC
  3 .rodata       0000000a  00000000  00000000  00000048  2**0
                  CONTENTS, ALLOC, LOAD, READONLY, DATA
  4 .comment      0000003a  00000000  00000000  00000052  2**0
                  CONTENTS, READONLY
  5 .comment.SUSE.OPTs 00000005 00000000 00000000 0000008c 2**0
                  CONTENTS, READONLY
  6 .note.GNU-stack 00000000  00000000  00000000  00000091  2**0
                  CONTENTS, READONLY
SYMBOL TABLE:
00000000 l    df *ABS*  00000000 hello.c
00000000 l    d  .text  00000000 .text
00000000 l    d  .data  00000000 .data
00000000 l    d  .bss   00000000 .bss
00000000 l    d  .rodata        00000000
.rodata
00000000 l    d  .comment.SUSE.OPTs
```

```
00000000 .comment.SUSE.OPTs
00000000 l      d   .note.GNU-stack
00000000 .note.GNU-stack
00000000 l      d   .comment          00000000
.comment
00000000 g      F .text  00000014 hello
00000000          *UND*  00000000 printf

RELOCATION RECORDS FOR [.text]:
OFFSET    TYPE               VALUE
00000009 R_386_32            .rodata
0000000e R_386_PC32          printf
```

The objdump command has many different options that are worth learning about [28]. It's highly recommended you become an expert in using objdump, especially if you're doing advanced work with compilers and linkers. This tool also provides the capability to disassemble machine code back into assembly language, which is important if you suspect that your assembler is generating bad machine code instructions.

As a final resort, you may also consider using the UNIX hexdump command to examine the raw bytes in the file. This is a primitive way to examine files, but if objdump fails for some reason (such as a corrupt file), it might be your only hope.

## Executable Programs

The final step in the C/C++ example is to link the object files into a single executable program. This is done by providing the name of the program (with the -o option) and listing all the object files that should be linked.

```
$ gcc -o hello hello.o main.o
```

For the sake of convenience, GCC enables you to execute the whole toolchain at once instead of explicitly listing each step (preprocess, compile, assemble, link). To use this feature, you specify the source code filenames instead of the object filenames.

```
$ gcc -o hello hello.c main.c
```

Although doing everything in one command is a useful feature for small programs, a large build system wouldn't do things this way. Instead, you'd need more control over when and how files are compiled and linked, especially if only some of the source files have changed. In most build systems, you see the compilation from .c files to .o files done using the -c option, followed by a separate linking phase that joins all the object files.

Finally, to make sure you generated a suitable executable file, use the UNIX `file` command again.

```
$ file hello
hello: ELF 32-bit LSB executable, Intel 80386, version 1
➥(SYSV), for
GNU/Linux 2.6.4, dynamically linked (uses shared libs), not
➥stripped
```

The `file` command's output is similar, except that you've now constructed an executable program. This file can be loaded into memory and executed.

## Static Libraries

The Linux operating system supports both statically and dynamically linked libraries. As a reminder, static libraries are just an archive of object files that can be linked into an executable program (if required), whereas a dynamic library is loaded at runtime and the program directly calls the required functions.

The following example shows how to create a static library containing four object files (`sqrt.o`, `sine.o`, `cosine.o`, and `tan.o`). Static libraries are also known as **archives**, given that all they're doing is collecting multiple files into a single larger file. The object files aren't modified in any way and can easily be extracted from the archive and returned to their original form.

```
$ gcc -c sqrt.c
$ gcc -c sine.c
$ gcc -c cosine.c
$ gcc -c tan.c

$ ar -rs mymath.a sqrt.o sine.o cosine.o tan.o
ar: creating mymath.a

$ ar -t mymath.a
sqrt.o
sine.o
cosine.o
tan.o
```

The UNIX `ar` command is responsible for creating the static library archive (with the `-rs` option) and can also be used to examine the content of the archive (with the `-t` option). Options exist for extracting object files and writing their content back to disk, but that's not a common operation for build systems.

In the final step, you specify both the `main.o` object file (the main program) and the `mymath.a` archive file on the GCC command line.

```
$ gcc -c main.c
$ gcc -o prog main.o mymath.a
```

GCC knows how to manage these archive files and can link them into the program, but only if it needs to. If `main.o` actually requires any of the archive's object files, they're included in the executable program. Conversely, other object files that `main.o` doesn't require are not linked.

## Dynamic Libraries

In the case of dynamically linked libraries, the process is more complex. In particular, you must allow for the fact that linking happens at runtime rather than when the program is compiled. This necessitates a change to the compilation sequence.

All object files must now be created using special **position-independent code** (PIC) so that they can be loaded at any memory location the program requires. The shared library is created as if it were an executable program in its own right, except that you use the `-shared` option to make it a dynamic library (with the `.so` suffix).

```
$ gcc -c -fPIC sqrt.c
$ gcc -c -fPIC sine.c
$ gcc -c -fPIC cosine.c
$ gcc -c -fPIC tan.c
$ gcc -shared -o libmymath.so sqrt.o sine.o cosine.o tan.o

$ file libmymath.so
libmymath.so: ELF 32-bit LSB shared object, Intel 80386,
version 1 (SYSV),
dynamically linked, not stripped
```

To make use of the new shared library, you specify the name of that library on the standard GCC linker line. The `-l` option asks the linker to include the `libmymath.so` library. Note that the `-L` option informs the linker of the directory where the library can be found—in this case, that is the current directory.

```
$ gcc -c main.c
$ gcc -o prog main.c -L. -lmymath
```

To verify that everything works correctly, you use the UNIX `ldd` command to see which dynamic libraries need to be loaded into memory when the main program is executed.

```
$ ldd prog
        linux-gate.so.1 =>   (0xffffe000)
        libmymath.so => not found
        libc.so.6 => /lib/libc.so.6 (0xb7f3a000)
        /lib/ld-linux.so.2 (0xb80ab000)
```

The first observation is that there are four libraries, with only one being yours. GCC implicitly added the remaining three libraries so that the program would execute correctly. One of these libraries (`libc.so.6`) is the standard C language library that provides the implementation of functions such as `printf`.

The second observation is that the `libmymath.so` library can't be found, and trying to run the `prog` executable will therefore fail. Although you used the `-L` option to tell GCC where the library is stored (the current directory), you also need to inform the operating system where it can be loaded. Directories such as `/lib` and `/usr/lib` are searched automatically, but for nonstandard locations, you first must set the `LD_LIBRARY_PATH` environment variable.

```
$ export LD_LIBRARY_PATH=.
$ ldd prog
        linux-gate.so.1 =>  (0xffffe000)
        libmymath.so => ./libmymath.so (0xb80a7000)
        libc.so.6 => /lib/libc.so.6 (0xb7f3a000)
        /lib/ld-linux.so.2 (0xb80ab000)
```

This time, the library can be found. Of course, in a real situation, you would set `LD_LIBRARY_PATH` to the absolute pathname where `libmymath.so` is installed, instead of asking the operating system to find the library in the current directory (which would be a major security hole).

As a reminder, using dynamic libraries enables you to upgrade them without recompiling the executable program. Dynamic libraries can also save a lot of the computer's memory, because it's possible to share a single copy among multiple programs instead of requiring each program to have its own copy (as is the case with static libraries).

## C++ Compilation

Given that C++ is a superset of the C language, every effort has been made to ensure that the object files are consistent between the two languages. However, the file formats are different in a few places. Most notably, C++ is capable of performing link-time type checking, whereas C programs must do all their type checking at compile time.

In the previous example, `hello.c` and `main.c` both included the prototype definition of the `hello` function, by including `hello.h`. The compiler could then ensure that the caller of the function (`main.c`) and the definer of the function (`hello.c`) are in total agreement about the type of parameters and return value expected.

On the other hand, if the two files used inconsistent definitions for the `hello` function (that is, they didn't both include `hello.h`), there would be no way for the linker to complain. After all, the object file states only that `hello` is defined, or required by that file, and never mentions that it has parameters. The linker would have no way to identify the parameter type mismatch.

For C++, the compiler (called g++) gets around this problem by generating more detailed object file information. In the following output, notice that the hello symbol has been **mangled** (yes, that's the technical term) to include extra characters that specify the type information.

```
$ g++ -c hello.c
$ nm hello.o
00000000 T _Z5helloPc
         U __gxx_personality_v0
         U printf
```

You end up with the symbol name Z5helloPc. If two object files don't use the same type information, the mangled names won't match when the program is linked, and the linking step will fail.

If you're observant, you notice that the printf function doesn't have a mangled name. This is because printf is a C-language function (not C++), and the compiler is explicitly instructed to treat it as a C function. This is an important feature that allows C++ and C object files to be linked correctly without causing type mismatch errors in legacy source code.

That completes the analysis of the files and compilation steps for C and C++ software. You haven't explored any of the language details, but when creating a build system, you care only about the sequence of compilation steps required to create an executable program, not the content of the software itself.

Let's now focus on Java-based software and learn how Java programs are compiled into executable form.

## Java

The Java programming language is now one of the most popular systems for developing new application code. Sun Microsystems (now Oracle) publicly released it in 1995, but Java was made famous when it was incorporated into the Netscape web browser. Although many people saw Java as a way of creating cute web page animations, it quickly became a full-fledged general-purpose language that could execute programs on a wide range of desktop and server machines (including Linux, Mac OS X, Windows, and Solaris).

Java was derived from a number of earlier languages, with C++ being a key contributor. However, many of the quirks in the C++ language were removed and replaced by "safer" features. For example, C++ developers can manipulate pointers using arithmetic, which is a frequent cause of memory corruption problems. Additionally, C++ developers often forget to deallocate memory when it's no longer required, potentially causing memory leaks. Both of these limitations have been removed from the Java language and replaced by safer mechanisms that enable faster and more accurate software development.

One big selling point of the Java language has been its "write once, run anywhere" philosophy. That is, it should be possible to compile a Java program on a Linux machine, yet run it on a Windows or Solaris machine without any modification. This is achieved by using a standard set of byte codes that are interpreted by the **Java Virtual Machine (JVM)** [29]. Also, because of Java's security features, it's possible to restrict the environment in which a Java program executes, therefore allowing untrusted programs to be executed without fear of harming the host computer.

Because of Java's general-purpose nature, it's currently used in a wide range of applications, including desktop applications, business applications, and web-based systems. One area in which Java is not so strong is in high-performance systems where execution time is highly optimized.

## Compilation Tools

Sun Microsystems (now a subsidiary of Oracle) maintains the standard Java programming environment. The Java Development Kit (JDK) has gone through numerous iterations since the inception of Java and is still actively being improved as the Java language grows. The JDK is shipped with both a set of compilation tools (specifically javac) and a number of standard Java libraries.

The JDK is often viewed as being a **reference implementation** of the language. Other vendors are welcome to create their own Java implementation, as long as it conforms to the JDK standard. The advantage of this approach is that each vendor is permitted to add platform support and performance optimizations, while ensuring that they can still execute programs compiled by other standard version of Java.

Although the JDK is the most popular implementation and can be downloaded for free [30], you can consider several other options. The OpenJDK implementation [31] is an open-source spinoff from the original JDK product, whereas the GNU Java Compiler [32] (from the Free Software Foundation) is a completely separate implementation. It's also worth considering the Eclipse Java Compiler (ECJ), which is mostly used within the Eclipse IDE [33]. Finally, vendors such as IBM (the Jikes compiler) and Microsoft (Visual J++) have provided Java implementations, although these are no longer actively supported.

The examples in this book use the JDK system on a Microsoft Windows environment. Given Java's cross-platform nature, the same concepts apply on all other operating system types (such as Linux and Solaris). Also, as with the discussion of C and C++, this book focuses exclusively on the language and tool features that are relevant to build systems.

## Source Files

In Java, the basic unit of source code is the `.java` file. These files contain Java class definitions (typically one class per source file), which, in turn, contain the definitions of constants, variables, and methods. Unlike C and C++, there's no concept of preprocessing a source file and no capability to include header files.

Sharing information between classes occurs when one class explicitly imports variables and methods that are defined within another class. A developer can control when a variable or method is available for export or may decide to keep it hidden for private use within a single class definition.

Consider an example in which the source code is stored in the file `com\arapiki\examples\Hello.java`. Note the Java convention in which files are stored within a hierarchy of directories that indicate which package the file belongs to. This encourages developers to think hard about the structure of their code (and, hence, their source tree) before they start to write their software.

In `Hello.java`, you define a new Java class, named `Hello`:

```
1   package com.arapiki.examples;
2
3   public class Hello {
4
5       private String words;
6
7       public Hello(String message) {
8           words = message;
9       }
10
11      public void speak() {
12          System.out.println("Hello " + words);
13      }
14  }
```

When an object of the `Hello` class is first created, the `Hello` method (lines 7–9) is implicitly executed (this is known as a **constructor**). Later, users of the `Hello` class can call the `speak` method (lines 11–13) to perform operations on the data that `Hello` encapsulates. Note that, on line 8, the constructor saves a string message to be displayed when `speak` is called.

The second source file, `com\arapiki\examples\Main.java`, is the main entry point of the program:

```
1   package com.arapiki.examples;
2
3   import com.arapiki.examples.Hello;
4
5   public class Main {
6
7       public static void main(String args[]) {
8           Hello speaker = new Hello("World");
```

```
 9              speaker.speak();
10        }
11   }
```

In the `main` method (lines 7–10), you create a new object of type `Hello` and pass in a `String`-typed message as a parameter. You then ask the newly created object to execute its `speak` method.

It's worth noting that, in `Main.java`, you use an explicit `import` directive (line 3) to ask the Java compiler to look for the definition of the `Hello` class. Using this information, the compiler determines the various types, constants, and methods that the `Hello` class defines. If mismatches arise between the definition of `Hello` and the reference to that class, they're flagged at compile time. This is similar to the concept of header files in C, except that there's no need for duplicated code between two different files (such as `hello.c` and `hello.h`).

Note that, on line 12 of `Hello.java`, you explicitly reference `System.out.println` by its fully qualified name instead of using an `import` directive. This approach has the same effect with respect to gathering type information and performing type checking.

The Java language also supports the concept of an **interface,** which is essentially a class that doesn't have any of its methods implemented. These ensure type compatibility between objects of different classes. From the perspective of the build system, little difference exists between interfaces and a true class, so this book doesn't discuss them further.

## Object Files

The object file format for a Java class is known as a **class file** and has the suffix of `.class`. Because of Java's "run anywhere" approach, a class file uses machine-independent byte codes to describe the flow of the program instead of compiling directly into native machine code. A Java Virtual Machine (JVM) is required to load and interpret these byte codes, although the JVM likely first translates them into native machine code before actually executing the program.

To translate Java source files into class files, you use the `javac` command. Because of Java's package system, you're required to invoke the compiler from the top of the directory hierarchy instead of starting in the directory containing the source files.

```
C:\Work> javac com\arapiki\examples\Main.java

C:\Work> dir com\arapiki\examples
Directory of C:\Work

07/24/2009  09:17 AM    <DIR>          .
07/24/2009  09:17 AM    <DIR>          ..
```

```
07/24/2009   09:47 AM                      632 Hello.class
07/24/2009   09:17 AM                      227 Hello.java
07/24/2009   09:47 AM                      391 Main.class
07/24/2009   09:18 AM                      210 Main.java
              4 File(s)            1,460 bytes
              2 Dir(s)    17,457,893,376 bytes free
```

Note that because the Main class imports definitions from the `Hello` class, the Java compiler also proceeds to compile `Hello.java`, even though it wasn't explicitly listed on the `javac` command line.

In general, a Java compilation produces one class file for each Java file. The exception is if you used Java's **inner class** concept, in which multiple classes can be defined within a single Java source file. As you'll see later, this mechanism can cause problems for your build system.

To check that you've generated a valid class file, you now use the `javap` command. Not many command-line options exist for `javap`, but it does provide the capability to list the methods defined in the file, as well as to view the byte codes for each method.

```
C:\Work\com\arapiki\examples> javap Hello

Compiled from "Hello.java"
public class com.arapiki.examples.Hello extends java.lang.
➥Object{
    public com.arapiki.examples.Hello(java.lang.String);
    public void speak();
}

C:\Work\com\arapiki\examples> javap -c Hello

Compiled from "Hello.java"
public class com.arapiki.examples.Hello extends java.lang.
➥Object{
public com.arapiki.examples.Hello(java.lang.String);
  Code:
   0:   aload_0
   1:   invokespecial    #1; //Method java/lang/
➥Object."<init>":()V
   4:   aload_0
   5:   aload_1
   6:   putfield         #2; //Field words:Ljava/lang/String;
   9:   return

public void speak();
  Code:
   0:   getstatic   #3; //Field java/lang/System.out:Ljava/io/
➥PrintStream;
   3:   new         #4;    //class java/lang/StringBuilder
   6:   dup
```

```
      7:   invokespecial   #5; //Method java/lang/
StringBuilder."<init>":()V
     10:   ldc        #6;          //String Hello
     12:   invokevirtual #7; //Method java/lang/StringBuilder.
append:
                            // (Ljava/lang/String;)Ljava/lang/
StringBuilder;
     15:   aload_0
     16:   getfield         #2; //Field words:Ljava/lang/String;
     19:   invokevirtual    #7; //Method java/lang/StringBuilder.
append:
                            //(Ljava/lang/String;)Ljava/lang/
StringBuilder;
     22:   invokevirtual    #8; //Method java/lang/StringBuilder.
toString:()
                            // Ljava/lang/String;
     25:   invokevirtual    #9; //Method java/io/PrintStream.
println:
                            //(Ljava/lang/String;)V
     28:   return
}
```

Examining these byte codes in detail gives you a rough idea of how they relate to the original Hello.java file. For more information about Java byte codes, refer to [29] in References.

## Executable Programs

One of the fundamental concepts in the world of Java programming is **dynamic class loading**. No build-time link step is required to produce an executable program. Instead, Java classes are individually loaded into memory when a running program needs them. Java executable programs are thus quite different in nature from C/C++ programs, and there's no single executable program image to be loaded.

In reality, Java programs are simply a collection of dynamic libraries, although individual classes are loaded one at a time instead of as part of much larger shared libraries.

A Java program requires two things to execute:

- The JVM must be provided with the name of a class that contains a main method. This is used as the starting point for execution.

- The JVM must also be provided with a **class path**, which is used to identify where additional classes can be located.

Let's see how the `java` tool (the JDK's virtual machine) executes the previous "Hello World" example. Note the use of the fully qualified class name (containing periods) rather than the directory path (containing slashes or backslashes).

```
C:\Work> java com.arapiki.examples.Main
Hello World
```

If you followed along when looking at the source code in `Main.java` and `Hello.java`, the program output shouldn't surprise you. What's more interesting is the sequence of events taking place under the covers of the JVM interpreter. If you run that same java command again, but this time with verbose output enabled, you see additional information on which classes are loaded.

```
C:\Work> javac –verbose:class com.arapiki.examples.Main
[Loaded java.lang.Object from shared objects file]
[Loaded java.io.Serializable from shared objects file]
[Loaded java.lang.Comparable from shared objects file]
[Loaded java.lang.CharSequence from shared objects file]
[Loaded java.lang.String from shared objects file]
. . .
[... lots of output removed ...]
. . .
[Loaded java.security.Principal from shared objects file]
[Loaded java.security.cert.Certificate from shared objects file]
[Loaded com.arapiki.examples.Main from file:/C:/Work/]
[Loaded com.arapiki.examples.Hello from file:/C:/Work/]
Hello World
```

The output is quite long because of all the built-in classes used. Toward the end of the output, you can see the Main class being loaded, followed shortly by `Hello`. Finally, you see the expected output displayed.

The remaining question is how the JVM knew where to find the `.class` files. In this example, the `Hello` class was located in a directory that was relative to the current directory. That is, when the JVM was asked to import the class named `com.arapiki.examples.Hello`, it simply looked for a file named `com\arapiki\examples\Hello.class` relative to the current directory.

In more complicated programs, you would need to explicitly set the class path to indicate where additional classes could be located. The class path can be specified either by setting the `CLASSPATH` environment variable before starting the JVM or by specifying the `–cp` command-line option. The class path is a semicolon-separated list (or colon-separated list, in UNIX) of all the directories to search to find class files.

## Libraries

In addition to specifying a list of directories in which .class files can be found, Java classes can be placed into larger archive files, known as **JAR files**. Most Java applications prefer the JAR file format (with a .jar suffix), simply because it's easier to manipulate JAR files than package and distribute a large number of .class files.

JAR files are similar to the archive (.a) files used with C and C++, because they're simply a container for a number of different .class files. They're also similar to C's dynamic libraries because they're loaded at runtime instead of being statically linked into the main program (a concept that isn't normally used in Java).

The following example demonstrates how a JAR file can be created. With the -cf option, you create a new .jar file containing all the .class files found within the com/ directory hierarchy.

```
C:\Work> jar -cf example.jar com
```

The jar command works silently in this case and doesn't produce any output. With the -tf option, you can examine the **table of contents** to make sure the .jar file was created properly.

```
C:\Work> jar -tf example.jar
com/
com/arapiki/
com/arapiki/examples/
com/arapiki/examples/Hello.class
com/arapiki/examples/Main.class
```

To use this JAR file, you provide the -cp option to the JVM and execute the program as you did earlier.

```
C:\Work> java -cp example.jar com.arapiki.examples.Main
Hello World
```

As you'll see in Part II when you look at Java-based build tools, the JAR file is commonly used as a means of distributing programs. Not only do you package your own software in JAR files, but you can incorporate third-party packages by obtaining other people's JAR files and adding them to your own class path. Because of the dynamic loading system, you can replace and upgrade JAR files whenever you want.

As an added bonus, the Java class loader ensures that a class's method names, parameters, and return types match what the rest of the program expects them to be. For example, during the compilation process, the compiler ensures that whenever an instance of the Hello class is created, it's done so by passing a single String value into the constructor. At runtime, when the Hello class is loaded and executed, there's an additional check to ensure that this constructor still exists and that the class's public API hasn't been modified. Invalid changes to the API cause a runtime error.

# C#

The third and final general-purpose programming language examined here is C# (pronounced "C Sharp"). This is an object-oriented language that uses the Microsoft .NET development framework [34]. Although it's primarily designed for use in the Microsoft Windows environment, it's also possible to compile and execute C# programs on UNIX-like environments, such as Linux and Mac OS X. C# and the .NET Framework first made their public appearance around 2001.

From a language design perspective, C# is derived from a number of previous object-oriented languages, most notably C++ and Java. It provides general-purpose object-oriented programming facilities, and important concepts such as type safety and multithreading support. C# can be used in a wide variety of software, ranging from desktop applications to large business systems. However, it's not optimized for high-performance computing in the way C and C++ are often used.

One interesting feature of C# is that it uses the same intermediate byte code standard as other Microsoft-based languages. In particular, C#, Visual Basic. NET, Visual C++, and Visual J# are all languages that can be compiled using the same set of byte codes (known as the **Common Intermediate Language**). Additionally, the **Common Language Infrastructure** [35] defines a standard set of data types and calling conventions that all .NET languages must implement. These standards enable source code from each language to be compiled and integrated into the same executable program, clearly benefiting the large number of existing users of Visual Basic and Visual C++.

## Compilation Tools

Because C# is a Microsoft-designed language, the most commonly used compilation tools are from the Visual Studio development environment. This provides both a graphical interface for authoring code and a set of command-line tools for each of the supported languages. Microsoft provides an "Express" version of these tools [36] that can be downloaded free of charge. All of this book's examples use the C# compiler (called csc), which is bundled with this edition of the Visual Studio environment.

For non-Microsoft environments, such as Linux and Mac OS X, you have the option to download the open-source .NET Framework, known as Mono [37].

The goal of this project is to enable users to develop and execute their Windows .NET applications on UNIX-like environments, therefore enabling the integration between Microsoft and UNIX platforms.

## Source Files

The basic unit of compilation in C# is the `.cs` file (for example, `main.cs`). These files store one or more class definitions, each of which is placed into a suitable **namespace**. As with other object-oriented languages, classes and namespaces are used to divide a program into logical units of work. Start by looking at an extended version of the example used for Java. What's important to understand from the build perspective is how the source code files are compiled and linked into a single executable program.

In the first source code file, `hello.cs`, you define the `Hello` class with a constructor and a single method:

```
1   using System;
2
3   namespace Arapiki.Greeters {
4
5       public class Hello {
6
7           private string words;
8
9           public Hello(string message) {
10              this.words = message;
11          }
12
13          public void speak() {
14              Console.WriteLine("Hello {0}", words);
15          }
16      }
17  }
```

The constructor (lines 9–11) takes a string as its only parameter and stores it for later use. When the `speak` method (lines 13–15) is invoked, it displays the stored message on the output console.

An important observation here is the use of a namespace (on line 3). That is, the `Hello` class is encapsulated inside the `Arapiki.Greeters` namespace, which keeps it separate from other definitions of the `Hello` class that might be defined within other programs or libraries. As you'll see later, to access this particular `Hello` class, a program needs to explicitly mention the class's namespace.

When it comes to storing source code on the file system, any C# class can be stored in any namespace, without limitations on where on the computer's disk the file is stored. Unlike Java, which requires that source code be stored in a subdirectory with the same name as its enclosing package, the C# compiler allows an arbitrary layout. Therefore, for the compiler to locate the necessary classes, the developer must explicitly state the list of libraries to be searched.

Note that the previous example uses the System namespace (via the using System statement on line 1). When you compile a C# program, you typically need to inform the compiler of which library file (with .dll suffix) the desired namespace is defined in. Luckily, the System library is automatically added to all C# compilations.

Continue the example by defining two more classes in a new source file, goodbye.cs. You also add these classes to the same Arapiki.Greeters namespace:

```
 1  using System;
 2
 3  namespace Arapiki.Greeters {
 4
 5      public class GoodBye {
 6
 7          private string words;
 8
 9          public GoodBye(string message) {
10              this.words = message;
11          }
12
13          public void speak() {
14              Console.WriteLine("GoodBye {0}", words);
15          }
16      }
17
18      public class Farewell {
19
20          private string words;
21
22          public Farewell(string message) {
23              this.words = message;
24          }
25
26          public void speak() {
27              Console.WriteLine("Farewell {0}", words);
28          }
29      }
30  }
```

The implementation of these classes is almost identical to the Hello class, so no further explanation is required. Of course, any C# programmer worth his or her paycheck would rewrite these classes using inheritance, but this is just an example.

Finally, you create the main.cs compilation unit that contains the GreeterApp class.

```
 1   using Arapiki.Greeters;
 2
 3   public class GreeterApp {
 4
 5       public static void Main() {
 6           Hello h = new Hello("stranger");
 7           GoodBye g = new GoodBye("my friend");
 8           Farewell f = new Farewell("you fool");
 9           h.speak();
10           g.speak();
11           f.speak();
12       }
13   }
```

This is the main entry point of the application. It creates an instance of each of the newly defined classes and then calls the speak method on each of them. For the compiler to locate these classes, you provide the using Arapiki.Greeters directive on line 1.

Now look at the different ways to compile this source code into an executable program.

## Executable Programs

Compilation of a C# program is not too different from that of a C or C++ program. As with these other languages, you provide a complete list of source files and libraries to be linked into an executable program. In the .NET environment, the resulting file is known as an **assembly**. These files collect various class definitions (in byte code format), along with other resources, such as graphic images and documentation files.

The following command line demonstrates the compilation and execution of the program.

```
C:\Work> csc /target:exe /out:prog.exe main.cs hello.cs
➥goodbye.cs

Microsoft (R) Visual C# 2008 Compiler version 3.5.30729.1
for Microsoft (R) .NET Framework version 3.5
Copyright (C) Microsoft Corporation. All rights reserved.

c:\Work> prog
Hello stranger
GoodBye my friend
Farewell you fool
```

One interesting observation is that this example didn't use intermediate object files, as you did for C/C++ compilation. Instead, the C# compiler hides this level of detail and converts the entire program into a single assembly file in one step. As an optimization, the compiler can skip the recompilation of a .cs file that hasn't been modified, but only if it can determine that the generated byte codes will be exactly the same as the last time they were compiled. The C# compiler does permit the generation of **netmodule** files (equivalent to C's object files), but this technique isn't commonly used.

A second observation is that executing a .NET program is done in exactly the same way as in a traditional machine code program. That is, a byte-code program is invoked by typing the name of the executable program into the command shell. This contrasts with the approach taken by a Java program, in which an external virtual machine must first be started. In the .NET environment, an executable program starts by executing native machine code instructions that implicitly call upon the .NET virtual machine (conveniently located inside a Windows dynamic library). The virtual machine then proceeds by JIT compiling the intermediate byte codes into machine code.

To ensure that you have a valid executable program, you can use the ildasm. exe tool to disassemble the intermediate language (byte codes). The ildasm.exe tool starts a GUI display by default, but it can also display output in a text-only format. Figure 4.2 shows the disassembly of prog.exe.

**Figure 4.2** *The disassembly of the statically linked prog.exe using IL DASM.*

You can see the Arapiki.Greeters namespace and the three classes it contains. You can also see the GreeterApp class that contains the Main method.

Double-clicking the speak method of the Hello class obtains a listing of the byte codes from that method (see Figure 4.3).

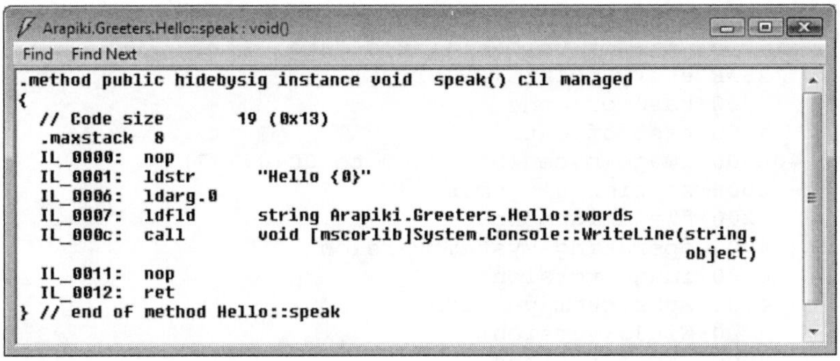

**Figure 4.3** *Disassembly of the speak method using IL DASM.*

For more details of the Common Intermediate Language instructions, refer to [35] in References.

As just mentioned, a .NET executable program is also a standard Windows program, so it is stored in Portable Executable (PE) format [38]. In this respect, you can use the same tools to analyze the content of the PE file as you can with any other Windows executable program. In the following example, the dumpbin.exe program disassembles the headers of the PE file. The dumpbin.exe program has numerous options, and becoming familiar with this tool is worthwhile if you do any type of work with compilers or build systems.

```
c:\Work> dumpbin /headers prog.exe
Microsoft (R) COFF/PE Dumper Version 9.00.30729.01
Copyright (C) Microsoft Corporation.  All rights reserved.

Dump of file prog.exe

PE signature found

File Type: EXECUTABLE IMAGE

FILE HEADER VALUES
             14C machine (x86)
               3 number of sections
        4A6F1190 time date stamp Tue Jul 28 07:56:16 2009
               0 file pointer to symbol table
               0 number of symbols
              E0 size of optional header
             102 characteristics
                 Executable
                 32 bit word machine

OPTIONAL HEADER VALUES
             10B magic # (PE32)
            8.00 linker version
             600 size of code
```

```
    800 size of initialized data
      0 size of uninitialized data
   253E entry point (0040253E)
   2000 base of code
   4000 base of data
 400000 image base (00400000 to 00407FFF)
   2000 section alignment
    200 file alignment
   4.00 operating system version
   0.00 image version
   4.00 subsystem version
      0 Win32 version
   8000 size of image
    200 size of headers
[... output truncated ...]
```

## Libraries

As you might expect, the .NET Framework also supports the concept of libraries. In the same manner as executable files, the **dynamic link library (DLL)** file can be used for storing either native code or .NET byte codes. This type of file also conforms to the Portable Executable format.

When developing C# code in the Visual Studio environment (the GUI interface that calls upon the .NET compilation tools), it's common to divide a large program into a number of smaller libraries. This contrasts with having all the program's source files compiled into a single executable program in one giant step. Many Visual Studio projects are thus made up of a collection of "Library" projects, as well as an "Application" project that depends on those libraries.

Now examine this mechanism by placing the `Arapiki.Greeters` namespace into a separate DLL. Again, the `csc` compiler is used, but this time you use the `/target` option to specify that a DLL be created.

```
c:\Work> csc /target:library /out:greeters.dll hello.cs goodbye.cs
```

You can now use the `ildasm.exe` tool to examine the content of the library file (see Figure 4.4). In this example, the library contains only the greeter classes and doesn't contain the main application (the `GreeterApp` class).

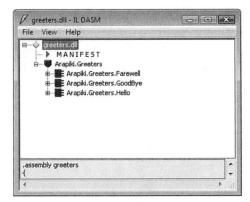

**Figure 4.4** *Disassembly of the greeters.dll dynamic library, using IL DASM.*

The next step is to reference this library when you compile `main.cs` into the `prog.exe` executable program. Note the use of the `/reference` option to inform the compiler of the additional library. It uses this library, as well as any built-in libraries, when searching for namespace and class definitions specified in the program's `using` directives.

```
c:\Work> csc /target:exe /out:prog.exe main.cs /reference:greeters.dll
```

Again, you can use `ildasm.exe` to examine the content of `prog.exe` to see which namespaces, classes, and methods exist (see Figure 4.5). This time, the program contains only the main `GreeterApp` class and doesn't contain any of the other classes, because they're now stored in the DLL.

**Figure 4.5** *Disassembly of prog.exe, now separate from greeters.dll.*

To locate the additional classes at runtime, the .NET Framework examines the **manifest** information that exists inside the `prog.exe` assembly. Double-clicking the `MANIFEST` entry in the ildasm.exe output informs you that `prog.exe` requires that `greeters.dll` also be loaded into memory and made available to the virtual machine (see Figure 4.6). This concept is identical to what you've already observed in C and C++ programs.

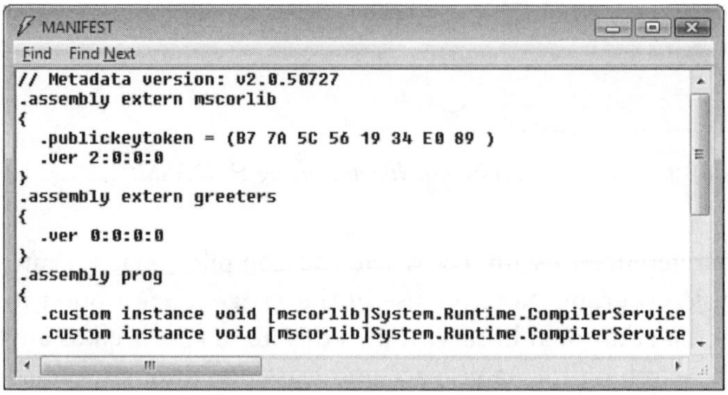

**Figure 4.6** *The manifest for prog.exe, showing that it depends on greeters.dll.*

Luckily for most C# developers, all this compilation process is conveniently hidden behind the user-friendly GUI interface. However, larger programs that have nontrivial build requirements require you to use a full-fledged build tool to automate the compilation of software. Part II briefly looks at the MS Build tool specifically designed for compiling .NET programs.

## Other File Types

Until now, this chapter has focused on the file types normally associated with compiled programming languages, including source files, object files, libraries, and executable programs. However, most software also includes scripts, documentation files, graphic images, and configuration files. The build system must also process these, even if only to include them in the final release package.

For example, a software product can include the following file types:

- **Program code, written in scripting languages:** This includes UNIX shell scripts, Windows batch scripts, and programs written using Perl or Python. As discussed in Chapter 3, "The Runtime View of a Program," these scripts don't require a compilation step, but are instead copied directly to the release package.

- **Web-centric files, including HTML, JavaScript, or PHP:** Depending on the exact file format, these are either interpreted and displayed by the end user's web browser, or compiled and executed by the web server. In either case, the build system is required only to package the files rather than compile them into object code.

- **Modeling language files, such as UML models:** As you'll see shortly, these are a high-level representation of the program, used to automatically generate code in more traditional languages such as Java, C++, or C#.

- **Documentation files such as online help or printable user manuals:** These can be in any format, ranging from UNIX-style nroff files, TeX files, or GNU info files, all the way through to PDF or HTML. Depending on the format used, the build system translates the input files into an output format suitable for displaying in a PDF viewer, rendering in a web browser, or sending to a printer.

- **Graphic image files:** These files are used to display anything from a small icon on a GUI window, to a program's splash screen or a full-size picture. You'll learn about these in more detail shortly.

- **Configuration files:** These files provide configuration data that controls the behavior of the program. These can be in plain text format, can be encoded using XML, or can be written in any customized format suitable for your program.

Let's now examine a few of these additional file formats, namely UML, graphic files, XML files, and language bundles.

## UML-Based Code Generation

The Unified Modeling Language (UML) [39] is a graphical language for describing the high-level design and flow of a program. It's considered to be a higher level than languages such as Java, C++, or C#, given that it focuses on the software's "big picture" and abstracts out the implementation detail. For example, the UML diagram shown in Figure 4.7 states that a program contains two classes (Student and Course), each having a set of methods that can be invoked on objects of that class. It also describes the relationship between the two classes. (For example, a student may be enrolled in zero or more courses.)

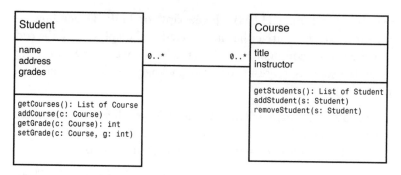

**Figure 4.7** *A Unified Modeling Language diagram.*

After developers create a UML model, they use tools to autogenerate an equivalent program in a lower-level language, such as Java, C++, or C#. As part of this process, each box in the diagram is translated into a single object-oriented class. The name of the class (such as Student or Course) is specified in the top third of each UML box, whereas the second section provides a list of the fields (such as name and address) that the class should contain. Finally, the third part of the box lists the method names for that class. Some UML tools enable the developers to provide the actual lines of code required to implement each of the methods.

If developers want to update their UML model for any reason, they can easily and quickly regenerate the source code by rerunning the code generator. Some UML tools enable **round-trip engineering** so that developers can change either the model or the source code, with the two kept synchronized.

From the perspective of a build system, Figure 4.8 shows the compilation steps required to generate source code from a UML model, using Java as the output language.

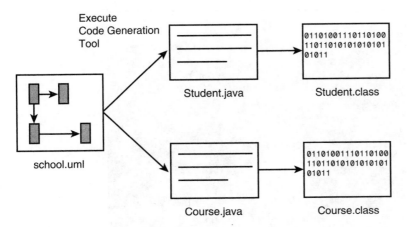

**Figure 4.8** *Generating Java source files from a UML model.*

In this diagram, the `school.uml` file is the only true source code, whereas the `.java` files are autogenerated code and should not be hand-modified by developers. The translation of Java source files into Java class files is the same as discussed earlier.

A number of development tools can construct and generate code from UML models. Common UML tools include Rhapsody (from IBM/Telelogic) and Poseidon for UML (from Gentleware).

## Graphic Images

Unless you're writing a text-only program, you'll almost certainly have reason to display some type of graphic image. This can be anything from a 320x200-pixel splash screen or a 16x16-pixel icon on the program's menu bar. In some cases, your program might need to display large multicolored images (see Figure 4.9). Regardless of their purpose, the graphic images must be available to the executable program, either as data that's embedded inside the program or as an external file that's read from disk.

**Figure 4.9** *A graphic image.*

The most popular programs used to create graphic images include The GIMP, Adobe Photoshop, Adobe Fireworks, and Windows Paint. Because these tools are graphics-oriented, they aren't run as part of the build process; instead, they're used in a standalone manner to generate GIF, JPEG, or PNG graphic files. These are either linked into the executable program or somehow packaged into the final release image.

One interesting alternative is that your build system can generate graphic files from other formats. For example, if your build system generates a set of web pages containing your software's online help, it might also generate a number of graphic image files, such as a graph or a pie chart. The content of these files is generated from raw input data rather than being hand-drawn using an artist's tool.

## XML Configuration Files

Many programs have some type of configuration file associated with them. When a program first starts, the user's configuration file is parsed to determine how the program should behave. If the user changes the configuration, such as by using the Tools, Options menu, the configuration is updated and saved back to disk. The user is unaware of this process, aside from noticing that the user preferences are maintained even when the program is shut down.

A configuration file can be stored in any format, but XML is becoming a common solution because of both standardization and the flexibility it provides in storing hierarchical data. The following example shows the type of information that can be stored in a configuration file.

```
<options>
  <font>
    <size>14<size>
    <family>Times New Roman</family>
  </font>
  <user-email>psmith@arapiki.com</user-email>
  <data-dir>C:\Users\Peter\Data\</data-dir>
</options>
```

From a build system perspective, you need to worry only about providing an initial version of this file. This is provided to each new user upon first executing the program because new users won't have a previous configuration of their own. The build process simply copies the default file into the software's release package, most likely without making any customizations.

## Internationalization and Resource Bundles

A second type of configuration file is known as a **resource bundle**. In a modern software package that is targeted for multiple countries and languages, it's important for the software to display content in the user's preferred language or country format. A resource bundle enables a developer to extract text-based messages out of the program code and store them in an external disk file.

For example, a Canadian English language bundle is a small text file that contains the following definitions:

```
color_choose=Please select the colour.
currency_name=Dollar
currency_code=CAD
flag_image=Canada_flag.gif
```

An American English bundle, on the other hand, would contain the following:

```
color_choose=Please select the color.
currency_name=Dollar
currency_code=USD
flag_image=USA_flag.gif
```

For Mexico, the resource bundle file would contain this:

```
color_choose=Seleccione por favor el color.
currency_name=Peso
currency_code=MXN
flag_image=Mexico_flag.gif
```

Selecting the appropriate resource bundle file is typically a runtime decision, but the build process needs to package all the bundle files, along with any other files they reference (such as Canada_flag.gif). Based on the user's preferred language or country choice, the software loads the appropriate bundle and uses the correct messages or graphics on the user interface.

In the examples, XML-formatted data was not used, even though that's a viable option. The data in our language bundle isn't hierarchical, so a flat file "properties" format is acceptable.

## Summary

This chapter covered an extensive range of file formats and compilation tools for a number of popular programming languages (C/C++, Java, and C#), as well as for both the Windows and Linux operating systems. It also discussed additional file formats, such as scripting languages, UML models, graphic images, and configuration files.

The goal of this chapter has been to describe the file formats used in a build system and to illustrate how compilation tools transform the input formats (such as source files) into output formats (such as object files). The output format is closer to what the target machine can understand or what is suitable to be executed in a virtual machine or rendered by a document viewer.

Learning these file transformation steps gives you a better idea of how to construct a build system. You also learned how to diagnose build-related problems when output files aren't generated as they should have been.

# Chapter 5

## Subtargets and Build Variants

So far, this book has assumed that each piece of software has its own unique build process. That is, it's assumed that there's only one way each source file is compiled and linked into an executable program and that only one type of release package can be generated. In reality, though, any number of variants can exist, each using a slightly modified build process and creating a slightly different release package. The word *slightly* indicates that the build process should still generate the same general program, but the behavior of that program could vary in a few minor ways.

The big picture (see Figure 5.1) has been drawing a one-to-one mapping from the source tree to the object tree. In practice, many mappings could exist, depending on which build options the developer selects. Additionally, there may be multiple object trees, one per build variant.

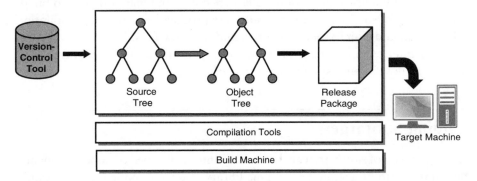

**Figure 5.1** *Big-picture diagram, showing multiple ways to create an object tree from a source tree.*

This chapter examines three different ways in which the mapping from source to object tree can vary:

1. **Building subtargets:** In a typical build process, you might expect the entire object tree to be compiled from source code and a corresponding release package to then be produced. This is usually a requirement if you intend to install and run the software on the target machine. However, developers who are making only incremental changes to one part of the build tree prefer to rebuild only the portion of the tree they're actively working on. This is known as building a **subtarget**.

2. **Building different editions of the software:** In this case, you still compile the full set of source files, but the output is customized to vary the software's behavior. These variations might include support for natural languages (such as French, German, or Japanese) or support for different combinations of product features, such as a Home or Professional edition.

3. **Building different target architectures:** To support a software product on different target machines, you must compile the same set of source files for a variety of different CPU types and operating systems. This includes CPUs such as x86, MIPS, and PowerPC, as well as operating systems such as Linux, Windows, and Mac OS X.

Each of these approaches modifies the build process in a different way. In the first case, you simply build a portion of the entire software product instead of compiling everything. In the second case, you build the entire product but selectively include or exclude source files depending on what you need to build. In the final case, you build the entire software product but vary the compilation tools used, in addition to including or excluding a few files.

This chapter examines each of these basic types of variation, paying special attention to how a build system supports each case.

## Building Subtargets

Any large piece of software can be divided into a number of subcomponents, often in the form of a static or dynamic library. Each component provides only a portion of the program's full functionality and is developed somewhat independently from other components. For large systems, the final software can contain different executable programs that work in cooperation. In this case, each of those programs itself is a subcomponent.

Figure 5.2 shows how a typical source tree is divided into multiple subcomponents.

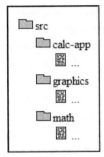

**Figure 5.2** *Dividing a source tree into multiple subcomponents.*

The directory layout of the tree is specifically designed to follow the structure of the program. That is, the `math` and `graphics` directories contain source code for the math and `graphics` libraries. Also, the `calc-app` source directory contains the main part of the application to be linked with the libraries to create an executable program.

By default, a developer builds the entire source tree to create the final executable program:

```
$ cd src
$ make all
... build output will be shown ...

$ ./calculator
... calculator program output will be shown ...
```

If you now imagine that the `calculator` program has many source files, an incremental build of the whole tree might still be time-consuming. Even though the build tool should recompile only files that have actually been modified, reading all the build description files (such as makefiles) and determining which object files are out of date requires effort. In some cases, an incremental build could take 2–3 minutes before it even starts to recompile anything.

As a tradeoff, developers might choose to limit the number of subcomponents they build instead of always rebuilding the whole source tree. To illustrate, if a developer made a small code change in the `math` library, he or she could optimize their build time by limiting their compilation to one directory.

```
$ cd src/math
$ make libmath.so
... build output will be shown ...

$ cd ..
$ ./calculator
... calculator program output will be shown ...
```

The important observation here is that the math library (`libmath.so`) is dynamically linked into the executable program (`calculator`). This enables certain types of change to the math library without the need to relink the program again. Simply recompiling the library and restarting the `calculator` program makes the code changes automatically take effect.

For a larger piece of software that contains multiple executable programs, you can also optimize the build process by compiling just one of those programs. Instead of generating and installing a new release package each time you invoke the build tool, you can save several minutes by manually copying the modified files directly to the target machine. The other files are already installed on the target and, in many cases, are still compatible with the newly added file.

## Building Different Editions of the Software

When developing software for a global market, it's important to consider the needs of all your end users. Unless you're writing software specifically for one customer, you need to consider factors such as language and culture, hardware variations, and differences in what the customers will pay for the software. Let's examine each of these in turn.

- **Language and culture:** Not all computer users speak the same language or have the same culture. To comfortably use a piece of software, users prefer to see the program's commands, menus, and error messages in their native language. They might also prefer to see words displayed in a right-to-left or top-to-bottom direction rather than the traditional Western left-to-right approach. They certainly expect to see monetary values written in their own currency. Even Canadian English speakers prefer to see the word *colour* instead of *color*.

  To enable this type of localization, the software team has additional work. Not only must all the text messages be translated into the supported languages, but also the software's user interface must be clever enough to display words and images in a variety of formats. Finally, the build process must select the necessary text strings or graphic images for each language and culture.

- **Hardware variations:** Software designed to execute on a variety of hardware platforms can be customized at build time to include the required functionality. Anyone familiar with the process of building a Linux kernel has seen how hardware variations are managed. The first step is to run a configuration tool that gives the user a set of choices. The second step is to invoke the build process to generate a customized kernel. The final kernel image includes all the selected drivers that the target hardware requires but doesn't include anything the user chose not to compile.

- **Pricing options:** Software vendors have learned that different customers are willing to pay different amounts of money for the same thing. For example, a home user might pay only $200 for a financial accounting package, whereas an accountant might comfortably pay $2,000 for the same package. To address both markets, the software supplier produces a Home Edition for the home user and a Professional edition for the accountant. The only difference is that some of the advanced features are disabled in the Home edition. This combination of price and features make both editions of the software attractive to each group of end users.

With these examples in mind, consider how you can add support for variation to your build system.

## Specifying the Build Variant

If you imagine your fictitious accounting package (with Home and Professional editions) in three different languages, you'd have the following six build variants. Note that not all options might be valid:

|          | Home  | Professional  |
|----------|-------|---------------|
| **English** | Valid | Valid         |
| **French**  | Valid | Valid         |
| **German**  | Valid | Not Supported |

When building the software, developers must select both a `Language` value and an `Edition` value. If they neglect to specify both, the build system either halts with an error message or instead defaults to something like `English/Professional`.

In some cases, supporting all build combinations might not make sense. In this example, the Professional edition doesn't support the German language; the fictitious software doesn't have the advanced features required in the German marketplace. The developers would never build that variant, and the testers would never test it. In fact, you might want to disallow anybody from building this combination and instead give an error message.

If you implemented this build system using the Make build tool, the developer would specify the variant by defining LANGUAGE and EDITION on the command line:

```
$ make all LANGUAGE=French EDITION=Home
... build output will be shown ...

$ make all LANGUAGE=French EDITION=Professional
... build output will be shown ...
```

As you might expect, typing the variant names can get tedious and error prone. You could write a small shell script or use a command-shell alias to repeat the same command, but it's also possible to store the configuration inside your build tree. With this approach, the build system defaults to the same values you chose last time, unless you decide to override those values.

In the following example, the first build command sets the configuration parameters, whereas all successive commands automatically use the same options.

```
$ make configure LANGUAGE=French EDITION=Home

$ make all
... build output for French/Home will be shown ...

$ make package
... build output for French/Home will be shown ...
```

To implement this feature, the configure target creates a short makefile fragment containing the stored definitions. For example, the following Make rule defines the configure target:

```
configure:
        @echo LANGUAGE=$(LANGUAGE) > .config
        @echo EDITION=$(EDITION) >> .config
```

This generates a .config file in the following format:

```
LANGUAGE=French
EDITION=Home
```

The main makefile parses this value whenever a build is invoked. If the user doesn't explicitly provide values for LANGUAGE and EDITION, the values saved in the .config file are used instead.

Incidentally, a similar method is used with great success when building the Linux kernel, given that it has hundreds of build-time options. Instead of providing them on the command line, developers use a separate configuration target to select all the build-time options they care about.

```
# gmake config
scripts/kconfig/conf arch/x86/Kconfig
*
* Linux Kernel Configuration
*
*
* General setup
*
Prompt for development and/or incomplete code/drivers
➥(EXPERIMENTAL)
[Y/n/?]
Local version - append to kernel release (LOCALVERSION)
[-0.1-pae]
Automatically append version information to the version
➥string [N/y/?]
Support for paging of anonymous memory (swap) (SWAP) [Y/n/?]
System V IPC (SYSVIPC) [Y/n/?]
POSIX Message Queues (POSIX_MQUEUE) [Y/n/?]
BSD Process Accounting (BSD_PROCESS_ACCT) [Y/n/?]
BSD Process Accounting version 3 file format [Y/n/?]
Export task/process statistics through netlink (TASKSTATS) [Y/n/?]
  Enable per-task delay accounting (EXPERIMENTAL)
➥(TASK_DELAY_ACCT) [Y/n/?]
  Enable extended accounting over taskstats (TASK_XACCT)[Y/n/?]
  Enable per-task storage I/O accounting [Y/n/?]
Auditing support (AUDIT) [Y/?] y
  Enable system-call auditing support (AUDITSYSCALL) [Y/n/?]
...
Remainder of output removed
...
```

After the user runs this command, a special configuration file records the user's options, ready for use by the build system. This cache of information is kept for future use, especially if the developers want to modify their previous choices.

Now focus on the accounting example again. To ensure that developers select a legal variant, you must carefully check the options they've entered. For example, if Japanese is not a valid language choice, you would expect to see a meaningful error message:

```
$ make configure LANGUAGE=Japanese EDITION=Home
Makefile: *** Invalid value for LANGUAGE. Must be one of:
➥English French German
```

The following makefile fragment demonstrates the type of safety check to be performed.

```
1  LANGUAGE := English
2  EDITION := Professional
3
4  VALID_LANGUAGES := English French German
```

```
 5  VALID_EDITIONS := Professional Home
 6
 7  ifeq ($(findstring $(LANGUAGE),$(VALID_LANGUAGES)),)
 8    $(error Invalid value for LANGUAGE. \
 9        Must be one of: $(VALID_LANGUAGES))
10  endif
11
12  ifeq ($(findstring $(EDITION),$(VALID_EDITIONS)),)
13    $(error Invalid value for EDITION. \
14        Must be one of: $(VALID_EDITIONS))
15  endif
16
17  ifeq ($(LANGUAGE)/$(EDITION),German/Professional)
18    $(error German language is not supported by Profession-
al Edition)
19  endif
```

If the user doesn't explicitly override the LANGUAGE and EDITION variables on the command line, the build system defaults to the English Professional version of the software. You also must disallow the German Professional version because that option doesn't make sense.

## Varying the Code

After selecting a build variant, you use it to configure the software's behavior accordingly. This involves selecting the specific directories, files, or lines of code that pertain to the variant you're building. Depending on the magnitude of the variation, you can configure the code in a number of ways.

- **Line-by-line variation:** This is the most fine-grained approach to introducing variation into the source code. In languages that allow it, conditionally compiling specific lines of code makes it possible to implement different behavior for each variant. The first step is for the build system to pass the necessary definitions to the compiler. In C/C++, this is done with preprocessor definitions. The required makefile fragment is as follows:

```
ifeq ($(LANGUAGE),English)
  CFLAGS += -DLANG_EN
endif

ifeq ($(EDITION),Professional)
  CFLAGS += -DEDITION_PROF
endif
```

Inside the C/C++ source code, you conditionally compile parts of the program by testing for those definitions. In the following case, you enable a more advanced feature if you're building the Professional edition.

```
int compute_costs()
{
    int total_costs = 0;
#ifdef EDITION_PROF
    total_costs += capital_cost_allowance();
#else /* not EDITION_PROF */
    total_costs += basic_costs();
#endif /* EDITION_PROF */
    ...
  }
```

Because of the simplicity of this method, many C/C++ programmers make heavy use of conditional compilation. Be warned that overusing the #ifdef directive can make the source code hard to follow, especially when multiple variants interact with each other.

- **Per-variant files:** If the source code for one variant differs significantly from other variants, you might find it simpler and cleaner to separate the source code into per-variant files. For example, you might have one source file named english.c that contains English-language functions, whereas the german.c file might contain similar functions for the German language. This approach makes it easier for developers to visualize the structure of the source code rather than intermixing variants into the same file using #ifdef. To conditionally compile the files, you modify the build description as follows:

```
SRCS := basic.c costs.c math.c interest.c ui.c
ifeq ($(LANGUAGE),English)
    SRCS += english.c
endif
ifeq ($(LANGUAGE),French)
    SRCS += french_france.c french_canada.c
endif
```

- **Per-variant directories:** A similar approach includes whole subdirectories rather than individual files. To simplify matters, naming the subdirectories after the variants keeps the build description compact. The following example assumes that you have subdirectories named English, French, and German, each containing language-specific source files.

```
DIRS := ui graphics math database $(LANGUAGE)
```

This approach is far more common in languages such as Java that don't support line-by-line conditional compilation. Instead, each variant has its own subdirectory of classes that are compiled into the program. All subdi-rectories contain the same list of Java source files, with each implemented differently.

```
English/Menus.java
English/Errors.java
English/Currency.java
French/Menus.java
French/Errors.java
French/Currency.java
German/Menus.java
German/Errors.java
German/Currency.java
```

In this example, the build system compiles the Java files from either the English, French, or German subdirectory. When the Java code executes, it simply references the Menus, Errors, or Currency class, without car-ing which source code directory those classes originally came from.

- **Per-variant build description files:** When each build variant is associated with different compilation flags, you might consider separating the build description into different files, with one file used per variant. The top-level build description file incorporates one or more of the variant-specific files, based on the user's settings. For example, the main file will contain the following include directive:

```
include $(LANGUAGE).mk
```

Each of the .mk files then provides all the variant-specific definitions. For example, English.mk would consist of nothing but definitions relevant for the English-language product:

```
CFLAGS += -DLANG_EN -DLEFT_TO_RIGHT_TEXT -DUSE_ASCII \
          -DSUPPORT_USA -DSUPPORT_UK -DSUPPORT_CANADA
CURRENCIES := USD CAD AUD GBP
SPLASH_SCREEN := ENGLISH_FLAG.jpg
OPTIONAL_DIRS := src/property_tax src/estate_tax
ERRORS_FILE := english-errors.list
PROPERTIES := english.properties
```

Separating the build description into multiple files makes it easy to add support for new variants and reduces the complexity of the main build description file. These files can become messy when they're littered with if/else statements for all the possible variants.

- **Packaging-time variation:** The next point at which variation can be applied is the packaging stage. To package a specific edition of the software, you selectively choose which files need to be copied into the final release package. Following the previous example, selecting a splash screen image for the accounting software depends on which language variant was chosen. This is the relevant portion of the build description:

```
$(COPY) $(SPLASH_SCREEN) splash_screen.jpg
```

  The `$(SPLASH_SCREEN)` variable was already defined in the build description file and refers to a suitable graphic image for the chosen language variant.

- **Installation-time variation:** Even if you had only one way to build the product—and, therefore, only one variant of the release package—you could still customize the behavior of the software at installation time. Software commonly identifies the end user's geographic location before installing the relevant files on the target machine. The release package contains all files required to support all variants, but only the files for the chosen variant are installed.

  Chapter 13, "Software Packaging and Installation," discusses packaging and installation systems in more detail.

- **Runtime variation:** The final way to customize software is to do it when the program is executing. The build system generates a release package that contains all functionality (all languages and all features), and every part of that functionality is installed on the target machine. However, when the program starts executing, it determines which variation is required and modifies its own behavior accordingly.

  One way to control variation is via the familiar `Tools, Options` menu, where end users can select the language or set of features they want to use. Alternatively, software that requires a license key can unlock certain features only if the appropriate license is available. This approach to customizing software has little to do with build systems, so this chapter doesn't go into further detail.

Naturally, these methods of implementing software variation (such as per-line or per-file variation) are not mutually exclusive. A build system is free to use any combination of these methods, depending on what makes the most sense. Indeed, you might find software that uses every one of these solutions, depending on which type of feature is impacted by each variant.

# Building Different Target Architectures

The third approach to varying the output of the build process is to generate code for more than one target architecture. This implies that the software supports multiple CPU types or operating systems. In general, the functionality of the program is identical in all cases, but the target computer is different. This type of variant is relevant only when programming in languages such as C and C++, which compile into native code. It's not relevant for Java and C#, which use machine-independent virtual machines.

## Multiple Compilers

The first important technique for varying the target architecture is to use more than one source code compiler. For example, if your product could be targeted for both the Linux environment and the Microsoft Windows environment, you'd likely use the GNU C Compiler to generate Linux code and then use the Visual Studio compiler to generate Windows code. Each compiler would require its own set of command-line options, but that could be handled in the same way, as follows:

```
ifeq ($(TARGET),Linux)
  CC := gcc-4.2
  CFLAGS := -g -O
endif
ifeq ($(TARGET),Windows)
  CC := cl.exe
  CFLAGS := /O2 /Zi
endif
```

Given that each compiler (gcc-4.2 and cl.exe) can be executed on only one type of build machine, you might be wondering whether the build system could automatically detect which compiler to use. That is, if the developer is building on a Linux build machine, you'd automatically use gcc-4.2. If the developer is on a Windows machine, cl.exe is used instead. The following example relies on the operating system itself to set the $(HOST) variable.

```
ifeq ($(HOST),Linux)
  CC := gcc-4.2
  CFLAGS := -g -O
endif
ifeq ($(HOST),Windows)
  CC := cl.exe
  CFLAGS := /O2 /Zi
endif
```

This type of autodetection is the correct approach for native compiling because the developer doesn't need to specify the TARGET= value.

On the other hand, the situation is quite different for cross-compilation. A single build machine can be used to generate code for more than one target platform, so developers must state which variant they want. The following example uses two variants of the GNU C Compiler: one that generates code for a Linux machine with an x86 CPU and a second that generates code for a Windows machine.

```
ifeq ($(TARGET),Linux)
  CC := i386-linux-gcc-4.2
  CFLAGS := -g -O
endif
ifeq ($(TARGET),Windows)
  CC := i386-windows-gcc-4.2
  CFLAGS := -g -O
endif
```

You no longer use the native Windows compiler because that doesn't run in a Linux-hosted environment. Instead, a purpose-built version of GCC generates Windows machine code.

## Platform-Specific Files/Functions

A second important technique when varying the target architecture is to recognize that not all source code is relevant for all platforms. Although you should usually try to write portable source code that executes on all machines, sometimes your code has no choice but to use OS-specific features. For example, the following code returns the name of the currently logged-in user, regardless of whether you use Linux or the Windows platform.

```
char * get_user_name()
{
#ifdef linux
  struct passwd *pwd = getpwuid(getuid());
  return pwd->pw_name;
#endif /* linux */
#ifdef WIN32
  static char name[100];
  DWORD size = sizeof(name);
  GetUserName(name, &size);
  return name;
#endif /* WIN32 */
}
```

In practice, unless you rely solely on standard libraries that are the same on all target machines (such as the POSIX standard), you need to do a fair amount of conditional compilation. The following methods are appropriate:

- Use line-by-line conditional compilation, such as `#ifdef` in C/C++.

- Use per-file variation to select the relevant source code for your specific architecture.

- Use per-directory variation to select whole directories of source code for your architecture.

Each of these methods was described earlier when discussing how to create different editions of the software. In essence, you're now creating a Linux edition and a Windows edition, although, as much as possible, you want to use the same source files and keep the same functionality for all platforms.

## Multiple Object Trees

A topic this book hasn't yet touched on is multiple object trees. If you're generating code for more than one operating system or CPU type, you might want to have the object code for different variants available at the same time. This is particularly useful when modifying parts of the source code that must be carefully tested on more than one target. A change that works for one architecture might not work on a second.

If you have only a single object tree, constantly rebuilding the whole tree whenever you needed to test your code for a different variant would be painful. If developers get lazy and don't bother testing on all target machines, there's a good chance that they'll break the code for somebody else. Making it easy to do the right thing is an important goal to aim for, so having multiple object trees is often the correct approach.

Figure 5.3 shows a single source code tree but two object trees.

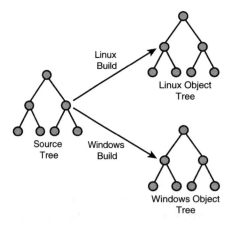

**Figure 5.3** *Compiling the same source code into multiple object trees.*

The structure of each object tree mirrors the structure of the source tree. Viewing this same arrangement as a directory listing produces the following layout:

```
src/math/*.c
src/graphics/*.c
src/calc-app/*.c
obj/Windows/math/*.obj
obj/Windows/graphics/*.obj
obj/Windows/calc-app/*.obj
obj/Linux/math/*.o
obj/Linux/graphics/*.o
obj/Linux/calc-app/*.o
```

In this example, the source files in the src directory can be compiled either into the obj/Windows directory by using the Windows compiler or into the obj/Linux directory by using the Linux compiler. Both object trees are kept indefinitely, so it's quick to incrementally compile the code for each platform, just to make sure that nothing has broken.

From the perspective of the build system, setting up multiple object trees is trivial. Assuming that all object files are stored into the $OBJDIR directory, you can set this directory on a per-variant basis.

```
OBJDIR := obj/$(TARGET)
```

Although this approach works well, it does limit you to storing object files within the top-level obj directory. A second approach is to allow developers to arbitrarily choose the location of their object tree. Developers must perform a configuration step to designate which variant of code should be built in that tree. For example:

```
$ mkdir /fast-disk/psmith/my-obj
$ cd /fast-disk/psmith/my-obj
$ configure --src=/home/psmith/source
$ make
... build output will be shown ...
```

In this example, the developer has chosen to store object files on a fast disk (/fast-disk/psmith/my-obj) instead of storing them in the same location as their source code (/home/psmith/source). The developer might have been done this to get better performance when building the software, or perhaps the /home disk is running short of free space. In either case, having the flexibility to select a location is often useful.

As a final note, the same benefits can be achieved when using the fixed-path approach, although less elegantly. Using symbolic links allows object files to be stored on a different disk, although the build system believes they're in the same place as the source code.

```
$ mkdir /fast-disk/psmith/my-obj
$ cd /home/psmith/source
$ ln -s /fask-disk/psmith/my-obj obj
$ make
... build output will be shown ...
```

In this example, you replace the fixed-path `obj` directory with a symbolic link to the `/fast-disk` directory. Symbolic links are great for this type of trick, although they can be confusing when overused.

---

## Summary

This chapter identified three main ways a build process can vary to provide additional functionality. These approaches involve building a subset of the whole tree (a subtarget), building different editions for different end users, and building for different CPU types and operating systems.

In compiling only a subset of the full code base, developers can optimize their workflow by reducing compilation time. This is a common approach when the program contains a number of shared libraries or a collection of executable programs.

Creating different editions of the software enables you to address different target markets. Many customers appreciate having software in their own native language or using their own cultural symbols. Other customers are willing to pay more for additional features that aren't part of the standard package. Build variants of this nature can be introduced on a per-line, per-file, or per-directory basis, or at packaging time, installation time, or runtime.

The need for your product to support multiple CPU types and operating systems can lead to multiple object trees. Each tree stores the object files for a single CPU or OS variant and must be kept and recompiled often.

# PART II

The Build Tools

Part I was an introduction to software build systems. You learned the basics of the GNU Make tool, considered the various components of a program, saw the compilation steps for three common programming languages, and explored subtargets and build variants.

However, aside from a few examples, you didn't learn about **build tools**. Recall that a build tool orchestrates the use of compilation tools to generate a complete software product. A build tool performs the full **build process** by reading the **build description** and acting upon the instructions.

The second part of this book examines a number of build tools in detail. Each tool was chosen because of both its popularity and the fact that it represents a particular class of build tools. These tools are discussed:

- **Chapter 6, "Make":** This is widely considered to be the first build tool created. GNU Make, a modern version of Make, is still the most common build tool used for C/C++ software products. If you're maintaining a legacy build system written using a Make-based tool, you should definitely read this chapter. However, it's not recommended that you create a new build system using GNU Make unless you're an expert in using the tool. In addition to GNU Make, this chapter discusses Berkeley Make, Microsoft's NMake, ElectricAccelerator®, and SparkBuild™.

- **Chapter 7, "Ant":** This is the most popular build tool for Java-based software products. It contains built-in features to support Java compilation and JAR-file creation. Ant differs from GNU Make in that it supports a more sequential **task-based** model. If you're creating a build system for a Java-based product, this is likely to be your first choice of build tool. This chapter also discusses NAnt and MSBuild as similar tools.

- **Chapter 8, "SCons":** This modern build tool uses Python as its build-description language. Build descriptions contain a sequence of method calls to explicitly state which objects must be built and which input files to use. SCons is interesting because build-description files are written in a general-purpose programming language. If you're creating a totally new build system for the C or C++ languages, consider using SCons instead of the older GNU Make tool. You'll also see examples of the Cons build tool (using Perl) and the Rake build tool (using Ruby).

- **Chapter 9, "CMake":** This is one of several tools that enable developers to write a high-level description of the build system but have that description translated into something that other build tools (such as Make) are capable of executing. You should learn about CMake (instead of using the older GNU Make tool) if you're creating a new build system for C or C++ software. This chapter also mentions Automake and Qmake, similar tools.

- **Chapter 10, "Eclipse":** This is one of the most popular graphical integrated development environment (IDE) tools used for editing source code. Eclipse contains its own build tool, but it can still interface with other external build systems. This chapter focuses on the JDT builder mechanism for Java support, but it briefly studies the CDT builder for C/C++ support. If you use Eclipse as your development environment, you should make a point of learning how the builder mechanisms work.

The goal of studying these five systems is to give you an appreciation of the variety of build tools available and to help you decide which of them is appropriate for your project. None of these tools is suitable for all projects, so understanding the advantages and disadvantages of each system is very important.

Unfortunately, it's not possible to discuss every build tool in existence; otherwise, this book would be twice as long. Some tools are very new and haven't yet proven to be successful or reliable. Other tools have been around for longer but are not as popular as those listed previously.

Each chapter in Part II follows a common outline designed to compare the five different systems. Each chapter covers these areas:

- A brief overview of the tool, describing the environment in which it's best suited

- A more detailed look at the tool's programming language (both syntax and semantics), showing how a developer can specify the build description

- A number of examples showing how the build tool can solve common build system problems

- Popular praise and criticism for the tool, taken from Internet web sites, other publications, and personal experience

- A description of other build tools that are similar in design

After you read each chapter, you should come away with a good appreciation of what it takes to use that tool in your own projects. Don't expect to know everything about the tool, but if you like what you see, you're encouraged to read the tool's user manual or perhaps another book that specifically covers the tool in detail.

Even if you consider yourself a build system expert, you might learn a thing or two about a new tool that changes your perspective or encourages you to try a new way of building software.

As a reminder, the following characteristics are important to think about when selecting a tool:

- **Convenience:** How easy is it for developers or build system maintainers to describe the build process using the tool's description language?

- **Correctness:** Will the build tool always generate a correct executable program, or will important dependencies be missed by mistake?

- **Performance:** Is the build tool efficient, or will the user often wait for slow builds to complete?

- **Scalability:** How does the tool perform with large-scale software projects containing thousands of source files?

Each software project is different, and every developer places a different level of importance on each of these characteristics. If you're a hobbyist developer building a project with fewer than 50 source files, you probably won't care too much about scalability or performance. On the other hand, a large software organization with hundreds of developers will care a lot.

In each chapter, you see a fair amount of discussion on the pros and cons of using each build tool. Table PII.1 summarizes the strengths and weaknesses of the tools covered.

**Table PII.1**   *Strengths and Weaknesses of Build Tools*

| Tool | Convenience | Correctness | Performance | Scalability |
|------|-------------|-------------|-------------|-------------|
| GNU Make | Poor | Poor | Excellent | Excellent |
| Ant | Good | Excellent | Good | Good |
| SCons | Excellent | Excellent | Good | Good |
| CMake | Good | Excellent | Excellent | Excellent |
| Eclipse | Good | Excellent | Good | Poor |

At the end of each chapter, you can read why the tool was assigned a particular rating.

## The Real-World Scenarios

A build tool would be no use if it weren't capable of supporting real-world applications. Most user manuals focus on the syntax and semantics of the tool's programming language, perhaps providing a few idioms for achieving certain tasks. However, without backing these up with realistic examples, you can never be sure whether the build tool is suitable for the long term.

To this end, each of the upcoming chapters illustrates how the build tools apply to real-world situations. The following scenarios are examined.

## Scenario 1: Source Code in a Single Directory

In this scenario, you use a small calculator program (see Chapter 2, "A Make-Based Build System") in which all source files are stored in the same directory. For GNU Make, SCons, and CMake, you use a C program, shown in Figure PII.1.

**Figure PII.1** *Single-directory build scenario for the C language.*

For Ant and Eclipse, you use the equivalent Java program, shown in Figure PII.2.

**Figure PII.2** *Single-directory build scenario for the Java language.*

You don't have to understand what this program does, because you're mainly interested in the file types and file system layout. All you actually need to know is that the .c files (or .java files) are combined into a single executable program.

## Scenario 2: Source Code in Multiple Directories

Next you use a larger calculator example, with the program's source code spread across multiple directories in a hierarchical build tree. This is common in nontrivial software products, so it's important for the build tool to handle the situation properly.

For GNU Make, SCons, and CMake, you use the C/C++-based tree, shown in Figure PII.3.

**Figure PII.3** *Multidirectory build scenario for the C language.*

For Ant and Eclipse, you use the equivalent Java source tree, shown in Figure PII.4.

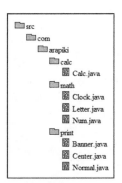

**Figure PII.4** *Multidirectory build scenario for the Java language.*

For some of the build tools, you'll look at several different ways of compiling these multidirectory trees. A large tree can contain thousands of directories, and a single type of build system might not be suitable for all source trees.

## Scenario 3: Defining New Compilation Tools

A large software project often incorporates nonstandard compilation tools. You must have a way to instruct the build system on how it can use the new tool and how it can predict a source file's set of dependencies.

The examples use a fictional tool named `mathcomp`. This tool takes a single input file with the suffix `.math` and generates either a C file or a Java file, depending on which output option you choose. The `.math` file contains a number of simple equations, whereas the output file computes the result of these equations and displays them on the program's output.

The examples use the following `equations.math` file as input:

```
#
# This test file has a number of equations in it, but
# it also includes some .mathinc files that also contain
# equations
#
1+2
4*5
6/2
import equ1.mathinc
10/2
100/4
import equ2.mathinc
10+20
```

Note that this example includes two other files, `equ1.mathinc` and `equ2.mathinc`, which also contain equations but don't contain further `import` directives. Using the `mathcomp` compiler with the `-j` flag to generate Java code creates the following output file (`equations.java`):

```
/* autogenerated - do not edit! */
public class equations {
    public static void math()
    {
        System.out.println("1 + 2 = " + (1 + 2));
        System.out.println("4 * 5 = " + (4 * 5));
        System.out.println("6 / 2 = " + (6 / 2));
        System.out.println("4 + 5 = " + (4 + 5));
        System.out.println("20 * 300 = " + (20 * 300));
        System.out.println("5 / 5 = " + (5 / 5));
        System.out.println("10 / 2 = " + (10 / 2));
        System.out.println("100 / 4 = " + (100 / 4));
        System.out.println("2 + 3 = " + (2 + 3));
        System.out.println("10 + 50 = " + (10 + 50));
```

```
        System.out.println("10 + 20 = " + (10 + 20));
    }
}
```

The C code generated by the -c option looks similar. Finally, when the -d flag is passed to mathcomp, the tool displays the set of input files that were scanned, including all the imported files.

```
equations.math equ1.mathinc equ2.mathinc
```

Each of the build tools uses this dependency information as it constructs the software's dependency graph.

## Scenario 4: Building with Multiple Variants

Large software products often have multiple variants that need to be supported. This includes multiple editions of the software and multiple CPU and operating system types. The user must have a means of specifying which variant to build.

For GNU Make, CMake, and SCons, you see how to generate code for multiple CPUs (i386, PowerPC, and Alpha); for Ant and Eclipse, you generate both Home and Professional editions of the software.

## Scenario 5: Cleaning a Build Tree

After a build tool has compiled all the software in the build tree, you need a way to remove all the generated files while still keeping the source code intact. You'll look at how each build tool approaches this problem.

## Scenario 6: Debugging Incorrect Builds

When a build tool fails to build (or rebuild) the software image, you need to understand why. Failure to fix problems causes further broken builds in the future or incorrectly compiled software images containing a number of subtle bugs. Each build tool must provide a way to trace execution of the build process and determine why things are not compiling the way they should.

Each of the following five chapters discusses how each build tool solves these real-world scenarios.

# Chapter 6

# Make

The first build tool this book examines in detail is Make [40]. You've already seen a basic example of using Make in Chapter 2, "A Make-Based Build System," and many developers are familiar with this popular tool. This chapter explores the syntax of Make-based build systems in more detail and presents a number of practical use cases.

Created in 1977, Make has revolutionized the way software is compiled. For many years, Make was the only build tool available; new tools created since that time (such as Ant, CMake, and SCons) introduced themselves as a "Make replacement." There's certainly no ignoring the valuable contribution Make has provided to the software industry.

Central to Make's operation is the concept of a **rule**, providing all the inter-file dependency information needed to compile a program. A developer must specify the name of a target file to be compiled, as well as all the input files for the compilation. In addition, the rule contains one or more shell commands that generate the target file from the source files.

As an example, the following rule indicates that myprog is a generated file that is created by running the gcc command with the prog.c and lib.c files as input.

```
myprog: prog.c lib.c
    gcc -o myprog prog.c lib.c
```

If either of the last-modified time stamps of prog.c and lib.c are more recent than the time stamp of myprog, Make assumes that the developer has modified the source files since myprog was last compiled. As a result, it reruns the gcc command to regenerate myprog from the latest source files.

The developer who writes a build description file (known as a **makefile**) must carefully specify the dependencies among all files in the system, along with all the intermediate steps. In a large system with thousands of source files and a large array of file types (such as executable programs, data files, and object files), the number of rules can be extensive.

Despite its age, Make is still the most commonly used tool for building software. A large percentage of C/C++ projects use Make as their build tool, particularly for UNIX/Linux environments and older Microsoft Windows systems. Because of this popularity, university courses continue to teach the theory and practice of Make to prepare students for future employment. In the software industry, many developers have heard only about Make, not about the alternative tools.

This chapter focuses on the GNU version of Make because of the large number of platforms it supports. Before GNU Make became popular, each operating system vendor provided its own version of the Make tool that accepted a slightly different syntax than the other variants. Naturally, this made constructing a multiplatform build system difficult. You'll take a look at other Make implementations at the end of the chapter.

As a reminder, the goal of this chapter is to give you an appreciation for the features and capabilities of the GNU Make tool. You won't examine the tool in too much detail, but by the end of this chapter, you'll have a better appreciation of how to use the GNU Make tool and how a makefile is written. If you plan to use GNU Make in your own build system, you should first refer to the tool's own documentation [16].

Because of the complexity of GNU Make, you might find some of the discussion challenging to follow if you don't already have experience writing a makefile. Make sure you've read and understood Chapter 2, or at least be prepared to work through the examples in great detail. Make-based build systems can be difficult to understand.

## The GNU Make Programming Language

The GNU Make tool is controlled by a user-written program script, stored in a file named `Makefile`. GNU Make provides a comprehensive programming language and gives a makefile developer enough functionality to describe the build process. You might find it useful to view the GNU Make language as three distinct programming languages integrated into one, each playing a slightly different role.

The three sublanguages are as follows:

- **File dependencies:** A rule-based syntax for describing the dependency relationships between files. A Make program is "executed" by matching disk filenames against the rules that generate them. Instead of sequentially executing rules, GNU Make performs a pattern-matching operation to decide which rule to evaluate next.

```
myprog: prog.c lib.c
```

- **Shell commands:** A list of shell commands encapsulated within each rule, to be executed if the target of the rule is "out-of-date." As with any shell script, each command invokes a separate program, such as `ls`, `cat`, or `gcc`. Commands are executed in the order they're listed and can use shell metacharacters to control sequencing and I/O redirection.

```
cp myfile yourfile && cp myfile1 yourfile1
md5 < myfile >>yourfile
touch yourfile.done
```

- **String processing:** A language for manipulating GNU Make variables, such as treating them as a list of values. This language uses the functional programming paradigm in which each function is passed one or more string values as input and returns a single string value as the result. By combining different function calls, complex expressions can be evaluated.

```
VARS := $(sort $(filter srcs-% cflags-%, $(.VARIABLES)))
```

With this combination of programming styles, it's possible to construct any type of build system, no matter how complex. Let's start by looking at GNU Make's syntax and basic concepts. Later you'll examine how these can apply to real-world build scenarios.

## Makefile Rules to Construct the Dependency Graph

To reiterate, a makefile consists of a number of rules, each describing how to generate a particular target file from one or more prerequisite input files. If the target file is out of date with respect to the input files, the sequence of shell commands is executed to bring it up-to-date. "Out-of-date" refers to the time stamp on the file being older than the files it was derived from. Therefore, the input files must have been changed more recently.

As you saw in Chapter 2, the following makefile is a simplistic way of translating the `calculator` program's dependency graph into code that GNU Make can understand.

```
1  calculator: add.o calc.o mult.o sub.o
2      gcc -g -o calculator add.o calc.o mult.o sub.o
3
```

```
 4   add.o: add.c numbers.h
 5       gcc -g -c add.c
 6
 7   calc.o: calc.c numbers.h
 8       gcc -g -c calc.c
 9
10   mult.o: mult.c numbers.h
11       gcc -g -c mult.c
12
13   sub.o: sub.c numbers.h
14       gcc -g -c sub.c
```

Keep in mind that GNU Make's rule-based language doesn't execute sequentially, as would a program written in a procedural language. Instead, the whole mechanism is based on matching target filenames against whichever rule happens to match the name. As you see later, the target of a rule (the left side) can also contain wildcards and variable names, so locating a matching rule is not always a simple matter.

Let's not go into too much detail quite yet; this chapter later examines GNU Make's pattern-matching and rule-searching algorithm. First you'll learn about the different rules you can create.

## Makefile Rule Types

In addition to the simple rules you've seen so far, you can express dependencies in several other ways, making it easier for makefile developers to get their job done. GNU Make is a flexible and powerful language with a number of syntactical features for expressing the relationship between files. Consider some examples:

- **Rules with multiple targets:** The previous example had a single target file on the left side of the rule. However, the following syntactical shortcut is also allowed:

```
file1.o file2.o: source1.c source2.c source3.c
        ... commands go here ...
```

  Of course, this works only if both targets have the same set of prerequisites and can be generated by the same list of shell commands.

- **Rules with no prerequisites:** Sometimes you want to define a target that doesn't depend on any prerequisites. You can use this approach to define pseudotargets that don't relate to actual disk files. In the following example, you're defining the `help` target to display a synopsis of the commands the developer can use:

```
.PHONY: help
help:
        @echo "Usage: make all ARCH=[i386|mips]"
        @echo "        make clean"
```

If the developer types gmake help, no file named help exists on the disk, and the shell commands shouldn't proceed to create that file. Additionally, the shell commands are executed every time the help target is invoked because no time stamp checking needs to be performed. Note the use of the PHONY directive to indicate that GNU Make should always execute the rule, even if somebody accidentally left a file named help sitting in the current directory.

- **Rules with patterns in the filename:** As you probably noticed, the previous calculator example contained a lot of repetition. For every object file, such as add.o, there was a dependency on the corresponding C file, such as add.c. Because there were four different source files, you had four different rules that all looked similar. You can use wildcard characters as a shortcut to specify that the target and prerequisite filenames must match.

```
%.o: %.c
        ... commands go here ...
```

This example matches any pair of files in which the target ends with .o and the prerequisite both ends with .c and also starts with the same sequence of characters (known as the **stem**). In other words, a file *stem*.o can be generated from the file *stem*.c by executing the list of shell commands. When first asked to build the calculator target, GNU Make determines that calc.o, add.o, mult.o, and sub.o must all be generated and that this rule is capable of doing so.

- **Rules that apply only to certain files:** To make the pattern matching in rules more useful, it's also possible to state which files the pattern applies to. For example:

```
a.o b.o: %.o: %.c
        echo This rule is for a.o and b.o

c.o d.o: %.o: %.c
        echo This rule is for c.o and d.o
```

By being more specific about the list of files, you can create more elaborate build systems. For example, you might want some object files to be compiled with an x86-target compiler, whereas other object files must be compiled with a MIPS compiler. Although you haven't explored GNU

Make variables in detail, this feature is a lot more useful if you have a list of several hundred files stored in a single variable.

- **Multiple rules with the same target:** It's often more useful to split the list of prerequisites for a target across multiple rules than to define them all on the same line.

```
chunk.o: chunk.c
     gcc -c chunk.c

chunk.o: chunk.h list.h data.h
```

In this example, the rule states that chunk.o is generated from chunk.c, and a separate rule states that chunk.o has dependencies on several other C header files. Only one of these rules can contain a set of shell commands; the other rule simply contributes to the list of prerequisites.

If you're curious about these and other ways of writing makefile rules, study the GNU Make reference manual for more examples.

## Makefile Variables

As with any other language, writing a nontrivial program without using variables is difficult. The examples seen so far in this chapter have used hard-coded file names, but that won't work in a large build system with hundreds of files. Let's now see how GNU Make variables can simplify a makefile.

GNU Make variables are similar to those in other programming languages, but they have a few unique behaviors of their own. The rules are listed here:

1. Variables are given a value by an assignment statement, such as X := 5. As you'll see shortly, several types of assignment exist, each with their own semantics.

2. Variable values are referenced using the syntax $(X).

3. All variables are of string type, with the valuecontaining zero or more characters. No mechanism exists for declaring variables before they're used, so assigning to them for the first time creates the variable.

4. Variables have global scope, which means that all assignments and references to the variable X (within a single makefile) refer to the same variable.

5. Variable names can contain upper- and lowercase letters, numbers, and punctuation symbols such as @, ^, <, and >. To make them more visible,

this book typically uses uppercase letters in the examples, but that's not a requirement.

To illustrate these rules, consider a simple example. You shouldn't see any real surprises in this code, although an unusual feature is that strings don't require quotation marks around them. Instead, they simply consume the remainder of the input line, with the exception of anything after the comment (#) character.

```
1   FIRST := Hello there
2   SECOND := World     # comments go here
3   MESSAGE := $(FIRST) $(SECOND)
4   FILES := add.c sub.c mult.c
5   $(info $(MESSAGE) - The files are $(FILES))
```

The last line, containing the $(info ...) directive, displays the following message on the output:

```
Hello there World - The files are add.c sub.c mult.c
```

Although this example shows only one type of assignment statement, several actually exist, each with its own semantics:

- **Immediate evaluation:** This is the case you've already seen, using the := operator. The right side of the assignment is fully evaluated to a constant string and then assigned to the variable listed on the left side. Most modern programming languages use this type of immediate evaluation in their assignment statements.

- **Deferred evaluation:** This second type of assignment, using = instead of := enables you to defer the evaluation of variables until they're actually used instead of immediately converting them to a constant string. Now look at a case in which a variable is defined in terms of other variables.

```
1   CC := gcc
2   CFLAGS := -g
3   CCOMP = $(CC) $(CFLAGS)   # observe the use of =
4   $(info Compiler is $(CCOMP))
5   CC := i386-linux-gcc
6   $(info Compiler is $(CCOMP))
```

Note that line 3 uses deferred assignment (the = sign). When you execute this makefile, the right side of line 3 isn't evaluated until the CCOMP variable is actually used (which, in this case, is on lines 4 and 6). Given that the CC variable is modified on line 5, the value of CCOMP changes when it's used the second time.

```
$ gmake
Compiler is gcc -g
Compiler is i386-linux-gcc -g
```

This feature might seem a little awkward, but the capability to define variables and then modify individual parts of the variable later can be useful. You'll see this again when you look at GNU Make's built-in rules.

- **Conditional assignment:** In a third situation, you assign a value if the variable doesn't already have one.

```
1   CFLAGS := -g
2   CFLAGS ?= -O
3   $(info CFLAGS is $(CFLAGS))
```

In this case, you supply a default value for CFLAGS (on line 2), which is used if the user hasn't already provided a value earlier in the program (on line 1 here). Although this is an oversimplified example, this feature is useful when you include one makefile from within another, where the parent makefile might or might not want to explicitly define the CFLAGS variable. If it chooses not to, the default value is used.

Now let's look at some of the variables and rules built into the tool, making it easier to construct a makefile.

## Built-In Variables and Rules

GNU Make provides built-in rules and variables to address common build system requirements. First examine **automatic variables,** so named because their value depends on the context in which they're used. Unlike many other programming languages, GNU Make variable names can contain punctuation symbols such as @, <, and ^.

- $@: Contains the filename of the current rule's target. Instead of hard-coding the name of the target into the sequence of shell commands, you use $@ to have it automatically inserted. This is handy when the rule uses wildcards to match the name of the target file and there's no specific name to be hard-coded.

- $<: Represents the first prerequisite of a rule. As shown in the following example, you use $@ to represent the target of the rule (the object file you're generating), and you use $< to represent the first source file in the list. (In this case, only one source file is mentioned in the rule.)

```
%.o: %.c
    gcc -c -o $@ $<
```

- $^: Similar to $<, but it evaluates to the complete list of prerequisites in the rule, with spaces between them.

- $(@D): Evaluates to the directory containing the target of the rule. For example, if the target is /home/john/work/src.c, then $(@D) evaluates to /home/john/work. This is useful when you have a shell command such as mkdir that needs to manipulate the target file's directory.

- $(@F): Similar to $(@D), but evaluates to the base name of the target file. If the target is /home/john/work/src.c, then $(@F) evaluates to src.c.

Of course, many more variables are available in GNU Make, but they aren't all listed here.

In addition to variables, GNU Make provides built-in rules. These are used for compiling C, C++, Yacc, and Fortran code, among others. Invoking GNU Make with the -p command-line option (gmake -p) shows you the rules built into the system. Here's the built-in rule for C compilation.

```
1   COMPILE.c = $(CC) $(CFLAGS) $(CPPFLAGS) $(TARGET_ARCH) -c
2   OUTPUT_OPTION = -o $@
3   %.o: %.c
4       $(COMPILE.c) $(OUTPUT_OPTION) $<
```

This fragment shows a wildcard rule (lines 3 and 4) for generating .o files from the correspondingly named .c files. The automatic variables $@ and $< represent the target and prerequisite of the rule, which could be any matching pair of filenames that end in .o or .c, respectively. Notice also that line 1 of this rule uses deferred evaluation (the = sign), permitting developers to add their own values for CC, CFLAGS, CPPFLAGS, and TARGET_ARCH later. In theory, each time this wildcard rule is used, it could be with a different combination of flags, as set by the makefile developer.

As you saw in Chapter 2, the calculator example can be rewritten to take advantage of this built-in C compilation rule.

```
1   calculator: add.o calc.o mult.o sub.o
2       gcc -g -o calculator add.o calc.o mult.o sub.o
3
4   add.o calc.o mult.o sub.o: numbers.h
```

That is, you can remove all the makefile rules that specify how to compile a C source file into an object file, because the implicit rule handles that case. To make the code even more readable, you can then define and reference a number of variables:

```
 1   SRCS = add.c calc.c mult.c sub.c
 2   PROG = calculator
 3   CC = gcc
 4   CFLAGS = -g
 5   OBJS = $(SRCS:.c=.o)
 6
 7   $(PROG): $(OBJS)
 8       $(CC) $(CFLAGS) -o $@ $^
 9
10   $(OBJS): numbers.h
```

Note that CC and CFLAGS (lines 3 and 4) are implicitly inserted into the built-in C compilation rule that you saw earlier because COMPILE.c used deferred evaluation.

Line 5 uses some clever syntax to set OBJS to the same value as the SRCS variable (defined on line 1) but with all the .c extensions changed to .o. As you know from programming experience, it's a bad idea to list all the filenames twice, so you instead define one variable in terms of the other.

Line 7 is still required to link the final executable, but this time you're making use of variables instead of hard-coding filenames. Note that CC and CFLAGS are the same variables used when compiling source files into object files. If you decide to change to a different compiler or add new compilation flags, only lines 3 and 4 need to be modified.

Finally, line 10 states that all object files depend on numbers.h. This is shorter than the previous version, in which all the object files had to be listed.

## Data Structures and Functions

All of GNU Make's variables are of string type but this needn't stop you from representing other data types, such as numbers, lists, and structures. The key to storing complex data is to find a way to represent information as a sequence of space-separated words. GNU Make has plenty of features for manipulating variables in this form.

The following are some typical data structures you might find yourself using:

```
1 PROG_NAME := my-calculator
2 LIST_OF_SRCS := calc.c main.c math.h lib.c
3 COLORS := red FF0000 green 00FF00 blue 0000FF purple FF00FF
4 ORDERS := 100 green cups 200 blue plates
```

Line 1 is a standard variable assignment of a simple string, and you'll see this type of assignment in almost every makefile. Line 2 is a common way of expressing lists of things, although, obviously, the elements of the list can't contain spaces. This can be painful if you were planning to store C:\Program Files in a list.

Lines 3 and 4 demonstrate more complex data structures that you probably won't use as often. For the ORDERS variable, element 1 is the quantity, element 2 is the color, and element 3 is the item to purchase. The pattern repeats itself for each additional order item. As long as you have a mechanism for extracting specific items out of a list, you can treat this variable like a structured data type.

Consider some of the most common functions for dealing with strings:

- words: Given a list as input, returns the number of space-separated words in that list. In this example, $(NUM_FILES) evaluates to 4.

```
NUM_FILES := $(words $(LIST_OF_SRCS))
```

- word: Given a list, extracts the nth word from that list. The list is 1-based, so $(SECOND_FILE) evaluates to main.c.

```
SECOND_FILE := $(word 2, $(LIST_OF_SRCS))
```

- filter: Returns the words from a list, which match a specific pattern. A common use is to select a subset of files that match a specific filename pattern (such as all C source files).

```
C_SRCS := $(filter %.c, $(LIST_OF_SRCS))
```

- patsubst: For each word in a list, replaces any that match a specific pattern with a replacement pattern. The % character identifies the part of each word that remains unchanged (the stem). Note that the first comma must not be followed by a space character; otherwise, the replacement list ends up with two spaces between each word.

```
OBJECTS := $(patsubst %.c,%.o, $(C_SRCS))
```

This example is similar to the $(C_SRCS:.c=.o) syntax you've already seen, with the resulting list being calc.o math.o lib.o.

- addprefix: For each word in a list, prepends an additional string. In the following example, you add the objs/ prefix to each element in the $(OBJECTS) list.

```
OBJ_LIST := $(addprefix objs/, $(OBJECTS))
```

In this case, $(OBJ_LIST) evaluates to objs/calc.o  objs/main.o objs/lib.o.

- foreach: Visits each word in a list and constructs a new list containing the "mapped" values. The mapping expression can consist of any combination of GNU Make function calls. The following example is identical to the addprefix case, in that you're constructing a new list in which all the filenames are mapped to the expression obj/$(file).

```
OBJ_LIST_2 := $(foreach file, $(OBJECTS),objs/$(file))
```

- dir/notdir: Given a file's pathname, returns the directory name component or the filename component.

```
DEFN_PATH := src/headers/idl/interface.idl
DEFN_DIR := $(dir $(DEFN_PATH))
DEFN_BASENAME := $(notdir $(DEFN_PATH))
```

In this case, $(DEFN_DIR) evaluates to src/headers/idl/ (including the final /) and $(DEFN_BASENAME) evaluates to interface.idl.

- shell: Executes a shell command and returns the command's output as a string. The following example demonstrates a nonportable way of determining the owner of the /etc/passwd file. This assumes that the third word in the output of the ls -l command is the name of the file's owner.

```
PASSWD_OWNER := $(word 3, $(shell ls -l /etc/passwd))
```

In addition to these functions, and the many other functions listed in the GNU Make documentation, certain language features are designed to keep GNU Make programs short and concise.

First, the concept of a **macro** enables you to associate a name with a complex GNU Make expression and to pass arguments into that expression. This enables you to write your own GNU Make functions, effectively extending the basic language. The following code defines a macro named file_size that returns the number of bytes in a file (again, this is nonportable). You use the $(1) syntax to reference the first parameter of the $(call) expression.

```
file_size = $(word 5, $(shell ls -l $(1)))
PASSWD_SIZE := $(call file_size,/etc/passwd)
```

Another shortcut is to define a canned sequence of shell commands by using the define directive. When specifying the shell commands to be executed in GNU Make rule, you call upon that canned sequence instead of writing it out every time.

```
define start-banner
    @echo ==============
    @echo Starting build
```

```
    @echo ==============
endef

.PHONY: all
all:
    $(start-banner)
    $(MAKE) -C lib1
```

These language features, and many more discussed in the GNU Make documentation, make it possible to construct powerful makefile-based build systems.

## Understanding Program Flow

This discussion of the GNU Make programming language finishes with a study of how a GNU Make program flows—that is, in which sequence the makefile is scanned and interpreted, and in which order the various parts of the program are executed. You've seen many of GNU Make's language features, but you also need to understand how and when these features are called into action.

You'll explore three topics that are somewhat unrelated, except that they all deal with the flow of a GNU Make program:

1. **Parsing a makefile:** Parsing a makefile involves two main phases: reading the makefile to build the dependency graph and then executing the compilation commands. Recall that a makefile is essentially a text-based representation of the dependency graph, which itself is a mathematical structure showing the relationship between files.

2. **Controlling the parsing process:** GNU Make provides a number of features for controlling how you include a submakefile, or conditionally compile parts of the makefile.

3. **Executing the rules:** The rule execution algorithm decides the order in which rules are applied and the corresponding shell commands are executed.

### Parsing a Makefile

For the first topic, consider what happens when a developer invokes the gmake command:

1. **The makefile parsing phase:** The makefile is parsed and validated, and the full dependency graph is constructed. All rules are scanned, all variable assignments are performed, and all variables and functions are evaluated.

Any problems that occur in the definition of rules or the construction of the dependency graph are reported at this time.

2. **The rule execution phase:** When the entire dependency graph is in memory, GNU Make examines the time stamps on all the files to determine which files (if any) are out of date. If it finds any such targets, the appropriate shell commands are executed to bring those targets up-to-date. Any problems that occur within the shell commands are reported at this time.

Although in many cases you don't need to be aware of these phases, this next example illustrates the difference between the two. Again, keep in mind that variables are assigned in the first phase and shell commands are executed in the second phase.

```
1  X := Hello World
2
3  print:
4       echo X is $(X)
5
6  X := Goodbye
```

This example should seem straightforward, although you might be surprised to see the result of invoking the `print` target:

```
$ gmake print
X is Goodbye
```

The reason is that line 4 (a shell command) is simply saved until the second phase, and $(X) is not evaluated at all. This means that the second assignment on line 6 dictates the value of $(X) to be used when the shell command is finally evaluated.

If you're going to become a makefile expert, it's important to feel comfortable with the operation of these two phases. Much of your build system's functionality can be implemented either by using GNU Make functions (processed during the first phase) or as part of a shell script (processed during the second phase). Also, when you need to debug your makefile problems, you must understand the distinction between the two phases because different problems arise at each point in time.

### Controlling the Parsing Process

Next, you must consider some additional flow-control features in GNU Make that impact the execution of a GNU Make-based program.

- **File inclusion:** Similar to how C and C++ use the `#include` directive, GNU Make enables you to read additional files as if they were part of the main makefile. Any rules and variables defined inside the included file are treated as if they're actually written inside the main file.

```
FILES := src1.c src2.c

include prog.mk     # content of prog.mk textually
                    # inserted here

src1.o src2.o: src.h
```

As you've seen, this approach can be used to include a framework file containing reusable sections of code. You'll see another practical case of file inclusion later in this chapter.

- **Conditional compilation:** Similar to C/C++'s #ifdef directive, you can conditionally include or exclude parts of the makefile. This inclusion is done within the first phase of the makefile parsing, so the conditional expressions need to be pretty simple (instead of using shell commands).

```
CFLAGS := -DPATH="/usr/local"
ifdef DEBUG
    CFLAGS += -g     # debug case if DEBUG is defined
else
    CFLAGS += -O     # non-debug case if DEBUG not defined
endif
```

### Executing the Rules

Finally, let's examine the algorithm GNU Make uses to construct a dependency graph, and see how the execution of the makefile flows as a result. Consider the main steps (with some of the detail left out for convenience).

1. The developer who invokes GNU Make (with the gmake shell command) must specify which target to build. This is typically the name of an executable program, although you can also create pseudotargets such as all or install that don't relate to actual disk files. If the developer doesn't state which target file to build, GNU Make attempts to build the first target listed in the makefile (such as calculator).

2. If GNU Make locates a rule to generate the target file, it examines each of the prerequisites listed in that rule and treats them recursively as targets. This ensures that each file used as an input to a compilation tool is itself up-to-date. For example, before linking add.o and calc.o into the calculator executable program, GNU Make recursively searches for rules that have add.o or calc.o on the left side.

3. If a rule is found for the target you're trying to satisfy (either the user-specified target or one that was found recursively), you have two options:

  **a.** If the target file for the rule doesn't yet exist (there's currently no disk file with that name), the rule's shell command sequence is executed and the file is created for the first time. This is often the case when you're compiling a completely fresh source tree and no object files have yet been created.

  **b.** On the other hand, if the target file already exists on the disk, the time stamp on each of the prerequisite files is examined to see if any are newer than the target file. If so, you proceed to regenerate the target, thereby making it newer than the input files.

4. If step 3 fails, meaning that the makefile doesn't contain a suitable rule to generate a target file, you also have two options:

  **a.** If the target file exists on the disk (but there's no rule to regenerate it), GNU Make can only assume that this is a source file that was handwritten by the developer. This is where the rule recursion stops.

  **b.** If the target file doesn't exist on the disk, GNU Make aborts with an error and the build fails. GNU Make doesn't know how to regenerate the file, and because it doesn't already exist on disk, you can't proceed any further.

Throughout this process, GNU Make doesn't preserve any state between invocations and doesn't maintain a database of file time stamps. It determines whether a file has changed by comparing the time stamps between the target and its prerequisites. As you'll see in later chapters, build tools that record time stamps in a database can detect changes only by looking at that one file.

## Further Reading

Although you've explored a number of GNU Make features, you need to learn more before you can create your own build system. The ultimate authority on GNU Make syntax and semantics is the online reference document [16]; this is fairly tough going for beginners, though, so you'll probably want to start with a more introductory guide [41]. For more advanced best practices for using GNU Make, refer to [42] in References.

To simplify the construction of a makefile, consider using the GNU Make Standard Library [43] which adds an extra layer of language support for logical operators; manipulation of lists, strings, and sets; and basic arithmetic.

Now let's study how to use the GNU Make language to address common build system scenarios.

## Real-World Build System Scenarios

As discussed in the introduction to Part II, "The Build Tools," it's important to compare how each of the available build tools can be used in realistic scenarios. After all, not until you actually solve a technical problem do you get a true sense of whether the tool is easy to use. From now on, this chapter focuses less on the syntax of GNU Make and more on how everything fits together.

### Scenario 1: Source Code in a Single Directory

In the simple case in which you have a C program stored entirely within a single directory, you have three solutions. The first is a repeat of what you saw earlier in the chapter. The second shows how to improve upon that solution, and the third uses an external scanner tool to find dependencies.

Consider the solution you've already seen:

```
1   SRCS = add.c calc.c mult.c sub.c
2   PROG = calculator
3   CC = gcc
4   CFLAGS = -g
5   OBJS = $(SRCS:.c=.o)
6
7   $(PROG): $(OBJS)
8       $(CC) $(CFLAGS) -o $@ $^
9
10  $(OBJS): numbers.h
```

This type of makefile is common for projects that start small. When developers first write their code, they often don't put much effort into planning their build system, given that a simple makefile will suffice. They can add new source files by appending to the SRCS variable, and everything continues to work perfectly—at least, for a while.

Focus on line 10, stating that all source files have a dependency on the numbers.h header file. What would happen if a newly added source file didn't actually include numbers.h? What if additional header files were added, but you forgot to list them in the makefile? In both cases, a lot of manual work is required to keep the makefile consistent with the source files; otherwise, you'd end up with an incorrect executable program.

The second approach is to automate the detection of header files. The following solution scans the source files and computes the correct set of dependencies.

```
1    SRCS = add.c calc.c mult.c sub.c
2    PROG = calculator
3    CC = gcc
4    CFLAGS = -g
5    OBJS = $(SRCS:.c=.o)
6
7    $(PROG): $(OBJS)
8        $(CC) $(CFLAGS) -o $@ $^
9
10   -include $(SRCS:.c=.d)
11
12   %.d: %.c
13       @$(CC) -MM $(CPPFLAGS) $< | sed 's#\(.*\)\.o: #\1.o
     \1\.d: #g' > $@
```

This code looks rather complex (and it is), so let's break it down in detail. The approach is to automatically generate a new dependency information file (with .d suffix), corresponding to each C source file. In this case, you generate add.d, calc.d, mult.d, and sub.d. Here's what these dependency files look like (in this case, it's add.d):

```
add.o add.d: add.c numbers.h
```

On line 10 of the makefile, you explicitly include all these .d files, ensuring that everything is added to the same dependency graph. On line 12, a new rule informs GNU Make how to generate these .d files if they're missing or if the corresponding .c or .h files have changed.

Line 13 works a bit of magic to obtain the dependency information in the first place. Most of the work is done by passing the -MM option to the GCC compiler. This asks the compiler to generate the list of .c and .h files that it reads in but to stop immediately after doing so (instead of doing any real compile work). Finally, the cryptic sed command adds the name of the .d file on the left side of the rule, because GCC won't put it there by itself.

To fully understand this example, you need to know that GNU Make determines when makefile fragments (such as .d files) have changed and restarts the entire parsing process as a result. That's more detail than you'll want to get into, but hopefully you can see what's involved in automatically detecting header file dependencies.

A third solution uses the makedepend command. This tool is similar in nature to gcc -MM, although it provides its own scanner for analyzing C source files instead of relying on the compiler itself. Chapter 19, "Faster Builds," discusses build system performance and covers makedepend in more detail.

Let's continue by addressing scalability and see how to write a makefile for multidirectory programs.

## Scenario 2(a): Source Code in Multiple Directories

Constructing a multidirectory build system is not as simple as the single directory case, so next you'll see three different attempts to achieve what you need. In these cases, the source code files are no longer colocated in the same directory, but are instead spread across a larger source tree. As a reminder, Figure 6.1 shows the tree for the example software described at the start of Part II.

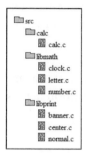

**Figure 6.1** *The source tree for the multidirectory calculator example.*

For the first attempt, you use a similar makefile to the single-directory program, but the SRCS variable now contains the full path to each file.

```
1   SRCS = libmath/clock.c libmath/letter.c libmath/number.c \
2       libprint/banner.c libprint/center.c libprint/normal.c \
3       calc/calc.c
4   ...
```

Although this is easy to understand and it works properly for simple programs, this approach doesn't work in a large-scale build environment, for several reasons:

1. **Harder dependency generation:** With automatic generation of .d files, the dependency rules are no longer created properly. Instead, you end up with a rule that doesn't contain the correct pathname on the left side (it's missing the directory component).

```
clock.o: libmath/clock.c libmath/math.h
```

Of course, this can be fixed by adding more complexity to the rule that generates .d files, but let's not look into that approach yet.

2. **Developer contention on the single makefile:** The SRCS variable is already spread over three lines in the makefile. What would happen if you had a hundred files or a thousand files? This single makefile would be unmanageable, becoming a point of contention when all software engineers (perhaps hundreds of them) needed to modify the same file at the same time.

3. **Inability to subdivide the program:** This makefile solution doesn't enable the use of libraries, such as libmath.a or libprint.a. For large programs, it's convenient to subdivide the code into libraries that help delineate areas of code, making it possible to reuse code across different executable programs.

For these reasons, it's uncommon to find a large build system that uses a single makefile. A more common solution is to divide the build description across more than one makefile. That leads to the next solution.

## Scenario 2(b): Recursive Make over Multiple Directories

The second approach, known as **recursive Make,** is a common solution in the software industry. The basic approach is to have a different makefile in each source directory, with the high-level makefile (in the high-level directories) recursively invoking each lower-level makefile. Figure 6.2 shows the revised directory tree, with each directory having its own makefile.

**Figure 6.2** *Multidirectory example, showing the location of makefiles and library files.*

Observe that the build tree now has four different files named `Makefile`: one at the top level and one within each of the `libmath`, `libprint`, and `calc` subdirectories. Going a step further, two static libraries, `libmath.a` and `libprint.a`, were added, each archiving the object files from their specific directories.

The advantage of recursive Make is that each makefile needs to list only the files in the current source directory. When necessary, a makefile can recursively call upon another makefile if there's a requirement to build other parts of the source tree. Listing long pathnames in the makefile is unnecessary because all file references are relative to the directory itself. Less contention also arises between different developers who need to make changes to a makefile. The odds of two developers changing the same small makefile are significantly less than with a single large makefile.

Now look at the content of each makefile, starting with `libmath/Makefile`:

```
1   SRCS = clock.c letter.c number.c
2   LIB = libmath.a
3   CC = gcc
4   CFLAGS = -g
5   OBJS = $(SRCS:.c=.o)
6
7   $(LIB): $(OBJS)
8       $(AR) cr $(LIB) $(OBJS)
9
10  $(OBJS): math.h
```

The code looks similar to the makefile used in the single-directory case, which, of course, is a major reason for using recursive Make. The files listed in the `SRCS` variable are all relative to the current directory, and you can use GNU Make's built-in rule for compiling C source files. Notice that the code is a bit lazy here: Line 10 contains an explicit dependency for the `math.h` header file instead of automatically detecting it.

The big difference is in lines 7 and 8, where, instead of linking together a final executable program, a static library is created by archiving the files listed in `$(OBJS)` into `libmath.a`. In another makefile that you'll see shortly, this archive is linked into the executable program.

The next makefile, in the `libprint` subdirectory, is essentially the same.

```
1   SRCS = banner.c center.c normal.c
2   LIB = libprint.a
3   CC = gcc
4   CFLAGS = -g
5   OBJS = $(SRCS:.c=.o)
6
7   $(LIB): $(OBJS)
8       $(AR) cr $(LIB) $(OBJS)
9
10  $(OBJS): printers.h
```

This makefile is so similar to `libmath/Makefile` that you might wonder whether you could factor out the common code. This is certainly the case, and many build systems extract the common code into a framework makefile. Each individual makefile uses the `include` directive to incorporate the shared functionality. For example, you could rewrite `libprint/Makefile` as follows:

```
1   SRCS = banner.c center.c normal.c
2   LIB = libprint.a
3   include lib.mk
4   $(OBJS): printers.h
```

The third makefile, in the `calc` directory, is different from the other two, in that it creates the final executable program by combining `libprint.a` and `libmath.a`, along with a small main program.

```
1   SRCS = calc.c
2   PROG = calculator
3   LIBS = ../libmath/libmath.a ../libprint/libprint.a
4   CC = gcc
5   CFLAGS = -g
6   OBJS = $(SRCS:.c=.o)
7
8   $(PROG): $(OBJS) $(LIBS)
9        $(CC) -o $@ $^
```

Note the use of relative paths on line 3 to access the static libraries from the `libmath` and `libprint` directories. An assumption is clearly being made that `calc/Makefile` is executed only after the two libraries have already been brought up-to-date. If the ordering of the steps was incorrect, you'd end up with a broken build, or worse, would build an executable program with outdated libraries.

To make sure everything is built properly, the top-level makefile recursively calls every other makefile in the correct order.

```
1   .PHONY: all
2   all:
3        $(MAKE) -C libmath
4        $(MAKE) -C libprint
5        $(MAKE) -C calc
```

This top-level makefile uses only the most basic features of GNU Make and doesn't have much of a dependency graph. Each of the shell commands is executed in the specified order, and there's no choice about whether they'll be executed. The `all` target has no prerequisites, so each of the recursive calls to `$(MAKE)` happens every time the developer executes the makefile.

Although recursive Make is simple to understand, it isn't the most efficient solution available. It might be commonly used in the software industry, but it still has a number of flaws that tend to cause slow or incorrect builds. Even though recursive Make enables developers to keep each makefile small and self-contained, with operations being done in an explicit sequence, those are the exact reasons the solution sometimes fails.

The example had only three directories to think about: libmath, libprint, and calc. The relationship between these directories was clearly defined, so the explicit sequence of $(MAKE) calls was easy to determine. On the other hand, what if you had a hundred directories with a complex network of dependencies between them? Trying to build everything in the correct order becomes an impossible task, especially if developers create more interdirectory dependencies as they write new code. After a while, you'd start wishing you'd used GNU Make's dependency-analysis system to figure out the correct ordering for you.

As an example, what would happen if the source code in the libmath directory started to use the libprint.a library. In the current system, libmath is compiled first and, therefore, runs the risk of using an outdated version of the libprint.a library or simply failing if the library didn't yet exist. The easiest solution is to modify the top-level makefile to build libprint first, but that solution doesn't scale to hundreds of directories with complex ordering requirements.

A similar problem occurs if you want to build only part of the program. Imagine if you tried to cut corners and not build the calculator example from the top-level makefile. If you started in the calc subdirectory and typed gmake, you'd simply be recompiling the calc.c source file (if required). Because calc/Makefile doesn't know how to build libprint.a, it doesn't attempt to rebuild any of those files even if they are out-of-date.

To phrase these problems in more technical terms, each makefile is executed by a separate instance of the $(MAKE) process and, therefore, has a completely different dependency graph. In no place in the build system is the entire dependency graph available, which, of course, is the root cause of invalid builds. If GNU Make isn't provided with full dependency information, it can't compile the correct set of files in the correct order.

In most large-scale recursive Make systems, developers end up seeing a lot of redundancy. To avoid risking the chance of building an executable program using outdated libraries, each makefile rebuilds the same libraries many times, just to make sure no dependencies were missed. For example, you might choose to build libmath.a, followed by libprint.a, and then repeat the compilation of libmath.a, just in case something in the libprint directory changed since the first time it was compiled. This type of paranoia is common when developers don't trust the build system to do the right thing.

This sequencing technique clearly results in building libmath.a twice, although because the library is already up-to-date, there's probably no extra work to do the second time—well, *almost* no work. In reality, there's still the overhead of starting a new GNU Make process, parsing the makefile to build the dependency graph, and then reading the file time stamps to see if anything has changed. Unfortunately, this overhead isn't free: It could slow the build by anything from a few seconds to a few minutes, depending on the size of libmath.a.

These problems and several others are detailed in a classic research paper titled "Recursive Make Considered Harmful" [44]. This paper also discusses solutions to the recursive Make problem, including the next solution you'll evaluate.

## Scenario 2(c): Inclusive Make over Multiple Directories

The third multidirectory solution adopts the good practices of the recursive Make approach, while ensuring that only one instance of the GNU Make process is ever executed. As a result, you benefit from the full power of GNU Make's dependency system so that important dependencies aren't missed. In contrast to the previous method, this new solution is called **inclusive Make**.

Consider the benefits:

- Only one instance of GNU Make is running, with a lower start-up time. This contrasts with starting hundreds of processes over the lifetime of the build.

- You still have a single makefile per directory to describe all the files in that directory. This makes it possible to encapsulate each directory's build description, and it reduces contention between developers when they modify each makefile.

- All source filenames are specified by their filename component only, so there's no need to include the full path to each file (as in the first example).

- A single dependency graph contains all dependencies in the entire build system, reducing the chance of incorrect builds.

- Because there's no recursion, you don't need to explicitly sequence all the recursive $(MAKE) calls and risk possibly getting it wrong. GNU Make executes the rules in the correct order.

Although this sounds like an excellent solution, the major downside is the additional complexity. If you're new to GNU Make, the solution you're about to see will stretch your knowledge of how the tool works. In most production build systems, an experienced GNU Make guru would create the inclusive build system in the first place, with junior GNU Make programmers scratching their heads to understand how everything works. This example just covers the basic framework and doesn't go into much detail.

Figure 6.3 illustrates the inclusive Make build tree. This is a larger example because a two-level directory structure doesn't show the full extent of this solution.

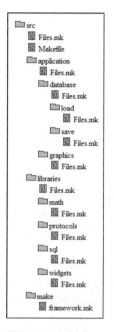

**Figure 6.3** *A larger source tree, illustrating the inclusive Make system.*

This example has one main makefile, at the top of the source tree. You can also see the `make/framework.mk` file, which contains most of the complexity of the build system. Finally, each source directory contains a short makefile fragment, named `Files.mk`, for describing the source files in that particular directory.

Because of the complexity of the inclusive Make framework, this separation of files is important. Software developers are only encouraged to view and edit `Files.mk` files where they can find the list of source files, the list of subdirectories to traverse, and the list of compiler flags. On the other hand, the GNU Make complexity is deliberately hidden inside the `make/framework.mk` file so that nonguru software engineers don't attempt to change the build mechanism by mistake.

Start by examining a few of the `Files.mk` files. These are designed to be readable and editable by software developers, and they contain only variables that developers care about:

- src/Files.mk:

```
1   SUBDIRS := libraries application
2   SRC := main.c
3   CFLAGS := -g
```

- src/libraries/Files.mk:

```
1   SUBDIRS := math protocols sql widgets
```

- src/libraries/math/Files.mk:

```
1   SRC := add.c mult.c sub.c
2   CFLAGS := -DBIG_MATH
```

First consider the SUBDIRS variable definitions. For directories (such as src and src/libraries) that contain subdirectories of their own, the SUBDIRS variable lists the directories to be included in the build process. As you can see, src/libraries/Files.mk includes the math subdirectory, so the inclusive framework must incorporate src/libraries/math/Files.mk into the build process. On the other hand, src/libraries/math/Files.mk doesn't contain a definition for SUDIRS, so the build system won't search any lower in the build tree.

Next, the SRC variable within each Files.mk fragment informs the build system about the C source files that should be included from that directory. Given that src/libraries/Files.mk doesn't include the SRC variable, none of the source files from that directory (if there were any) would be included.

Finally, the CFLAGS variable states which C compiler flags should be used for all the source files in this directory. Each directory can have a different set of C flags instead of using a global set of flags for all files in the build tree.

In the inclusive Make example, these Files.mk fragments are all that an average software developer is interested in seeing. The question remains of how GNU make interprets these Files.mk files  and how the SRC, SUBDIRS, and CFLAGS variables are used.

Continue by examining src/Makefile, which is the main entry point to the GNU Make program. As a reminder, only build gurus would be interested in reading or modifying this file.

```
1   _subdirs :=
2   _curdir :=
3   FRAMEWORK := $(CURDIR)/make/framework.mk
4   include Files.mk
5   include $(FRAMEWORK)
6
7   VARS := $(sort $(filter srcs-% cflags-%, $(.VARIABLES)))
8   $(foreach var, $(VARS), $(info $(var) = $($(var))))
```

```
 9
10   .PHONY: all
11   all:
12       @# do nothing
```

Again a detailed explanation is in order. The inclusive Make solution is complex, so now examine each line in detail.

On line 1, the `_subdirs` variable is initialized to the empty string. This variable is used as a space-separated list of subdirectories to be traversed. Within each of these directories, you can expect to find a `Files.mk` file, which itself could potentially include a definition for the `SUBDIRS` variable. Each time you find another `SUBDIRS` definition, you append the new subdirectories onto `_subdirs`, effectively creating a queue of directories to visit.

For example, after you've visited `src/Files.mk`, the `_subdirs` variable contains the following:

```
libraries applications
```

In the next step, you pop the `libraries` path off the front of the queue and parse `src/libraries/Files.mk`. After discovering the new definition for `SUBDIRS` in that file, the `_subdirs` variable changes to this:

```
applications libraries/math libraries/protocols libraries/sql \
    libraries/widgets
```

Following this process repeatedly, you end up traversing the entire build tree and reading every `Files.mk` file. Note that the `src` directory name isn't included in these pathnames because that's the current working directory. Everything is already relative to the `src` directory.

Line 2 of `src/Makefile` initializes `_curdir` to the empty string. This variable represents the current directory you're traversing. It starts empty because you're at the top level of the build tree (inside the `src` directory). As you traverse the build tree, by popping entries off the start of the `_subdirs` queue, the value of `_curdir` reflects the current point of traversal.

Line 3 defines `FRAMEWORK` to be the path of the framework makefile. You'll be calling upon this makefile often, so it's convenient to have a variable referring to it.

Line 4 starts everything in motion by including the `src/Files.mk` file. From this, you get the top-level definition of `SRC`, `SUBDIRS`, and `CFLAGS`. Note the distinction here between including a file with the `include` directive and calling upon another makefile using `$(MAKE)`. Because you're using `include`, the same Make instance is used, and you'll be adding to the same dependency graph each time (instead of creating a new one).

Line 5 calls the inclusive Make framework to process the content of the SRC, SUBDIRS, and CFLAGS variables; the framework then continues traversing the remainder of the source tree. By the time you return from this particular include directive, all the Files.mk files will have been processed.

Lines 7 and 8 are executed after the entire tree of Files.mk fragments has been processed. This code takes the complete list of variables that GNU Make knows about (automatically stored in $(.VARIABLES)) and filters all variables names that start with srcs- or cflags-. It then displays each one on the program's output so that you can see the computed values. You haven't seen it yet, but the framework file defines the srcs-* and cflags-* variables as it traverses the build tree.

This mechanism isn't normally part of the build system, but it's used as a means of debugging the inclusive Make algorithm to ensure that everything is working correctly. You'll take a look at the output shortly.

Now examine the content of make/framework.mk, which is the main algorithm for traversing the build tree and collecting the values from each Files. mk fragment:

```
1   srcs-$(_curdir)  := $(addprefix $(_curdir),$(SRC))
2   cflags-$(_curdir) := $(CFLAGS)
3   _subdirs := $(_subdirs) $(addprefix $(_curdir), $(SUBDIRS))
4
5   ifneq ($(words $(_subdirs)),0)
6       _curdir := $(firstword $(_subdirs))/
7       _subdirs := $(wordlist 2, $(words $(_subdirs)),
        $(_subdirs))
8       SUBDIRS :=
9       SRC :=
10      CFLAGS :=
11      include $(_curdir)Files.mk
12      include $(FRAMEWORK)
13  endif
```

As with the previous file, this makefile framework requires detailed explanation. Recall that this file is included immediately after one of the Files.mk files has been parsed. Therefore the SRC, SUBDIRS, and CFLAGS variables have just been set to the appropriate value for the directory you're currently processing.

Line 1 records the set of source files for the current directory. The variable name on the left side of the assignment also contains a variable, so you'll be creating a different GNU Make variable for each directory you visit. This syntax seems odd at first, but having the capability to dynamically construct variable names is equivalent to defining arrays or hashes in other languages. That is, the srcs- variable has many subelements, each indexed by the name of the directory.

On the right side of line 1, you take the current definition of the `SRC` variable and add the current directory as a prefix to each element in that list. For example, if `_curdir` is set to `libraries/math/`, then you've just finished parsing the `src/libraries/math/Files.mk` file. Line 1 of the framework makefile is therefore equivalent to this:

```
srcs-libraries/math/ := libraries/math/add.c \
    libraries/math/mult.c libraries/math/sub.c
```

Although it might seem odd, it's perfectly acceptable to have punctuation within variable names.

Line 2 is similar and stores the current directory's `CFLAGS` definition inside a directory-specific `cflags-*` variable. In the simple inclusive framework, you won't be doing anything with these variables aside from displaying them for debugging purposes.

Line 3 is responsible for queuing up any additional `SUBDIRS` values that the current `Files.mk` fragment might contain. Again, you prefix the elements in `SUBDIRS` with the current directory, but this time you append these values to the end of the existing `$(_subdirs)` value.

Lines 5–13 are where the tree traversal takes place. Assuming that there are more entries in the queue of pending subdirectories, you'll extract the first of them and visit the `Files.mk` file in the corresponding source code directory.

Lines 6 and 7 remove the first queue element. Line 6 sets the first item in the `_subdirs` list as the current directory (`_curdir`). Line 7 deletes this first element from the queue by reassigning `_subdirs` with all the words from position 2 to the end of the current `_subdirs` value.

Line 11 now includes the `Files.mk` fragment that resides within the current directory. Given that `Files.mk` isn't required to contain all the variable definitions (`SRC`, `SUBDIRS`, `CFLAGS`), you first set them to the empty string (lines 8–10) to make sure that the values from the previous directory don't "leak through" to the current directory.

Finally, Line 12 repeats the whole framework file, which stores the values of `SRC` and `CFLAGS` and then traverses any additional directories listed in `SUBDIRS`.

That's the end of the example. For completeness, let's see the output of executing the makefile on the example build tree. The values for the `srcs-` and `cflags-` variable should match the original diagram.

```
cflags- = -g
cflags-application/ =
cflags-application/database/ =
cflags-application/database/load/ =
cflags-application/database/save/ =
cflags-application/graphics/ =
cflags-libraries/ =
```

```
cflags-libraries/math/ = -DBIG_MATH
cflags-libraries/protocols/ = -DFAST_SEND
cflags-libraries/sql/ = -O2
cflags-libraries/widgets/ = -DCOLOR="red"
srcs- = main.c
srcs-application/ =
srcs-application/database/ = application/database/
➥persistence.c
   application/database/backup.c application/database/
➥optimize.c
srcs-application/database/load/ = application/database/load/
➥loading.c
srcs-application/database/save/ = application/database/save/
➥saving.c
srcs-application/graphics/ = application/graphics/line-
➥drawing.c
   application/graphics/vector-size.c application/
graphics/3d.c
srcs-libraries/ =
srcs-libraries/math/ = libraries/math/add.c libraries/math/
➥mult.c
   libraries/math/sub.c
srcs-libraries/protocols/ = libraries/protocols/tcp.d
   libraries/protocols/udp.c libraries/protocols/ip.c
srcs-libraries/sql/ = libraries/sql/select.c libraries/sql/
view.c
   libraries/sql/create.c libraries/sql/drop.c
srcs-libraries/widgets/ = libraries/widgets/button.c
   libraries/widgets/list.c libraries/widgets/window.c
   libraries/widgets/tree.c
```

At this point, it should be clear that you haven't built a complete inclusive Make system, but you should have a basic idea of how it could be done. The important factors are that each directory has its own Files.mk files (with paths specified relative to that directory) and that using one instance of the GNU Make process enables you to have a single unified dependency graph.

To make a fully functional build system, you need to add the following features:

- GNU Make code to define the dependencies between object files, source files, and header files (using automatic dependency analysis).

- Rules for compiling the code (You'd need to override the built-in rules for C compilation.)

- Code to link object files into static libraries.

- Code to link together the final executable programs (possibly more than one program could be compiled).

- The capability to start the GNU Make process from a subdirectory (Currently, the only makefile is in the top-level `src` directory.)

- Support for compiling on multiple CPU architectures.

- C compiler flags on a per-file basis instead of just on a per-directory basis.

- Inheritance of compiler flags from parent directories to child directories.

Certainly, the list goes on. In summary, an inclusive Make build system is not an easy system to create. Definitely budget plenty of time if you decide to create your own. Luckily, several experts [42][44] have provided systems you can use as a starting point.

## Scenario 3: Defining New Compilation Tools

The next real-world scenario looks at adding a new type of compilation tool into the makefile. So far, this chapter has focused exclusively on compiling C-language source files, but the same concepts extend nicely to other languages. In fact, this GNU Make code will appear simple compared to some you've seen so far.

To make use of the `mathcomp` compiler (discussed in the introduction to Part II), you need to add the following:

1. A list of source files that are in `.math` file format, to be read by the `mathcomp` compiler

2. A GNU Make rule that describes how to compile `.math` files into `.c` files

3. A new type of dependency file (with `.d1` suffix) to record the relationship between `.math` files and the `.mathinc` files they depend upon

Now jump right into the final solution, which isn't too different from what you've already seen.

```
1   MATHCOMP := /tools/bin/mathcomp
2   CC := gcc
3   MATHSRC := equations.math
4   CSRC := calculator.c
5   PROG := calculator
6   OBJS := $(CSRC:.c=.o) $(MATHSRC:.math=.o)
7
8   $(PROG): $(OBJS)
9       $(CC) -o $@ $^
10
11  %.c: %.math
```

```
12        $(MATHCOMP) -c $<
13
14    -include $(CSRC:.c=.d)
15    -include $(MATHSRC:.math=.d1)
16
17    %.d: %.c
18        @$(CC) -MM $(CPPFLAGS) $< | sed 's#\(.*\)\.o: #\1.o
      \1.d: #g' > $@
19
20    %.d1: %.math
21        echo -n "$@ $(*F).c: " > $@; \
22        $(MATHCOMP) -d $< >> $@
```

Here's a line-by-line explanation, but only for the new portions of the makefile. Everything else should look familiar.

Line 1 defines the path of the mathcomp compiler. An absolute path is used for the tool here instead of relying on users to have their $PATH variable set correctly.

Line 3 defines the list of source files (MATHSRC) in the .math file format, just as line 4 defines the list (CSRC) of C-language source files. Line 6 forms a list of object files by replacing .c and .math file extensions with the .o extension.

Lines 11 and 12 define a dependency rule to generate .c files from their corresponding .math files. For example, to generate equations.o (required by line 8), you first need to generate equations.c (defined by the built-in C compilation rule). To do this, GNU Make triggers the rule on line 11 to generate equations.c from equations.math.

Lines 15 and 20–22 perform the magic necessary for autodetecting makefile dependencies. Similarly to the C compiler, you pass the -d option to the mathcomp compiler and have it generate the list of source files it includes (namely, .mathinc files). The additional echo command on line 21 adds a small amount of extra information that mathcomp doesn't provide by default. The resulting equations.d1 file looks like this:

```
equations.d1 equations.c: equations.math equ1.mathinc \
    equ2.mathinc
```

With those key points covered and all the previous examples you've seen, the rest of the makefile should be easy to understand. In summary, adding a new compilation tool in GNU Make is not too difficult, except perhaps when it comes to automatically detecting dependencies.

## Scenario 4: Building with Multiple Variants

GNU Make is the most common means of compiling C and C++ code, and both of these languages usually compile to native machine code. Clearly, you need a way to select which CPU type to use. This example allows the software developer to compile for the Intel x86 series, the PowerPC series, or the Alpha CPUs. In fact, you allow them to compile for all three architectures within the same build tree at the same time.

To select a target architecture, developers should provide a value for the PLATFORM variable. If they don't provide a value, the compilation defaults to using the x86 architecture. For example:

```
$ gmake PLATFORM=powerpc      # build for PowerPC CPUs
$ gmake                       # build for i386 CPUs
$ gmake PLATFORM=xbox         # OOPS! Not allowed.
Makefile:8: *** Invalid PLATFORM: xbox. Stop.
```

Here's the necessary GNU Make code for compiling platform-specific code:

```
1   SRCS = add.c calc.c mult.c sub.c
2   PROG = calculator
3   CFLAGS = -g
4   PLATFORM ?= i386
5   VALID_PLATFORMS = i386 powerpc alpha
6
7   ifeq ($(filter $(PLATFORM), $(VALID_PLATFORMS)),)
8       $(error Invalid PLATFORM: $(PLATFORM))
9   endif
10
11  OBJDIR=obj/$(PLATFORM)
12  $(shell mkdir -p $(OBJDIR))
13
14  CC := gcc-$(PLATFORM)
15  OBJS = $(addprefix $(OBJDIR)/, $(SRCS:.c=.o))
16
17  $(OBJDIR)/$(PROG): $(OBJS)
18      $(CC) $(CFLAGS) -o $@ $^
19
20  $(OBJDIR)/%.o: %.c
21      $(CC) -c -o $@ $<
22
23  $(OBJS): numbers.h
```

This makefile example includes a few new concepts. Line 4 provides the default value for the PLATFORM variable. If the user doesn't set the variable on the command line, it defaults to i386. You don't technically need to use the ?= operator here; any variable defined on the command line automatically overrides the default value provided in the makefile.

Lines 7–9 tests whether $(PLATFORM) is one of the acceptable values. The $(filter) function returns the empty string if it's unable to find $(PLATFORM) in the list of valid platforms. The ifeq directive tests for this empty string and displays an appropriate error message.

Lines 11 and 12 determine the directory in which the object files will be placed. All the examples so far have stored the object files in the same directory as the source files because that's the default behavior. However, with object files from three different architectures, you need to explicitly store them in an architecture-specific location (obj/i386, obj/powerpc, or obj/alpha). Line 12 ensures that the selected object directory already exists.

Line 14 selects the appropriate C compiler to use and assigns the name to the CC variable. Assume that each CPU architecture requires a different version of GCC, as opposed to a single compiler instance supporting multiple targets.

Line 15 computes the list of object files to be compiled. Given that each CPU's object files are stored in a different object directory, you need to explicitly state which object files are to be built. In this case, you prefix each element in the object file list with $(OBJDIR).

Finally, lines 17–21 rewrite the rules you've seen many times before. The only difference is that here you've added $(OBJDIR) on the left side of each rule, whereas in the past you've assumed that object files are placed in the source directory. This code uses an interesting feature of GNU Make that permits the source and object files to be located in different places.

With this additional functionality, you now can support multiple CPU architectures. To help clarify how this build system works, examine the output:

```
$ gmake
gcc-i386 -c -o obj/i386/add.o add.c
gcc-i386 -c -o obj/i386/calc.o calc.c
gcc-i386 -c -o obj/i386/mult.o mult.c
gcc-i386 -c -o obj/i386/sub.o sub.c
gcc-i386 -g -o obj/i386/calculator obj/i386/add.o obj/i386/
calc.o
        obj/i386/mult.o obj/i386/sub.o

$ gmake PLATFORM=powerpc
gcc-powerpc -c -o obj/powerpc/add.o add.c
gcc-powerpc -c -o obj/powerpc/calc.o calc.c
gcc-powerpc -c -o obj/powerpc/mult.o mult.c
gcc-powerpc -c -o obj/powerpc/sub.o sub.c
gcc-powerpc -g -o obj/powerpc/calculator obj/powerpc/add.o
        obj/powerpc/calc.o obj/powerpc/mult.o obj/powerpc/sub.o
```

Of course, in a realistic environment, you'd integrate this code into a recursive Make or inclusive Make solution; otherwise, you're limited to compiling files in a single source directory.

## Scenario 5: Cleaning a Build Tree

The next real-world scenario involves cleaning a build tree by removing all the generated files. Sometimes you want this functionality on a per-directory basis, but in other cases, you're happy to remove all objects files from the build tree. In either case, it's important that your cleaning operation remove the exact set of object files your build process created in the first place.

The way a build system cleans a build tree depends entirely on how your build system was constructed. For recursive Make systems, each makefile is responsible for generating the object files in its own directory; therefore, it should be responsible for removing them, too.

For example, in the top-level makefile, you'd have a rule that recursively cleans the subdirectories.

```
.PHONY: clean
clean:
        $(MAKE)  -C libmath clean
        $(MAKE)  -C libprint clean
        $(MAKE)  -C calc clean
```

And in each of the subdirectories, you'd have a rule to actually remove the files.

```
.PHONY: clean
clean:
        rm -f $(OBJS) $(LIB)
```

One advantage of this system is that developers can easily clean the content of any subdirectory by simply issuing the gmake clean command at that level.

For inclusive Make systems, you can take advantage of the fact that the entire dependency graph is available within the single GNU Make process. Because you have a complete list of source files being compiled, you also know the complete set of object files. Things get a little more complicated when you have other generated files (such as equations.c being generated from equations. math), but this simply requires additional logic to record the relevant filenames. Cleaning specific subdirectories is also possible by filtering each file based on its pathname.

The tricky part about cleaning a build tree is that you're not always aware of which files are generated. Sometimes this is a sign that your interfile dependencies are not well understand, but sometimes a compilation tool creates extraneous files that you don't really care about. Although these files are never used and are never included in the dependency graph, they still need to be deleted from the build tree.

One good practice for testing your clean target is to fully build a source tree and then fully clean that same tree. Next, compare the list of disk files against a completely fresh source tree and see if any discrepancies arise. If any files are left over, you can explicitly add them to the clean target to make sure they're properly deleted. On the other hand, you might wonder why those files weren't already accounted for in $(OBJS) and, therefore, already deleted.

Finally, one advantage of storing all generated files in a special object directory instead of the source code tree is that a single delete command (such as `rm -rf` in UNIX) is guaranteed to remove all generated files.

## Scenario 6: Debugging Incorrect Builds

Locating bugs in your GNU Make build system is often challenging. Given the nature of the pattern-matching algorithm, GNU Make doesn't use the line-by-line sequencing that most programmers are comfortable with. Rules from any part of the makefile system can be triggered at any time.

In a real-world development project, you'll likely experience the following makefile problems:

- A target file isn't being generated when it should be. In this case, there's probably a missing link in the dependency graph, and you need to add an additional rule.

- A file is being generated when it shouldn't be, which makes you wonder if an incorrect dependency is causing too much work to be performed.

- The content of the target file is incorrect, which suggests that a compilation tool is being invoked with the wrong command-line options.

- GNU Make is reporting that no rule is available to create a specific target. You need to add the missing rule or determine why an existing rule isn't triggering when it should.

- Rules are being triggered in the wrong order, most likely when you're trying to build multiple jobs in parallel. This is also because you have links missing in the dependency graph.

You can resolve each of these problems by first determining which compilation tool has the incorrect behavior and then working backward to determine where the associated rules and variables are defined. The steps are as follows:

1. Examine the build output log to determine which of the compilation tools is doing the wrong thing. This might involve scanning through hundreds or thousands of lines of output to find the offending command.

2. Locate the makefile rule that's responsible for generating the bad command line. Given that rules (including the built-in rules) can be spread across a number of different makefiles in a build system, finding where everything is defined can take time.

3. Check that the command-line options in this rule are valid. If necessary, double-check the variable definitions used in the rule. This can be challenging if some of the variables use deferred evaluation, making use of subvariables that are defined in other parts of the build system.

4. Examine the dependencies in the rule to make sure they're correct. This might involve searching for related rules to ensure that prerequisite files are also being created.

To help with this debugging effort, GNU Make provides a number of command-line options:

- `gmake -n`: Displays the list of shell commands to be executed, without actually executing them. This saves you a lot of time when trying to find an offending compilation tool, without waiting for a long build to complete.

- `gmake -p`: Displays the content of GNU Make's internal database. This contains the complete list of rules and variables defined in each makefile, as well as GNU Make's built-in rules. Line number information is recorded so you can easily track down where something is defined.

- `gmake -d`: Displays a trace log of GNU Make's pattern-matching algorithm as it parses and executes a makefile. The output can be extremely verbose, but it provides everything you need to know.

In addition to these command-line options, you can use the **print debugging** approach to display useful messages on the program's output. The exact sequence in which these messages appear helps the developer understand how the makefile is executing. The `$(warning)` function displays a text message, along with information on where in the makefile the function was called.

```
$(warning CFLAGS is set to $(CFLAGS))
```

This function doesn't return a value, so it can be inserted at any point in the makefile where a function is permitted. Another clever trick is to use `$(warning)` within the definition of variables. Whenever the variable is accessed, a suitable message is displayed.

```
CFLAGS = $(warning Accessing CFLAGS) -g
```

Also, if you redefine the `$(SHELL)` variable to include a `$(warning)` directive, you display a message on the program's output whenever a rule is triggered.

```
SHELL = $(warning Target is $@) /bin/sh
```

Now see how all this fits together. Going back to the first `calculator` program, you now get a much better view of when variables are accessed, what they're defined as, and when the rules are being triggered.

```
Makefile:8: Accessing CFLAGS
Makefile:8: CFLAGS is set to  -g
Makefile:13: Accessing CFLAGS
Makefile:13: Target is add.o
gcc  -g -c -o add.o add.c
Makefile:13: Accessing CFLAGS
Makefile:13: Target is calc.o
gcc  -g -c -o calc.o calc.c
Makefile:13: Accessing CFLAGS
Makefile:13: Target is mult.o
gcc  -g -c -o mult.o mult.c
Makefile:13: Accessing CFLAGS
Makefile:13: Target is sub.o
gcc  -g -c -o sub.o sub.c
Makefile:16: Accessing CFLAGS
Makefile:16: Target is calculator
gcc  -g -o calculator add.o calc.o mult.o sub.o
```

Finally, to make life much easier, the third-party GNU Make debugger tool [45] uses these underlying tricks to provide a more traditional debugging environment. You can interactively print the value of variables, find out how they're defined, and set breakpoints on specific makefile rules. Consider using this tool when debugging a nontrivial makefile.

## Praise and Criticism

Having been around for more than 30 years, the Make tool (GNU Make being a modern version) has had plenty of opportunity to gather praise and criticism. Clearly, Make offers many benefits; otherwise, it would no longer be the most popular tool for C/C++ development. On the other hand, plenty of empirical experience has shown that Make has a number of flaws.

Let's now review what users of Make have been saying. The following comments were either found on Internet web sites, published in books, or gathered via personal experience.

### Praise

- **Wide support:** Make (particularly GNU Make) is widely supported on a large number of operating systems. Most software engineers have at least a passing knowledge of makefile construction, and quite a few people consider themselves to be makefile experts. Part of this widespread knowledge results from universities teaching Make as a standard build tool. The significant number of legacy build systems using Make is also a contributing factor.

If you were starting a new software project, the fact that so many developers are already familiar with Make would likely convince you to use the same tool again. In addition, numerous Make-related tools (such as automatic makefile generators, automatic parallelization tools, and makefile editors) are available either commercially or for free. Make is clearly the best-supported build tool, at least for C/C++ development.

- **Very fast tool:** Being written in C, GNU Make is fast and highly optimized. Compared to other tools, GNU Make is extremely fast for computing and traversing the dependency graph. As a side note, some people counter this benefit by questioning whether speed is important if accuracy of the tool's dependency information can't be guaranteed.

- **Portable syntax:** GNU Make has a portable syntax and is available on a wide range of platforms, including Microsoft Windows. Before the introduction of GNU Make, developers were required to write a makefile that was compatible with every operating system's variant of Make. They often were limited to using only the small subset of features that all Make implementations had in common. With GNU Make, the syntax is the same across all platforms, and you can use the entire set of the GNU Make's features.

- **Fully featured programming language:** As a general-purpose dependency engine, Make can be used for any type of dependency analysis. As long as you can write a rule that maps input files to output files, there's no limit on the type of compilation you can perform. Whereas other build tools might focus on C, C++, Java, or C# compilation, Make enables you to compile any type of file (such as creating PDF files from TeX source).

  It's worth noting that GNU Make's language is **Turing complete**. This means that any program written in a general-purpose programming language can also be written as a GNU Make program. It would be incorrect to claim that "GNU Make can't do that" because any feature of any other build tool can be implemented in GNU Make. (Just ask a Make guru how it can be done.)

- **The first tool:** Being the first build tool ever invented, Make paved the way for automated build systems. Newer tools would never have been able to improve on Make if it hadn't first demonstrated what was possible.

## Criticism

On the flip slide, there are many criticisms of the Make tool to be aware of:

- **Inconsistent language design:** GNU Make's language has clearly grown over time, and the design hasn't always stayed consistent. Some of the language features (such as rules) were part of the original Make design, but many other features were added over time as people found a need. In addition, the syntax for each of the features isn't always consistent with the syntax of other features. This makes the language difficult for new developers to learn.

  Some of the common concerns include the following:

  - When writing a makefile rule, the shell commands must be indented by a tab character instead of by spaces. This syntactical rule has impacted almost everyone, especially if their editor automatically converts tabs to spaces.

  - All makefile variables are global, so it can be challenging to determine where a variable is defined and whether you're conflicting with a different variable that accidentally has the same name.

  - Some parts of the makefile syntax ignore whitespace; in other parts, whitespace must be included.

  - It can be confusing to determine which parts of a makefile enable you to write shell commands and which parts enable GNU Make functions.

  - When invoking shell commands within a Make rule, you need to be familiar with the syntax of each command being invoked. Often a lot of inconsistency arises in the command-line arguments and return values each tool provides.

  - For developers familiar with procedural programming (sequencing, loops, conditionals, and function calls), it can be challenging to write GNU Make code. In particular, it's difficult to fit together the necessary shell commands, GNU Make functions, and user-defined macros to achieve the desired effect.

  As a result of these syntax and semantic issues, a number of additional tools such as Automake and CMake (see Chapter 9, "CMake") automatically generate a makefile from a higher-level description. This alleviates the need to learn the GNU Make syntax.

- **No standard framework:** Although this chapter discussed using inclusive Make to solve a number of build system problems, no standard framework can be used as a starting point. GNU Make provides a powerful set of language features, but it wasn't designed to work out-of-the-box for large software projects. In particular, the following important features must be implemented by hand:

  - Automatic dependency analysis for common languages such as C/C++. Without a good dependency system, the chance of introducing build failures is much higher.

  - Multidirectory support with a single dependency graph for the whole build tree.

  - C compiler flags that can be set on a per-directory or per-file basis.

  - A mechanism for rebuilding object files if the C compiler flags are modified.

  - A mechanism for abstracting out values such as SRCS, SUBDIRS, and CFLAGS, as was done with the Files.mk fragments.

  Unfortunately, anybody using GNU Make is required to implement these features for themselves or perhaps borrow an existing framework from some other software project. In reality, it's common to see each project using an entirely different framework that grows over time as new features are required. None of this is easy work.

- **Lack of portability:** Although GNU Make provides a consistent syntax across all operating systems, it's unlikely that the syntax of the shell commands will be consistent. Each operating system is free to store its standard tools (such as ls, cat, sed, and grep) in whichever directory it likes, and it's free to implement whichever optional tool features it desires. Even with modern versions of UNIX and Linux, some amount of inconsistency always seems to arise between shell commands.

  To make things easier, follow a couple good practices:

  - Use the standard GNU versions of command-line tools instead of the operating system's own version. This at least guarantees that command options are consistent.

  - Use makefile conditionals (such as ifdef SOLARIS) to select an appropriate tool or tool path that works on each operating system, and then use a variable to access the tool instead of hard-coding the name. For example, use $(RM) foo.o instead of rm foo.o.

- **Challenging debugging:** Many developers find it difficult to follow Make's flow of control when filenames are being pattern-matched against rules. In contrast to most other programming languages, the flow of control isn't sequential. This means that the next rule to be triggered could be defined at any point within the makefile system, including built-in rules and those included in `Files.mk` fragments. Before the use of the GNU Make debugger (a recent creation), developers were left to interpret confusing errors messages or to scan through complex listings of the dependency graph.

- **Language completeness versus ease of use:** Even though any general-purpose program can be implemented within the GNU Make programming environment, the real question is how much work needs to be done to make that happen. As you've seen already, constructing a complete GNU Make framework isn't trivial and requires the author to have "guru" status. The authors must have a perfect understanding of GNU Make's flow of control, as well as an intimate knowledge of GNU Make's syntax and built-in functions. Finally, they need to have a handful of clever tricks to convince GNU Make to perform certain operations that aren't officially supported.

If you decide to create an inclusive Make framework for yourself, be prepared to devote a large amount of time (months, not weeks). You need to support your development team on an ongoing basis when it requests that new functionality be added. After all this work, you'll end up with a solid build system, but be prepared for average software engineers to not have any understanding of how it works. After all, many people never get beyond the much simpler recursive Make systems, even with all the associated problems.

## Evaluation

To summarize the GNU Make tool, let's evaluate it against the build system quality measurements discussed in Chapter 1, "Build System Overview."

- **Convenience:** *Poor*. As you've seen, creating a fully functioning build system is difficult. This includes the detection of implicit dependencies and the traversal of a full build tree. Although a simple makefile is quick and easy to construct, the tool is much less convenient for nontrivial build systems.

- **Correctness:** *Poor*. Because of the poor level of convenience, GNU Make is notorious for not producing a correct build image. It's possible to guarantee a correct build, although the effort to do so can be enormous.

- **Performance:** *Excellent.* GNU Make is written in optimized C code and has an efficient algorithm for dependency analysis. Compared to other build tools discussed in later chapters, GNU Make is extremely fast.

- **Scalability:** *Excellent.* As with the performance criteria, GNU Make is highly scalable. The assumption is that you've already created a makefile framework that adequately supports multiple directories.

As a general rule, consider using GNU Make for legacy software that already uses a Make-based build system. However, if you're writing a new build system for C/C++ software, first consider using SCons (Chapter 8) or CMake (Chapter 9). If you're writing a build system for Java, consider using Ant (Chapter 7). For C# code, use MSBuild (discussed briefly in Chapter 7). If none of these tools meets your needs, especially for performance reasons, writing a new build system using GNU Make is a possibility.

Note that these evaluation criteria are subjective in nature, so your value judgment could be quite different.

---

# Similar Tools

Although this chapter's focus has been the GNU Make tool, several other tools conform to Make's original premise. Let's now look briefly at the Berkeley Software Distribution's version of Make, Microsoft's version of Make, and the more recent ElectricAccelerator and SparkBuild tools.

## Berkeley Make

The Berkeley Software Distribution (BSD) is a version of the UNIX operating system first developed at the University of California in the mid-1970s. Although other UNIX-like systems, such as Linux and Solaris, tend to get more publicity, you've likely heard of the NetBSD, FreeBSD, and OpenBSD systems. In fact, the Apple Mac OS X operating system is based on BSD technology, making it a common version of UNIX.

In addition to an operating system kernel, the BSD systems include a number of user-space utilities, including a variant of the Make tool known as Berkeley Make (also known as `bmake` or `bsdmake`) [46]. If you find yourself modifying existing code in a BSD environment, you'll likely use Berkeley Make, even though GNU Make is also available on those platforms.

Much of Berkeley Make's syntax is identical to GNU Make's syntax, especially for basic features. This includes the definition of makefile rules, the list of shell commands, and the definition and usage of variables. In fact, a number of makefile features can be executed by either Berkeley Make or GNU Make.

One of the most noticeable syntax differences is the way variables are manipulated. The GNU Make system uses the concept of functions that manipulate string values. The Berkeley Make system instead uses **modifiers**. For example:

- $(MY_VAR:E): For each space-separated word in $(MY_VAR), returns the file name's suffix, such as .c or .h. This is similar to GNU Make's $(suffix) function.

- $(MY_VAR:H): For each word in $(MY_VAR), returns the pathname component of the word. This is similar to the $(dir) function in GNU Make.

- $(VAR:M<*pattern*>): Returns only the list of words that match the specified pattern. This is similar to GNU Make's $(filter) function.

In addition, the Berkeley Make language has syntax to support both conditional execution and looping. The following example demonstrates the use of a for loop (line 4) that traverses a list of subdirectories, and an if statement (line 6) to test whether a particular file exists.

```
1   SUBDIRS = application database libraries storage
2   ALLTARGS =
3
4   .for SUBDIR in $(SUBDIRS)
5   SUBMK = $(SUBDIR)/Sub.mk
6   .if exists($(SUBMK))
7   .include "$(SUBMK)"
8   ALLTARGS += make-$(SUBDIR)
9   .endif
10  .endfor
11
12  all: $(ALLTARGS)
13        @echo All targets up to date
```

The net effect of this makefile is that all Sub.mk files residing within any of the subdirectories are included in the top-level makefile.

To effectively use Berkeley Make, you'll probably find yourself learning a few new syntax tricks. You might also find yourself limited by the number of features available, especially if you're used to GNU Make's wide range of built-in functions.

## NMake

The NMake tool [47] is another variant of Make, typically used as part of Microsoft Visual Studio. Whereas developers use the Visual Studio graphical interface for their day-to-day development, NMake can be used more for batch-oriented tasks that are performed from a command line, such as in software packaging.

NMake provides the same basic syntax as GNU Make and Berkeley Make, particularly for the definition of rules and variables. However, any sequences of shell commands will obviously be targeted for the Windows command prompt and use the Visual Studio compilation tools.

Users of the GNU Make tool will find NMake's syntax limiting because it contains only a few advanced features. With the introduction of Microsoft's MSBuild tool (discussed briefly in Chapter 7, "Ant"), the use of NMake has become less common.

## ElectricAccelerator and SparkBuild

ElectricAccelerator [48] and SparkBuild [49] are two products created by Electric Cloud, Inc. ElectricAccelerator is a commercially available tool that accelerates the software build process. It achieves this goal by dispatching jobs onto multiple CPUs in a networked cluster and coordinating access to disk files to make sure jobs are executed in the correct order. Given that ElectricAccelerator can parse GNU Make and NMake syntax, customers with legacy build systems see a dramatic increase in performance with little extra work.

SparkBuild is a feature-limited version of ElectricAccelerator that solves some of GNU Make's basic weaknesses, even though it doesn't support cluster-based builds. Earlier, this chapter identified problems with recursive Make in starting a compilation within a subdirectory of the source tree. Given that GNU Make doesn't have a global view of all the dependencies, it's likely to miss some of the important recompilation steps.

When using SparkBuild, you start by explicitly asking the tool to generate a database of dependency information. This knowledge remains even after the build completes.

```
$ emake --emake-gen-subbuild-db=1
[ ... output hidden ... ]
```

When the build is complete, the `emake.subbuild.db` file contains all the dependency information for the whole build tree.

```
$ ls
emake.subbuild.db  libmath  libprint  Makefile calc
```

If a developer rebuilt the software from within the `calc` subdirectory, SparkBuild would have enough intelligence to first rebuild the `libmath` and `libprint` subdirectories, even though the developer didn't explicitly request it.

```
$ cd calc
$ emake --emake-subbuild-db=../emake.subbuild.db
emake -C libmath
make[1]: Entering directory '/home/psmith/sparkbuild/libmath'
make[1]: 'libmath.a' is up to date.
make[1]: Leaving directory '/home/psmith/sparkbuild/libmath'
emake -C libprint
make[1]: Entering directory '/home/psmith/sparkbuild/lib-
        print'
make[1]: 'libprint.a' is up to date.
make[1]: Leaving directory '/home/psmith/sparkbuild/libprint'
        make: 'calculator' is up to date.
```

Another nice feature of SparkBuild is that it records useful information for
later analysis of the build process. For example, it records which commands
were executed, which makefile each command was listed in, and how long it
took to execute each of the steps. Feeding this information into the SparkBuild
Insight graphical interface produced a comprehensive view of the entire build
process (see Figure 6.4).

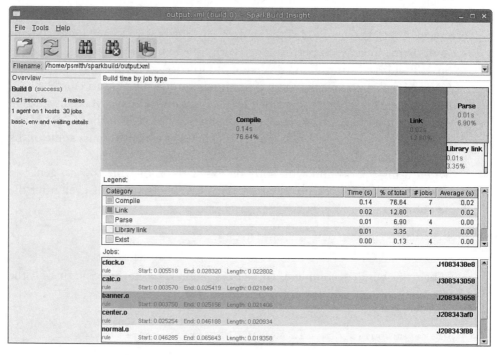

**Figure 6.4** *The SparkBuild Insight GUI, showing the analysis of the build process.*

The SparkBuild Insight interface also provides the capability to query the build steps and to examine the underlying command and path information (see Figure 6.5).

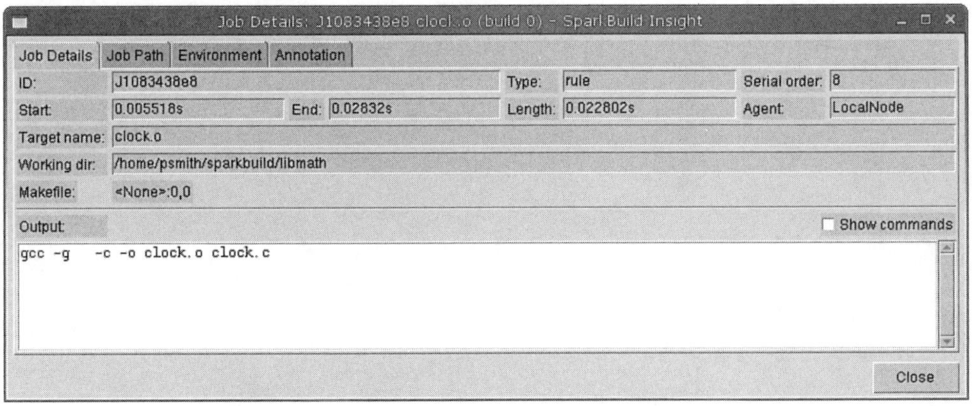

**Figure 6.5** *The SparkBuild Insight GUI, showing the detail of an individual job.*

Although SparkBuild and SparkBuild Insight are relatively new products, they'll likely become a value resource for makefile developers. They're particularly useful when trying to debug makefile problems such as missing dependencies or slow builds.

## Summary

A Make-based build system is created by defining rules to piece together a program's complete dependency graph. Each rule specifies a target file, a list of prerequisite input files, and the necessary shell commands to generate the target from the inputs.

The GNU Make tool is a modern version of Make that supports a wide range of features. Among these features is the capability to manipulate string-valued variables and treat them as more complex data types. In particular, a variable can be treated as a list of filenames, and various functions can manipulate that list.

Although GNU Make is a powerful language, you still need to add support for automatic dependency analysis and for building software that spans multiple file system directories. Although it's possible to implement these features by hand, they aren't built into the basic language, making it challenging for developers to construct a reliable build system.

Other Make-based tools include Berkeley Make, NMake for Microsoft environments, and the more modern SparkBuild and SparkBuild Insight tools.

# Chapter 7

---

# Ant

The second build tool to examine is Apache Ant [50], maintained by the Apache Software Foundation. Ant is one of the most popular build tools for Java-based projects and has numerous features for compiling code in that environment. Few Java developers would consider using GNU Make for building Java code, even though it's technically possible.

Ant was originally created as part of Apache Tomcat because existing build tools were too hard to use in multiplatform Java projects. Since being released as a standalone tool in 2000, Ant now runs on a diverse set of operating systems such as UNIX, Windows, OS/2 Warp, OpenVMS, and Mac OS X.

One of the challenges in writing build systems for multiple operating systems (OS) is that each platform has its own peculiar set of commands and services. For example, in UNIX-like systems, the shell command for copying files is cp, whereas in the Windows environment, the command is copy. Naturally, writing a makefile rule that works smoothly on both platforms becomes difficult.

The approach Ant follows is to encapsulate each activity in the build system into a high-level **task**. Instead of specifying the exact shell commands to be executed, you use a task to handle interaction with the operating system. Most of the time, end users don't need to know or care which machine their build system is running on because an Ant-based build description works cleanly on all platforms.

The following Ant fragment defines a **target** that contains a list of three tasks to be performed:

```
  . . .
  3        <target name="all">
  4            <mkdir dir="pkg"/>
  5            <jar basedir="obj" destfile="pkg/prog.jar"/>
  6            <copy file="index.txt" tofile="pkg/index.txt"/>
  7        </target>
  . . .
```

The first task (line 4) creates a new directory named pkg. The task on line 5 finds all the files inside the obj directory and packages them into a Java JAR file named prog.jar. Finally, line 6 copies the index.txt file into the pkg directory. Given that Ant build descriptions are written in a platform-neutral way (using XML syntax), each operating system's implementation of the Ant tool knows how to map the high-level task into an underlying shell command (such as cp or copy) or the relevant system calls.

Also note that no mention was made of interfile dependencies, which is a fundamental building block of GNU Make. Each task is responsible for knowing whether the underlying command actually needs to be executed. For example, the <copy> task first checks whether pkg/index.txt is newer than index.txt; if it is, it completes without actually copying any data.

An attractive quality of the Ant tool is the wide support from Java tool vendors. Most vendors supply additional Ant tasks to interact with their tool. Not only do these tasks manage the low-level interaction with the operating system, but they also perform the necessary dependency analysis. This approach enables seamless integration of the vendor's tool into any existing Ant-based solution.

Additionally, all popular Java integrated development environments (IDEs) have the capability to create and execute Ant scripts, providing a strong integration into the development process. The breadth and depth of Ant's support is a major reason for using Ant in your build projects.

This chapter starts by looking at Ant's programming language and then shows how Ant solves a number of common build problems. Finally, it examines the pros and cons of using Ant and discusses a few similar build tools.

## The Ant Programming Language

Using the term **programming language** might seem a little misleading when comparing Ant to general-purpose languages such as C# or Java. The basic Ant language doesn't have many of the standard constructs, such as variables, loops, if/then/else statements, or pointers. Luckily, it's still possible to extend the language. You might prefer to think of an Ant script as more of a sequence of build tasks than a fully fledged program.

Ant's build description is written using an XML-based format, with the default filename being build.xml. Although XML is not always the easiest format for new developers to learn, and a number of experienced developers consider it too verbose, it's still a well-supported data format. Many tools exist for editing XML, including some that were designed specifically for viewing and editing Ant description files. This chapter assumes that you at least have a passing knowledge of XML.

As you'll see in more detail, each of Ant's XML files contains a **project**. Each project contains one or more **targets** that represent something the user can build. Finally, each target contains an ordered sequence of tasks that perform the real work, such as making a directory or compiling a Java source file.

## A Little More Than "Hello World"

To illustrate how an Ant build description file is structured, consider a simple example that does nothing but display messages on the output. Instead of starting with the typical "Hello World" example, skip ahead to see a program that has multiple targets, dependencies between those targets, and a few simple constant definitions.

Here's the `build.xml` file for the simple program.

```
1   <project name="ant-project" default="all">
2
3       <property name="country" value="New Zealand"/>
4       <property name="city" value="Christchurch"/>
5
6       <target name="print-city">
7           <echo message="The nicest place in the world is"/>
8           <echo message="${city}, ${country}"/>
9       </target>
10
11      <target name="print-math">
12          <echo message="Two plus two equals four"/>
13      </target>
14
15      <target name="all" depends="print-city, print-math">
16          <echo message="Thank you!"/>
17      </target>
18
19  </project>
```

Line 1 defines the overall project that's stored inside the `build.xml` file. The name attribute is useful for identification purposes and is displayed by any of Ant's graphical front-end tools. The `default` attribute specifies the target to run if the user doesn't specify a target (that is, if the user just types ant by itself on the command line).

Now skip ahead to the default target (`all`) on lines 15–17, which is where execution actually starts. Line 15 defines the name of the target and lists the prerequisite targets that must first be executed. That is, before the tasks listed within the `all` target are executed, Ant must go to the `print-city` and `print-math` targets to make sure all those tasks are performed.

Now jump back to the definition of the `print-city` target on lines 6–9. This time, there are no dependencies on other targets, so Ant immediately starts executing the task on line 7. The first `<echo>` target is fairly simple: It displays only a constant string on the program's output. The task on line 8 is a little more complex because the echoed message refers to a couple of property names, each identified by the ${...} syntax.

Back on lines 3 and 4, you see these Ant properties defined. You should consider these properties to be constant because it's not possible to change their values after they've been assigned. As you'll see later, property definitions can be quite complex and can contain a lot more than simple string values.

Lines 11–13 don't add anything new; the `print-math` target simply echoes a constant string.

Finally, after the `print-city` and `print-math` targets have been executed, the `<echo>` task on line 16 is the only action performed in the `all` target. Now finish by reviewing the output of the `ant` command:

```
$ ant
Buildfile: build.xml
print-city:
     [echo] The nicest place in the world is
     [echo] Christchurch, New Zealand
print-math:
     [echo] Two plus two equals four
all:
     [echo] Thank you!
BUILD SUCCESSFUL
Total time: 218 milliseconds
```

As you can see, it's not too hard to determine which target from the `build.xml` file is responsible for generating each line of the output, or to figure out which task generates each message. In this case, you use only `<echo>` tasks, but in other programs, you'll see different tasks names displayed.

By reading through the output, it's straightforward to understand the ordering in which the tasks are executed. For any developer with experience in procedural programming (which is almost everybody), the flow of control within the `build.xml` file should be obvious.

At this point, you might think that a makefile written in GNU Make syntax would look similar to this Ant example, and you'd certainly be right. Given that this example contains only `<echo>` tasks and doesn't need to deal with interfile dependencies, a GNU Make program would be just as easy to follow.

Now that you've seen the basic concepts of targets, properties, and tasks, let's examine each of them in more detail.

## Defining and Using Targets

In an Ant-based build system, a target is a convenient way to group tasks that need to be executed sequentially. To invoke an Ant target, a developer provides the name of that target on the command line. Target names should be designed for ease of use and readability, and must describe the operation being performed. For example, the following targets are commonly used for building software:

ant `compile`: For compiling all the Java source files into class files

ant `jar`: For packaging the class files into a single Jar file

ant `package`: For creating a full software release package, complete with a version number

ant `clean`: For removing all generated files from the build tree

ant `javadoc`: For generating API documentation using the Javadoc tool (Chapter 12, "Building with Metadata," discusses this more)

ant: For executing the default target, which is most likely the same as the `package` target

In contrast to a Make-based build system, the name of an Ant target isn't related to the name of any disk files. An Ant target is similar to a GNU Make `.PHONY` target, where the target's filename isn't considered part of the dependency graph.

In addition to these publicly visible targets, the project can contain a number of internal targets. These are never invoked directly from the command line but are instead used as dependencies of public targets. For example, when the `java` target is invoked, it could have a dependency on the `init` target that defines a number of Ant properties and a `make-directories` target that creates all the necessary build directories. In this case, you would use the following syntax:

```
 ...
 3    <target name="java" depends="init, make-directories">
            ...
12    </target>
 ...
```

It might help to think of `init` and `make-directories` as function calls executed before the tasks in the `java` target are executed.

To add more flexibility, you can conditionally choose whether to invoke a list of tasks. If you specify the name of an Ant property in the target's `if` attribute, Ant executes the tasks only if the property has been defined. In the following example, the tasks in the `append-to-log` target are executed only if the `log-enabled` property is set to a value (instead of not being set to anything).

```
 ...
 3        <property name="log-enabled" value="1"/>
 4
```

```
5       <target name="append-to-log" if="log-enabled">
6           <echo message="Appending..."/>
7       </target>
...
```

This mechanism is somewhat like an `if` statement in other languages and is useful for controlling whether optional parts of the build process are executed. As you'll see later, properties can also store the result of more complex conditions, using features such as string comparison. In the example, the log feature is simply enabled or disabled by manually setting the property.

In addition to invoking a target from the user's command line or listing a target as a dependency of other targets, you can use the `<antcall>` task. This is useful for executing a few tasks before calling upon another target to do the rest of the work.

```
...
3     <target name="java" depends="init, make-directories">
      ...
7         <antcall target="check-rules"/>
      ...
12    </target>
...
```

This approach can even extend across multiple build files, using the `<ant>` task instead of `<antcall>` (which is limited to calling targets in the same `build.xml` file).

```
...
3     <target name="java" depends="init, make-directories">
      ...
9         <ant antfile="utilities.xml" target="perform-check-
sum"/>
          ...
12    </target>
...
```

As you might expect, dividing your Ant targets into separate build files and invoking them with the `<ant>` task allows a fair amount of modularity in your build. It's possible to construct concise build files by factoring out sequences that would otherwise be repeated multiple times. As you'll see later, `<antcall>` actually creates a new execution environment with a new set of properties, so performance can suffer if this method is used too often.

In contrast to `<ant>`, you can also use the `<import>` task, which is similar to the `#include` directive from C/C++. That is, importing an external build file effectively inserts the body of that file into the current file. This technique can be used to inherit a set of default targets and override them within the body of the main `build.xml` file.

## Ant's Flow of Control

Before looking at more of Ant's syntax, stop to reflect on how an Ant program executes. From a high-level view, Ant has a sequential flow of control in which tasks are executed in the order they're specified within a target. In addition, targets are invoked in the order in which they're specified on the command line or listed in a target's depends attribute.

When you stop to consider the GNU Make system, the flow of control is based on triggering rules that match the name of a file you're trying to build. If the target name matches, you check the prerequisites and potentially execute a sequence of shell commands to bring everything up-to-date. The flow of control isn't sequential because rules can spread across multiple parts of a makefile or even across different framework files. Determining which rule will be triggered next can sometimes be challenging.

The key feature behind Ant's sequential execution is that each task must determine whether any work needs to be done. In the case of the <echo> task, no files are involved, so the task is always executed. However, in the case of the <copy> task, Ant first checks whether the source file is newer than the target file; if not, it silently completes without executing any copy operations. As you'll see later, the compilation of Java code using the <javac> task uses a much more complicated algorithm for determining whether work needs to be done.

As an outcome of this approach, Ant developers have much less work to do when writing a build.xml file. Instead of focusing on the dependency relationships between source and targets files, they simply list the tasks in the order they should be executed. Ant then determines which of those tasks are required and which can be skipped. This is another reason Ant discourages the use of ordinary shell commands when writing build.xml files.

As a final note, a target listed as a dependency of another target is executed, at most, once. In Figure 7.1, you can see that target A depends on both targets B and C, and target B depends on target C. In this case, Ant executes target C only once.

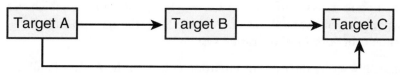

**Figure 7.1** *Ant's target dependencies, with target C used twice but executed once.*

The key assumption here is that Ant targets should always produce the same output, regardless of how many times they're executed. Naturally, they need to be invoked only a single time.

## Defining Properties

An earlier example introduced the concept of an Ant property that associates a value with a property name. This is similar to a constant definition in other programming languages because the value can't be modified after it's defined. You might consider this a limitation, but because build systems implement a consistent and repeatable process, the need to change a value occurs less than you might think.

Ant properties can be defined in a number of different ways:

1. **As a string:** These can reference other properties by using the ${...} syntax. For example:

```
<property name="wife" value="Grace"/>
<property name="dog" value="Stan"/>
<property name="request"
    value="${wife}, please take ${dog} for a walk"/>
```

2. **As a file system location:** You can set the property to the absolute path of the file or directory. This is useful if your build system makes relative paths unusable by changing to a different "current" directory.

```
<property name="obj-dir" location="obj/i386/debug"/>
```

In this example, ${obj-dir} evaluates to

```
C:\Users\Peter\workspace\Ant_Builds\properties\obj\i386\debug
```

which is an absolute path on the Windows system used to test this example. To support cross-platform build.xml files, you can use whichever path separator you want (\ or /). Ant modifies the path to match the requirements of your local operating system.

3. **Automatically set by the runtime environment:** Both the Ant tool and the Java runtime environment define a standard set of properties than can be accessed via the familiar ${...} syntax.

```
<echo>${os.name}</echo>
<echo>${ant.file}</echo>
<echo>${user.name}</echo>
```

Naturally the output of these commands differs on each machine and for each user, but here are some typical values:

```
[echo] Windows Vista
[echo] C:\Users\Peter\workspace\Ant_Builds\properties\build.
xml
[echo] Peter
```

4. **As the result of a** `<condition>` **task:** This evaluates nontrivial decisions. In this example, the `${is-windows}` property is set if the build machine's operating system is in the Windows family (including Windows Vista and Windows 2000).

```
<condition property="is-windows">
    <contains string="${os.name}" substring="Windows"/>
</condition>
```

5. **Defined on the user's command line:** This is particularly useful because a developer can customize the build process by manually specifying a property value instead of hard-coding that property into the `build.xml` file.

```
$ ant -Dname=Jones print-name
```

6. **Loaded from an external properties file:** This is useful when a common set of properties is defined in an external file and can read into any Ant build file that needs to reference those values.

```
<loadproperties srcfile="values.prop"/>
```

Although this is a fairly detailed list of ways properties can be defined, it's certainly not a complete list. In addition, each of these approaches comes with a number of optional flags to provide even more flexibility.

The scope of property definitions is important to understand. A property may be defined either within the top-level scope of an Ant project or inside a particular target. Consider some rules regarding scope:

- If a property is defined at the top level of a project (not within a target definition), the property is available throughout the entire project.

- A property defined inside a target definition is also available throughout the entire project but only after that target is executed.

- Properties can be defined only once in a given project, so the first definition is used. If there's a top-level definition (executed before any targets are executed), that definition takes precedence. If there's no top-level definition, the first target that executes the necessary `<property>` task provides the property's value.

These rules can be a bit confusing at first, especially if you're familiar with other languages in which scope is based on the lexical structure of the program. In Ant's case, the dynamic order of the program's execution is important when defining properties.

To make things even more interesting, the `<ant>` and `<antcall>` tasks enable you to pass property values into the newly invoked target as if they were function parameters. These parameters override any previous definition of the property, but only during the execution of that target. This is more in line with the scope rules you're familiar with in other languages.

```
<antcall target="print-name">
    <param name="name" value="John"/>
</antcall>
```

You'll see more examples of passing parameters between targets later in this chapter when you look at real-world build scenarios.

## Built-In and Optional Tasks

One of the most attractive qualities of Ant is the range of tasks either built into the standard tool or available for download from third-party sites. Ant wouldn't have become one of the most popular tools if it didn't support such a wide range of compilation tasks. Even the standard set of Ant tasks support the following features:

- Basic file operations such as `mkdir`, `copy`, `move`, and `delete`

- The creation of file archives using an array of different formats (such as `.tar`, `.gz`, `.zip`, `.jar`, and `.rpm`)

- The compilation of Java code, including special tools for RMI and JSP compilation

- The automatic generation of API documentation, using the Javadoc tool

- Direct access to version-control tools such as CVS, Perforce, and Clear-Case

- Build lifecycle features, such as updating build version numbers, sending email messages, and playing sounds to indicate the completion of the build process

And the list goes on. If you created a new compilation tool for the Java environment, there's a good chance that Ant-integration would be on your feature checklist.

There's no way to discuss all of Ant's features, but let's now look in more detail at three frequently used tasks. It's interesting to note which optional features each task provides and to consider how each solves the dependency analysis problem.

### The <javac> and <depend> Tasks

The following example shows how to compile Java source code, using the <depend> and <javac> tasks.

```
 . . .
  9            <depend srcdir="${src}" destdir="${obj}" />
 10            <javac srcdir="${src}" destdir="${obj}"/>
 . . .
```

For now, ignore the <depend> task and focus on the <javac> task on line 10. This task finds all the Java source files that reside within the ${src} directory and generates the corresponding class files (.class suffix) into the ${obj} directory. This process traverses the entire hierarchy of directories beneath ${src} and creates a corresponding hierarchy within ${obj}. To perform the actual compilation, the <javac> task invokes either the javac compiler or whatever compiler you've configured.

The <javac> task uses a familiar algorithm for determining whether any work needs to be done. It searches the source tree to find files that don't yet have a corresponding class file, but it also finds cases where the source file is newer than the class file, indicating that a recompile is required.

After the underlying Java compiler is invoked, some further dependency work takes place. In the Java language, classes are free to **import** or **extend** other classes, meaning that the other classes contribute important type information, such as method signatures. Before it can finish compiling the current Java source file, the compiler must examine the other class files to obtain those type definitions. As a result, the compilation of one source file automatically triggers the compilation of other source files.

To clarify, if you're compiling class A, which imports or extends class B, the compiler needs to examine the content of B.class to discover the exported type definitions. If no class file is found but the B.java source file is available, the compiler proceeds to generate B.class from the source code. The same thing happens if the class file can be found but the source code is newer.

Although this importing/extending algorithm might be repeated recursively, the compiler stops the process whenever it locates an up-to-date class file. That is, if the B.class file is newer than the corresponding B.java file, the compiler uses the B.class file without recompiling it. As a result, nothing that B.java imports or extends is ever recompiled.

This algorithm works properly in many cases, but it causes incorrect builds in other cases. (And this is where things get complex.) Imagine a case in which class A imports class B, which then imports class C (see Figure 7.2). If both A.java and C.java have been recently modified, the Java compiler is asked to recompile both those files. When compiling class A, the compiler examines B.class (because B is imported by A), but because B.class is up-to-date with respect to B.java, it's never recompiled. Class A therefore uses the existing version of class B.

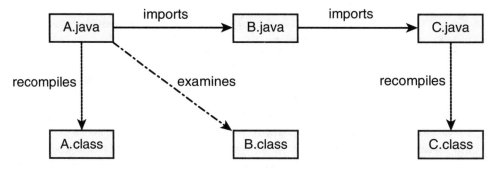

**Figure 7.2** *The <javac> task doesn't recompile B.java, even though C.java has changed.*

In the next step, the Java compiler recompiles C.java, resulting in a change to its external interface. Unfortunately, the Java compiler doesn't notice that class B imports class C, so it doesn't proceed to recompile class B. The glitch here is that class B has an outdated view of C's external interface, which will likely cause a runtime error.

To solve this limitation of the <javac> task, first use the <depend> task to remove any outdated class files.

```
9              <depend srcdir="${src}" destdir="${obj}" />
```

The <depend> task has a more extensive knowledge of which classes import or extend other classes and is better at determining when a class needs to be recompiled because of an external interface change. The <depend> task also understands Java's inner class feature (a single .java file can generate multiple .class files) and can handle long chains of import or extends directives.

All this complexity can be confusing (you might need to reread this section a couple times), so it's lucky that it's hidden inside the `<javac>` and `<depend>` tasks. Ant developers don't need to worry about specifying the dependencies for themselves because the combination of these tasks should do the right thing.

### The `<chmod>` Task

The second task to study is `<chmod>`, which sets the access permissions on a file or directory. This task is UNIX-centric and has no effect on Windows systems. Anyone with experience of the UNIX `chmod` command can understand the following:

```
      . . .
4       <chmod dir="pkg" perm="750"/>
5       <chmod file="pkg/data.file" perm="640"/>
      . . .
```

Note the distinction between the first and second uses of `<chmod>`, where line 4 changes the permissions on a directory and line 5 changes the permissions on a file. It's also possible to modify many files at one time, either within a directory hierarchy or by selecting the list of files using regular expressions. You learn more about this technique shortly.

In the case of `<chmod>`, the dependency analysis is quite straightforward. Given that there's no input file to compare time stamps against, the `chmod` operation is always performed. The only concern is that updating the underlying file system takes times, so you don't want to do it too often. Depending on the build machine, it might be an optimization to first read the existing permission bits to see if any changes are actually required.

### The `<copy>` Task

The third task to examine in detail is `<copy>`, which is similar to the Windows `copy` command and the UNIX `cp` command. This task isn't too hard to understand, but it does have some optional parameters that change the way it behaves.

In the following example, the README file is copied from the current working directory into the subdirectory named pkg.

```
<copy file="README" todir="pkg"/>
```

This is fairly straightforward, but now see how the `<copy>` task's optional attributes can change the default behavior.

- **tofile:** In the earlier example, the target file will have the same name as the original README file but is stored within the pkg directory; therefore, it'll be copied to pkg/README. If you want to change the name of the file, use the `tofile` attribute instead of the `todir` attribute. For example:

```
<copy file="README" tofile="pkg/Documentation.txt"/>
```

- **preservelastmodified:** If the copied file will be used as input to some other task, you might want the last modified time of the target file to be the same as that of the source file. This probably isn't a common thing to do, but you can achieve it by setting the preservelastmodified attribute to true.

- **overwrite:** By default, the <copy> task doesn't perform the action if the target file already exists and is newer than the original. However, if you set the overwrite attribute to true, the copy takes place anyway. This behavior is useful when your <copy> task also inserts a dynamic value into the file, such as the current date or time. If the copy operation didn't happen every time, you'd be left with stale values.

- **flatten:** If this attribute is set to true, the <copy> task discards the original file's pathname when it creates the target file. This is useful when you're copying a number of files that are spread around the source tree, but you want them copied to the same target directory. If you don't set flatten to true, the original directory hierarchy is kept, which you don't want.

The following table demonstrates the two cases:

| Source Filename | With flatten=false | With flatten=true |
|---|---|---|
| src/europe/england-flag.jpg | pkg/europe/england-flag.jpg | pkg/england-flag.jpg |
| src/americas/canada-flag.jpg | pkg/americas/canada-flag.jpg | pkg/canada-flag.jpg |

The <copy> task has several more attributes, but this section doesn't examine them. Refer to the Ant user manual [50] to see the full set of available options.

In finishing the discussion of the <copy> task, it's worth pointing out that you've only seen how to copy a single file at a time. In reality, you often want to copy multiple files at once, or perhaps copy an entire directory hierarchy. Ant has support for this feature, but it's worth a whole section of its own.

## Selecting Multiple Files and Directories

Most Ant tasks focus on creating or manipulating files, processing a file's content, or combining files into an archive. Where it makes sense, these same tasks can process multiple input files in a single operation. This section covers how to select a large number of files, known as a `fileset` or a `dirset`, and incorporate them into a single Ant task.

Let's extend the previous case, which talked about copying two files (england-flag.jpg and canada-flag.jpg) into a target directory. The following example shows how it's possible to copy multiple files with a single `<copy>` task. You'll also set the `flatten` attribute so that all `.jpg` files are placed in the same target directory.

```
...
5         <copy todir="pkg" flatten="true">
6             <fileset dir="src">
7                 <include name="**/*.jpg"/>
8             </fileset>
9         </copy>
...
```

This example replaces the `<copy>` task's `file` attribute with an embedded `<fileset>` directive. You can think of a `<fileset>` as a collection of files that reside within the `src` directory. To identify exactly which files the set contains, the `<include>` directive provides a regular expression that matches all the filenames you care about.

The syntax of the regular expression is generally what you'd expect, with `?` matching a single character and `*` matching zero or more characters, but not crossing the boundary between directories. That is, the regular expression a/*/b matches a/x/b and a/y/b, but it won't match a/x/y/b because the `*` wildcard can't match more than one directory component.

Given that matching multiple directories is a useful feature in build systems, the regular expression can also use the `**` pattern. This matches zero or more path components. In the example, the regular expression **/*.jpg matches both src/file.jpg and much longer paths, such as src/a/b/c/d/e/f/file.jpg. Of course, if you use a Windows system, it'll also match src\file.jpg.

In addition to the `<include>` directive, it's possible to exclude files that you don't want to have in the set. You first use `<include>` to select a superset of the files, followed by an `<exclude>` directive to extract the files you don't want.

The following example shows how to include all the `.jpg` and `.png` files from the `src` directory and all the `.gif` files from within the `lib` directory. However, you don't want to include any files that contain the string `flag` in their name.

```
...
14        <copy todir="pkg" flatten="true">
15            <fileset dir="src">
16                <include name="**/*.jpg"/>
17                <include name="**/*.png"/>
18                <exclude name="**/*flag*"/>
19            </fileset>
```

```
20          <fileset dir="lib">
21             <include name="**/*.gif"/>
22             <exclude name="**/*flag*"/>
23          </fileset>
24       </copy>
...
```

As you can see, it's possible to include multiple `<fileset>` directives within the same `<copy>` task, with a new set created by merging the two smaller sets. If it made sense, you could also use the `<dirset>` directive to select a number of directories, in contrast to `<fileset>`, which includes only files.

The possible combinations are endless, and you might end up with a complex set of `<include>` and `<exclude>` directives, making your tasks appear rather messy. If that's the case, you can define a `<patternset>` in a separate part of the build file and reference that set with a user-friendly name.

```
...
32    <patternset id="imagefiles-1">
33       <include name="**/*.jpg"/>
34       <include name="**/*.png"/>
35       <exclude name="**/*flag*"/>
36    </patternset>
37
38    <patternset id="imagefiles-2">
39       <include name="**/*.gif"/>
40       <exclude name="**/*flag*"/>
41    </patternset>
42
43    <target name="copy-refid">
44       <copy todir="pkg" flatten="true">
45          <fileset dir="src">
46             <patternset refid="imagefiles-1"/>
47          </fileset>
48          <fileset dir="lib">
49             <patternset refid="imagefiles-2"/>
50          </fileset>
51       </copy>
52    </target>
...
```

You can specify sets of files or directories in other ways, but they won't be discussed here. The key point is that Ant provides a powerful mechanism for stating which files or directories you want your task to act upon.

## Conditions

One class of feature that's noticeably missing from the basic Ant language is control-flow statements, such as `if` and `while`. Most programming languages treat these as a fundamental part of the language, but with Ant they're significantly less important. After all, you usually want your build process to behave in a repeatable way, so a linear sequence of tasks is often enough.

On the other hand, Ant does provide a mechanism for testing basic conditions and setting properties to reflect the result. If the condition is true, the property is set to the value `true`; otherwise, it's left undefined. When used with the `if` or `unless` attributes in a target definition, you can effectively create an `if` statement.

```
...
13     <condition property="common-name">
14       <or>
15           <equals arg1="${surname}" arg2="Smith"/>
16           <equals arg1="${surname}" arg2="Brown"/>
17           <equals arg1="${surname}" arg2="Wong"/>
18       </or>
19     </condition>
20
21     <target name="check-name" if="common-name">
22         <fail>You have a common name, you can't proceed!</fail>
23     </target>
...
```

Lines 13–19 of this example set the `common-name` property to `true` if `${surname}` is set to either `Smith`, `Brown`, or `Wong`. On line 21, the target definition tests `${common-name}` and executes the body of the target only if the property is defined. In this case, the `check-name` target causes the build to fail if the user has a common surname.

In addition to using the standard Boolean operations (such as `not`, `and`, and `or`), you can interact with the build environment in the following ways:

Testing whether a specific disk file exists

Testing whether a particular URL is accessible on the target web server

Testing whether a string contains a specific substring or matches a regular expression

Testing the value of operating system environment variables

Ant certainly has some powerful ways to test conditions, but the syntax to do so is rather cumbersome. As you'll see in later examples, it's possible to extend the basic Ant language to add new tasks that make your code more readable, such as `<if>`, `<then>`, and `<else>`. Let's now continue by seeing how the basic Ant language can be enhanced.

## Extending the Ant Language

In addition to the built-in Ant language features you've seen so far, you can extend the language in a number of ways. This section looks at five different mechanisms for adding new language features, ranging from defining new Ant tasks to executing scripts written in other languages.

- **The `<exec>` task:** This built-in task enables you to invoke a shell command, just as you would with GNU Make. The output of the command can be stored in an Ant property for further processing by other tasks. The following example shows how to execute the Windows `dir` command by explicitly invoking the DOS shell.

```
...
15      <target name="dir">
16          <exec executable="cmd">
17              <arg value="/c"/>
18              <arg value="dir"/>
19          </exec>
20      </target>
...
```

- **The `<java>` task:** This approach is similar to the `<exec>` method, although the purpose is to invoke an arbitrary collection of Java code by specifying the class path and class name. This is a common technique in which the build process compiles a Java-based program (using `<javac>`) and the resulting program then acts as a compilation tool in the second phase of the build process.

- **The `<macrodef>` task:** In this approach, you create a new type of task, with the definition of that task written in Ant syntax. You can customize how the task behaves by allowing the user to pass in parameter values. The following example defines the `<greet>` task that simply displays a welcome message.

```
1   <project name="macrodefs" default="all">
2
3       <macrodef name="greet">
4           <attribute name="surname"/>
5           <attribute name="firstname"/>
6           <sequential>
7               <echo>Hello @{firstname} @{surname}, how are
                    you?</echo>
8           </sequential>
9       </macrodef>
10
11      <target name="all">
12          <greet surname="Jones" firstname="Lloyd"/>
```

```
13        </target>
14
15   </project>
```

- Lines 3–9 define the new `<greet>` macro, with lines 4 and 5 providing the names of the two attributes that customize the macro's behavior. Line 7 invokes the `<echo>` task and uses the `@{...}` syntax to reference the user-supplied attribute values. Finally, line 12 invokes the `<greet>` macro as if it were a regular Ant task.

- **The `<taskdef>` task:** This is somewhat similar to the `<macrodef>` task, although it enables you to implement a task using the full power of the Java language instead of being limited to using Ant's built-in syntax. Most third-party vendors provide their task definitions in the form of Java `.jar` files, which can be plugged into Ant using a simple `<taskdef>` directive. This is also similar to the `<java>` task you saw earlier, but in this case, you invoke the task by defining a new XML tag and set of attributes instead of explicitly invoking a standalone Java program.

  You'll see a detailed example of `<taskdef>` in a later section.

- **The `<script>` task:** This is a recent addition to the Ant language that permits code from other scripting languages (such as JavaScript, Python, and Ruby) to be directly embedded inside a `build.xml` file. The script can access and manipulate the Ant program's properties, thereby creating a powerful programming environment. An embedded script can do anything a Java-based task can do, so if you're undertaking a serious Ant-based project, you'll definitely want to learn more about this feature.

If you think about it, these extension methods make Ant a powerful language, in the same way that GNU Make is powerful. The notable difference is that Ant tasks are designed to encapsulate complexity. Average developers don't need to worry about the underlying compilation tool or its dependency-analysis requirements. On the other hand, anyone who needs to add more functionality still can have the full power of general-purpose languages.

## Further Reading

Although you can find many sources of information about the Ant tool, you'll likely find that the Ant web site [50] contains enough documentation to get you started. After all, writing a `build.xml` file is somewhat similar to writing a shell script, with Ant targets acting like shell function definitions and tasks like individual shell commands. You should have no problem constructing a simple build.xml file after reading through the examples in the Ant manual.

On the other hand, if you want to learn more about the best practices of using Ant in larger projects, read one of the many books on the topic, including [51] in References.

## Real-World Build System Scenarios

You've now seen enough of Ant's syntax to understand how to apply the tool in real-world scenarios. The most common activities, such as compiling Java code, tend to be easy to implement in Ant, so this section doesn't give too much explanation. On the other hand, more adventurous activities such as adding new compilation tools and supporting multiple variants are much harder than they were in the GNU Make examples.

### Scenario 1: Source Code in a Single Directory

In the first scenario, the goal is to compile a Java program in which the source files (.java suffix) are all stored in the same directory. In this case, you'll use a separate classes directory for storing the .class files and you'll package them into a single JAR file, called scenario-1.jar. Here's the complete code:

```
1   <project name="scenario-1" default="package">
2
3       <property name="src" location="."/>
4       <property name="obj" location="../classes"/>
5       <property name="jarfile" location="../scenario-1.
        jar"/>
6
7       <target name="compile">
8           <mkdir dir="${obj}"/>
9           <depend srcdir="${src}" destdir="${obj}" />
10          <javac srcdir="${src}" destdir="${obj}"/>
11      </target>
12
13      <target name="package" depends="compile">
14          <jar basedir="${obj}" destfile="${jarfile}">
15              <include name="*.class"/>
16          </jar>
17      </target>
18
19  </project>
```

Lines 3–5 define each of the important file system locations. ${src} is the location of the source code (the current directory), ${obj} is the directory where the object files will be stored, and ${jarfile} is the full path of the JAR file you're going to create. Even though the code uses forward slashes (/) when specifying the paths, these are silently translated to work correctly on Windows systems.

Lines 7–11 define an Ant target for compiling the `.java` files into `.class` files. You first ensure that the object directory already exists and then use the familiar `<depend>` and `<javac>` sequence to compile the source code.

Lines 13–17 locate all the `.class` files within the `${obj}` directory and archive them into the single `scenario-1.jar` file. Note that, on line 1, the `package` target was declared as the default for this Ant project, so the program's execution starts here. However, given that the `package` target depends on the `compile` target (see line 13), code compilation always occurs before the packaging step.

Finally, to execute this program, you invoke the `java` command-line tool:

```
$ java -cp scenario-1.jar Calc
```

Now consider the case in which the program's source code is spread across multiple directories.

## Scenario 2(a): Source Code in Multiple Directories

As it turns out, the solution for the first scenario almost works correctly when source code is stored in multiple directories. The reason is that `<depend>`, `<javac>`, and `<jar>` are all designed to support multiple directories by default, assuming that you're happy to store the entire program in a single `.jar` file.

In practice, though, one minor change is needed. The `<include>` directive on line 15 must include `.class` files from anywhere within the hierarchy, not just from the top-level directory. The new `package` target is therefore:

```
...
13          <target name="package" depends="compile">
14              <jar basedir="${obj}" destfile="${jarfile}">
15                  <include name="**/*.class"/>
16              </jar>
17          </target>
...
```

## Scenario 2(b): Many Directories, with Multiple `build.xml` Files

As you saw in Chapter 6, "Make," in the discussion of recursive Make, it's often nice to have your build description spread across multiple files instead of having everything in the same place. Even though Ant is capable of building multidirectory programs with a single `build.xml` file, larger programs typically split their build description across multiple files. This approach avoids cluttering a single `build.xml` file and provides better modularity by keeping the relevant Ant targets nearer to the source code.

Now extend the calculator example to build three JAR files, one each for the `print` and `math` libraries, and a third for the main program. As in Figure 7.3, the source for each JAR file is stored in a separate directory hierarchy, each of which has its own `build.xml` file.

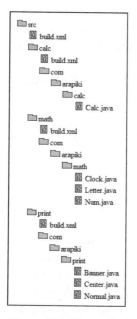

**Figure 7.3** *The multidirectory calculator example, using a different package hierarchy for each component.*

Because of the way in which the directory hierarchy must match the Java package name, you end up with the `com/arapiki` structure repeated multiple times. This might seem odd for such a small example, but it would make sense if each of the libraries contained hundreds of files. A developer working on the `com/arapiki/print` library could have a workspace containing only those files instead of a copy of the entire source tree.

Note also that you aren't required to have a separate `build.xml` in every directory. Large software systems might have thousands of source code directories but only five to ten `build.xml` files total. Each file manages the build process for an entire subsystem instead of just a single directory.

Start the example by looking at the `src/build.xml` file. This file doesn't do any compilation on its own; instead, it uses the `<ant>` task to dispatch work to the remaining three `build.xml` files.

```
1   <project name="scenario-2b" default="package">
2
3       <property name="src" location="."/>
4       <property name="obj" location="../classes"/>
5       <property name="jars" location="../jars"/>
6       <property name="math-jar" location="${jars}/math.
        jar"/>
7       <property name="print-jar" location="${jars}/print.
        jar"/>
8       <property name="calc-jar" location="${jars}/calc.
        jar"/>
9
10      <path id="library-classpath">
11          <pathelement path="${math-jar}"/>
12          <pathelement path="${print-jar}"/>
13      </path>
14
15      <target name="package">
16          <mkdir dir="${jars}"/>
17          <ant dir="math" antfile="build.xml"
            target="package"
18                  inheritall="false">
19              <property name="obj" location="${obj}/math"/>
20              <property name="jarfile" location="${math-
                jar}"/>
21          </ant>
22          <ant dir="print" antfile="build.xml"
            target="package"
23                  inheritall="false">
24              <property name="obj" location="${obj}/
                print"/>
25              <property name="jarfile" location="${print-
                jar}"/>
26          </ant>
27          <ant dir="calc" antfile="build.xml"
            target="package"
28                  inheritall="false">
29              <property name="obj" location="${obj}/calc"/>
30              <property name="jarfile" location="${calc-
                jar}"/>
31              <reference refid="library-classpath"/>
32          </ant>
33      </target>
34
35  </project>
```

Lines 3–8 define the locations of the source tree, the object tree, and the
JAR files. In this case, you explicitly name the three .jar files you're going to
build. In addition, lines 10–13 define a class path for linking against the math
and print libraries. Separating out this path definition and giving it a name
(library-classpath) makes it easier to reference the path in other parts of the
build system.

The package target on lines 15–33 does little other than invoke the lower-level build.xml files. On lines 17–21, the <ant> task calls on the package target defined in the math/build.xml file. Note the use of the inheritall="false" directive to indicate that top-level properties should not automatically be passed to the lower-level build.xml file. Limiting the scope of these properties makes the build description more modular.

The <property> task on lines 19 and 20 shows how to explicitly pass property values into the lower-level build.xml files. In this case, line 19 informs the math/build.xml file that any object files it creates should be stored in the ${obj}/math subdirectory. Line 20 asks it to store the resulting JAR file in the location specified in ${math-jar}.

The remaining two <ant> tasks in the package target simply repeat the first case. The notable difference on line 31 is that you pass a reference to the math and print libraries (stored within the library-classpath path) so that the main program knows which JAR files to link against.

The src/math/build.xml file is similar to examples you've already seen:

```
1   <project name="scenario-2b-math" default="package">
2
3       <property name="src" location="."/>
4
5       <target name="compile">
6           <mkdir dir="${obj}"/>
7           <depend srcdir="${src}" destdir="${obj}"/>
8           <javac srcdir="${src}" destdir="${obj}"/>
9       </target>
10
11      <target name="package" depends="compile">
12          <jar basedir="${obj}" destfile="${jarfile}">
13              <include name="**/*.class"/>
14          </jar>
15      </target>
16
17  </project>
```

Note how the code defines the ${src} property to compile the source code in the current directory, but uses the ${obj} and ${jarfile} properties to store the object files and .jar file in the location requested by the caller.

The src/print/build.xml is almost identical; the only change is in the project name:

```
1   <project name="scenario-2b-print" default="package">
    ...
17  </project>
```

Finally, the src/calc/build.xml file is a little different: It uses the library-classpath reference that was passed down by the caller. This class path is required because the `Calc.java` source file imports code from the `math` and `print` libraries.

```
   ...
   9        <javac srcdir="${src}" destdir="${obj}"
   10           classpathref="library-classpath"/>
   ...
```

To execute this example, you use the `java` command-line tool, but this time with all `.jar` files listed.

```
java -cp jars\calc.jar;jars\math.jar;jars\print.jar com.arapiki.
➥calc.Calc
```

It's interesting to note that Ant also suffers from the subbuild problem you saw with recursive Make. If the developer invokes the build process from one of the lower-level `build.xml` files, Ant won't know how to rebuild the dependent JAR files. The developer must instead invoke the top-level `build.xml` file to make sure everything else is up-to-date.

Even with this same problem, it's less likely to be a problem than with GNU Make. Even the largest software products have only a few `build.xml` files, so the problem of sequencing the build steps in the correct order is significantly less.

## Scenario 3: Defining New Compilation Tools

Now consider how to define a task to invoke the `mathcomp` tool, the custom compiler you need to add to the build process. In the same way as most tool vendors, you'll use `<taskdef>` to declare the new XML tag and you'll write a Java class to implement the task's functionality.

Start with a simple `build.xml` file that shows how the task is defined and then used.

```
1   <project name="scenario-3" default="compile">
2
3       <taskdef name="mathcomp" classname="MathcompTask"
4           classpath="mathcomp-task.jar"/>
5
6       <target name="compile">
7           <mathcomp file="equations.math"/>
8       </target>
9
10  </project>
```

Lines 3–4 use `<taskdef>` to define the new `<mathcomp>` task. All that's required is that you identify the name of the Java class that implements the feature and the name of the JAR file containing that class. Line 7 then uses the

`<mathcomp>` task to compile the `equations.math` source file into a corresponding `equations.java`.

Luckily, end users don't need to specify the output filename or spend any time worrying about dependency analysis. Of course, the complexity has to be dealt with somewhere, so here's the Java source code for the `Mathcomp` class:

```
1   import org.apache.tools.ant.*;
2   import java.io.*;
3   import java.util.*;
4
5   public class MathcompTask extends Task {
6
7       private File srcFile;
8
9       public void setFile(File file) {
10          srcFile = file;
11      }
12
13      private String execMathcomp(String flag, File srcFile) {
14          try {
15              Process p = Runtime.getRuntime().exec(
16                  "python.exe mathcomp.py -" + flag +
17                  " \"" + srcFile + "\"");
18              BufferedReader progOutput = new BufferedReader(new
19                  InputStreamReader(p.getInputStream()));
20              String resultLine = progOutput.readLine();
21              return resultLine;
22          } catch (IOException ex) {
23              throw new BuildException(
24                  "Can't execute the mathcomp compiler. " +
                    ex);
25          }
26      }
27
28      private File getTargetFile(File file) {
29          String fileName = file.getName();
30          if (!fileName.endsWith(".math")) {
31              throw new BuildException("Input file '" +
                fileName
32                  + "' must end with .math");
33          }
34          String targetFileName =
35              fileName.replaceFirst("\\.math$", ".java");
36          return new File(file.getParentFile(), target-
                FileName);
37      }
38
39      private List<File> getAllSourceFiles(File file) {
40          List<File> sources = new ArrayList<File>();
41          String sourceFileString = execMathcomp("d", src-
                File);
```

```
42          StringTokenizer tokens =
43              new StringTokenizer(sourceFileString);
44          while (tokens.hasMoreTokens()) {
45              sources.add(new File(tokens.nextToken()));
46          }
47          return sources;
48      }
49
50      public void execute() {
51          if (srcFile == null) {
52              throw new BuildException(
53                  "Missing 'file' attribute for <math-
                    comp>");
54          }
55          if (!srcFile.exists()) {
56              throw new BuildException("Input file '" +
                srcFile
57                  + "' doesn't exist.");
58          }
59
60          File targetFile = getTargetFile(srcFile);
61          List<File> allSources =
            getAllSourceFiles(srcFile);
62          if (allSources == null) {
63              throw new BuildException(
64                  "Unable to determine all source files
                    used by '" +
65                  srcFile + "'");
66          }
67
68          boolean targetOutOfDate;
69          if (!targetFile.exists()) {
70              targetOutOfDate = true;
71
72          } else {
73              targetOutOfDate = false;
74              long targetModifiedDate = targetFile.last-
                Modified();
75              for (File thisSourceFile : allSources) {
76                  if (thisSourceFile.lastModified() >
77                          targetModifiedDate) {
78                      targetOutOfDate = true;
79                      break;
80                  }
81              }
82          }
83
84          if (targetOutOfDate) {
85              log("Compiling " + srcFile);
86              execMathcomp("j", srcFile);
87          }
88      }
89  }
```

This class is quite complex, so break it down into smaller sections. Lines 7–11 state that the end user can set the `file` attribute. The fact that the `setFile` method is defined in this class lets Ant know that it's a settable field. You store the string value in the `srcFile` field for later use.

The `execute` method, defined on lines 50–88, is the main entry point. Ant calls this method whenever somebody invokes the `<mathcomp>` task.

Lines 51–58 perform error checking to make sure that the `file` attribute was defined and that it refers to a disk file that already exists. If either of these checks fails, a `BuildException` error is thrown and the error message becomes part of Ant's error report.

Line 60 calls the `getTargetFile` method to translate the source file's name into the corresponding target filename. For example, if the source file is a/b/c/ equations.math, the corresponding target file will be a/b/c/equations. java. The `getTargetFile` method is defined on lines 28–37 and performs a significant amount of error checking to make sure the name is valid.

Line 61 calls the `getAllSourceFiles` method to determine which additional source files will be read during the compilation process. This method is defined on lines 39–48 and does its work by calling the `mathcomp` compiler with the `-d` option. The output looks something like this:

```
equations.math equ1.mathinc equ2.mathinc
```

In this case, the `getAllSourceFiles` method divides this string into individual filenames and returns them in a list. Unfortunately, the simple method fails if a filename contains spaces, so a more realistic tool would need to do a better job.

Now that you have the list of source files and you know the name of the target file you're about to create, the rest of this method double-checks whether any compilation work is required. Lines 69–70 check whether the target file already exists; if not, a compilation is definitely required.

Lines 73–81 perform the time stamp comparison of each of the source files to see whether any are newer than the target file. If so, a recompilation is forced.

Finally, you reach lines 85–86, but only if you've decided to actually invoke the `mathcomp` tool. On line 8, you log a message to inform the end user that work is about to take place. On line 86, you call the `execMathcomp` method (defined on lines 13–26) to invoke the `mathcomp` compiler. This compiler is just a Python script, so you first invoke the Python interpreter.

Note that you've already used the `execMathcomp` method as part of the `getAllSourceFiles` method, but this time you're passing the `-j` option to generate a .java file instead of returning the list of dependencies.

That completes the definition of the `<mathcomp>` task. If you count the number of lines of code, this is certainly a much larger solution than the GNU Make case—it would be even larger if you included all the possible error cases (some were left out, for the sake of convenience). This is largely because Make is proficient at pattern matching and deriving the name of the target files from the corresponding source file. Also, the dependency list produced by `mathcomp -d` was tailored for Make. Finally, the time stamp comparison is a fundamental part of GNU Make's language, whereas you needed to hand-code the algorithm in Java.

## Scenario 4: Building with Multiple Variants

Given that Java class files use CPU-independent byte code, it's not possible to show a multivariant example that compiles for different CPU types. Instead, you can consider a program that's compiled into two different editions:

1. **Professional edition:** A software package containing the complete set of program functionality

2. **Home edition:** A smaller edition of the software, with some of the advanced features stubbed out

In the source tree (see Figure 7.4), you'll maintain two parallel sets of Java source files. The `professional` directory includes the program's entire set of functionality. The `home-stubs` directory contains stubbed-out versions of any classes that shouldn't be included in the Home edition. For example purposes, `Clock.java` and `Letter.java` are stubbed out.

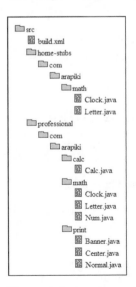

**Figure 7.4** *A separate directory hierarchy for each of the professional and Home editions.*

To keep things simple, this example uses a single `build.xml` file to compile the entire product. Here's the complete listing:

```
1   <project name="scenario-4" default="package">
2
3       <property name="obj-prof" location="../classes/pro-
        fessional"/>
4       <property name="obj-home" location="../classes/home-
        stubs"/>
5       <property name="src-prof" location="professional"/>
6       <property name="src-home" location="home-stubs"/>
7       <property name="jarfile" location="../scenario-4.
        jar"/>
8
9       <target name="check-edition" depends="check-edition-
        helper"
10              unless="edition-ok">
11          <fail message="You must set 'edition' to either
            'home'
12              or 'professional'"/>
13      </target>
14
15      <target name="check-edition-helper">
16          <condition property="edition-ok">
17              <or>
18                  <equals arg1="${edition}" arg2="home"/>
19                  <equals arg1="${edition}"
                    arg2="professional"/>
20              </or>
21          </condition>
22          <condition property="edition-home">
23              <equals arg1="${edition}" arg2="home"/>
24          </condition>
25      </target>
26
27      <target name="compile">
28          <mkdir dir="${obj-prof}"/>
29          <depend srcdir="${src-prof}" destdir="${obj-
            prof}"/>
30          <javac srcdir="${src-prof}" destdir="${obj-
            prof}"/>
31          <mkdir dir="${obj-home}"/>
32          <depend srcdir="${src-home}" destdir="${obj-
            home}"/>
33          <javac srcdir="${src-home}" destdir="${obj-
            home}"/>
34      </target>
35
36      <target name="jar-prof" unless="edition-home">
37          <echo message="Packaging the Professional edi-
            tion."/>
38          <jar basedir="${obj-prof}" destfile="${jarfile}">
39              <include name="**/*.class"/>
```

```
40              </jar>
41          </target>
42
43          <target name="jar-home" if="edition-home">
44              <echo message="Packaging the Home edition."/>
45              <jar destfile="${jarfile}">
46                  <fileset dir="${obj-prof}">
47                      <include name="**/*.class"/>
48                      <exclude name="com/arapiki/math/Letter.
                        class"/>
49                      <exclude name="com/arapiki/math/Clock.
                        class"/>
50                  </fileset>
51                  <fileset dir="${obj-home}" includes="**/*.
                    class"/>
52              </jar>
53          </target>
54
55          <target name="package" depends="check-edition,
            compile,
56              jar-prof, jar-home">
57              <copy file="run.bat" toFile="../start-calc.bat">
58                  <filterset>
59                      <filter token="EDITION"
                        value="${edition}"/>
60                  </filterset>
61              </copy>
62          </target>
63
64  </project>
```

Plenty of decision making takes place in this build.xml file, and because some of the operations occur twice means the build description is quite long.

Execution starts with the package target on line 55. The depends attribute asks Ant to first execute the check-edition, compile, jar-prof, and jar-home targets, in that order.

The check-edition target, defined on lines 9–13, immediately calls the check-edition-helper target, which is defined on lines 15–25. This helper target uses the <condition> task to define two different properties. The first property, ${edition-ok}, is set to true if ${edition} is either home or professional, whereas the ${edition-home} property is set to true if ${edition} is equal to home.

For these conditions to make sense, the ${edition} property must have been defined on the command line when the build was invoked:

```
ant -Dedition=home
```

The ${edition-ok} value is therefore a true/false indicator of whether a valid definition was provided on the command line. On the other hand,

${edition-home} is a true/false value to indicate whether the user selected home for the edition. With Ant's limited capability to test conditions, it's important to express these properties as true/false values instead of keeping them as strings.

Back in the check-edition target (line 9), you use the unless attribute to state that the body of the target should be executed, unless the ${edition-ok} property was set. This effectively states that unless the user specified the home or professional edition properly, you'll fail with an error message.

The next top-level target is compile, on lines 27–34. This uses the familiar <depend> and <javac> combination, except that now you're compiling both the home-stubs and professional source trees while taking care to keep the generated class files separate.

We next execute the jar-prof target on lines 36–41. By using the unless="edition-home" attribute, you execute the body of this target only if the user elected to build the professional version. In this case, you store all the class files into the resulting .jar file.

In contrast, the jar-home target on lines 43–53 does quite a bit more work and is executed only if the user selected the home edition. You first package all the professional class files, with the exception of the Letter.class and Clock.class files that aren't shipped in the home edition. Then you add the stubbed-out version of those class files, which exist solely so you don't get a runtime error when the program executes. As an optimization, the list of excluded classes could have been determined by scanning the ${obj-home} directory.

The final step is to return to the body of the package target, on lines 55–62, which prepares the start-calc.bat script. You've seen this type of script many times already:

```
java -cp scenario-4.jar -Dedition=@EDITION@ com.arapiki.calc.Calc
```

What's different in this case is that you customize the -Dedition= portion of the command line, to pass either of the values home or professional into the executable program. This allows the program to make an intelligent decision on which set of features to provide to the user.

To make this all work correctly, the <copy> task on line 57 reads the template command line (stored in the run.bat file) and creates a new file (named start-calc.bat), where the string @EDITION@ is replaced by the value of the ${edition} property. As a result, the start-calc.bat file ends up with this content:

```
java -cp scenario-4.jar -Dedition=home com.arapiki.calc.Calc
```

for the Home edition or this for the Professional edition:

```
java -cp scenario-4.jar -Dedition=professional com.arapiki.
➥calc.Calc
```

Of course, in the Home edition, the real classes would have been replaced by the stub versions, so it's important to pass in the correct value for the `edition` property.

Here's some sample Java code that reads the property value and customizes its runtime behavior accordingly.

```
String edition = System.getProperty("edition");
if (edition == null){
    System.err.println("Error: 'edition' property is not de-
    fined");
    System.exit(1);
}
...
if (edition.equals("professional")) {
    /* perform professional features */
    ...
}
```

As an alternative, instead of defining this property on the command line, you could have defined a method in one of the stub classes that records the edition's name. By querying this method at runtime, you could determine which edition is being used.

In summary, you can see that Ant's capability to support decision making is somewhat limited, resulting in substantially longer code than you might expect. If you compare the length of code to the similar program in GNU Make syntax, you might find the makefile much easier to read.

On the brighter side, Ant enables you to extend the basic language. One third-party package, `ant-contrib` [52], introduces the `<if>` and `<then>` tasks:

```
...
15       <target name="check-edition">
16           <if>
17               <not>
18                   <or>
19                       <equals arg1="${edition}"
                         arg2="home" />
20                       <equals arg1="${edition}"
                         arg2="professional" />
21                   </or>
22               </not>
23               <then>
24                   <fail message="You must set 'edition' to
                     either
25                           'home' or 'professional'" />
26               </then>
27           </if>
28       </target>
...
```

Ant's flexible set of tasks, including a wide range of third-party plug-ins, comes to the rescue by making the code much more readable than in the first attempt.

## Scenario 5: Cleaning a Build Tree

Removing the object files from a build tree is a matter of defining an additional clean target to explicitly remove files or directories:

```
...
19      <target name="clean">
20          <delete file="${jarfile}" />
21          <delete dir="${obj}" />
22      </target>
...
```

It's common practice in Ant to store all .class files and .jar files in a special object directory, which is separate from the source directory. It's usually possible to delete the entire object directory in a single command and be confident that all generated files have been removed. Of course, any failure to follow this rule means you must explicitly delete the generated files with a <delete> task.

If you use multiple build.xml files, you need to define a suitable clean target in each lower-level file. The top-level clean target invokes each of the lower-level targets in turn.

## Scenario 6: Debugging Incorrect Builds

Although Ant hides all the detail of constructing a dependency graph, errors can still creep into a build.xml file. These are some of the most common errors you'll encounter:

- **Missing input files:** If a task fails because it can't locate one of the required input files, it's usually because you've invoked the targets or tasks in the incorrect order. Just as you'd expect in a shell script, files can't be used if they don't already exist. This is different from GNU Make, which attempts to generate a missing file, assuming that there's a suitable rule defined.

- **Files not building when they should:** Either you're not invoking the targets or tasks in the correct order, or your <fileset> directives aren't accurate enough. All Ant tasks are supposed to check their own dependencies, but the tasks can't do a good job if you haven't included all the necessary input files.

- **Too many files rebuilt:** Again, check your `<fileset>` directives to make sure they're specific enough. If you include too many files in the input, you'll end up building too often. It's also possible (although unlikely) that your Ant tasks aren't doing a good job of dependency analysis.

- **Failed compilation or invalid output image:** If a task fails to generate a valid output file even though the input files are correct, you likely haven't provided the correct task attributes. Many tasks have attributes for controlling their behavior, and finding suitable settings might take time.

- **Incorrect Java classes included:** The behavior of a Java program (such as Ant) is highly dependent on your CLASSPATH variable settings. If your program is behaving badly, that's always the first thing to check.

- **Missing task definition:** If you're making use of Ant tasks that aren't built into the standard distribution, there's a chance that they'll be reported as missing. Make sure that the correct third-party JAR files are installed and the correct `<taskdef>` directives are provided.

If any of these problems cause the build to fail, Ant provides a fully detailed stack trace:

```
BUILD FAILED
/home/psmith/debugging/build.xml:4: The following error
    occurred while executing this line:
/home/psmith/debugging/src/build.xml:4: The following error
    occurred while executing this line:
/home/psmith/debugging/src/lib/build.xml:4: Warning: Could
    not find file
/home/psmith/debugging/src/lib/run.bat to copy.
```

It's easy to identify the exact line number and source file causing the problem. Often the bug is on the line being reported, but sometimes it's necessary to scan backward through the file to make sure that all your properties are defined correctly.

In reality, though, a number of the bugs you encounter don't cause the build to fail. Instead, they generate invalid output files, or things just don't rebuild when they should. In this case, you need to spend more time tracing the flow of the program.

When you use the `ant -d` command, Ant provides copious amounts of detail about what it's doing:

```
Adding reference: ant.projectHelper
Adding reference: ant.parsing.context
Adding reference: ant.targets
parsing buildfile /home/psmith/debugging/build.xml with URI =
file:///home/psmith/debugging/build.xml
Setting ro project property: ant.project.name -> debug-app
Adding reference: debug-app
Setting ro project property: ant.file.debug-app ->
/home/psmith/debugging/build.xml
Project base dir set to: /home/psmith/debugging
 +Target:
 +Target: package
```

The log shows you every time a new `build.xml` is parsed, a property is defined, or a task is executed. If you locate the failed task and then search backward through the debug output, you usually can identify the source of the problem.

Ant doesn't show you the underlying shell commands that each task performs, so it isn't possible to cut and paste a command from the build log and run it in isolation. This technique is quite common with GNU Make, where you often find a rule that isn't doing what it should and need to manually rerun the shell command to debug the problem.

In an Ant-based build system, you need to have a lot more faith that the tasks will invoke the correct underlying commands (or system calls). If you want to narrow your debugging focus, you might need to "touch" specific input files and then invoke the required Ant targets.

If you use an IDE such as Eclipse, you can use the Ant debugger mode. This enables you to view the `build.xml` files, set breakpoints on specific lines, display the value of properties, and then single-step through the targets and tasks. Given the popularity of IDEs, this is probably the best place to start.

Another debugging technique is to use the `ant  -v` command to understand Ant's decision to rebuild one or more files. The following excerpt shows what the `<javac>` task does in the single-directory `calculator` example.

```
. . .
[javac] Add.java omitted as Add.class is up to date.
[javac] Calc.java added as Calc.class doesn't exist.
[javac] Mult.java omitted as Mult.class is up to date.
[javac] Sub.java omitted as Sub.class is up to date.
[javac] build.xml skipped - don't know how to handle it
. . .
```

In summary, debugging Ant-based build problems can be significantly easier than dealing with GNU Make problems. This is largely because of Ant's sequential programming model, in which it's easier for a developer to understand the program flow. Also, having each task handle its own dependency analysis relieves much of the opportunity for making mistakes.

# Praise and Criticism

Ant has been around long enough to gather a large group of supporters, as well as plenty of people who dislike its programming model. Much of this discrepancy centers on whether they're trying to use the well-supported Java compilation tasks or whether they're creating a more complex build system that pushes Ant to its limits. Now see what people say about Ant.

## Praise

Praise for Ant includes the following:

- **Cross-platform support:** Because Ant doesn't use a shell-centric language, it has fewer cross-platform issues. By instead using the task abstraction, Ant developers no longer need to worry about each build machine's specific commands and behavior.

- **Hidden dependency analysis:** Dependency analysis isn't a key part of the language; instead, it's handled within the implementation of each task. The end user doesn't need to think about the dependency graph or debug problems related to missing dependencies.

- **Easy-to-learn the language:** Ant has few language constructs to learn, and most developers are familiar with the sequential model of execution. A clear separation also exists between the use of tasks and their underlying definition. Developers care about only the external behavior of each task and the set of configurable attributes. The complex implementation of each task is hidden away from view.

- **Extensive third-party support for Java:** Ant has the widest range of Java compilation tool and plug-in support. Although other Java build tools are starting to appear, Ant will likely continue to be the most popular tool in the Java world.

- **Important build system features are standard:** Build system features such as automatic dependency analysis and multidirectory support are a standard part of the build tool. In contrast to GNU Make, it's not necessary to add an additional framework.

## Criticism

Points of criticism include the following:

- **Lack of a full programming language:** Ant isn't a scripting language, which makes it harder to perform nontrivial activities. Variables, looping, and conditionals are limited in support and often need to be emulated using confusing control structures.

- **Ugly and verbose XML:** Many people don't like XML and find it hard to read or too verbose. This can be a barrier for new developers to adopt the tool and is a definite point of resistance for people who prefer the more concise syntax of GNU Make.

- **Not a dependency-based language:** Many developers prefer to add new pattern-based dependencies to trigger a compilation instead of wading through the Ant documentation to find a suitable task. If no task is available, they might waste a full day trying to piece together existing features to achieve the same result. In the end, the job could've been done in five minutes using GNU Make.

- **No visible shell commands:** Ant doesn't show which shell commands the tool is executing, so you don't know exactly what's happening. Instead, you need to trust the task implementation to do the right thing.

- **Nontrivial process of adding new tasks:** Adding a new compilation tool is much harder than with GNU Make. As you saw earlier, you need to write a Java-based plug-in instead of just matching the file extension. This can be a significant amount of work if you're using a nonstandard compilation tool.

- **Lacking support for other languages:** Ant is Java-centric, with minimal support for other programming languages.

- **Confusing variable scope:** The scoping rules for Ant properties are quite different from rules in other programming languages and can therefore be confusing for new Ant developers.

- **Undefined variables that aren't trapped:** When accessing an Ant property that hasn't yet been assigned a value, the name of the property is used instead of reporting an error. For example, if careless programmers type `${destfiel}` instead of `${destfile}`, they'll end up with a file in their local directory named `${destfiel}`. This happens instead of having the `${destfile}` property expanded to whatever value it contained.

- **No persistent state:** Ant doesn't cache any of the dependency information between builds, so all dependency analysis must be repeated each time the `ant` tool is invoked.

## Evaluation

The Ant build tool clearly focuses on supporting build systems for Java-based software. The tasks are designed to support common operations such as Java compilation and the manipulation of JAR files. Each Ant task contains implicit knowledge of how to compute interfile dependency relationships, removing this from the developer's list of things to worry about.

According to the build system quality metrics discussed in Chapter 1, "Build System Overview," Ant receives the following evaluation:

- **Convenience:** *Good.* Ant simplifies the creation of a build system for Java-based software. It provides a wide range of tasks for common Java-related activities and alleviates the need to specify dependencies. However, Ant doesn't provide a general-purpose programming language, making complex build systems challenging to implement.

- **Correctness:** *Excellent.* Ant's automatic dependency analysis makes creating a correct and reliable build system easy. There's little chance of incorrect dependencies being introduced. The only limitation is that tasks can be listed in the wrong order, but this problem is easy to detect.

- **Performance:** *Good.* Ant provides adequate performance, although it is not known for being exceptionally fast. The fact that each task is responsible for checking its own set of dependencies makes the invocation of tasks slower than GNU Make.

- **Scalability:** *Excellent.* Ant can scale to support large build systems. By interconnecting multiple `build.xml` files, any size of build system can be supported.

Ant clearly has a well-established place in the world of build systems, but only for Java-based software. If you're building C/C++ code, consider using SCons (Chapter 8) or CMake (Chapter 9). For small and simple Java projects, consider using Eclipse to build your software within the IDE environment. For Microsoft languages, such as C#, consider using the MSBuild tool discussed shortly.

## Similar Tools

The introduction of the Ant tool has clearly made people think differently about constructing build systems, with a few newer tools taking a similar approach. The first tool, NAnt, is a direct copy of Ant for the .NET environment, whereas the MSBuild tool has taken a slightly different approach with both syntax and semantics.

## NAnt

The NAnt tool [53] is extremely similar to Ant but focuses on the .NET range of languages instead of Java. The following example shows a `NAnt.Build` file that compiles and links a simple C# program:

```
1   <project name="hello" default="compile">
2
3      <target name="compile">
4         <csc target="exe" output="hello.exe">
5            <sources>
6               <include name="*.cs" />
7            </sources>
8         </csc>
9      </target>
10
11  </project>
```

The basic language features are mostly the same, and Ant developers won't have trouble reading or writing a NAnt script. Unfortunately, the NAnt tool is not as well documented or supported as the original Ant tool.

## MSBuild

The MSBuild tool from Microsoft is most commonly used as part of the Visual Studio development environment, replacing the much older NMake tool (see Chapter 6). From a syntax perspective, Ant and MSBuild have many similarities, along with some interesting differences. The official Microsoft documentation for MSBuild [54] provides a fair amount of technical information, although, for a gentler introduction, you should refer to [55].

Just as Ant uses `build.xml` files, MSBuild uses `.proj` files to store the build description. Visual Studio can automatically generate these, or you can write them by hand. Here's a simple example of compiling three C# files into a `HelloWorld.exe` program.

```
1   <Project DefaultTargets="Build"
2      xmlns="http://schemas.microsoft.com/developer/
       msbuild/2003" >
3
4      <PropertyGroup>
5         <ExeFile>HelloWorld.exe</ExeFile>
6      </PropertyGroup>
7
8      <ItemGroup>
```

```
 9           <MySource Include="goodbye.cs;hello.cs;main.cs"/>
10      </ItemGroup>
11
12      <Target Name = "Build" Inputs="@(MySource)"
        Outputs="$(exeFile)">
13           <CSC Sources="@(MySource)"
             OutputAssembly="$(exeFile)"/>
14      </Target>
15
16   </Project>
```

Although the syntax is a little different from an Ant program, you should be able to get the general idea of what this program does. Looking in detail at each part of this file reveals a few differences.

Lines 4–6 define a new property named `ExeFile` and assigns it the value `HelloWorld.exe`. This syntax is a bit unusual because the `<ExeFile>` tag provides the name of the new property instead of being a tag that's already built into the XML schema. With Ant, you would have used the predefined `<property name="ExeFile">` sequence.

Lines 8–10 define the list of source files to be compiled, similar to Ant's `<fileset>` concept. Note again that the `<MySource>` tag defines the name of this group of items.

Lines 12–14 define the `Build` target that performs the compilation work. Line 13 uses the `<CSC>` task to compile the source files into an executable program (assembly). Note the use of `@(...)` to refer to the group of source files, and the `$(...)` syntax to refer to a property's value.

The significant difference between Ant and MSBuild appears on line 12. The `Inputs` and `Output` attributes are explicitly listed here because MSBuild doesn't require that each task implement its own dependency checking. The MSBuild tool contains a full dependency engine, which is similar to that of GNU Make. Failure to supply these attributes causes the `<CSC>` task to execute every time, regardless of whether the source files have changed.

Although this dependency-analysis technique places a greater burden on the developer, MSBuild completely skips targets with up-to-date files. This is in contrast to Ant, in which each task must be partially executed each time, even if Ant determines there's no work to be done. The value of this approach depends entirely on whether you care about build performance (when you manually provide the dependencies) or the reduced effort of having each task do its own analysis.

MSBuild will clearly continue to be the most popular build tool in the .NET development environment, largely because of its integration with Visual Studio and support for Microsoft compilers.

## Summary

Ant build description files are organized around the concept of targets, each containing a sequential list of tasks. The flow of control in an Ant program is familiar to most developers, making it easy for new users to construct and debug `build.xml` files.

Ant provides a wide range of built-in and optional tasks to support common build system activities, specifically for the Java development environment. These include moving and copying files, changing file permissions, creating archives, and compiling source code into object code.

Although Ant provides a number of off-the-shelf tasks, you could also write your own plug-in to support additional tools. Writing plug-ins is best done in Java, which gives you the expressive power of a full programming language. However, the occasional need to write Java code adds to the complexity of creating an Ant-based build system.

An interesting feature of Ant is that tasks are required to perform their own dependency analysis and to decide whether they need to do any real work. This alleviates the need for Ant developers to think about the program's dependency graph. Programs are thus easier to write and debug.

Unfortunately, Ant's lack of variables and loops, and its unusual way of implement conditions, can make constructing nontrivial programs difficult. This can be a deterrent for developers who prefer a more powerful language.

# Chapter 8

# SCons

The SCons build tool [56] provides a third approach to compiling software. It blends the expressive power of the Python scripting language with some of the stronger features of other build tools. SCons uses high-level **builder methods** to describe the work to be performed, just as in Ant tasks. Additionally, it takes GNU Make's approach of generating a dependency graph for the full program. The decision to base the SCons tool on the Python language was an important choice. Python is a fully featured programming language with expressive power equivalent to Java, C++, or C#, making it easy for new users to adopt the language. This contrasts with GNU Make and Ant, which use a completely unique language. Not only must users learn that new language, but they also need to overcome the language limitations.

The object-oriented features in Python enable SCons to encapsulate data types, while providing access to the data via **methods**, similar to functions in nonobject-oriented languages. SCons provides classes for files, directories, and environment settings, with each having methods to manipulate the objects of that class. For example, the following SCons program compiles the `prog.c` source file to create the `prog` executable program:

```
env.Program('prog', ['prog.c'])
```

In this case, `env` is a **build environment** object, `Program` is a builder method, `'prog'` is the name of the executable program to be constructed, and `['prog.c']` is a list of source files.

As you'll see, a SCons program is usually much shorter and easier to write than an equivalent program for GNU Make or Ant. Not only is the SCons language relatively concise, but also the built-in methods make it easy to perform common operations. If it's necessary to extend the language, you can do so in Python instead of breaking out into a second programming language.

197

The SCons tool was designed with a number of principles in mind. Clearly, the creators of SCons have learned a lot from the mistakes made by other build tools. The guiding principles are listed here:

- **Correctness:** SCons focuses on making sure the final build results are correct, even at the cost of performance. Not only is dependency analysis fully automated, but also any change to compiler flags, include paths, or library paths cause the impacted object files to be recompiled. In addition, the usual time stamp method of detecting file changes is replaced by a more accurate MD5 digest comparison.

- **Performance:** Although it's not as fast as GNU Make, SCons does attempt to execute as quickly as possible. This sometimes conflicts with the primary goal of build correctness, but you can speed up the build process in a number of ways.

- **Convenience:** The SCons language is designed to be easy to use, with minimal effort required to create a build system. As you'll see in the real-world examples, this is certainly true in most cases.

In addition to these core principles, SCons has been designed to support a wide range of compilation tools and build environments. The main focus is clearly C/C++–based development environments, for a wide range of UNIX-like systems, and Microsoft Windows. It offers some support for Java compilation, although that's not yet as powerful as Ant's support.

Finally, it's worth noting that SCons has been under active development since the year 2000. Not only are bugs and weaknesses fixed on a regular basis, but also a number of new features are currently planned.

## The SCons Programming Language

This overview of the SCons build tool covers a number of topics to give you an appreciation of the basic language. You'll start with a simple C compilation that includes the creation and use of libraries. You'll then consider compilation tools and how other environment settings are managed, as well as how various parameters can control the build steps.

Program flow and dependency analysis are interesting topics, largely because they're a combination of the methods used by GNU Make and Ant. You'll also look at the rather unique way in which SCons decides whether an object file is out-of-date. This includes the case in which a change in compiler options or include paths is considered.

Finally, you'll touch on a number of the more advanced features in the SCons build tool. These include managing the compilation tool options, the cross-platform support features, and the capability to share object files with other developers.

Before diving into the details of the SCons tool, let's take a quick overview of the underlying Python language. You've studied the unique GNU Make and Ant languages in great detail, so it's only reasonable to spend time learning the basics of Python.

## The Python Programming Language

The concepts used in the Python language are similar to those in Java, C++, and C#, making it easy for developers to adopt the tool. On the other hand, the syntax is quite different, which introduces a bit of a learning curve. In this introduction, you'll learn the language by studying a couple of short programs. Pay careful attention to each of these examples, and you'll learn most of the concepts you need in a build system.

In the first example, you create a Python function that uses a regular expression to filter the content of a list. The list contains a number of filenames, and the regular expression matches only names that end with `.c`. In addition, the function returns the list of matching names in reverse order.

```
 1   import re
 2
 3   def extractAndReverse(pattern, inputList):
 4       newList = []
 5       for i in inputList:
 6           if re.match(pattern, i) != None:
 7               newList.insert(0, i)
 8       return newList
 9
10   reversedList = extractAndReverse(r'.*\.c$',
11       ['dog.c', 'cat.h', 'tiger.y', 'cat.c', 'bear.y',
       'wolf.c'])
12
13   for animal in reversedList:
14       print animal
```

Now study this example line by line, paying attention to both the syntax and semantics of the language:

Line 1 asks the Python interpreter to import the `re` (regular expression) module. The `re.match` function will be used on line 6.

The `extractAndReverse` function is defined on line 3, using the `def` statement. This function has two parameters, `pattern` and `inputList`, which are declared in the function heading. Python uses dynamic typing, so you don't specify the type of these variables.

Line 4 defines the `newList` variable and initializes it to an empty list. You use this variable to accumulate the names that match the regular expression.

Line 5 iterates through the content of the `inputList` variable, with the variable `i` being set appropriately for each iteration of the loop. Python uses dynamic typing, so an error is reported on this line if the `inputList` variable doesn't actually contain something you can iterate over.

An `if` statement is used on line 6 to determine whether the current element of the list matches the regular expression. The `re.match` function either returns a special object to describe the match's detail or, if there's no match, returns the null value (`None`). All you need to care about in this case is whether there's a match.

If the current filename matches the regular expression, you insert the name at the start of `newList` (on line 7). Because you're prepending the value (instead of appending), `newList` ends up in the reverse order of the original list. This line of code also demonstrates how a method (`insert`) is invoked on an object (`newList`).

Line 7 introduces the block structure of a Python program. It's important to note that neither the `if` statement nor the `for` statement contains a corresponding `end` statement to indicate where each block finishes. Python doesn't use curly braces to mark the start and end of a block; instead, the source code must be indented to indicate which lines of code belong to each of the blocks. This is not just good coding style—it's mandatory.

Because of the indentation on line 8, the `return` statement executes only when the entire loop is complete. `newList` therefore contains all the members of the original `inputList` variable that match the regular expression. This marks the end of the `extractAndReverse` function.

Lines 10 and 11 are part of the main program instead of a separately defined function. The `extractAndReverse` function is called and the return value is assigned to the `reversedList` variable. (Variables are declared when they're first assigned to.) The first parameter of the function call provides the regular expression (you're searching for any string ending with `.c`), and the second parameter is the list of filenames.

Finally, lines 13 and 14 traverse the resulting list and display each element on the standard output. As before, the indentation on line 14 indicates that it's part of the loop body.

This completes the first example. Although it might seem rather contrived, manipulating a list is an important part of a build system. Python has numerous built-in functions and methods (such as `re.match` and `newList.insert`) to help make the job easier.

Now look at a second example that generates a copyright message file. This is definitely something build systems need to do.

```
 1   import sys
 2
 3   def makeCopyright(holder, year, filename):
 4       try:
 5           file = open(filename, 'w')
 6       except IOError:
 7           print >> sys.stderr, "Error: Can't open %s" %
             filename
 8           sys.exit(1)
 9
10       print >> file, "This software is Copyright (C) %d by
         %s." % \
11           (year, holder)
12
13       file.close()
14
15   makeCopyright("Arapiki Solutions Inc", 2010, "copyright.
     txt")
```

Let's examine the interesting parts of the program, without going into too much detail on the concepts you've already seen.

Line 3 defines the makeCopyright function, which takes three parameters. The holder variable contains the name of the copyright holder, year contains the year of the copyright, and filename is the name of the disk file you'll create. Jump forward to line 15 to see an example of how to invoke this function.

Line 5 opens the output file in write mode, with the file variable holding the file object. You'll use this object later when you write to the file.

Lines 4–8 introduce the concept of an exception. Python tries to execute the open function on line 5, but if an IOError occurs, the body of the except block handles the error. Line 7 uses formatted printing to display an error message, and the program terminates on line 8.

Line 10–11 write the copyright message to the file you just opened. The concept of formatted printing is familiar to most developers, although the % (year, holder) syntax might take a little getting used to.

Line 13 invokes the close method on the file object. Because of the change in indentation on line 15, this also marks the end of the function.

At this point, you should be feeling quite comfortable with the basic Python concepts and syntax. Reading a SCons script will now be easy, given the syntax rules you've learned about. When you start writing your own scripts, you might still need to refer back to the Python documentation to recall the exact detail.

In addition to what you've seen so far, numerous Python libraries are available, both packaged with the tool and available from third parties. A Python program can do all the following and more:

- Create complex data structures, such as dictionaries

- Define object-oriented classes and create new objects

- Define code packages to help modularize larger programs

- Create disk-based databases as a persistent storage mechanism

- Access any of the underlying operating system services

- Define strings in Unicode format

- Interact with other machines over the Internet

This chapter can't cover all these topics, so you're encouraged to refer to the Python documentation [57] for more detail.

## Simple Compiling

Now see how the basic Python concepts are applied to building C programs. This section looks at a number of ways to compile the `calculator` example, including using static and dynamic libraries. In each case, you'll write a `SConstruct` file, which is equivalent to the `Makefile` and `build.xml` files in previous chapters.

### *The First Program*
Start with the simplest way of generating the `calculator` program:

```
1 Program('calculator', ['calc.c', 'add.c', 'mult.c', 'sub.c'])
```

The `Program` builder method is passed two different arguments. The first provides the name of the executable file, whereas the second lists the source files to compile and link together. When you invoke the `scons` tool in the same directory as the `SConstruct` file, you see the following output:

```
$ scons
scons: Reading SConscript files ...
scons: done reading SConscript files.
scons: Building targets ...
gcc -o add.o -c add.c
gcc -o calc.o -c calc.c
gcc -o mult.o -c mult.c
gcc -o sub.o -c sub.c
gcc -o calculator calc.o add.o mult.o sub.o
scons: done building targets.
```

The `Program` builder is obviously doing a lot of work and actually invokes a couple of subbuilders to get the whole job done. Each source file is compiled into object code and they're all linked together to create the executable program. Although it's not clear in this example, the `Program` builder also detects any source code dependencies. Any change to `numbers.h` triggers all source files to be recompiled.

By default, SCons builds all the files in the current directory. To limit what gets built, specify the name of the target file:

```
$ scons calc.o
scons: Reading SConscript files ...
scons: done reading SConscript files.
scons: Building targets ...
gcc -o calc.o -c calc.c
scons: done building targets.
```

In this case a target is an actual disk file, which matches GNU Make's concept of a target instead of Ant's definition.

Without going any further, you can see that SCons makes simple build systems easy to construct. Users just need to say what they want built and which source files should be used, and SCons handles all the detail. Contrast this with GNU Make, where compiler names need to be hard-coded and automatic dependency analysis is challenging to implement.

### Cross-Platform Builds

With the cross-platform nature of the SCons tools, the program can also be compiled on a Microsoft Windows system using the Visual Studio tools. Using the exact same `SConstruct` file as before, we see the following output:

```
scons: Reading SConscript files ...
scons: done reading SConscript files.
scons: Building targets ...
cl /Foadd.obj /c add.c /nologo
add.c
cl /Focalc.obj /c calc.c /nologo
calc.c
cl /Fomult.obj /c mult.c /nologo
mult.c
cl /Fosub.obj /c sub.c /nologo
sub.c
link /nologo /OUT:calculator.exe calc.obj add.obj mult.obj
sub.obj
scons: done building targets.
```

SCons automatically detects which compilers are available on the build machine and invokes them with suitable command-line options. Note that the `.exe` extension was automatically added to the name of the executable program, and `.obj` was used instead of `.o`.

### Modifying Compiler Options

To make the example a little more interesting, modify the C compiler flags to override the default settings. Here you use the `Program` builder again, but you pass a third parameter to set the `CFLAGS` variable:

```
1  Program('calculator',
2         ['calc.c', 'add.c', 'mult.c', 'sub.c'],
3         CFLAGS='-g')
```

When you invoke the `scons` build tool, you can see that `-g` has been added to the appropriate `gcc` command line:

```
$ scons
scons: Reading SConscript files ...
scons: done reading SConscript files.
scons: Building targets ...
gcc -o add.o -c -g add.c
gcc -o calc.o -c -g calc.c
gcc -o mult.o -c -g mult.c
gcc -o sub.o -c -g sub.c
gcc -o calculator calc.o add.o mult.o sub.o
scons: done building targets.
```

As you'll see shortly, SCons has many settings to control the build process. You'll also look at how these settings can be encapsulated inside a build environment object instead of providing the additional `CFLAGS` argument each time.

### Variations of the Basic Syntax

In addition to the syntax you've seen so far, you can use many variations. First, you can specify the list of object files instead of naming the source files.

```
1  Program('calculator',
2         ['calc.o', 'add.o', 'mult.o', 'sub.o'],
3         CFLAGS='-g')
```

SCons uses built-in rules to figure out that `calc.o` can be built from `calc.c`, so it already knows how to do that. This approach works fine in a UNIX environment but fails on a Windows system that uses `.obj` files. It's better to list the source files and let SCons determine the intermediate files.

As you might expect, you can also use a variable to store the list of filenames. This is useful if you make reference to the same list more than once.

```
1  sources = ['calc.c', 'add.c', 'mult.c', 'sub.c']
2  Program('calculator', sources, CFLAGS='-g')
```

It's even possible to list all the files as a single Python string and then separate the filenames using the `split` function.

```
1  Program('calculator',
2          Split('calc.c add.c mult.c sub.c'),
3          CFLAGS='-g')
```

Finally, you can use Python's keyword-based argument passing to give meaningful names to each of the arguments. This enables you to state the values in a different order, if you prefer.

```
1  Program(source = ['calc.c', 'add.c', 'mult.c', 'sub.c'],
2          target = 'calculator',
3          CFLAGS='-g')
```

Plenty of variations on this basic SConstruct file exist, with the exact syntax you choose depending largely on convenience or personal preference. They all produce the same executable program in the end.

### C Compilation with Libraries

Keeping with our calculator example, let's consider how to build static and dynamic libraries. In this case, you store add.c, mult.c, and sub.c in a library, and use calc.c as the main program. Here's the SConstruct file that creates and uses a static library:

```
1  myCalcLib = StaticLibrary('libcalc', ['add.c', 'mult.c',
   'sub.c'])
2  Program('calculator', ['calc.c'], LIBS = [myCalcLib],
   CFLAGS='-g')
```

Line 1 introduces the StaticLibrary builder method to construct a static library, named libcalc.a on UNIX systems. The return value from StaticLibrary is an object of type Node, which refers to the library you just built. A Node object can be used anywhere filenames are expected. In the example, the myCalcLib variable is a reference to the libcalc.a file, or whatever it's called on the specific build machine.

On line 2, you use the Program builder again but this time set the LIBS option to link against the library named in the myCalcLib variable. The corresponding build output follows:

```
$ scons
scons: Reading SConscript files ...
scons: done reading SConscript files.
scons: Building targets ...
gcc -o add.o -c add.c
gcc -o calc.o -c -g calc.c
gcc -o mult.o -c mult.c
gcc -o sub.o -c sub.c
ar rc libcalc.a add.o mult.o sub.o
ranlib libcalc.a
gcc -o calculator calc.o libcalc.a
scons: done building targets.
```

As you might expect, the `StaticLibrary` builder method knows how to compile the source files and then uses the `ar` command to create a static library. The `Program` builder knows how to link against this library.

The `SharedLibrary` builder can be used in a similar way to build dynamic libraries:

```
1   myCalcLib = SharedLibrary('libcalc', ['add.c', 'mult.c',
    'sub.c'])
2   Program('calculator', ['calc.c'], LIBS = [myCalcLib],
    CFLAGS='-g')
```

This time, you see a slightly different set of compilation options used:

```
scons: Reading SConscript files ...
scons: done reading SConscript files.
scons: Building targets ...
gcc -o add.os -c -fPIC add.c
gcc -o calc.o -c -g calc.c
gcc -o mult.os -c -fPIC mult.c
gcc -o sub.os -c -fPIC sub.c
gcc -o libcalc.so -shared add.os mult.os sub.os
gcc -o calculator calc.o libcalc.so
scons: done building targets.
```

Observe that the `SharedLibrary` builder is actually generating object files with the `.os` extension to distinguish them from nonshared object files. This is not the case for `calc.o` file, which the `Program` builder generates. Note also that the `gcc` compiler uses the `-fPIC` option to generate position-independent code.

At this point, you've seen enough examples of compiling C code. You're ready to think more about customizing the build environment.

## Managing Build Environments

Previous examples touched on the idea of setting **construction variables** such as `CFLAGS` and `LIBS` to configure the behavior of the compiler. In each case, you explicitly added the `CFLAGS` or `LIBS` argument when invoking the `Program` builder. Unfortunately, this solution doesn't scale well for large build systems because you'd need to repeat the same variables every time you invoked a builder.

SCons uses the concept of an `Environment` object to encapsulate the list of construction variables, making it easier to reuse settings:

```
1   env = Environment(CFLAGS = '-g')
2   env.Program('calculator', ['calc.c', 'add.c', 'mult.c',
    'sub.c'])
```

The `Environment` object stores the detail of which compiler should be used, which command-line options should be passed to that compiler, and which filename extensions should be used on the build machine (such as `.o` versus `.obj`). This example starts with the default environment that includes most of this information but then adds a custom definition for the `CFLAGS` variable. All the default variables are set to whatever makes sense on the user's build machine.

### *Using Multiple Environments*

You can extend the example by considering how SCons could selectively build either a debug version or a production version of our code. You can achieve this goal by creating two different environments and then selecting the environment needed for your specific purpose. To build a debug version of `calculator` that uses static libraries, you'd use this:

```
$ scons
```

For the production version that enables optimization and uses shared libraries, invoke the tool as follows:

```
$ scons production=1
```

Here's the code to implement this feature:

```
1   env = Environment()
2
3   if ARGUMENTS.get('production', 0):
4       env['CFLAGS'] = '-O'
5       env['CPPDEFINES'] = '-DPRODUCTION'
6       myLibraryBuilder = env.SharedLibrary
7   else:
8       env['CFLAGS'] = '-g'
9       env['CPPDEFINES'] = '-DDEBUG'
10      myLibraryBuilder = env.StaticLibrary
11
12  myLib = myLibraryBuilder('libcalc',
13          ['add.c', 'mult.c', 'sub.c'])
14
15  env.Program('calculator', 'calc.c', LIBS = [myLib])
```

Line 3 tests whether the `production` variable was provided on the command line and then chooses the appropriate block of code to execute. The first block on lines 4–6 sets the `CFLAGS` and `CPPDEFINES` variables to indicate that code optimization should be enabled in the compiler and that the `PRODUCTION` C preprocessor symbol must be defined. You also set the `myLibraryBuilder` variable to indicate that you need to build a shared library.

The second block of code, lines 8–10, enables the generation of debug symbols and defines the DEBUG preprocessor symbol. You also indicate here that a static library should be built, because they're often easier to use when debugging code.

Lines 12–13 use either the StaticLibrary or SharedLibrary builder methods, depending on what the user requested. Each of these builders is invoked as part of the environment (env) and thus pick up the necessary values for CFLAGS and CPPDEFINES.

Finally, you invoke the Program builder and pass in the library you've just constructed. This builder also uses the same environment and builds the calc.c source file using the same settings as the other files.

If you're observant, you might have realized that the -g and -o options won't actually work on a Windows system because the Windows cl compiler uses different options for debugging and optimization. Clearly, you still need to do a bit more work to make sure you're passing in the correct flags.

### Construction Variables

Without going into too much detail, let's examine some of the commonly used construction variables. Literally hundreds of variables exist, so the following are just a few of the basics:

- CC: Provides the path to the C compiler executable on the build system. This defaults to gcc on a Linux system or cl on a Windows system that uses Visual Studio. The value can be overridden to use a different C compiler.

- CCVERSION: Provides the version of the C compiler. For example, this is set to 4.3.2 if the build machine uses GCC version 4.3.2.

- CFILESUFFIX: C-language source files have this file suffix. The default on most machines is .c.

- PROGSUFFIX: Specifies the file suffix to be used for executable programs. This variable is empty on UNIX systems and is set to .exe on Windows systems.

- CCCOM: Specifies the command-line options to be passed to the C compiler. The following default value is used for GCC compilers on Linux.

```
'$CC -o $TARGET -c $CFLAGS $CCFLAGS $_CCCOMCOM $SOURCES'
```

When the CCCOM variable is accessed, each of the variables in the definition is expanded to its current value (similar to GNU Make's deferred evaluation). The $TARGET and $SOURCES variables are set appropriately each time the builder invokes the underlying compiler.

Although each of the construction variables just listed comes with a default value, this isn't true for all of them. The following variables are initially empty and can be defined by the user:

- CCFLAGS : Options that are passed to both C and C++ compilers.

- CFLAGS : Options that are used only when compiling C code, not for C++ code.

- CPPDEFINES : A list of C preprocessor symbols to be passed to the C compiler. These are prefixed with -D or /D, depending on which compiler is used.

- CPPPATH : The list of directories to search when an #include directive is used in a C program.

- LIBPATH : Likewise, the list of directories to search when a library is linked against a program.

Finally, here's a construction variables that doesn't impact how the compilation tool is invoked but that does impact what the user sees on the standard output:

- CCCOMSTR : If this variable is defined, display the specified message to the user instead of showing the actual compilation command. For example:

```
env['CCCOMSTR'] = "Compiling $SOURCES"
```

In this case, you'll see Compiling calc.c in place of gcc -o calc.o -c calc.c when the program is compiled.

Refer to the SCons user guide or man page for a complete list of supported variables.

## Construction Variable Defaults

For any of the construction variables that come with default values, the SCons tool does a fair amount of upfront work to decide what those values should be. SCons detects which operating system is running on the build machine and then searches all the standard file system locations to find out which tools are installed. In many cases, users will be happy with the default set of tools, but each time they create a new environment, they're welcome to override the defaults.

It's worth noting that SCons won't use the developer's $PATH or %PATH% environment variables when searching for local tools. This is a great example of how SCons focuses on the correctness of the build process. It removes any chance that the user's personal search path includes a compilation tool that other developers don't have in their path.

## Program Flow and Dependency Analysis

At first glance, a SCons builder method appears to be similar to an Ant task. You provide a high-level directive that lists the inputs and outputs of a particular build step, and the SCons builder method invokes the necessary compilation tool. All the dependency analysis is hidden inside the builder, so the user doesn't need to think about constructing the dependency graph.

Things start to differ when the actual work is performed. Whereas Ant invokes the compilation tools when the task is first invoked, SCons uses the same two-phase approach you saw with GNU Make. When a builder is invoked, it does nothing more than compute the dependency information for that build step. In the second phase, SCons traverses the entire dependency graph and invokes the compilation tools necessary to bring files up-to-date.

With this two-phased approach in mind, SCons developers can easily read through a program as if it were any other Python program. They can follow the sequential flow of execution from top to bottom and can see how values returned by one builder method are passed as input into the next. The overall construction of the dependency graph is therefore easy to understand, and most developers have no problem seeing how the software is constructed.

Things get a little more complex in the second phase, where the compilation tools are actually invoked. Unlike Ant, the compilation tools are invoked in whatever order SCons decides, and this can be quite different from the order in which the builders were listed in the source file. As you'll see later, SCons provides a mechanism for viewing and understanding the dependency graph, so it's still possible to debug a misbehaving SCons program.

### Multiple Directory Support

To handle SCons programs that are split across multiple directories, you use the SConscript function to join multiple files into one. In this case, the build description files that appear in lower-level directories must be named SConscript, in contrast to the top-level file, which is called SConstruct:

```
SConscript('subdir/SConscript')
```

Given that SCons was designed with correctness in mind, the builders that are invoked from within the `subdir/SConscript` file contribute to the same global dependency graph. You therefore don't have the problems you saw with recursive Make. Any filenames mentioned in the `SConscript` file are interpreted as being relative to the `subdir` directory, making it unnecessary to list a long pathname to each file. Later in this chapter, you'll see a number of examples that use the `SConscript` function.

### Dependency Analysis

It's worth noting that although much of the dependency analysis is done for you, SCons provides a few functions for directly manipulating the dependency graph:

- `Depends`: If the builder method you're using doesn't seem to get the dependencies correct, you can use the `Depends` function to explicitly add a link in the dependency graph. In this example, you want the `calculator` program to also depend on the `headers.h` file (which is different from the existing `number.h` file).

```
target = Program('calculator',
                 ['calc.c', 'add.c', 'mult.c', 'sub.c'])
Depends(target, 'headers.h')
```

If `headers.h` changed, even if it's not included by any of the source files, the `calculator` program will be relinked. Hopefully you won't need to use this function often, but it's nice to know that it's available.

- `Ignore`: This is the opposite of `Depends` and is used where a link in the dependency graph must be explicitly removed.

```
Ignore(target, 'calc.o')
```

This example causes the `calculator` program to not recompile, even if `calc.o` changed. Note that `calc.o` would still be linked into the executable program, but only if some other file changed, causing the link step to be triggered.

- `Default`: By default, SCons always builds all the targets within the current directory. To override this behavior and have a specific file (or files) built by default, use the `Default` function.

```
Default('calculator')
```

If the user invokes the scons command-line tool without a target name, the calculator program is built.

- Alias: As we noted earlier, a SCons target is normally the name of a disk file that you're going to build. By using the Alias function, you create a named target that resembles a target in the Ant language or one of GNU Make's phony targets that don't relate to a real disk file.

```
Alias('all', 'calculator')
```

In this case, you're defining the all target to be an alias for the calculator program. You can also have a list of files as the second argument, making it possible to build multiple targets with a single alias name.

Now look at the unique ways in which SCons decides whether a file is up-to-date.

## Deciding When to Rebuild

Compared to other build tools, SCons places a considerable amount of effort into deciding whether a generated file needs to be rebuilt. Instead of using the traditional method of comparing time stamps, SCons can use MD5 checksums to determine whether a file has changed. It also looks for changes in compilation tool flags and search paths, to predict whether a generated file might end up with different content.

A SCons program can use the Decider function to specify how decisions are made, giving a fully customizable process. SCons is shipped with a number of built-in deciders, but it's also possible to create your own, based on whichever criteria is important for your code. The following deciders are built into SCons, with the first approach being the default:

- Decider('MD5'): To determine whether a source file has changed, SCons computes the MD5 checksum of the file and compares it with the file's checksum from the last time the build was started. If there's no difference in checksum, there's a high likelihood that the file content hasn't changed. This approach requires that SCons keep a persistent database of MD5 signatures, which is stored in the .sconsign file.

- Decider('timestamp-newer'): To determine whether a source file has changed, SCons checks whether the time stamp on the source file is newer than the time stamp on the object file. If so, it's quite likely that the source file has changed. On the other hand, there's still a chance that the file was written to, but the content didn't actually change. This is the same approach used by the GNU Make tool.

- `Decider('timestamp-match')`: Similar to the previous case, but instead of comparing the source file and object file time stamps, SCons remembers the source file's time stamps between consecutive builds. This approach doesn't require you to check as many time stamps, but SCons must record time stamp information in a database.

- `Decider('MD5-timestamp')`: The default MD5 decider can be rather slow, so this approach tests each file's time stamp before computing the MD5 checksum. You'll learn more about this approach shortly.

Of course, you can also write your own decider functions. If your build system generates web pages containing financial stock information, you could even write a decider that checks whether stock prices have changed. It would be pointless to regenerate HTML files each time a build was invoked, even if the financial data was the same.

In addition to testing for file changes, SCons checks for environment changes. These include the flags that are passed into compilation tools and the file system paths that are searched to find libraries or header files. Now consider the cases:

- `CFLAGS`: Most C compiler options have some type of impact on the generated object code. If you compiled a number of object files with the -O flag enabled but then you changed it to -O2 to get better optimization, SCons must regenerate all the object files.

- `CPPPATH`: This variable is used as the search path for locating C header files. If the program included `numbers.h` but you then changed the search path, the possibility exists that a different file called `numbers.h` could be used instead. In this case, the object file needs to be regenerated.

- `LIBPATH`: Similar to the previous case, except that the search path is used to find library files. If this variable changes, there's a chance of including a different library.

As you might expect, this focus on build correctness reduces the number of incorrect builds you'll see. However, these features don't come for free and, unfortunately, tend to slow the build system. SCons developers need to carefully consider whether they care about performance or whether correctness is more appealing. Think about these tradeoffs:

- Even though MD5 checksum calculations can be time-consuming, it's possible to disable this feature by using a time stamp–based decider. On the other hand, you might find that time stamp–based methods are less accurate and, therefore, cause a lot more files to rebuild, even when they don't need to. As a compromise, the MD5-timestamp decider combines the best of both worlds by performing a fast time stamp comparison and performing a slower MD5 computation only if the time stamp indicates that the file might have changed.

- Even though MD5 computation is slower than time stamp checking, it could save you time. For example, if you modify a comment in the source code, the source file's content changes and the corresponding object file is regenerated. However, because the object file content isn't affected (you changed only a comment), the build process can stop at that point. There's no need to relink the executable program because SCons has already determined that none of the object files have changed.

- If you're not too worried about changes in your CPPPATH and LIBPATH variables picking up the wrong files, you can disable this feature by using the implicit_cache option. This stops SCons from rescanning each of the source files when it tries to determine which headers or libraries to use. The information is instead cached between consecutive builds, thus increasing the overall build performance.

As you'll see in Chapter 19, "Faster Builds," using the MD5-timestamp and implicit_cache options makes the SCons build tool almost as fast as a GNU Make build system.

## Extending the Language

As you've seen with other build tools, it's often important for users to extend the basic language by adding more features of their own. These can include new builder methods or the addition of normal Python functions that make the SConstruct file easier to write. SCons offers a number of extension points, including the following:

- Writing normal Python functions

- Creating a builder method using a shell command

- Creating a builder method using only Python code

- Directly invoking shell commands

- Writing a source code scanner

In each of these cases, the extension is written in the Python programming language; although, you're free to use shell commands if you need to invoke specific compilation tools. Unlike many other build tools, there's no need to break out into using a different programming language: The combination of Python code and shell commands is powerful enough for most applications.

### *Writing Normal Python Functions*

Although writing a SConstruct file is relatively easy in the first place, you might need extra helper functions to make it even simpler. For example, the extractAndReverse function you looked at earlier could easily be used from within a SConstruct file:

```
reversedList = extractAndReverse('.*\.c$', fileList)
```

In your build system, you might have a similar approach to processing a list of source files or deciding which files need to be generated. The more complex your build system is, the more likely you are to write this type of function to make your build description easier to read.

Keep in mind that this code is executed during the first phase of parsing the SConstruct files, so the goal should be to construct the dependency graph. Therefore, you'd use the reversedList variable as input into a builder method that could trigger additional work to happen in the second phase.

If you need to invoke a compilation tool to actually do some work, you should create a builder method.

### *Creating a Builder Method Using a Shell Command*

When extending the SCons language by adding a new compilation tool, perhaps the easiest way is to defer most of the work to a shell command. Even then, you need to do some work to build up the dependency graph. Here's a simple example of adding a new builder method. In this case, you use a fictitious rpctool compiler to generate .c files from higher-level .rpc files.

```
1   env = Environment()
2   rpc_builder = Builder(action = '/tools/bin/rpctool -o
    $TARGET $SOURCE',
3                        suffix = '.c', src_suffix='.rpc')
4   env['BUILDERS']['RPC'] = rpc_builder
5
6   env.RPC('fast_messages.rpc')
```

Line 2 does most of the hard work in this example. The `Builder` function takes an `action` string containing the shell command to be executed. This command won't be executed yet, but it will be at a later time when the tool is called into action. The `$SOURCE` and `$TARGET` variables will be expanded to their appropriate values, and the whole string is passed to the command shell.

The `suffix` and `src_suffix` parameters are used to build up the dependency graph. This builder can be used on input files with the `.rpc` extension, and the resulting output file will have a `.c` extension.

Line 4 adds this new builder to the construction variable environment. By adding the RPC builder name, you can invoke the tool using the syntax shown on line 6. When you execute this script, you'll see the following output:

```
$ scons
scons: Reading SConscript files ...
scons: done reading SConscript files.
scons: Building targets ...
/tools/bin/rpctool -o fast_messages.c fast_messages.rpc
scons: done building targets.
```

This approach to adding new builders is similar to the technique used in GNU Make. Matching filename patterns is certainly a convenient way to add new build tools.

### Creating a Builder Using Only Python Code

Although the capability to have a builder method invoke a shell command is good enough in many situations, you might find that invoking a single command is rather limiting. If you think about the standard `Program` builder, a lot of work went on behind the scenes to generate all the object files and to process all the command-line options. In these complex cases, you might appreciate having the full power of the Python language.

The following example makes use of the `makeCopyright` function defined earlier. In this case, the entire builder method is written in Python, although there's nothing to stop you from invoking one or more shell commands if you need to.

```
1   from MakeCopyright import makeCopyright
2   from time import localtime
3
4   def copyright_function(target, source, env):
5       target_file = str(target[0])
6       holder_file = source[0]
7       holder_name = holder_file.get_contents().strip()
8       year = localtime()[0]
9       makeCopyright(holder_name, year, target_file)
10
11  env = Environment()
```

```
12   builder = Builder(action = copyright_function)
13   env['BUILDERS']['Copyright'] = builder
14
15   env.Copyright('LICENSE.txt', 'holder.txt')
```

Skip over the first part of this file for now and focus on lines 11–13. This is similar to the previous example, except that you're providing the name of a Python function instead of a shell command. You're also not including the `suffix` or `src_suffix` parameters, although you could if you needed to.

Looking back at lines 4–9, there you define the `copyright_function` function. The three parameters are as follows:

- `target`: The list of `Node` objects (and special SCons data type) that describe the files to be generated. Line 5 fetches the first `Node` object and determines the file's name (using the `str` function).

- `source`: The list of `Node` objects describing the input files you should read. Lines 6–7 fetch the first source file from the list and then read the content of that file into the `holder_name` variable (taking care to strip the trailing newline).

- `env`: The `Environment` object to be used when building things. You don't use the environment in this case.

The builder method finishes on line 8 by retrieving the current year (such as `2010`) and invoking the `makeCopyright` function that you've already seen. Finally, line 15 invokes the `Copyright` builder using the usual syntax, so the file is then written to disk.

### Directly Invoking Shell Commands

In some cases, your build system might invoke a specific compilation tool only once, in which case you don't need to define a new `Builder` object. Instead, you can use the `Command` method to invoke a one-time shell command on a particular pair of files:

```
env.Command("data.txt.gz", "data.txt", "gzip -c < $SOURCE >
➥$TARGET")
```

In this example, the `data.txt.gz` file is generated from the `data.txt` file by running the `gzip` command. The shell command isn't executed immediately but is added to the dependency graph in case it's needed later.

On the other hand, if you really did want the shell command to be executed in the first phase of parsing the `SConstruct` files, you should instead use the standard Python `os.system` function.

*Writing a Source Code Scanner*

Earlier in this chapter, you touched on the idea that SCons automatically discovers a source file's dependencies. For example, a C source file can include a number of header files by using the #include directive. To complete the RPC builder, you'd also need to add a scanner to identify which other files are included. You'll learn more about this technique when you look at adding the mathcomp compiler to SCons builds.

## Other Interesting Features

SCons has a lot of interesting features that this chapter hasn't discussed but that are certainly worth a brief mention.

- **Manipulating compilation tool flags:** SCons provides a wide array of functions for manipulating lists of compilation tool options. This includes the capability to append and prepend flags to an existing list, overwrite existing flags with a new value, ensure that there's no repetition of flags in a list, and parse a string of compiler flags and have each of them passed to the appropriate compilation tool.

- **Displaying a progress indicator:** For large builds, it's possible to call a user-defined method to display an update on how the build is progressing.

- **Building code from central code repositories:** Instead of each developer having a copy of all files, it's possible to share a common source tree. SCons looks for source files in this shared tree if they can't be found in the developer's own tree. This is similar to GNU Make's VPATH feature.

- **Caching prebuilt object files:** By utilizing MD5 checksums, SCons can determine a fingerprint for each object file it compiles. If another developer has already compiled the exact same source code file using the same header files and compilation flags, SCons obtains the object file from a shared repository instead of recompiling it again. Chapter 19 covers this mechanism in more detail.

- **Probing the build machine:** SCons includes a number of functions for analyzing the build machine to ensure that it supports the required build environment. A SConstruct program can detect the presence of specific library and header files and can compile a small test program to validate which features exist in the build environment.

The SCons system has plenty more features, and the list is growing over time. Although SCons is still relatively young, the growing user base is likely to increase the number of available features.

## Further Reading

The best place to learn more about SCons is the tool's own user guide and manual page [56]. The user guide provides a gentle introduction for first-time users, whereas the manual page is more suitable for experts who need to be reminded of the function parameters or construction variables.

Not much additional documentation exists for the SCons tool, but that's likely because of the high quality of the existing user guide.

Anybody writing a SConstruct file should also become familiar with the Python language, for which numerous books are available [58].

---

# Real-World Build System Scenarios

Now let's look at our standard collection of real-world build system scenarios. As you'll see, the SCons tool designers have obviously thought about these common cases, making it easy to implement these examples. These SConstruct files are much shorter than the equivalent programs in GNU Make or Ant.

## Scenario 1: Source Code in a Single Directory

You've already seen the solution to the single directory calculator example:

```
1   Program('calculator',
2           ['calc.c', 'add.c', 'mult.c', 'sub.c'],
3           CFLAGS='-g')
```

As discussed earlier, the Program builder manages all the dependency analysis for you and rebuilds the object files if the numbers.h header file is modified. Object files also are recompiled if the CFLAGS variable is changed, ensuring the correctness of the resulting object files.

## Scenario 2(a): Source Code in Multiple Directories

If you spread the source files across multiple directories, the SConstruct file is almost the same:

```
Program('calculator',
        ['libmath/clock.c', 'libmath/letter.c', 'libmath/
        number.c',
```

```
'libprint/banner.c', 'libprint/center.c', 'libprint/
normal.c',
'calc/calc.c'],
CFLAGS='-g')
```

SCons handles the dependency analysis correctly, and the object files are stored in the same hierarchical structure as the source files.

The obvious downside to this approach is that the SConstruct file can become long and hard to maintain, especially when dealing with thousands of source files. The contention among developers who need to change this file makes it difficult to coordinate changes.

## Scenario 2(b): Multiple SConstruct Files

To avoid having all source files listed in the same SConstruct file, you can divide the build description into multiple files. This approach limits the size of each file, reduces the contention when making changes, and keeps the build description in the same directory as the source files.

Here's the top-level SConstruct file:

```
1   env = Environment()
2   env['CFLAGS'] = '-O'
3   Export('env')
4
5   libmath = SConscript('libmath/SConscript')
6   libprint = SConscript('libprint/SConscript')
7   Export('libmath libprint')
8
9   SConscript('calc/SConscript')
```

Lines 1–3 create a build environment (env) that'll be used across the entire system. In this case, you're changing only the CFLAGS variable, but nothing is stopping you from creating an elaborate environment containing a number of customizations. The Export function on line 3 states that this environment should be made available to any SConscript file that chooses to import it.

Line 5 includes the libmath/SConscript file, and line 6 does the same for the libprint/SConscript file. The content of these files is parsed, and the dependencies are all added to the same global dependency graph. On line 7, the variables containing the values return from these SConscript calls are both exported so that other SConscript files can import them.

Finally, line 9 includes the calc/SConscript file to link together the final calculator executable. In this case, you needn't care about the return value.

Now jump to the libmath/SConscript file:

```
1   Import('env')
2
```

```
3  lib = env.StaticLibrary('libmath',
4          ['number.c', 'clock.c', 'letter.c'])
5
6  Return('lib')
```

This file imports the `env` variable, containing the environment object, and uses it when creating the `libmath` library. This ensures that all compiler options are used consistently throughout the build system. Line 6 returns the resulting `Node` object that stores the name of the library you've just created.

As you'd expect, the `libprint/SConscript` is similar.

```
1  Import('env')
2
3  lib = env.StaticLibrary('libprint',
4          ['normal.c', 'center.c', 'banner.c'])
5
6  Return('lib')
```

Finally, the `calc/SConscript` file imports the `libmath` and `libprint` variables (the `*` wildcard imports everything) and uses them to create the `calculator` executable program:

```
1  Import('*')
2
3  env.Program('calculator',
4          ['calc.c'],
5          LIBS=[libmath, libprint])
```

This completes the entire build system, spread across multiple directories. At this point, you might be wondering whether SCons is capable of solving the sub-build problem that both GNU Make and Ant suffer from. Luckily, the SCons tool does have a clever way of solving this common dilemma, and it all comes down to the choice of filenames: `SConstruct` versus `SConscript`.

It's important to note that SCons accepts only a `SConstruct` file as input and won't look at `SConscript` files unless the `SConscript` function explicitly includes them. If you invoke `scons` in a lower-level directory, you'll see the following output:

```
$ scons
scons: *** No SConstruct file found.
```

You might think it's impossible to do anything other than top-level software builds, but that's not quite the case. If you invoke `scons` with the –u option, it searches up through the chain of parent directories to locate the nearest `SConstruct` file. It can therefore parse the entire build description and form a complete dependency graph.

However, this doesn't mean that the entire software image will be compiled. By default, SCons builds the targets only in the current directory (and below), and because you invoked SCons from a subdirectory, you'll build the content of only that directory. The good news is that SCons has a complete copy of the dependency graph and proceeds to build the other subdirectories first, but only if they're necessary to compile the files in the current directory. The subbuild problem is thus solved.

## Scenario 3: Defining New Compilation Tools

Our solution for adding the `mathcomp` tool to the SCons environment is more complex than the equivalent GNU Make solution, but definitely simpler than the Ant solution. Part of the complexity is that you'll write your own source code scanner to determine the dependencies instead of using the built-in `mathcomp -d` flag.

Here's the complete source code:

```
1   import re
2   reg_exp = re.compile(r'^import\s+(\S+)$', re.M)
3
4   def scan_math(node, env, path):
5       import_nodes = [ node ]
6       import_list = []
7
8       while len(import_nodes) != 0:
9           this_node = import_nodes.pop()
10
11          new_imports = reg_exp.findall(this_node.get_
            contents())
12          for file in new_imports:
13              import_list.append(file)
14              import_nodes.append(File(file))
15
16      return import_list
17
18  env = Environment()
19  math_scanner = Scanner(function = scan_math, skeys =
    ['.math'])
20  env.Append(SCANNERS = math_scanner)
21
22  math_builder = Builder(action = '/tools/bin/mathcomp
    $SOURCE',
23                         suffix = '.c', src_suffix='.math')
24  env['BUILDERS']['Math'] = math_builder
25
26  extra_c_src = env.Math('equations')
27  env.Program('calc', ['main.c', extra_c_src])
```

For convenience, let's start the discussion at the end of the program and work backward. Lines 26–27 show how to use a new builder method, named Math. You pass in the name of the equations.math file (excluding the suffix), and the builder generates a C source file to be passed into the Program builder.

Back on lines 22–24, the new Math builder was added to the environment, using a shell command as the builder's action. In this case, you need to pass only the $SOURCE variable to the mathcomp tool because the tool automatically determines the target file's name.

Lines 19–20 define a new source code scanner. This definition informs SCons that a source file ending in .math can be scanned for dependencies by calling the scan_math function. This function must return the list of .mathinc files that are referenced by import statements.

Now review the scan_math function on lines 4–16. On line 4, scan_math accepts three parameters provided by the SCons dependency-analysis system. The first is a Node object that represents the file to be scanned, the second is the construction environment, and the third is the search path for finding additional include files. The example uses only the first parameter.

Line 5 creates the import_nodes variable used to track which sources files still need to be scanned. Given that .mathinc files can include other .mathinc files, you could end up searching a long chain of import statements.

Line 6 creates the import_list variable to track the list of filenames found so far. This is similar to import_nodes, except that the goal is to collect a list of filenames to return, whereas the import_nodes list contains Node object that aren't yet processed.

The while loop on line 8 continues until you run out of Node objects still to be processed. Each time around the loop, you pop off a single Node object (this_node), making the import_nodes list smaller.

Line 11 is where the magic happens. First you read the content of the file referenced by the this_node variable and pass it through a regular expression that matches lines in the file (see line 2 for the definition). Any lines that start with the import statement, followed by a filename, are returned in the new_imports list.

For each element of the new_imports list, lines 12–14 add the newly found filename to the list of files to be returned and add the corresponding Node object to the list of nodes still to be processed.

When the import_nodes list is empty, you can be sure that you've done a complete traversal of all the import statements in the .math and .mathinc source files. This solution doesn't handle the case in which files can't be found or the case in which the import statements create an infinite cycle, but those are straightforward to add.

## Scenario 4: Building with Multiple Variants

As you did for the corresponding GNU Make example, you'll now see what it takes to generate code for three different CPU variants (i386, PowerPC, and Alpha). You'll store each set of object files in a CPU-specific directory.

Figure 8.1 shows the build tree layout you'll be using.

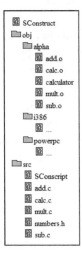

**Figure 8.1** *The build tree for the multivariant build system, supporting three different CPU types.*

The SConstruct file in the top-level directory validates the command-line arguments and sets up the required environment. It then defers to the lower-level src/SConscript file to perform the actual compilation. The user invokes the build tool by specifying the CPU type:

```
$ scons platform=powerpc
```

Start with the top-level SConstruct file:

```
1  vars = Variables()
2  vars.Add(EnumVariable('PLATFORM', 'CPU type', 'i386',
3           allowed_values = ('i386', 'powerpc',
             'alpha')))
4
5  env = Environment(variables = vars, CFLAGS='-g',
6                    CC='/tools/bin/gcc-${PLATFORM}')
7  Export('env')
8
9  Help(vars.GenerateHelpText(env))
10
11 platform = env['PLATFORM']
12 SConscript('src/SConscript',
13            variant_dir='obj/%s' % platform)
```

Luckily, SCons contains built-in functions for evaluating command-line options, as well as for compiling into variant-specific directories. Now look at each line in detail. Lines 1–2 create a new `Variables` object and add the `PLATFORM` variable. You also provide some help text (`'CPU Type'`), the default value if no platform type is provided (`'i386'`), and the list of legal values. If you add this amount of detail, SCons can perform all the input validation for you. The build description can therefore reference the `PLATFORM` variable with full confidence that it contains a meaningful value.

Line 5 creates a new `Environment` object, using the `vars` object to define the list of user-supplied input values. Note the use of the `${PLATFORM}` variable on line 6, which expands to either `i386`, `powerpc`, or `alpha`.

Line 9 is another SCons feature that generates user-friendly help text. If users pass in the `–help` command-line option, they'll see the following:

```
$ scons --help
scons: Reading SConscript files ...
scons: done reading SConscript files.

PLATFORM: CPU type (i386|powerpc|alpha)
    default: i386
    actual: i386

Use scons -H for help about command-line options.
```

Lines 11–13 defer the actual compilation work to the `src/SConscript` file. The only new concept is that you're using the `variant_dir` flag to specify where the compiled object files should be stored. Typically, they're stored in the same directory as the source code, but in this case, you're storing them in a platform-specific location within the `obj` subdirectory.

Finish this scenario by looking at the `src/SConscript` file:

```
1  Import('env')
2  env.Program('calculator', ['calc.c', 'add.c', 'mult.c',
   'sub.c'])
```

As you can see, there's nothing surprising in how the builder methods are invoked. The top-level `SConstruct` file has handled all the environment settings, as well as decided where object files are stored. The `Program` builder just does the right thing, based on what the `env` variable contains.

For the sake of completeness, here's the output of building the `alpha` variant:

```
$ scons platform=alpha
scons: Reading SConscript files ...
scons: done reading SConscript files.
scons: Building targets ...
/tools/bin/gcc-alpha -o obj/alpha/add.o -c -g src/add.c
/tools/bin/gcc-alpha -o obj/alpha/calc.o -c -g src/calc.c
```

```
/tools/bin/gcc-alpha -o obj/alpha/mult.o -c -g src/mult.c
/tools/bin/gcc-alpha -o obj/alpha/sub.o -c -g src/sub.c
/tools/bin/gcc-alpha -o obj/alpha/calculator obj/alpha/calc.o
obj/alpha/add.o obj/alpha/mult.o obj/alpha/sub.o
scons: done building targets.
```

The other variants provide similar output.

## Scenario 5: Cleaning a Build Tree

The act of cleaning a build tree is common, and SCons provides an easy way of doing so. Given that a builder methods know exactly which files it's supposed to compile, SCons uses that same information to delete all the generated files. Cleaning a build tree is done by passing the -c option.

```
$ scons -c
scons: Reading SConscript files ...
scons: done reading SConscript files.
scons: Cleaning targets ...
Removed calc/calc.o
Removed libmath/number.o
Removed libmath/clock.o
Removed libmath/letter.o
Removed libmath/libmath.a
Removed libprint/normal.o
Removed libprint/center.o
Removed libprint/banner.o
Removed libprint/libprint.a
Removed calc/calculator
scons: done cleaning targets.
```

If SCons doesn't know about all the files that the build system creates, you can explicitly invoke the Clean function to add more files to the list. Although it's not common for C compilation, some tools generate additional files that the build process doesn't know, so additional Clean directives might be required. It's also possible to invoke the NoClean function to ask SCons not to remove a particular file from the build tree, just in case it's important.

## Scenario 6: Debugging Incorrect Builds

A SCons program is largely just a sequence of builder methods invoked against environment objects, so many of the problems you'll encounter are centered on those constructs. As a result, SCons provides a number of built-in features for viewing the dependency graph, analyzing the content of environment objects, and tracing the sequence of decisions that cause SCons to rebuild a generated file.

Let's look at a few ways of debugging a SCons program to find out why builders might not trigger when they should, why they cause the generated output files to have invalid content, or why they sometimes trigger an unnecessary rebuild.

## Builders Not Triggering When They Should

In this scenario, a developer modifies a source file or the build system regenerates an object file, but the program's behavior doesn't seem to reflect the code change. The generated files further downstream in the dependency graph aren't correctly updated.

The first thing to check is whether the file has really changed or whether the same content has been written back without modification. Given that SCons uses MD5 checksums by default, simply "touching" the file (a common practice with GNU Make) won't make the content any different and nothing rebuilds. Likewise, simply adding a comment to a source file could cause the object file to regenerate, but SCons won't relink the executable program if the machine code is exactly the same.

If you're confident that your files really have changed, the next step is to validate the dependency graph. There's always a chance that the builder's arguments were incorrect or that the source code scanner function (for your particular type of source code) isn't picking up all the dependencies. You can validate the dependency graph with the `--tree=all` command-line option:

```
$ scons --tree=all calc
scons: Reading SConscript files ...
scons: done reading SConscript files.
scons: Building targets ...
scons: 'calc' is up to date.
+-calc
  +-main.o
  | +-main.c
  | +-/usr/bin/gcc
  +-equations.o
  | +-equations.c
  | | +-equations.math
  | | +-equ1.mathinc
  | | +-equ2.mathinc
  | | +-equ3.mathinc
  | | +-equ4.mathinc
  | | +-/tools/bin/mathcomp
  | +-/usr/bin/gcc
  +-/usr/bin/gcc
scons: done building targets.
```

In this example, you need to check that the `calc` program has a dependency on all the necessary object files, which, in turn, depend on the relevant source files. If there's a discrepancy, it's possible that the builder method hasn't been given the correct list of input files or that the builder method itself contains a bug. If it's absolutely necessary, use the Depend function to force a missing dependency to appear in the graph.

You can also see that the .math file scanner is detecting a number of .mathinc include files, so take care to double-check that list. For scanner problems, you need to either fix the scanner (if you have the source code) or perhaps modify your source files slightly so that the scanner can locate the include or import directives.

### Builders Triggering When They Shouldn't

The reverse of the previous problem is files being regenerated even though you don't think they've changed. The dependency graph is a great place to start, but you also have the --debug=explain to tell you why SCons believes a certain file is out-of-date.

```
$ scons --debug=explain
scons: Reading SConscript files ...
scons: done reading SConscript files.
scons: Building targets ...
scons: rebuilding 'calc.o' because 'calc.c' changed
gcc -o calc.o -c -g calc.c
scons: rebuilding 'calculator' because 'calc.o' changed
gcc -o calculator calc.o add.o mult.o sub.o
scons: done building targets.
```

The extra annotation makes it easy to figure out what caused SCons to make the wrong decision. You need to revisit your builder's arguments or check the builder or scanner source code to understand where the problem could be. If necessary, use the Ignore function to remove a dependency from the graph.

### Failed Compilation Step or Invalid Output Files

In the final debugging scenario, a file is generated at the correct point in time, but the content is incorrect. This is usually because the compilation tool was invoked with the wrong arguments. The first step is always to double-check the output from the SCons build log and rerun the command line (such as gcc -c) to make sure it's doing what you need.

If you find an incorrect command line, the problem is likely with one or more of the construction variables stored in an environment object. By using the --debug=presub option, SCons shows exactly which environment variables are being expanded to form the command lines:

```
$ scons --debug=presub
scons: done reading SConscript files.
scons: Building targets ...
```

```
Building calc.o with action:
  UnlinkFunc(target, source, env)
Building calc.o with action:
  $CC -o $TARGET -c $CFLAGS $CCFLAGS $_CCCOMCOM $SOURCES
gcc -o calc.o -c -g calc.c
Building calculator with action:
  UnlinkFunc(target, source, env)
Building calculator with action:
  $LINK -o $TARGET $LINKFLAGS $SOURCES $_LIBDIRFLAGS
  $_LIBFLAGS
gcc -o calculator calc.o add.o mult.o sub.o
scons: done building targets.
```

From this output, you can see which of the variables is providing the incorrect value. Perhaps it's even one of the command-line template variables, such as $CCCOM, that's passing an incorrect list of options and arguments to the compiler. In either case, use the environment object's Dump function to check all the variables and their values. The full set of variables is enormous, but here are the first few:

```
{ 'AR': 'ar',
  'ARCOM': '$AR $ARFLAGS $TARGET $SOURCES',
  'ARFLAGS': ['rc'],
  'AS': 'as',
  'ASCOM': '$AS $ASFLAGS -o $TARGET $SOURCES',
  'ASFLAGS': [],
  ...
```

One unfortunate limitation of SCons is that it doesn't appear possible to trace a builder output back to the line of source code where the builder method was invoked. This makes it difficult to narrow the scope of a problem, when all you have is the SCons output log showing the incorrect behavior. The best solution might be to search all the SConstruct and SConscript files to try to identify the offending line of code.

As a final note, it's always possible to use the standard Python debugging tools to trace a SConstruct file. This is another benefit of using a general-purpose programming language as the basis for a build tool.

# Praise and Criticism

Although SCons is a relatively young tool, there's enough of a user base that many strengths and weaknesses have been identified. On the other hand, SCons is still in active development, so some of the weaknesses have already been resolved or will be addressed in upcoming releases of the tool.

## Praise

The praise includes the following:

- **Uses a general-purpose programming language:** Using Python as the basis for SCons was a good choice. It enables developers to write code in a familiar style, using a full-featured programming language. To express the nuances of their build description, users aren't forced to use cryptic syntax or to work around the limited language. This is often the case with other build tools.

- **Makes constructing a build system simple:** Only a couple of minutes are needed to construct a fully functional build system for a small project, complete with dependency checking and a `clean` target. Even for larger builds, it's relatively easy to create a hierarchy of `SConscript` files, with the assurance that a single dependency graph will be created. It isn't necessary to create a complex framework as it is with GNU Make.

- **Uses builder methods to improve portability:** Builder methods hide many of the underlying compilation tools, making SCons a portable build tool. The default construction environment is automatically configured to use the build machine's local toolsets, with the developer focusing on what needs to be done, not how it'll be done on each specific build machine.

- **Uses tool extensions written in Python:** When a SCons extension needs to be written, Python can also be used instead of breaking out into a shell script or writing a Java method. This includes all builders, scanners, and other helper functions that make `SConstruct` files easier to write. Python makes it easy to hide a complex piece of code logic inside a function, enabling the end user to invoke that function without understanding the internal details.

- **Focuses on correctness:** One of the most important goals of SCons is that the build process must be followed as accurately as possible. It therefore uses MD5 checksums to detect file changes, uses scanner functions to determine file dependencies, and rebuilds object files if the compilation flags have changed. In contrast to other tools, SCons is much less likely to build the wrong thing.

- **Still in active development:** SCons might be a young tool, but improvements are continuously being added, based on a growing amount of experience with the tool. Future bugs likely will be fixed quickly and new features will be added regularly.

- **Easy to debug programs:** SCons provides a number of debugging options, making it straightforward to identify and resolve any problems in the build process.

## Criticism

The criticism includes the following:

- **Too slow, especially for incremental builds:** The focus SCons places on build correctness is also responsible for decreasing the performance, especially for incremental builds in which only a few files have changed. Using the default settings, SCons computes the MD5 checksum of each file to see if it changed and then scans each source file to identify its header file usage. In addition, SCons always builds the full dependency graph before starting to compile anything. Even if a single source file has changed, all this extra work can take a while.

- **Builders can be too restrictive:** The standard builder methods can often feel too restrictive. You might need a sequence of build steps that don't appear to be possible using the default builders. In this case, either you end up studying the user guide in great detail to figure out the desired behavior, or you write your own builder to do the same thing. Sometimes providing an explicit list of shell commands is the easiest way to get the job done.

- **Inadequate support for Java and .NET languages:** SCons is effective for the C and C++ languages in UNIX and Windows environments, but it's not as strong for languages such as Java and C#. In those situations, it currently makes sense to use Ant or MSBuild.

- **Excessive memory footprint:** When compared to approaches such as recursive GNU Make, an equivalent SCons-based build uses considerably more memory on the build machine. However, this is not necessary true when compared to inclusive Make, which stores the entire dependency graph in memory.

## Evaluation

To summarize the SCons build tool, let's evaluate it against the build system quality measurements discussed in Chapter 1, "Build System Overview."

- **Convenience:** *Excellent*: SCons uses the general-purpose Python programming language as the basis of writing build description files, making it easy to configure the build system. In addition, build methods encapsulate high-level build operations in a simple function call, without requiring a developer to worry about multidirectory support or computing dependency information.

- **Correctness:** *Excellent*: The automatic generation of dependency information and the use of MD5 checksums are among the many SCons features designed to ensure a correct build process. Compared to other build tools, SCons is much less likely to produce a release package that doesn't match the source files.

- **Performance:** *Good*: Although SCons focuses heavily on the correctness of the build process and isn't as fast as GNU Make, it has adequate performance for most purposes. For developers requiring a faster build system, it's possible to disable some of the correctness features.

- **Scalability:** *Good*: SCons can support large build systems while still guaranteeing correctness, although the tool's memory footprint can be excessive for extremely large systems. Some users have replaced their SCons-based build system with a GNU Make solution to improve performance and scalability.

SCons is an ideal tool for building C/C++ code and is highly recommended for new software products or when replacing troublesome GNU Make build systems. However, SCons is not suitable for compiling Java and C# code; Ant and MSBuild are the best choices in that situation.

## Similar Tools

As it turns out, most of the popular build tools have their own special-purpose language included, and few are built on top of existing programming languages. Two notable exceptions are the Cons tool, upon which SCons is based, and the Rake tool, which is based on the general-purpose Ruby language.

### Cons

The Cons build tool [59] is based on the Perl language and provided much of the inspiration for the SCons tool. Cons hasn't been actively developed since 2001 because SCons superseded it. The Cons web site even encourages people to switch to the newer tool.

If you decide to use Cons, perhaps if you prefer the Perl language, you'll already be familiar with many of the tool's concepts. Construction environments, builders, scanners, and MD5 checksums are among the many concepts that were reused in SCons. Here's the calculator example again:

```
 1   @lib_sources = ('add.c', 'sub.c', 'mult.c');
 2   @main_sources = ('calc.c');
 3   $exe_name = 'calculator';
 4
 5   $env = new cons(
 6       CC => 'gcc',
 7       LIBS => 'libmath.a'
 8   );
 9
10   Library $env 'libmath', @lib_sources;
11   Program $env $exe_name, @main_sources;
```

You'll find the syntax to be slightly different, but the ideas are generally the same. There's no need to describe how this program works.

## Rake

The Rake build tool [60] is based on the Ruby scripting language, which provides a number of interesting language features. These features might not seem familiar at first, but they're not hard to follow when you understand the syntax. Now look at an example program and explain it carefully.

Rake is quite different from SCons and Cons because it doesn't provide any automatic dependency analysis. It instead relies more on the model GNU Make uses, in which the developer provides the source and target dependencies, as well as the list of commands to be executed. The commands can be written in pure Ruby code or can use the sh method to invoke a shell command.

Here's the calculator example again, but written in Rake/Ruby syntax:

```
 1   require 'rake/clean'
 2
 3   exe_name = 'calculator'
 4   sources = FileList['*.c']
 5   objects = sources.ext('o')
 6
 7   task :default => [exe_name]
 8
 9   rule '.o' => '.c' do |t|
10       sh "gcc -c -o #{t.name} #{t.source}"
11   end
12
13   desc "Build the #{exe_name} program"
14   file exe_name => objects do
15       sh "gcc -o #{exe_name} #{objects}"
```

```
16   end
17
18   objects.each do |object|
19     file "#{object}" => ["numbers.h"]
20   end
21
22   CLEAN.include('*.o')
23   CLOBBER.include(exe_name)
24   verbose(true)
```

Spend some time looking through this example, because the syntax needs some explanation if you've never seen Ruby.

Lines 3–5 provide a number of useful definitions, using Ruby's variable assignment syntax. The exe_name variable provides the name of the program you're creating, whereas sources is defined to include all the .c files in the current directory (a wildcard operation). The objects variable is derived from the sources variable by replacing all the .c extensions with .o.

Line 7 is the first example of Rake's rule definitions. In this case, you're stating that, to build the default target, you first need to build the program whose name is stored in the exe_name variable.

Lines 9–11 provide a suffix rule that states how to generate object files from source files. For each .c file, you invoke the gcc compiler with the –c flag. If you're not familiar with Ruby, it's interesting to know that rule is a Ruby method that takes two parameters. The first, '.o' => '.c', is actually a hash that maps the .o string to the .c string. Likewise, the second parameter takes a code block, which appears between the do and end keywords. There's nothing unusual about this in the Ruby language, where constant hash mappings and code blocks can be passed into a method.

Lines 14–16 are similar and state that the executable program depends on all of the object files. Lines 18–20 use a looping construct to state that each of the object files has a dependency on the numbers.h header file. Finally, the remaining lines define which files will be cleaned when the user invokes the clean or clobber build targets.

It's also interesting to note that Rake supports both file-based target names (as in GNU Make) and symbolic target names (as with Ant). The example mainly uses the file-based approach, with the exception of the :default target. The colon prefix indicates that it's a symbol instead of a filename. Additional symbols can be created just as easily.

Here's the output from running the rake tool:

```
$ rake
(in /home/psmith/Rake)
gcc -c -o calc.o calc.c
gcc -c -o sub.o sub.c
gcc -c -o add.o add.c
```

```
gcc -c -o mult.o mult.c
gcc -o calculator calc.o sub.o add.o mult.o

$ rake -T
(in /home/psmith/Rake)
rake calculator  # Build the calculator program
rake clean       # Remove any temporary products.
rake clobber     # Remove any generated file.

$ rake clean
(in /home/psmith/Rake)
rm -r calc.o
rm -r sub.o
rm -r add.o
rm -r mult.o
```

The first case shows the regular build sequence. The second shows how each Rake target can be enhanced with useful help text (see line 13). The third case shows how the `clean` target is automatically defined for you when you include the appropriate library (see line 1).

For developers who are familiar with Ruby, Rake is definitely a tool to consider using.

## Summary

The SCons build tool uses a standard Python script to describe a build process instead of taking the usual approach of creating a domain-specific language. A number of Python functions, known as builder methods, are used to compile source code, create libraries, and link together executable programs. Each of these builder methods accepts a list of input files and any number of compilation tool flags.

Given the wide range of construction variables used to configure the build process, SCons uses environment objects to encapsulate the detail. You create a single environment object and reuse it for each different builder method to ensure that a consistent set of compiler flags is used. To support multiple build machine types, SCons creates a default environment that references the build machine's locally installed tools.

SCons uses a two-phased approach to perform the build process. The first phase involves executing all the builder methods and constructing a dependency graph. In the second phase, SCons invokes the underlying compilation tools necessary to bring the generated files up-to-date. By default, SCons calculates an MD5 checksum for each file in the build tree and uses that information to determine whether a file has changed from one build to the next.

A number of mechanisms are available for extending the basic SCons language. By writing standard Python code, developers can create their own builder methods, as well as source code scanners that automatically determine a source file's dependencies.

SCons takes the goals of correctness, performance, and convenience seriously, and many of the language features reflect this approach. Unfortunately, one of the main criticisms of SCons is that the focus on correctness is responsible for the tool's degraded performance.

# Chapter 9

# CMake

The next build tool to discuss is CMake [61]. This tool differs from GNU Make, Ant, and SCons because it doesn't actually execute the build process. Instead, it translates a high-level build description into a lower-level format accepted by other tools. For example, a CMake **generator** can translate the high-level build description into a makefile, ready for execution by the GNU Make tool.

The goals of this approach are to simplify the construction of build systems and support cross-platform development. As you saw in Chapter 6, "Make," constructing a GNU Make build system is challenging, especially when dealing with large code bases. It's also hard to construct a single build system that works across a range of different platforms.

CMake addresses these problems by providing a high-level language to describe the build process. A generator then translates this description into a native build tool's own language, hiding all the complexity from developers. Although Ant and SCons also provide a high-level abstraction (using tasks and builder methods), those tools execute the build process directly, whereas CMake delegates the execution to another tool.

Several CMake generators are available, running on a wide range of build machine types, including Microsoft Windows, Mac OS X, Linux, and numerous variants of UNIX. Given that each operating system has different native build tools, CMake's generators support many popular development environments. For example, CMake can create a makefile for GNU Make or NMake, as well as project descriptions for Microsoft Visual Studio or Eclipse CDT (discussed in Chapter 10, "Eclipse").

CMake build descriptions are stored in a `CMakeLists.txt` file, using a platform-neutral language. Figure 9.1 shows the overall workflow of using the `cmake` tool to produce a **native build system**, which is then invoked by running the **native build tool**.

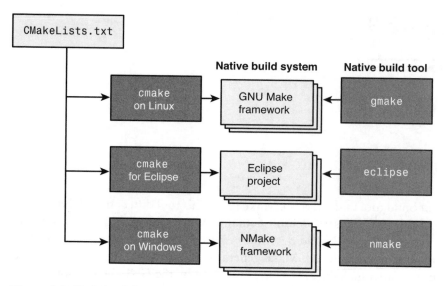

**Figure 9.1** *High-level flow of the CMake tool, generating a native build system.*

When executed on a UNIX system, the default behavior is to create a makefile-based framework (a main makefile and a number of supporting framework files). If you override the default and instead generate an Eclipse-based project, extra project-related files are added. Finally, when executed on Windows, the default behavior is to use Visual Studio's compilers and the NMake build tool.

This chapter reviews CMake's syntax and features. The syntax of the CMake language is unique to CMake and is therefore worth some discussion. As usual, you'll also spend time evaluating real-world scenarios.

The CMake build description provides support for the C and C++ languages, with limited support available for Java and various scripting languages.

## The CMake Programming Language

This section provides an overview of the CMake language syntax and features, but it discusses only a few of them in detail. After all, the language might at first seem different from GNU Make, Ant, or SCons, but you'll quickly realize that most of the concepts are the same. This section covers the following topics:

- **CMake language basics:** The basic syntax of invoking commands, setting and accessing variables, and managing source and object file properties

- **Building executable programs and libraries:** How to compile C source files into libraries or executable programs

- **Control flow:** How to test conditions, repeat operations in a loop, and define macros

- **Cross-platform support:** Locating tools, libraries, and header files on the native build machine

- **Generating a build system:** Generating a native build system (such as a makefile)

Throughout this discussion, keep in mind that the CMake build description must be easy to map into an equivalent description for other build tools. It's not reasonable for CMake to have too many advanced language features of its own. For example, if the CMake language provided support for a general-purpose scripting language, such as Python, it would be challenging to translate this into an equivalent GNU Make build description.

## CMake Language Basics

The syntax of the CMake build description file (CMakeLists.txt) isn't too hard to understand, so you can learn the basics by looking at an example. This example defines a couple variables, sets a property on two different source files, and then displays some messages:

```
1   project (basic-syntax C)
2
3   cmake_minimum_required (VERSION 2.6)
4
5   set (wife Grace)
6   set (dog Stan)
7   message ("${wife}, please take ${dog} for a walk")
8
9   set_property (SOURCE add.c PROPERTY Author Peter)
10  set_property (SOURCE mult.c PROPERTY Author John)
11  get_property (author_name SOURCE add.c PROPERTY Author)
12  message("The author of add.c is ${author_name}")
```

The first observation is that all commands are invoked using a standard syntax, with arguments separated by spaces.

```
command ( arg1 arg2 ... )
```

The arguments can be numbers, filenames, strings, or property names, with the exact syntax requirements depending on which command is used. To group multiple words into a single argument, place quotation marks around the entire string.

The `project` command (on line 1) provides a name to uniquely identify the build system. This is used by native build tools (such as Eclipse) that require a project name. It also states which programming languages (such as C, C++, or Java) are to be compiled.

The `cmake_minimum_required` command (on line 3) states that the build description uses commands supported only by CMake version 2.6 or higher. Note that `cmake_minimum_required` expects two arguments, with the first being the VERSION keyword. This informs CMake to interpret the second argument (2.6) as a version number.

Lines 5 and 6 demonstrate the creation of variables. The first argument is the variable's name, and the second is the value. Line 7 uses the familiar `${...}` syntax to access each variable's value.

Line 9 introduces the concept of a **property**, using the `set_property` command. Properties enable you to assign a value within the scope of a specific disk file. The build system simply associates the value with that file's name instead of modifying the file content itself. Other commands are free to reference the property's value.

This example sets the Author property on the `add.c` source file. This value is limited in scope to `add.c`, so it's possible to assign different Author values to other source files. Line 10 sets the Author property on `mult.c`, but to a different value.

On line 11, the `get_property` command fetches the Author property associated with the `add.c` file. The resulting value is assigned to the `author_name` variable and is displayed on line 12.

Now that you understand the basic syntax, let's see how libraries and executable programs are created.

## Building Executable Programs and Libraries

As usual, the most popular operation is to compile source files into libraries and executable programs. CMake provides a number of commands that appear similar to builder methods in SCons but still have a few interesting features of their own.

### Creating Executable Programs and Libraries

The following line of code shows how the `calculator` program is compiled from the four source files:

```
1  add_executable (calculator add sub mult calc)
```

This looks simple, but based on past experience with build tools, you can imagine that `add_executable` does a lot of work in the background. This includes constructing a suitable compiler command line, as well as adding the filenames into the dependency graph.

Another observation is that none of the filenames is given a file extension, so CMake must know the correct extension to use for each build machine. For example, when using Microsoft Windows, the resulting program is named `calculator.exe`.

Creating a new library is also similar to SCons, although with a few syntax differences:

```
1  add_library (math STATIC add sub mult)
2  add_executable (calculator calc)
3  target_link_libraries (calculator math)
```

Line 1 produces a static library by compiling `add.c`, `sub.c`, and `mult.c`. The resulting library is given a name that makes sense on the build machine, such as `libmath.a` for UNIX systems. Lines 2 and 3 state that the `calculator` program is created by compiling `calc.c` and then linking it with the `math` library.

To assist the `add_executable` and `add_library` commands, you could use `include_directories` and `link_directories`. These commands inform the C compiler where to find additional header files and tell the linker where it can find additional libraries. As you might expect, these directives are translated into the appropriate compiler flags (such as `-I` and `-L`) in the native build system.

One topic this chapter hasn't mentioned is how CMake determines the dependencies for each source file. In reality, the native build system and build tool do much of this work. If the native build tool already automates the dependency analysis, CMake has nothing to do. On the other hand, for Make-based tools that don't contain this feature, CMake adds the required functionality into the auto-generated build framework.

### Setting Compilation Flags

Varying a compilation tool's options is also a useful activity. In contrast to build tools that are more platform-dependent, CMake discourages the use of hard-coded compiler flags. Instead, the build description states which type of output is required and CMake determines the compiler flags to use.

For example, to request that CMake produce a "debug" build in which the executable program contains source-level debugging information, you add the following command to the `CMakeLists.txt` file.

```
set (CMAKE_BUILD_TYPE Debug)
```

Even though the platform-specific flags are abstracted away, CMake generates a native build system with the correct flags for that machine. For example, on a UNIX system, the `-g` flag is added to the C compiler command line.

The same approach is used for adding C preprocessor definitions because each C compiler has its own set of command-line options. This time, you set a property on either the whole directory or an individual file.

```
set_property (DIRECTORY
      PROPERTY COMPILE_DEFINITIONS TEST=1)

set_property (SOURCE add.c
      PROPERTY COMPILE_DEFINITIONS QUICKADD=1)
```

In the first case, you ask the build system to define the TEST symbol when compiling all the C files in the current directory. In the second case, you ask that the compilation of add.c also include the QUICKADD symbol. The native build system adds the required command-line options to make this happen.

### Adding Custom Commands and Targets

For more complex build requirements, you can define new compilation tools and have CMake add them to the native build system. Now look at add_custom_command, which resembles a standard GNU Make rule, and the add_custom_target command, which is similar to GNU Make's concept of phony targets.

The following example shows how the /tools/bin/make-data-file UNIX command translates the data.dat source file into the data.c output file. In this case, data.c is an autogenerated source file.

```
1   project (custom_command)
2   cmake_minimum_required(VERSION 2.6)
3
4   set (input_data_file ${PROJECT_SOURCE_DIR}/data.dat)
5   set (output_c_file data.c)
6
7   add_custom_command (
8     OUTPUT ${output_c_file}
9     COMMAND /tools/bin/make-data-file
10                < ${input_data_file}
11                > ${output_c_file}
12    DEPENDS ${input_data_file}
13  )
14
15  add_executable (print-data ${output_c_file})
```

The bulk of the work is done on lines 7–13, where the custom tool is added to the dependency graph. The OUTPUT directive (line 8) states which file will be created, whereas the DEPENDS directive (line 12) indicates the input for the command. Lines 9–11 contain the UNIX-dependent shell command to execute. This code is thus equivalent to the following GNU Make program:

```
$(output_c_file) : $(input_data_file)
    /tools/bin/make-data-file < $(input_data_file) >
$(output_c_file)
```

Line 15 is required to make sure there's a top-level target that causes the new tool to be invoked. If you don't define an executable program, the dependency graph won't be complete and you'd have no way to request that data.c be created. Unlike many other build tools, CMake makes a clear distinction between top-level targets and individual files in the build tree.

To focus more on this top-level target concept, the add_custom_target command facilitates the creation of new top-level targets and specifies the order in which they'll be executed. These are similar to GNU Make phony targets because they're not dependent on whether files are up-to-date and they don't produce any output. They're also similar to Ant targets that use the depends attribute to control the order in which targets are invoked.

```
1    project (custom_target)
2    cmake_minimum_required(VERSION 2.6)
3
4    add_custom_target (print-city ALL
5        COMMAND echo "Vancouver is a nice city"
6        COMMAND echo "Even when it rains")
7
8    add_custom_target (print-time
9        COMMAND echo "It is now 2:17pm")
10
11   add_custom_target (print-day
12        COMMAND echo "Today is Monday")
13
14   add_dependencies (print-city print-time print-day)
```

An interesting part of this code is that line 4 contains the ALL keyword to state that print-city should be invoked as part of the default build (when the developer doesn't explicitly choose a target). Also, line 14 states that print-city depends on print-time and print-day.

## Control Flow

Control flow (conditions, loops, and macros) is similar to other programming languages and doesn't require much explanation. The distinction with CMake is that the CMake generator, not the native build system, evaluates and executes control-flow commands. This might seem a little odd at first, but as long as the native build system ends up with the same behavior described in CMakeLists.txt, no problem should occur.

The syntax of the if command is fairly standard, perhaps with the exception that () is required after the else and endif statements.

```
set (my_var 1)
if (${my_var})
    message ("my_var is true")
else ()
    message ("my_var is false")
endif ()
```

It's also possible to perform Boolean operations, including NOT, AND, and OR, which, incidentally, don't require the standard ${...} syntax around variable names.

```
if (NOT my_var)
...
endif ()
```

Variables can be tested against other variables or constant values:

```
if (${my_age} EQUAL 40)
...
endif ()
```

The existence of files can be tested, although keep in mind that the test is performed at the time the native build system is created; it isn't performed by the native build tool itself.

```
if (EXISTS file1.txt)
...
endif ()
```

Likewise, you can test whether one file is newer than a second file.

```
if (file1.txt IS_NEWER_THAN file2.txt)
...
endif ()
```

Finally, for more complex scenarios, it's possible to match a variable's value against a regular expression.

```
if (${symbol_name} MATCHES "^[a-z][a-z0-9]*$")
...
endif ()
```

The macro construct is similar to a function or method definition in other languages, making it possible to reuse common code. The macro syntax is easy to understand:

```
1  project (macro)
2  cmake_minimum_required (VERSION 2.6)
3
4  macro (my_macro ARG1 ARG2 ARG3)
```

```
5     message ("The my_macro macro was passed the following
      arguments:")
6     message ("${ARG1}, ${ARG2} and ${ARG3}")
7  endmacro (my_macro)
8
9  my_macro (1 2 3)
10 my_macro (France Germany Russia)
```

Finally, the `foreach` loop iterates through a list of values:

```
1  project (foreach)
2  cmake_minimum_required (VERSION 2.6)
3
4  foreach (source_file add.c sub.c mult.c calc.c)
5    message ("Calculating cksum for ${source_file}")
6    add_custom_target (cksum-${source_file} ALL
7        COMMAND cksum ${PROJECT_SOURCE_DIR}/${source_file}
8    )
9  endforeach (source_file)
```

This last example requires more explanation. Line 6 adds a new top-level target for each of the source files in the list. Invoking one of these targets invokes the `cksum` command for the associated source file. Assuming that you generate a makefile-based build, you can invoke either all targets at once or each target individually. (The percentages are part of the autogenerated makefile framework.)

```
$ gmake
615245502 109 /home/psmith/loops/src/add.c
[ 25%] Built target cksum-add.c
2090159248 294 /home/psmith/loops/src/calc.c
[ 50%] Built target cksum-calc.c
4029979682 113 /home/psmith/loops/src/mult.c
[ 75%] Built target cksum-mult.c
3864170835 124 /home/psmith/loops/src/sub.c
[100%] Built target cksum-sub.c

$ gmake cksum-add.c
615245502 109 /home/psmith/loops/src/add.c
[100%] Built target cksum-add.c

$ gmake cksum-calc.c
2090159248 294 /home/psmith/loops/src/calc.c
[100%] Built target cksum-calc.c
```

As mentioned earlier, this looping construct isn't translated into the native build tool's looping construct. Instead, it provides the equivalent functionality by adding a number of different rules to the makefile.

## Cross-Platform Support

Continuing with the approach that a CMake build description should be platform neutral, consider how to deal with build machine differences. CMake enables you to locate specific tools and files, and also to identify which features the underlying compiler supports.

### *Locating Files and Tools on the Build Machine*

To create a build system that works on any type of build machine, you can't be too specific about where tools and files are located. At the very least, the tool or file must exist somewhere on the file system, but each machine might store it in a different location.

CMake provides a number of commands to search for files and tools in all the standard paths. The following code locates the `ls` program, the `stdio.h` header file, and the standard C math library.

```
1   project (finding)
2   cmake_minimum_required (VERSION 2.6)
3
4   find_program (LS_PATH ls)
5   message ("The path to the ls program is ${LS_PATH}")
6
7   find_file (STDIO_H_PATH stdio.h)
8   message ("The path to the stdio.h file is ${STDIO_H_
    PATH}")
9
10  find_library (LIB_MATH_PATH m /usr/local/lib /usr/lib64)
11  message ("The path to the math library is ${LIB_MATH_
    PATH}")
```

When this build description is translated into the native build system (by running the `cmake` tool), you see the following output:

```
The path to the ls program is /bin/ls
The path to the stdio.h file is /usr/include/stdio.h
The path to the math library is /usr/lib/libm.so
```

Each type of build machine might give different results, so the build description must reference these variables to access the tool instead of using a hardcoded pathname.

Note that line 10 explicitly asks the `find_library` command to search for the math library in `/usr/local/lib` and `/usr/lib64`. These paths are searched in addition to CMake's default locations.

To make it easier to write build description files, CMake provides code modules for locating popular tools and libraries. As an example, by including the `FindPerl` module, you can easily locate your build machine's Perl interpreter:

```
1   project (find-perl)
2   cmake_minimum_required (VERSION 2.6)
3
4   include (FindPerl)
5   if (PERL_FOUND)
6     execute_process (
7         COMMAND ${PERL_EXECUTABLE} ${PROJECT_SOURCE_DIR}/
          config.pl
8     )
9   else ()
10    message (SEND_ERROR "There is no perl interpreter on
      this system")
11  endif ()
```

The FindPerl module (on line 4) contains a small amount of CMake build description code, which is included by the CMakeLists.txt file. This module detects the presence of the Perl interpreter no matter what type of build machine you're executing on (such as Linux or Windows). If Perl can be located, the PERL_EXECUTABLE variable contains the absolute path of the program, and the PERL_FOUND variable is set to a true value.

Notice that the execute_process command (on line 6) passes the config. pl file into the Perl interpreter. This invocation takes place as part of *generating* the native build system. In contrast, the add_custom_command directive you saw earlier adds references to Perl *within* the native build system, to be invoked when the native build tool is used.

### Testing for Source Code Capabilities

A second type of cross-platform support is the capability to test the underlying compilers. Before attempting to compile a program, you must determine whether the build machine's compiler provides all the required functions and header files. If it doesn't, you must substitute your own implementation or even abort the build process.

CMake provides the try_compile and try_run commands, enabling you to determine whether a snippet of C/C++ code compiles correctly. If it does compile, you can try to execute the program to see if it provides the correct output. To make it easy to use these commands, CMake wraps them in a number of prewritten macros. For example:

```
1   project (try-compile)
2   cmake_minimum_required(VERSION 2.6)
3
4   include (CheckFunctionExists)
5   include (CheckStructHasMember)
6
7   CHECK_FUNCTION_EXISTS(vsnprintf VSNPRINTF_EXISTS)
8   if (NOT VSNPRINTF_EXISTS)
```

```
 9    message (SEND_ERROR "vsnprintf not available on this
      build machine")
10    endif ()
11
12    CHECK_STRUCT_HAS_MEMBER("struct rusage" ru_stime wait.h
      HAS_STIME)
13    if (NOT HAS_STIME)
14      message (SEND_ERROR "ru_stime field not available in
        struct rusage")
15    endif ()
```

Lines 7–10 demonstrate the use of the CHECK_FUNCTION_EXISTS macro, as defined in the CheckFunctionExists module (line 4). By using the try_compile command, this macro sets the VSNPRINTF_EXISTS variable to indicate whether the vsnprintf function was available to the underlying C compiler or linker.

Lines 12–15 perform a similar operation, but this time to determine whether the definition of struct rusage contains the ru_stime field. If not, the associated variable is left undefined and the build system fails with an error message.

## Generating a Native Build System

As discussed earlier, using CMake involves two main phases. The first is to process the CMakeLists.txt file and generate a native build system. The second phase is to use a native build tool to actually compile the software. This generation process is a key part of CMake's design, providing support for a wide range of operating systems and native build tools.

### Generating the Default Build System

The easiest way to generate a build system is to accept the default configuration. The developer simply creates a directory for the object files and then invokes the cmake tool within that directory. No file in the source directory is ever modified, making it possible to generate more than one object directory from the same source tree.

```
$ mkdir obj
$ cd obj
$ cmake ../src
-- The C compiler identification is GNU
-- The CXX compiler identification is GNU
-- Check for working C compiler: /usr/bin/gcc
-- Check for working C compiler: /usr/bin/gcc -- works
-- Detecting C compiler ABI info
-- Detecting C compiler ABI info - done
-- Check for working CXX compiler: /usr/bin/c++
```

```
-- Check for working CXX compiler: /usr/bin/c++ -- works
-- Detecting CXX compiler ABI info
-- Detecting CXX compiler ABI info - done
-- Configuring done
-- Generating done
-- Build files have been written to: /home/psmith/obj
```

CMake attempts to locate each of the required development tools and determines which version of each tool is in use. Any `try_compile` and `try_run` commands in your `CMakeLists.txt` file are also executed at this time.

Assuming that you generated a Make-based native build system (the default for Linux and UNIX), the object directory now contains the following directory structure:

```
Makefile
cmake_install.cmake
CMakeCache.txt
CMakeFiles
CMakeFiles/calculator.dir
CMakeFiles/calculator.dir/cmake_clean.cmake
CMakeFiles/calculator.dir/build.make
CMakeFiles/calculator.dir/depend.make
CMakeFiles/calculator.dir/progress.make
CMakeFiles/calculator.dir/link.txt
CMakeFiles/calculator.dir/flags.make
CMakeFiles/calculator.dir/DependInfo.cmake
...
CMakeFiles/progress.make
CMakeFiles/Makefile.cmake
CMakeFiles/CMakeDetermineCompilerABI_C.bin
CMakeFiles/CMakeOutput.log
CMakeFiles/CMakeCXXCompiler.cmake
```

This build framework certainly includes a lot of files, but the most important files to notice are these:

- `Makefile`: The main entry point for the native build system.

- `CMakeCache.txt`: A text-based configuration file that contains the auto-discovered settings for this build machine. (You'll learn more about this shortly.)

- `CMakeFiles/`: A directory that contains all the autogenerated framework files. These are included by the main makefile.

The final step is to invoke the native build tool; in this case, you use `gmake`.

```
$ gmake
Scanning dependencies of target calculator
[ 25%] Building C object CMakeFiles/calculator.dir/add.c.o
[ 50%] Building C object CMakeFiles/calculator.dir/sub.c.o
[ 75%] Building C object CMakeFiles/calculator.dir/mult.c.o
[100%] Building C object CMakeFiles/calculator.dir/calc.c.o
Linking C executable calculator
[100%] Built target calculator
```

Notice how the autogenerated build framework displays a significant amount of customized output instead of simply showing the underlying commands as in the GNU Make examples.

### Generating a Nondefault Build System

One of CMake's strengths is flexibility in selecting the type of native build system to be generated. By passing the -G option to the cmake command, you can override the default selection. For example, to generate a Visual Studio 10 project, enter the following command on your Windows build machine:

```
cmake -G "Visual Studio 10" ..\src
```

Likewise, to generate a build system for Eclipse CDT version 4 on Linux, use the following:

```
cmake -G "Eclipse CDT4 - Unix Makefiles" ../src
```

Naturally, it's possible to add more CMake generators if your choice of development environment isn't already supported, but doing so isn't an easy task.

### Customizing the Generation Step

Although CMake's default behavior is to autodetect the build machine's compilation tools, it often makes sense to overwrite these values. In addition to the basic cmake command, you can use the ccmake command (see Figure 9.2) to interactively configure the native build system.

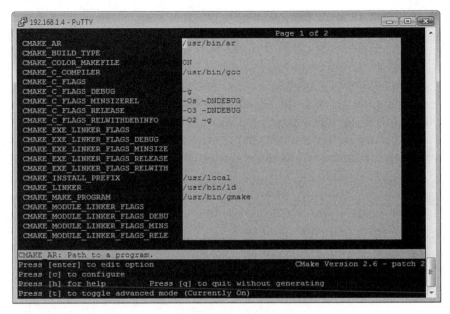

**Figure 9.2** *Configuration using the ccmake configuration tool.*

The variables in this list are collectively known as the **cache** and are stored in the object directory's `CMakeCache.txt` file. Each variable has a default value but can easily be modified to customize the build process. The following are some of the most commonly used cache variables:

- `CMAKE_AR`, `CMAKE_C_COMPILER`, and `CMAKE_LINKER`: The absolute path to the library archiver tool, the C compiler, and the object file linker. These can be overwritten if your build system uses custom tools in place of the build machine's standard tools.

- `CMAKE_MAKE_PROGRAM`: The absolute path to the native build tool, such as `/usr/bin/gmake`. This can be overwritten to use a nonstandard version of the tool.

- `CMAKE_BUILD_TYPE`: The type of the build tree you want to create. Possible values include these:

  - `Debug`: The generated object files and executable program will contain debugging information.

  - `Release`: The resulting executable program will be fully optimized and won't contain debug information.

- • RelWithDebInfo: The executable program will be optimized but will also contain debug information.

- • MinSizeRel: The executable program will be optimized to require as little memory space as possible

- • CMAKE_C_FLAGS_*: For each of the four build types just listed, these variables state which C compilation flags should be used. That is, depending on the value in the CMAKE_BUILD_TYPE variable, CMake will use the C compiler flags listed in the corresponding cache variable.

- • CMAKE_EXE_LINKER_FLAGS_*: Similar, but provides the linker flags for each of the four build types.

As you'll see later, it's possible to define your own cache variables and initialize them to a default value. The CMakeLists.txt build description can read all cache values as if they were normal variables. The values can also be written to using the standard set command.

### Translation from CMakeLists.txt to the Native Build System

A final consideration in using CMake is to understand when and how each of the CMake commands is translated into the native build system. The chapter has already touched on this topic briefly, but it's worth mentioning the detail a second time.

CMake commands can be divided into two main groups:

1. Commands that take effect immediately when the cmake tool is invoked. These include control-flow commands such as if, foreach, and macro, as well as commands for setting and displaying variable values.

2. Commands that are translated into native build system constructs. These include add_executable, add_library, add_custom_command, and add_custom_target.

As you can imagine, the second category of commands contributes to the native build system's dependency graph. On the other hand, the first set of commands enables you to control what gets added. You can use variables to control the filenames that are added, loops to individually add a large number of files, and macros to simplify the build description. The important fact is that only the commands that impact the dependency graph are directly translated to the native build system.

Here's a simple example to illustrate the concept. The following build description compiles two separate programs, `calc` and `calculator`, both using the same source files.

```
1   project (generating)
2   cmake_minimum_required(VERSION 2.6)
3
4   set (prog1 calculator)
5   set (prog2 calc)
6
7   execute_process (
8     COMMAND date
9     OUTPUT_VARIABLE TIME_NOW
10  )
11
12  foreach (prog_name ${prog1} ${prog2})
13    message ("Constructing program ${prog_name} at ${TIME_
      NOW}")
14    add_executable (${prog_name} add sub mult calc)
15  endforeach ()
```

To make things interesting, the description is more complex than it needs to be, although you shouldn't have trouble following along. When the `cmake` tool is invoked, you'll see the following output (note the additional messages):

```
$ cmake ../src
-- The C compiler identification is GNU
-- The CXX compiler identification is GNU
-- Check for working C compiler: /usr/bin/gcc
-- Check for working C compiler: /usr/bin/gcc -- works
-- Detecting C compiler ABI info
-- Detecting C compiler ABI info - done
-- Check for working CXX compiler: /usr/bin/c++
-- Check for working CXX compiler: /usr/bin/c++ -- works
-- Detecting CXX compiler ABI info
-- Detecting CXX compiler ABI info - done
Constructing program calculator at Sun Jun  6 16:05:28 PDT
➥2010
Constructing program calc at Sun Jun  6 16:05:28 PDT 2010
-- Configuring done
-- Generating done
-- Build files have been written to: /home/psmith/obj
```

You can learn from this output that both `set` commands were executed, the `execute_process` command invoked the `date` shell command, the body of the `foreach` loop was executed twice, and the `message` command displayed two messages on the output. Effectively, the entire program was executed at the same time the native build system was generated.

If you also take the view that `add_executable` is supposed to do nothing more than add information to the native build system, its task is also complete.

However, the executable programs (two of them) aren't actually created until you invoke the native build tool.

```
$ gmake
Scanning dependencies of target calc
[ 12%] Building C object CMakeFiles/calc.dir/add.c.o
[ 25%] Building C object CMakeFiles/calc.dir/sub.c.o
[ 37%] Building C object CMakeFiles/calc.dir/mult.c.o
[ 50%] Building C object CMakeFiles/calc.dir/calc.c.o
Linking C executable calc
[ 50%] Built target calc
Scanning dependencies of target calculator
[ 62%] Building C object CMakeFiles/calculator.dir/add.c.o
[ 75%] Building C object CMakeFiles/calculator.dir/sub.c.o
[ 87%] Building C object CMakeFiles/calculator.dir/mult.c.o
[100%] Building C object CMakeFiles/calculator.dir/calc.c.o
Linking C executable calculator
[100%] Built target calculator
```

It looks odd that all C files are compiled twice, but that's exactly what CMake is asked to do here. This makes sense, given the way the underlying makefile framework stores object files in `calc.dir` or `calculator.dir` instead of a directory that all programs share.

In summary, the commands in the CMake build description file aren't translated directly into commands in the native build system. (There's no one-to-one mapping of commands.) Instead, the native build system provides the same behavior, but using a different set of commands.

## Other Interesting Features and Further Reading

CMake is certainly a complex and powerful tool, although this chapter hasn't gone into too much detail on all the features. This chapter has focused on the generation of the native build system instead of everything CMake supports. Following are a few other features that the CMake tool supports:

- **String manipulation:** The `string` command provides regular expression matching, substring replacement, string comparison, and conversion to upper- or lowercase.

- **List manipulation:** The `list` command provides support for inserting, removing, searching, and sorting values within a list.

- **File manipulation:** The `file` command enables a CMake build description to read or write external data files, as well as to create new directories or remove old files.

- **Mathematical expressions:** The `math` command provides a simple interface for computing expressions. Only the basic arithmetic, logical, and bitwise operations are supported.

- **Customizing data files:** The `configure_file` command generates a data file from a template by replacing all occurrences of `${VAR_NAME}` or `@VAR_NAME@` with the value of that variable.

- **Testing of executable programs:** The CTest module is an extension of CMake that provides automated testing of executable programs. By adding test information into the `CMakeLists.txt` file, executable programs can be sanity-tested immediately after they're built.

- **Packaging and installation:** The CPack module is another extension that supports the creation of software release packages, ready for installation on the target machine. Chapter 13, "Software Packaging and Installation," discusses packaging and installation in more detail.

- **Platform-neutral shell commands:** CMake provides built-in support for common shell script operations. In many build tools, a developer is left to deal with the difficulties of using shell commands that vary from one machine to the next. To solve this problem CMake provides a uniform interface for invoking common shell operations. This is particularly important when compiling software for both Windows and UNIX when the shell commands are significantly different.

If you're interested in using CMake's more advanced features, you're strongly encouraged to learn more from the product's own documentation. The online wiki pages are available on the CMake web site [61], although advanced users should consider reading a book on the topic [62].

---

# Real-World Build System Scenarios

As with the other build tools described in this book, this section considers how CMake can address a number of real-world build system scenarios. CMake's language features are similar to those in other build tools, so this section describes the detail of these solutions when it's not already obvious.

## Scenario 1: Source Code in a Single Directory

The first scenario is extremely simple to implement, making CMake a great tool to use for small projects.

```
1   project (scenario-1)
2   add_executable (calculator add sub mult calc)
```

Keep in mind that when CMake generates a native build system, it adds a number of standard features, such as automatic dependency analysis.

## Scenario 2: Source Code in Multiple Directories

The second scenario shows how to use CMake for larger projects in which the build description is divided across multiple directories. You haven't yet seen the add_subdirectory command, but there should be no surprises in the way it works.

The first build description file, src/CMakeLists.txt, appears at the top level of the build tree and recursively includes content from the subdirectories.

```
1   project (scenario-2)
2
3   cmake_minimum_required(VERSION 2.6)
4
5   add_subdirectory(libmath)
6   add_subdirectory(libprint)
7   add_subdirectory(calc)
```

The second build description file, src/libmath/CMakeLists.txt, builds the Math library using the add_library command.

```
1   add_library(Math clock letter number)
```

Next, src/libprint/CMakeLists.txt builds the Print library in the same way.

```
1   add_library(Print banner.c center.c normal.c)
```

Finally, src/calc/CMakeLists.txt pulls everything together by creating an executable file and linking it with the Math and Print libraries.

```
1   add_executable (calculator calc.c)
2   target_link_libraries (calculator Math Print)
```

To make use of this build description, you again execute the cmake tool. This step is the same as in previous examples, so the output isn't interesting to show. Finally, you use the native build tool (in this case, GNU Make) to compile the finished product.

```
$ gmake
Scanning dependencies of target Math
[ 14%] Building C object libmath/CMakeFiles/Math.dir/
clock.c.o
```

```
[ 28%] Building C object libmath/CMakeFiles/Math.dir/
       letter.c.o
[ 42%] Building C object libmath/CMakeFiles/Math.dir/
       number.c.o
Linking C static library libMath.a
[ 42%] Built target Math
Scanning dependencies of target Print
[ 57%] Building C object libprint/CMakeFiles/Print.dir/
       banner.c.o
[ 71%] Building C object libprint/CMakeFiles/Print.dir/
       center.c.o
[ 85%] Building C object libprint/CMakeFiles/Print.dir/
       normal.c.o
Linking C static library libPrint.a
[ 85%] Built target Print
Scanning dependencies of target calculator
[100%] Building C object calc/CMakeFiles/calculator.dir/
       calc.c.o
Linking C executable calculator
[100%] Built target calculator
```

One of the many advantages of using a CMake-generated build system is that the subbuild problem is solved and dependencies into other subdirectories are dealt with correctly. For example, if you build in the libmath directory, only that library is rebuilt:

```
$ cd obj/libmath
$ gmake
[100%] Built target Math
```

However, if you build in the calc directory, both the Print and Math libraries are also considered for recompilation:

```
$ cd obj/calc
$ gmake
[ 42%] Built target Print
[ 85%] Built target Math
[100%] Built target calculator
```

As you can see, CMake generates a fully featured Make-based build system without requiring the developer to understand anything about the underlying framework.

## Scenario 3: Defining New Compilation Tools

Adding the mathcomp compiler into a CMake-based build system requires using the add_custom_command directive. In addition, you use the execute_process command to gather the dependencies. Finally, you wrap the whole solution inside a macro to make it more convenient to use.

```
1    project (scenario-3)
2
3    cmake_minimum_required(VERSION 2.6)
4
5    macro (mathcomp FUNC_NAME INPUT_FILE OUTPUT_FILE)
6       execute_process(
7           COMMAND /tools/bin/mathcomp -d ${INPUT_FILE}
8           OUTPUT_VARIABLE DEPS
9       )
10      separate_arguments(DEPS)
11
12      add_custom_command(
13          OUTPUT ${OUTPUT_FILE}
14          COMMAND /tools/bin/mathcomp -c -o ${OUTPUT_FILE}
15                  -f ${FUNC_NAME} ${INPUT_FILE}
16          DEPENDS ${DEPS}
17      )
18   endmacro (mathcomp)
19
20   mathcomp(equations ${PROJECT_SOURCE_DIR}/equations.math
         equations.c)
21   add_executable (calculator calculator.c equations.c)
```

Lines 5–18 define a macro that encapsulates the complexity of this solution. Line 20 invokes this macro to generate the equations.c output file from the equations.math input file. The build system executes from within the object directory, so you use the PROJECT_SOURCE_DIR variable to access the source file.

Looking now at the macro definition, lines 6–9 invoke the mathcomp compiler with the -d option, to determine the dependencies present in the .math file. The output from this command is placed in the DEPS variable. On line 10, this space-separated output is translated into a list of separate filenames.

The add_custom_command directive on lines 12–17 is now fairly straightforward. You already know the name of the output file, and you've just computed the list of dependencies. The /tools/bin/mathcomp compiler is ready to be invoked in the same way you did for GNU Make, Ant, and SCons.

One final observation is that add_custom_command makes the new tool available for use by the native build system. That is, when the native build system needs to create the equations.c file, it directly invokes the mathcomp compiler. However, notice that the execute_process command determines the source file dependencies. This command is used only when the cmake tool is initially invoked, which is before the native build tool is ever called into action.

The limitation here is that when source files are modified, the native build system won't notice if any dependencies have changed. Before long, the build system starts using outdated information. CMake solves this problem for C and C++ files by requiring the IMPLICIT_DEPENDS keyword for the add_custom_command directive. To support this same feature for the mathcomp tool, the standard CMake system must be modified.

## Scenario 4: Building with Multiple Variants

The multivariant scenario takes advantage of the configuration cache, where the user can indicate which CPU type to compile for (i386, powerpc, or alpha). The build system then validates the selection and chooses a suitable compiler for that CPU type. Unlike the GNU Make and SCons solutions, there's no requirement to create a per-CPU build directory. Instead, CMake already requires users to create their own directory for object files.

```
$ mkdir obj-alpha
$ cd obj-alpha
$ cmake -DPLATFORM=alpha ../src
```

Alternatively, the ccmake command (refer to Figure 9.2) can provide a more interactive user experience. The CMake build description is as follows:

```
1   project (scenario-4)
2
3   set (PLATFORM i386 CACHE STRING "CPU Type: i386, powerpc
    or alpha")
4
5   if (NOT ${PLATFORM} MATCHES "^(i386|powerpc|alpha)$")
6     message(SEND_ERROR
7         "Invalid PLATFORM. Must be one of i386, powerpc or
        alpha")
8   endif ()
9
10  message("Compiling code for platform ${PLATFORM}")
11
12  set (CMAKE_C_COMPILER /tools/bin/gcc-${PLATFORM})
13
14  add_executable (calculator add sub mult calc)
```

Line 3 demonstrates the creation of a new cache variable named PLATFORM. This command is similar to a standard set command, except that you use the CACHE keyword to indicate that the user can configure the value when generating a new native build system. As usual, the default CPU type is i386; in this case, a text string ("CPU Type: i386, powerpc or alpha") is provided as a prompt to the user.

The rest of the build description is easy to understand. Lines 5–10 validate the user's input and provide a suitable message. Line 12 selects the compiler to be used (CMAKE_C_COMPILER is another standard cache variable). Finally, line 14 generates the executable program.

## Scenario 5: Cleaning a Build Tree

As you might expect, the native build system created by CMake already supports a "clean" target for any object files it knows about. If `add_executable` or `add_library` is used to compile source files, CMake already knows the name of the executable or library file, as well as any intermediate object files. For generated files that aren't automatically detected, the name can be listed in the `ADDITIONAL_MAKE_CLEAN_FILES` property. This is a per-directory property that contains the list of files to be removed from that directory.

## Scenario 6: Debugging Incorrect Builds

CMake's two-phase approach to building software makes debugging a little more challenging. In some cases, the problem lies in the original `CMakeLists.txt` file, but in less common cases, a problem might arise in the native (auto-generated) build system. Even if the bug was caused by an error in the high-level description, you might locate the problem only when running the native build tool.

Start by focusing on the debug facilities that the CMake tool provides. These are used to analyze CMake's flow of control as it generates the native build system:

- The `--system-information` **flag:** Provides an extensive dump of information about the build machine as it executes the `cmake` command. This includes the location of compilation tools, the choice of command-line options to pass to each tool, and various other system-dependent parameters. If you suspect that an invalid tool or command-line option is used, start by validating this output.

- The `--trace` **flag:** Provides a line-by-line trace of CMake's execution. Every variable assignment, condition, loop, macro, and command is displayed in the order in which it's executed. By following along with the trace output, you can validate your expectations on how the program should execute.

If observing the CMake generator in action didn't solve your problem, try using the native build tool's debugging features. Each build tool, such as GNU Make, has its own range of options for tracing the build system's execution. If you manage to locate the source of the problem, you need to work backward and identify which lines in the `CMakeLists.txt` are causing the issue.

The tricky part is when the native build system contains a complex framework that you had no involvement in writing. You might be able to scour the framework to locate the problem, but executing the build and watching the output is usually much easier. Invoking `gmake` with the `VERBOSE=1` flag provides a nicely formatted output to show each of the compilation commands.

In the worst case, the native build system might contain a bug, even though the `CMakeLists.txt` file is correct. In this case, you have no choice but to fix the CMake tool itself. Some people might find it tempting to fix the bug directly in the native build system, but the CMake generator would soon overwrite any changes.

## Praise and Criticism

CMake isn't as well known as other build tools, such as GNU Make and Ant, so there isn't as much feedback on the use of the tool. However, vocal users have provided the following opinion.

### Praise

- CMake can use the same description file to generate a build system for a range of different platforms. This is particularly important for Microsoft Windows systems, which haven't typically received much support in the open-source world.

- The CMake build description language is simple to use, and creating a new build system is trivial.

- The generation of native build systems is high quality, with a lot of focus placed on the correctness of the build process. This contrasts with a standard GNU Make build system, in which developers must create and debug their own framework.

- CMake is just as easy to use as the SCons build tool, and the resulting build system is much faster.

- The integration of CPack for packaging and installation and CTest for testing purposes allows for a complete end-to-end build system.

- The special-purpose build description language is built into the `cmake` tool. Therefore, there's no need to install an additional language interpreter (such as Python) on the build machine.

## Criticism

In contrast, the following concerns have been raised regarding the CMake tool:

- Autogenerated build systems don't give you the complete power you might expect. If you're creating a complex build system, you might feel inclined to develop directly with the native build tool. This is also true if the autogenerated build system is buggy.

- The CMake tool introduces yet another language instead of building upon the power of an existing language. The learning curve for CMake is quite high, especially with all the advanced features that use an unfamiliar syntax.

- The CMake documentation is not as readable as the documentation for other build tools. You might find that some of the examples aren't explicit enough to provide the help you need; in some cases, the documentation doesn't match the tool's behavior.

- Although CMake does support cross-platform development, in many places it's still necessary to write different build description code for a Linux environment versus a Windows environment.

## Evaluation

Let's evaluate CMake against the build system quality measurements discussed in Chapter 1, "Build System Overview."

- **Convenience:** *Good*: CMake wins points for supporting a high-level abstraction of the build system, making it easy for developers to describe their build process. However, CMake doesn't provide a general-purpose programming language, making it hard to express complex requirements. Additionally, the capability to debug build problems largely depends on the native build tool (such as GNU Make), as well as an understanding of CMake's autogenerated framework.

- **Correctness:** *Excellent*: Regardless of which native build tool is used, CMake ensures that multidirectory support is enabled, along with automatically detecting dependencies.

- **Performance:** *Excellent*: Although it depends entirely on the native build tool, CMake has the potential to create a high-performance build system.

- **Scalability:** *Excellent*: For the same reason, CMake can generate a highly scalable build system supporting a large number of source files and file system directories.

CMake is an excellent choice of build tool for C/C++-based projects, and directly competes with SCons in this area. CMake however has the added value of supporting native build tools, enabling the use of platform or vendor-specific optimizations for those tools, some of which we'll discuss in Chapter 19, "Faster Builds." CMake isn't a good choice for Java or C# development.

## Similar Build Tools

CMake isn't the only build tool that generates a native build system, and it certainly wasn't the first. This section briefly discusses the Automake and Qmake build tools, which both take a similar approach.

### Automake

The Automake build tool is part of the Autotools suite [63], which is discussed in Chapter 15, "Build Machines." The most common tool from the suite is Autoconf, which is responsible for generating the GNU `configure` script that many UNIX developers are familiar with. In contrast, Automake focuses on creating a makefile framework based on a high-level description of the build process.

The Autotools suite is tightly coupled to the GNU development environment and is therefore dependent on UNIX-like systems. The build description for Automake is simple to understand, at least for small programs. Here's the `Makefile.am` file for the `calculator` program:

```
1  bin_PROGRAMS = calculator
2  calculator_SOURCES = add.c sub.c mult.c calc.c
```

The syntax of each variable name indicates the purpose of the values on the right side. For example, `bin_PROGRAMS` indicates that the `calculator` program should be installed into the default `bin` directory whenever the user issues the `make install` command. Also, the `calculator_SOURCES` variable provides the list of files to be compiled and linked into the `calculator` program.

As you might expect, running the `automake` tool on this build description creates a makefile that provides all the default targets (including `all`, `clean`, and `install`). It also hides the complexities of creating a makefile framework, such as automatic dependency analysis.

CMake is generally considered as a replacement for the Autotools suite, especially for software that needs to run on non-UNIX systems. CMake's capability to adapt to different build machines makes it a worthy competitor for Automake. On the other hand, the large amount of legacy software that uses Autotools suggests it'll continue to be one of the most popular makefile-generation systems.

## Qmake

The Qmake build tool is part of the Qt development environment [64]. Qt was specifically designed for cross-platform application development, providing a uniform set of GUI functions across all supported platforms. Naturally, the Qmake tool was also designed with this goal in mind.

The build description file for Qmake is similar to that of other tools, at least for simple programs:

```
1  TARGET = calculator
2  SOURCES = add.c sub.c mult.c calc.c
3  HEADERS = numbers.h
```

Qmake can generate either a makefile framework or a Visual Studio project. Because Qmake is targeted at Qt developers, the build system automatically includes the necessary C/C++ header file directories and libraries to support a Qt-based application.

If you're planning to develop a cross-platform application, both Qt and Qmake are definitely worth investigating.

## Summary

A key feature of the CMake build tool is that it can generate a native build system for a wide range of supported platforms. The software developer can focus on creating a single platform-neutral build description (CMakeLists.txt) and rely on CMake to generate the native build system.

The CMake language provides support for conditions, loops, and macros, as well as more advanced commands for compiling executable programs and libraries. CMake doesn't need to map these constructs directly into those supported by the native build tool, but instead it provides a build system with equivalent functionality.

CMake variables are similar to those in other programming languages, but the use of per-file and per-directory properties is somewhat unique. Among other things, properties control which compilation flags are used when compiling each of the source files.

Support for cross-platform development is also available. A CMake program can query the build machine to locate tools, header files, and libraries and can test the C/C++ compilers to discover which language features are supported.

CMake is certainly a build tool to be taken seriously for C/C++ development because it removes much of the complexity involved in creating a build framework. CMake's support for a wide range of operating systems and native build tools makes it a strong candidate for developing cross-platform software.

# Chapter 10

# Eclipse

The fifth and final build tool this book studies isn't actually a build tool at all. The Eclipse integrated development environment (IDE) [33] provides a complete set of development tools for code editing, compilation, version control, testing, and tracking of tasks. The build functionality in Eclipse is just one part of the wider toolset, and in many cases, the compilation happens behind the scenes; you don't even know it's taking place.

Although Eclipse is most well known for its Java support, it also provides development tools for C, C++, Python, Perl, PHP, UML, and many other languages. Eclipse is fully extensible, and any vendor can add support for its own tools and languages. Since 2001, Eclipse has been an open-source product, but it continues to be sponsored by IBM (the original owner) and a number of other industry leaders.

If you haven't considered using Eclipse in your own development environment, you should definitely do so. Even if you're an expert with editors such as `vi` or `emacs`, Eclipse can still increase your productivity. Eclipse can suggest what you might want to type next; it can collapse parts of the code you're not interested in seeing; it enables you to browse the classes defined within your program; and it can highlight compilation errors a few seconds after you type the bad code. Eclipse comes with a learning curve to use these exciting features, but most users see their productivity increase in the long term.

As you might expect, this chapter focuses exclusively on the compilation features built into Eclipse. Although Eclipse can compile a wide range of Java programs, including web services and JSF and JSP code, this chapter focuses on building standard Java classes and JAR files, using the Java Development Tools (JDT) plug-in. As usual, you'll consider how Eclipse can be used in real-world scenarios.

The key observation to make as you study Eclipse is that the edit-compile-run cycle is dramatically different. No longer are these phases clearly defined: They don't have to be, because the Eclipse GUI makes them work together seamlessly. You'll also notice that you don't write a build description file (such as a make-file): Eclipse already knows enough about the structure of the software. Relying on the GUI to provide the build functionality makes constructing a build system easy but also limits the set of available features.

This chapter follows the same format as for the previous build tools.

## The Eclipse Concepts and GUI

Eclipse doesn't provide a programming language to describe the build process, so it's not possible to summarize the syntax of the language. Instead, this section looks at the GUI operations that enable the tool to infer which build steps are required. For example, if the developer adds a new source file into an Eclipse project, the build system automatically compiles that source file and makes it part of the application. On the other hand, if the user wants to exclude a source file, there's also a menu item to allow that.

For more complex build environments, Eclipse provides a number of prefer-ences to configure the tool. This covers much of the same functionality that a text-based tool provides; although, everything is configured by clicking on GUI widgets instead of setting variables or writing commands.

In studying the Eclipse JDT build environment, you'll follow the workflow of a typical programmer:

- **Creating projects:** How a new project is created, and how the source and object files are managed within the build tree

- **Building a project:** How an Eclipse Java project is compiled, how that project can depend on other projects, and how compiler options are speci-fied

- **Running a project:** How an Eclipse project can be executed in one of the many supported runtime environments

- **Utilizing the internal project model:** How Eclipse can improve productivity by constantly updating an internal model of the program

- **Other build features:** Other interesting Eclipse features related to building software

Let's start with the basics to create a new project and add source files.

# Creating Projects

Before you can do any development work in the Eclipse environment, you must start a new **project**. This creates a directory on your file system in which to store files, and configures Eclipse to use the appropriate Java runtime environment and build options.

When Eclipse first starts, you're prompted to select a directory for your **workspace**. That is, you must decide which file system directory should contain all your source files. A single workspace can contain any number of projects, with each project potentially being a different type. Figure 10.1 shows a workspace with five Java projects, with only the first project (`Example Project`) expanded to show the Java source files.

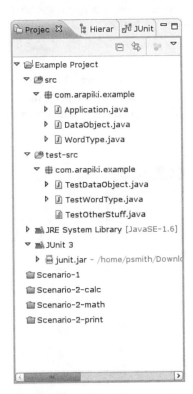

**Figure 10.1** *The Project Explorer view, showing the current Eclipse projects and the files they contain.*

If you look carefully, you can see that Example Project has a different icon from the `Scenario` projects at the bottom of the listing. This indicates that only `Example Project` is available to be edited; the remaining projects are in the closed state.

Looking at that first project more closely, you can see two top-level directories named `src`, for the main application code, and `test-src`, for the unit-testing code. It's useful to keep these separate so you don't confuse the production code with the test code. Note, however, that both sets of source files are stored within the `com.arapiki.example` package, so the test code still has access to package-private classes.

One point that's not so obvious is that `TestOtherStuff.java` has been excluded from the build process. Even though the file is still in the project's directory, the different icon tells you that it won't be compiled and linked into the final application. In the Eclipse environment, it's important to notice icons because they often provide important detail.

Finally, you can see that this project uses version 1.6 of the JRE System library, as well as version 3 of the JUnit library, for unit-testing purposes. An Eclipse project can contain any number of third-party JAR files.

### Selecting a Project Type

To get this new project started, you use the `File, New, Project` menu option and select the type of project you need (see Figure 10.2). Eclipse provides a wide array of project types, and you can extend this list by adding third-party plug-ins.

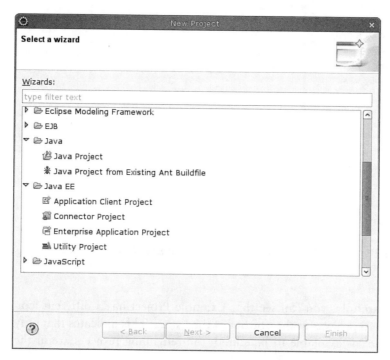

**Figure 10.2** *Selecting the type of a new Eclipse project.*

Even though all projects contain source code, the project's type dictates how those files can be edited or compiled. As an example, a code editor must know how to perform syntax coloring on the source code, as well as how to suggest code completion hints. The project must also be aware of how to compile the source code into an executable program.

A regular Java project contains a collection of `.java` files that are compiled and built into a Java application or JAR file. On the other hand, a Java Enterprise Edition (JEE) project automatically includes a deployment descriptor, the necessary Java EE libraries, and a means to deploy the program on an application server. Clearly, it pays to understand what each type of project can offer you.

In this case, the example focuses on simple Java applications, so see what happens when you create a Java project. The next step in the sequence is to provide some high-level detail (see Figure 10.3).

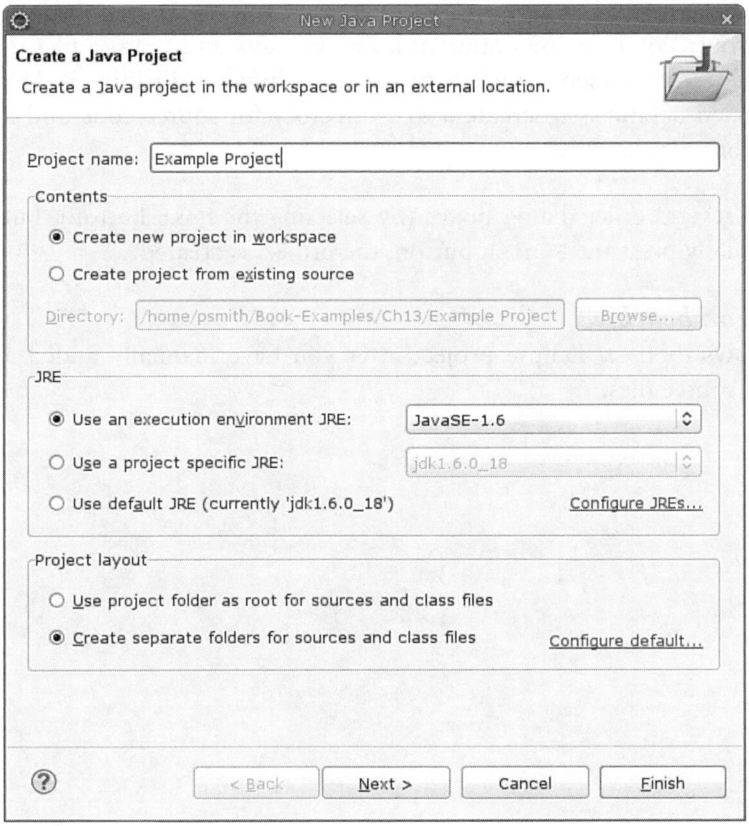

**Figure 10.3** *Creating a new Java project.*

This figure shows the basic dialog box where the user can specify the detail of the new project. Plenty of options are available for configuring more advanced parameters, but let's focus on the basics:

- **Project name:** This is the name of the underlying file system directory (within the workspace). It's also used when changing the project's configuration options.

- **Contents:** In many cases, you'll start with an empty project directory, although it's also possible to start with source code that's already on your file system. Another option is to populate the project directory from a version-control system, such as CVS.

- **JRE:** Your source code might depend on a particular version of the Java Runtime Environment. You can specify the exact file system path to your JRE or simply let Eclipse choose any of the JREs that match your version requirements.

- **Project layout:** You have the option of keeping `.java` and `.class` files in the same directory or separating them into two different directories. The recommended default is to create a `src` directory for source code and a `bin` directory for class files.

You can use several other dialog boxes (by selecting the `Next` button), but when you eventually press the `Finish` button, the project is created.

### The Eclipse Workbench

Figure 10.4 shows the new Eclipse project after you have manually added a number of Java source files.

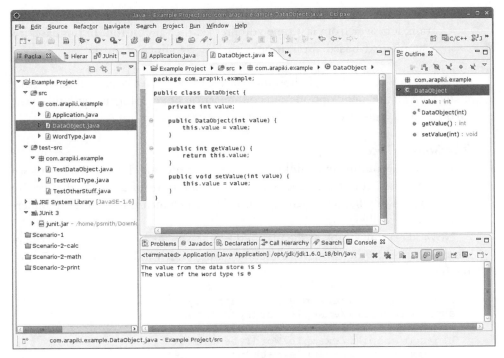

**Figure 10.4** *The main Eclipse workbench window.*

The entire Eclipse GUI consists of a number of smaller windows, containing both **editor windows** and **views**. The layout of these windows is fully configurable, but this is what a typical Java developer starts with:

- **The package explorer view:** On the left side, you see the Package Explorer view, which, for Java projects, is similar to the project explorer you saw earlier. This is used for navigating around the project's source tree and opening the source files for editing.

- **The editor window:** In the center of the GUI is the source code for the `DataObject.java` file. Developers with a large screen space normally expand this window to cover most of their desktop.

- **The outline view:** On the right side is an overview of the `DataObject` class. When you click on the various method names, the editor jumps to that part of the source code. This is one of Eclipse's many productivity features.

- **The console view:** At the bottom of the screen is the output of the program, left over from last time you pressed the Run button. In this case, it's a simple text-based application with only two lines of output.

To the novice user, the Eclipse interface can be rather overwhelming, especially with all the menu options and configuration boxes. Starting with this basic GUI layout is a good way to get familiar with the tool.

### The Source Tree

If you're more comfortable thinking about source files and lines of code, let's see how an Eclipse project is stored. One of the limitations of a GUI is that you're not in control of what's happening internally, which means it's harder to understand what's really going on.

Now take a quick look at the files in the Example Project subdirectory. Pay close attention to the top-level directory name, which indicates the purpose of the file.

```
src/com/arapiki/example/Application.java
src/com/arapiki/example/WordType.java
src/com/arapiki/example/DataObject.java
bin/com/arapiki/example/WordType.class
bin/com/arapiki/example/DataObject.class
bin/com/arapiki/example/Application.class
test-src/com/arapiki/example/TestDataObject.java
test-src/com/arapiki/example/TestOtherStuff.java
test-src/com/arapiki/example/TestWordType.java
test-bin/com/arapiki/example/TestDataObject.class
test-bin/com/arapiki/example/TestWordType.class
.project
.settings/org.eclipse.jdt.core.prefs
.classpath
```

The src and test-src directories were visible in the Package Explorer window, so there's no surprise there. On the other hand, bin and test-bin were hidden from view. Developers don't normally need to see the .class files, as long as they trust the build system to keep everything up-to-date.

This approach of having two source directories and two output directories is easy enough to configure using the Java Build Path GUI window (see Figure 10.5).

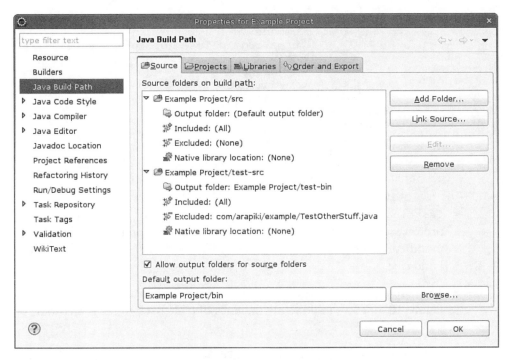

**Figure 10.5** *The Java Build Path window.*

In the center of the screen, you see the definition of the two source locations. For the `src` directory, you use the default output location (`Example Project/bin`); for the `test-src` directory, you explicitly provide the name of the `test-bin` directory. The `Included:` and `Excluded:` fields, similar to the `<fileset>` task in Ant, enable you to select which source files are included in the build process. In this case, `TestOtherStuff.java` is explicitly not compiled.

The final three files in the project directory are a text-based view of the GUI configuration. You're discouraged from hand-editing these files, but it doesn't hurt to understand what they're used for.

- `.project`: This file contains an XML description of how this project should be configured. Given that this is a Java project, the `javabuilder` feature is used for compiling code and the `javanature` feature describes all the characteristics of the project.

```
<?xml version="1.0" encoding="UTF-8"?>
<projectDescription>
      <name>Example Project</name>
      <comment></comment>
      <projects>
      </projects>
```

```
<buildSpec>
        <buildCommand>
                <name>org.eclipse.jdt.core.javabuilder</
                name>
                <arguments>
                </arguments>
        </buildCommand>
</buildSpec>
<natures>
        <nature>org.eclipse.jdt.core.javanature</
        nature>
</natures>
</projectDescription>
```

- .settings/: This directory contains a number of files that store the project's configuration. In this case, only the core preferences have been modified, so only the org.eclipse.jdt.core.prefs file appears in the build tree.

- .classpath: An XML version of the Java Build Path GUI you saw in Figure 10.5. You should relate the lines of code back to the screenshot.

```
<?xml version="1.0" encoding="UTF-8"?>
<classpath>
   <classpathentry kind="src" path="src"/>
   <classpathentry excluding="com/arapiki/example/TestOther-
Stuff.java"
                   kind="src" output="test-bin" path="test-
                   src"/>
   <classpathentry kind="con"
        path="org.eclipse.jdt.launching.JRE_CONTAINER/org.
        eclipse. \
        jdt.internal.debug.ui.launcher.StandardVMType/Java-
        SE-1.6"/>
   <classpathentry kind="con"
        path="org.eclipse.jdt.junit.JUNIT_CONTAINER/3"/>
   <classpathentry kind="output" path="bin"/>
 </classpath>
```

If you look carefully, none of this information describes the build process, but it still gives Eclipse enough information to compile the Java classes. Now continue by seeing how Eclipse JDT performs a build.

## Building a Project

Keeping in line with the IDE philosophy, building a project is done directly in the GUI environment. Whenever a source file is saved to disk, the Java compiler is invoked and the build results are shown immediately. As any experienced programmer knows, it's important to compile your code frequently to make sure that errors don't get out of hand. The Eclipse build process has been optimized so that compilation takes only a few seconds.

If the Java compiler encounters any errors or warnings, they're reported in the `Problems` window at the bottom of the Eclipse GUI (see Figure 10.6).

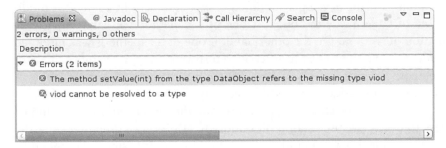

**Figure 10.6** *The Problems window, showing a compilation error.*

When you click on the error report, the Eclipse editor opens the offending source file and jumps to the line containing the error. This is another way to make sure that errors are resolved quickly.

Another good practice is to run the software on a regular basis, which is also easy in the Eclipse environment. When the `Run` button is pressed, Eclipse saves any modified source files and compiles any recent changes. Assuming that no errors arise, the program starts executing and the output is shown in the `Console` window.

Eclipse is fully configurable, so if you prefer a more traditional build environment, you can disable the `Build Automatically` option. If you do so, you need to press the `Build All` toolbar button every time you want to compile your code.

### Dependency Analysis

As with every other build tool, Eclipse uses dependency analysis to figure out which source files have changed and whether they depend on other files that have changed. What's interesting about the Eclipse Java builder is that it uses information stored by the IDE framework instead of recalculating the dependencies for itself. This speeds up the compilation process, which is important if you compile the program each time you save a file.

Whereas other build tools use time stamp or MD5 checksum comparison, Eclipse already knows which files were edited. After all, the tool itself was responsible for saving the file to disk, so it simply keeps track of everything that was modified. If you edit a file using a different editor, Eclipse won't know about the change and, therefore, won't rebuild that file.

The next optimization is in the recompilation of source files that depend on other source files. For example, if A.java contains an import directive for class B, then you might expect that A.java will be recompiled whenever B.java is changed. However, the Eclipse build tool is smart enough to know whether the change in B.java is actually relevant.

For example, if the developer modified only a comment in B.java or modified a line of code inside the body of one of B's methods, it can't impact the compilation of A.java. On the other hand, if one of B's methods was modified to include new parameters or a different return type, A.java is more likely to be impacted.

Given that most code changes impact only a single source file and don't modify a method's type signature, these are valuable optimizations. It would be pointless to check the time stamp on hundreds of files when the user typically saves one at a time. It's also pointless to recompile other files simply because they might be impacted by a change, even though they're usually not affected at all. Chapter 19, "Faster Builds," talks more about these optimization techniques.

## Compiler Options

Another aspect of Eclipse's integration is that the Java compiler is actually built into the IDE; it's not a third-party addition. In contrast, build tools such as Ant delegate to an external compiler, such as the Sun JDK. Eclipse's approach might seem strange at first, but having the compiler built into the IDE adds significant value. You'll hear more about this shortly.

Eclipse provides a variety of GUI dialog boxes for modifying the compiler settings, similar to an external compiler's command-line options. For example, a developer can change the following things:

- **JDK compliance level:** Specifies the version of the Java Development Kit, such as 1.4, 1.5, or 1.6, that the Eclipse compiler should comply with. This impacts the Java syntax accepted by the compiler and affects the format of the .class files.

- **Java runtime:** Enables you to control which Java runtime environment (JRE) is used when executing the program. At compile time, it's important to link against this same set of JRE libraries that you'll use at runtime.

- **Debugging information:** Specifies the level of debugging information to be inserted into .class files.

- **Compiler error/warning handling:** The developer can control whether each type of compilation problem is reported as an error or a warning, or whether it's ignored completely.

- **Maximum number of errors:** Enables you to control the maximum number of errors to be reported in each source file.

- **Javadoc tags:** Instructs the compiler on how to handle errors in Javadoc tags.

Take a look at a couple GUI dialogs. First, Eclipse enables you to select a particular instance of the JRE to be used when running the software (see Figure 10.7). Not only does the JRE provide a virtual machine to execute the `.class` files, but it also includes a number of standard Java libraries.

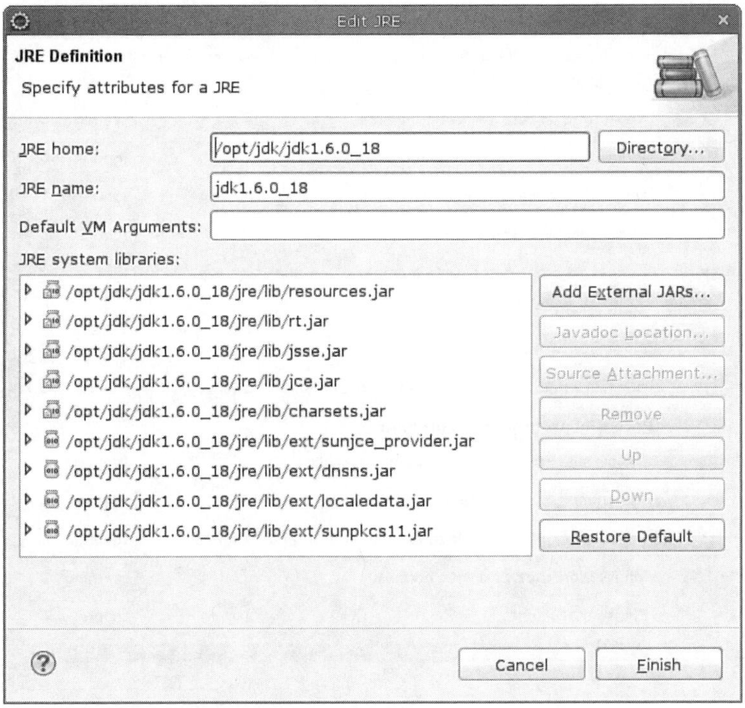

**Figure 10.7** *The Edit JRE window.*

In this example, you're explicitly using the version 1.6.0_18 runtime environment that was installed into /opt/jdk. Of course, the Eclipse compiler must be configured to generate .class files of the correct compliance level for this JVM. If for some reason you decide to use a JDK 1.4 virtual machine, you need to ask the compiler to generate the older .class file format.

A second feature of the Eclipse Java compiler is that each compilation message can be set as either an error or a warning, or perhaps can just be ignored completely (see Figure 10.8). An error message halts the compilation process, whereas a warning simply displays the message on the Problems window. Most of these warnings encourage good programming style instead of being serious errors.

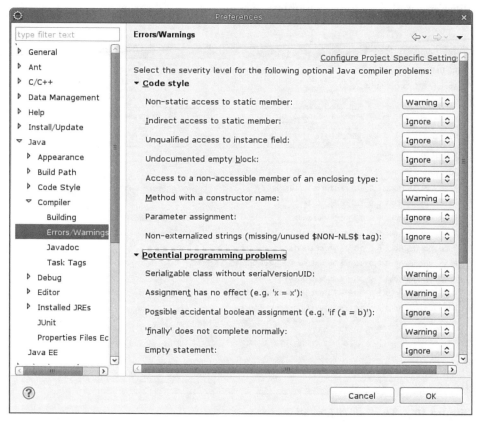

**Figure 10.8** *The compiler's Errors/Warnings preference page.*

When compiling legacy software, or code written by someone else, it may be necessary to ignore some of these messages until you get a chance to fix the code. On the other hand, your newly written source code should have as many of these options enabled as possible, as long as you believe that the errors or warnings are worth paying attention to.

## Packaging

The Eclipse incremental build system, which compiles a file when it's saved, generates only `.class` files. When a program is executed, the JVM uses those class files to execute the program. At no point in time are the class files packaged into a JAR file because this normally isn't required during development.

If you want to make your program available outside the Eclipse environment, you need to explicitly export the classes into a JAR file. As you might expect, the export process requires you to fill out a number of GUI forms. You need to specify the files you want to include in the archive (source files or class files), and you can optionally include a manifest that contains extra metainformation.

Depending on the type of Eclipse project you're using, you might export more than just plain JAR files. For example, an Enterprise Java Beans (EJB) project can export the project content to an EJB format file. Likewise, a Java Web Application project can export to the WAR format file.

## Project Build Paths

Although you've seen only a small example, Eclipse can actually manage thousands of source files. For the sake of productivity, it's a good idea to break large programs into smaller components, using a separate Eclipse project for each part of the software. It's also common to use third-party JAR files downloaded from the Internet.

As an example, a large application could be logically divided into a number of libraries, each providing an API to the main application code or to other libraries. Each library would be stored in a separate Eclipse project, as would the main program. In addition, a project is free to use one or more third-party JAR files instead of rewriting that same functionality.

To make all this happen, the Eclipse build tool must know all the class files and JAR files required to run the project. If one project depends on another project, the two lists of files must be merged. A project's **build path** can be configured to include any combination of the following:

- **Any directory of class files within the project's build tree:** This is normally the `bin` directory or any other output directory you've defined.

- **A JAR file that resides in your project's build tree:** You saw this case earlier, when the JUnit JAR file was added to the project.

- **An external class directory or JAR file that isn't part of your project:** You can use this to access files from anywhere on your build machine instead of inside your workspace. Because each machine can store the files in a different location, the build path should be accessed via a variable. Developers must therefore set the variable appropriately for their own machine.

When a project is compiled and executed on a virtual machine, Eclipse sets the Java class path to include each of the class directories or JAR files. This is essentially the same as defining the Java CLASSPATH environment variable, except that the GUI manages the content and order of entries.

For larger programs in which a project might depend on one or more other projects, the build paths are combined. That is, if project A depends on both projects B and C, the CLASSPATH variable contains all the directories and JAR files that all three projects require.

To make this project dependency system more usable, developers can indicate that only part of a project should be used. By providing Ant-like regular expressions, you can state that certain classes from the imported project are either discouraged or completely forbidden. Depending on your project settings, using any of the discouraged or forbidden classes will result in a build warning or error.

You can see another example of this multiproject approach in the real-world build scenarios. For now, let's examine the final development step, which is to actually run the compiled program on a Java Virtual Machine.

## Running a Project

Running a project in the Eclipse environment can be as simple as pressing the Run Application button on the toolbar. This assumes that you've already configured the project to use a suitable JRE and the correct command-line arguments. Eclipse provides a wide range of configuration parameters for controlling how a program should be executed.

Back when you compiled the project, you needed to state which JRE will be used when the program executes. This gives the compiler the knowledge of which runtime libraries are available to compile against, as well as which format the generated class files should use. Newer class file formats can be read only by newer virtual machines, whereas using an older machine gives a runtime error.

Assuming that you run the program within the Eclipse environment, you can be confident that a matching JRE will be used. If you change the JRE configuration, Eclipse prompts you to rebuild all the class files, just to make sure they match.

The next step in running a program is to select a **run configuration.** A Java program can execute in many ways, so you first need to select the suitable environment. After all, the program is really just a collection of Java classes, so you need to decide what should be done with those classes.

Figure 10.9 shows the `Run Configurations` window.

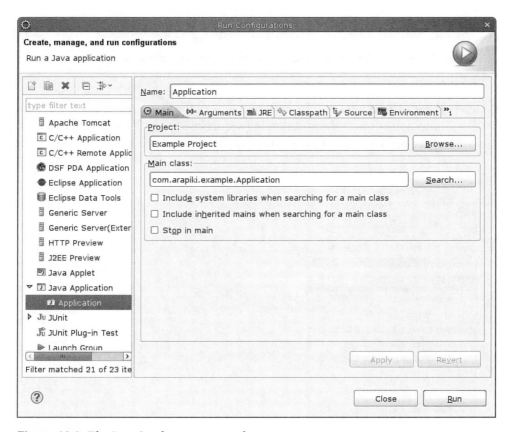

**Figure 10.9** *The Run Configurations window.*

On the left side is a list of runtime environments, including the following:

- **Java application:** The classes are loaded into a Java Virtual Machine, with the program's standard output appearing in the `Console` window (see Figure 10.10). This environment can also be used for GUI-based Java code, with new top-level windows popping up on the user's desktop.

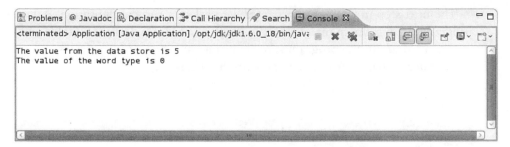

**Figure 10.10** *The Console window, showing the program's output.*

- **JUnit:** The classes will be executed within the JUnit test framework. The output of running the program is a sequence of pass/fail indicators for each of the test cases, as shown in the JUnit window (see Figure 10.11).

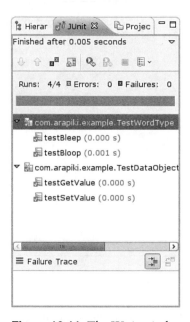

**Figure 10.11** *The JUnit window, with the result of running JUnit tests.*

- **Apache Tomcat:** A Tomcat application server is started, and the classes are loaded as a new web application. The program can be accessed by pointing a web browser at the Tomcat server's HTTP port.

- **Java applet:** A new web browser is started, and the project's classes are treated as a Java web applet. The classes are executed entirely within the web browser's internal JRE.

- **Eclipse application:** The classes implement a new plug-in for Eclipse, so a child instance of Eclipse is started in a separate process, with classes being loaded as a plug-in.

In addition to selecting this environment, it's common to specify the name of the main class (where execution starts), provide any command-line arguments to the program, provide command-line options for the JVM, or add new entries to the `CLASSPATH` variable. All this is possible in the `Run Configurations` GUI.

For the sake of convenience, you need to set this configuration only when the program is first executed. If the user presses the `Run Application` button a second time, the same configuration is used. As you saw earlier, running a project also saves and compiles your source files, which reduces the Eclipse edit-compile-run cycle to a single button press.

## Using the Internal Project Model

As mentioned earlier, Eclipse contains its own built-in Java compiler instead of invoking an external tool. Having an integrated compiler provides significant benefit to developers, above and beyond creating class files. Not only does Eclipse compile each source file when it's saved, but it also constantly watches what the user is typing to provide feedback on the work. This includes features for syntax checking, content assistance, and cross-referencing symbols from where they're used to where they're defined.

To enable these features, Eclipse constantly updates its internal model of the program. This model is queried whenever the developer needs help. Although these productivity features aren't what you'd normally consider as part of a build system, they use the same technology and are interesting to think about.

Consider some of the features:

- **Reporting of compilation errors:** Instead of reporting errors only when a source file is saved, Eclipse can provide feedback as soon as the code is typed. If the user enters invalid syntax or references a variable that isn't defined, the Java editor highlights the offending code. Underlining the text in red (for errors) or yellow (for warnings) informs the user of the mistake. If the user hovers the mouse pointer over the underlined code, a more detailed error message is provided.

- **Symbol/identifier cross-reference:** By clicking on any symbol in the program's source code and then selecting an option from the context menu, a user can find out where the symbol is defined. Eclipse immediately opens the relevant source file. For class names, you can examine the inheritance hierarchy to learn about the super classes and child classes. Finally, it's also possible to find all the places in the program where a symbol is used.

- **Content assistance:** If you press `Ctrl-Space` while editing code, Eclipse provides hints on what you might want to type next. If you're partway through typing a variable name, Eclipse suggests possible completions for that name. This is useful if you can't remember the full spelling of the name or for long names that take time to type.

  Additionally, if you've just finished typing the name of an object, followed by a period character, pressing `Ctrl-Space` provides a complete list of methods that can be invoked. This is extremely useful when navigating the extensive range of Java libraries, as opposed to looking up the Java API on the Internet. After you've selected a method to call, Eclipse prompts you with the list of arguments required for that method.

- **Refactoring support:** To clean up source code that has become messy over time, Eclipse supports a number of refactoring operations. For example, the `Extract Method` operation enables you to highlight a section of code within the body of one method and create a totally new method from that fragment. During this process, Eclipse identifies where each variable in the code fragment is defined and may end up passing it into the new method as a parameter.

It's interesting to note that each of these productivity improvements relies on the internal model of the compiled program. Many of these features wouldn't be available if Eclipse didn't come with a built-in Java compiler (at least, the syntax and semantic portions of the compiler).

## Other Build Features

Eclipse JDT has a couple of build-related features that are worth mentioning.

### Scrapbook Pages

In contrast to source files that contain a Java class definition, a **scrapbook** page allows individual statements or expressions to be evaluated. The user can enter a Java code fragment into the scrapbook editor, without needing to create a full class definition or even a method definition. Next, the user highlights the lines of code to execute and then presses the `Display` button. The code fragment is invoked, and the return value is displayed.

This scrapbook concept moves Java much closer to interpreted languages such as Python and Perl. The user can dynamically create objects, invoke methods, and study return values without too much overhead. This is somewhat like unit testing, although without the repeatability that a unit test framework provides.

### Using `build.xml` *Files*

Unlike most build tools, the Eclipse build system focuses heavily on interactive development. The build description is entirely GUI-based and is derived from a user's operations, such as adding a new source file to the project. Numerous GUI dialog pages exist for configuring the exact behavior of the compiler and build tool.

Unfortunately, this approach doesn't scale well for large and complex build systems that require a more detailed sequence of steps. If you're using a non-standard build tool or you have specific requirements for packaging your software, the Eclipse build system might not support your needs. A better option might be to use an external tool such as Ant.

In the JDT environment, a user is free to create an Ant `build.xml` file to build a project. The Ant plug-in for Eclipse shows a list of build targets (see Figure 10.12), which can be invoked by double-clicking on the target name.

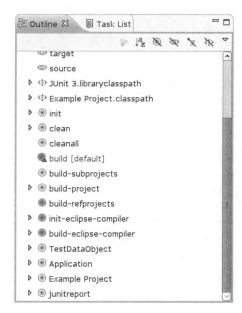

**Figure 10.12** *The Outline window for the autogenerated build.xml file.*

To make life easier, a `build.xml` file can be automatically generated from an existing Java project. The exported file provides the same features as the Eclipse builder, including targets for cleaning a build tree and running JUnit tests. When a `build.xml` file is generated for multiple projects, with one project depending on another, the top-level `build.xml` file uses the `<ant>` task to include the child project's build description.

Although the autogenerated file is a good starting point, you'll need to modify it by hand to include your additional build steps. Any project of medium to high complexity will almost certainly use a hand-coded Ant build system.

## Further Reading

As usual, we've touched on just the highlights of the Eclipse build system, enough to give you an idea of how the tool works and when it should be used. To gain a better understanding, you'll find the online documentation and tutorials [33] to be a good starting point. The tool includes a lot of documentation in the help pages, along with context-sensitive help for common tasks.

If you prefer to learn about Eclipse in a more structured style, books are available on the topic [65]. If your ambitions go beyond basic usage, you'll need to invest some time in learning about the Plug-in Development Environment (PDE) [66], which enables you to create new Eclipse features.

# Real-World Build System Scenarios

Now that you've seen the basic operation of creating an Eclipse project and building the software, let's see how you can use these features in a number of realistic situations. Unlike other build tools, the description of the steps relies heavily on GUI screenshots. You'll be provided with a detailed explanation on how to enter the information into the GUI forms.

## Scenario 1: Source Code in a Single Directory

The first scenario fits exactly into the Eclipse project model. Eclipse automatically compiles the `.java` files into `.class` files, and the default run configuration executes the program. The following steps are therefore required to create your first build system:

1. Create a new Java project with the name Scenario-1. Choose to start with an empty project, use the default JRE, and elect to use different directories for source and class files. This creates an empty src directory and an empty (and hidden) bin directory.

2. Add the Add.java, Mult.java, Sub.java, and Calc.java files to the src directory. The files are automatically added to the default Java package (see Figure 10.13).

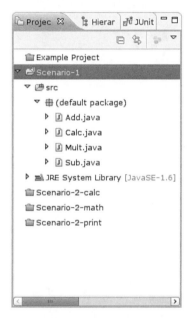

**Figure 10.13** *The Project Explorer window for the single-directory scenario.*

3. Press the Run button on the toolbar. The .java files are compiled (if they weren't already), and the application is executed. Eclipse identifies the main method inside the Calc class and starts executing from that point. The program's output appears in the Console window.

Most Java projects start out small and, therefore, fit into this scenario. You really didn't need to think much about the build system.

## Scenario 2: Source Code in Multiple Directories

For the multiple-directory case, you can still use a single Eclipse project, because it's capable of managing thousands of files. Of course, it's interesting to see how to combine multiple projects into a single application. As with the previous build tools, you should separate the `math` and `print` libraries into their own directories.

Figure 10.14 shows the three new Java projects (`Scenario-2-calc`, `Scenario-2-math`, and `Scenario-2-print`). The source files are stored within their respective project and Java package (such as `com.arapiki.calc`).

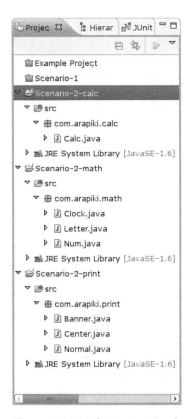

**Figure 10.14** *The Project Explorer window for the multidirectory scenario.*

This directory layout looks similar to what you used with the Ant build tool. However, you won't be creating intermediate JAR files, because Eclipse doesn't do that by default. Instead, you'll configure the Java build path for the `Scenario-2-calc` project to include the build paths for `Scenario-2-math` and `Scenario-2-print` (see Figure 10.15).

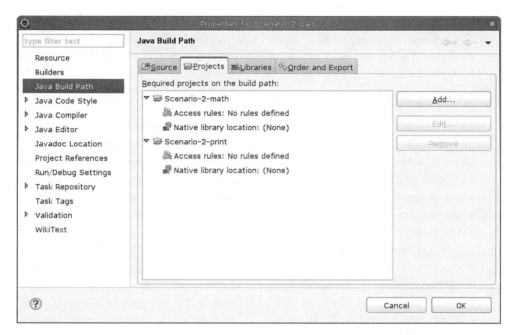

**Figure 10.15** *The Java Build Path window for the multidirectory build tree.*

To configure the build path, you press the Add button and select each of the child projects. When compiling Scenario-2-calc, Eclipse ensures that the class path includes the bin directories for each of these child projects. This means that Calc.java can make use of the math and print library methods, both at compile time and at runtime.

## Scenario 3: Defining New Compilation Tools

Defining a new compilation tool in the Eclipse environment is not an easy proposition. It's so complex that this chapter doesn't attempt to discuss the mathcomp compiler. If you're interested in the topic, you should learn how to create your own Eclipse plug-in [66].

Due to the nature of Eclipse, you wouldn't simply be adding the mathcomp tool into the build system. Instead, you'd want to create a new type of source code editor that could handle .math and .mathinc files and then provide some amount of added value for editing these files (such as content assistance or cross-referencing). None of this is easy to implement.

Perhaps the best solution is to defer to problem to an external build tool, such as Ant, where the problem is much easier to solve. Chapter 7, "Ant," already discussed the Ant solution for using the mathcomp tool.

## Scenario 4: Building with Multiple Variants

For the multivariant scenario, you'll revisit the Java application you built with the Ant tool. The idea is to have a calculator program with both home and professional editions. The two editions are largely the same, except that the home edition has a couple of the Java classes (Clock.java and Letter.java) stubbed out to remove those advanced features. Additionally, you use the edition runtime property to inform the program which set of features should be available to the user.

The key to implementing this solution using Eclipse is to recognize that each edition requires it own Eclipse project, with a slightly different build system. For the home edition, you include both src/home-stubs and src/professional in the build process, but for the professional edition, you need only src/professional. Figure 10.16 shows the two projects, Scenario-4-home and Scenario-4-prof.

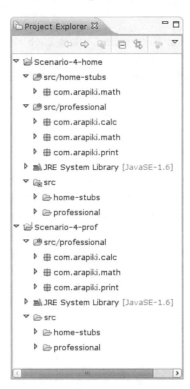

**Figure 10.16** *The Project Explorer window for the multivariant scenario.*

Pay careful attention to how these two projects were configured. If you look at the bottom of the `Scenario-4-prof` project, you'll see the `src` directory where all the source code is kept. This includes both the `src/home-stubs` and `src/professional` directories.

Near the top of the `Scenario-4-prof` project, you'll see an additional directory labeled `src/professional`, with a slightly different folder icon. Eclipse has chosen to show `src/professional` at the top of the project, because it was marked as a source folder from which you'll compile `.java` files. Note that `src/home-stubs` isn't shown in the same way, because you aren't building any source code from that directory.

If you now move further up the to the `Scenario-4-home` project, you'll see a similar set up, although this time you're building code from both the `src/professional` and `src/home-stubs` directories. Adding this additional source directory can be done via the Java build path GUI.

Before leaving this particular screenshot, it's worth noting that the icon next to the `src` directory in the `Scenario-4-home` project is slightly different from the corresponding icon in the `Scenario-4-prof` project. In the home edition, the `src` directory is configured to be a link to the `src` directory of the professional edition. This gives you a single source code directory (on the underlying file system) and also ensures that it will be compiled and executed via two different projects. As you might expect, editing a source file in one project immediately changes the file in the other project.

Moving on to Figure 10.17, you can see how another problem is solved. In the home edition, you need to ship your stubbed-out versions of `Clock.java` and `Letter.java`, not the full version from the `src/professional` directory. By modifying the Java build path, we exclude the two files we don't want (see the `Excluded` field), yet include all the source files from `src/home-stubs`.

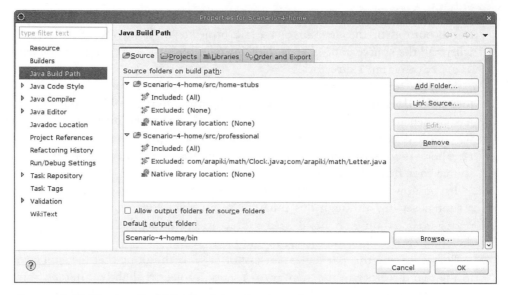

**Figure 10.17** *The Java Build Path window for the multivariant scenario.*

In contrast, the Java build path configuration for the Scenario-4-prof project (not shown) includes the src/professional directory and doesn't exclude any of the source files.

Finally, think about the runtime settings. In both editions, you need to pass a Java property value into the virtual machine so that the program knows which set of functionality should be provided to the user. To do this, you add the additional -Dedition=home or -Dedition=professional flag to the JVM command-line options.

Figure 10.18 shows the Run Configurations GUI.

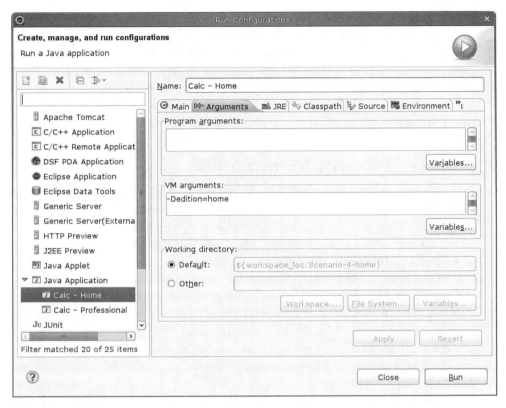

**Figure 10.18** *The Run Configurations window for the multivariant scenario.*

You've create two configurations, `Calc - Home` and `Calc - Professional`, visible at the bottom left of the screen. Both of these configurations set the `edition` property (center of the screen) to an appropriate value. Each of the two Java projects now has its own default run configuration for invoking the software.

Before completing this scenario, it's important to realize that most developers wouldn't use this approach to solve this real-world problem. Even though it's possible to build multiple variants within the Eclipse framework, it's more complex than you'd like. In a realistic situation, developers would only edit and compile the full professional edition in Eclipse. To create both the home and professional editions, they'd instead use a more powerful build tool, such as Ant.

## Scenario 5: Cleaning a Build Tree

Given that an Eclipse project is responsible for managing the list of source files and is able to compile those source files into class files, it should be no surprise that cleaning a build tree is automatic. Selecting the `Project,` `Clean` menu item removes all the `.class` files in the project.

One interesting behavior is that if you have the `Build Automatically` option enabled, Eclipse immediately proceeds to rebuild those class files. This might seem odd at first, but often the reason you clean the build tree is to generate completely fresh class files (such as for a JRE version change). If you do only want to keep the source files, it's a simple matter of deselecting the option.

### Scenario 6: Debugging Incorrect Builds

In many respects, the Eclipse JDT build system is simple. You don't have much control over which source files are compiled, because that's all managed by the Java builder. As discussed earlier, Eclipse knows which source files have been modified and which changes in one file might impact other files, so it usually does a good job of performing the correct compilation steps.

On the other hand, you do have a lot of control over the compiler's configuration, including the Java compliance level and various other compilation options. This makes it possible to use the wrong settings or to generate the wrong type of output files. If the program doesn't build correctly, try changing the available options to see if it makes a difference. You can always use the standard Java command-line tools, such as `javap`, to examine the class files and see if they look reasonable.

In the worst case, you can end up with Eclipse providing a build error that doesn't make any sense. Sometimes you'll find red error markers in parts of your source code that don't seem to have problems. If you can't figure out the issue within a couple minutes, it might be worth performing a clean build and starting again (hopefully your project is small). In these situations, forcing a clean build triggers Eclipse to reset its internal project model, which could make the errors go away.

If you've tried all these options and you still can't get Eclipse to build things correctly, try using an external build tool such as Ant. Eclipse wasn't designed to be a fully-featured build tool.

## Praise and Criticism

An IDE-based build tool is certainly an interesting idea and provides a great deal of productivity improvement. However, plenty of developers have never considered using an IDE, for a number of reasons. Let's now examine some of the pros and cons of using the Eclipse JDT build tool.

## Praise

The praise includes the following:

- **You don't need to write a build description file:** A large part of what makes the Eclipse JDT build system easy to use is that you often don't even know that it exists. Instead of writing a text-based build description, as you would for other tools, large parts of the build system are automatically constructed. This is all based on how you've configured your source code directories. When you do need to configure the build system, it's done via a user-friendly GUI.

- **Compilation is integrated with the full development environment:** The build process is no longer a separate step but is tightly integrated with the overall development environment. As a result, Eclipse incrementally compiles source files when they're saved to disk and can provide features such as content assistance and symbol cross-referencing.

- **A wide range of project types are supported:** Many languages and programming frameworks have Eclipse plug-in support. These plug-ins provide knowledge of how to edit and compile the associated source code, as well as how to execute the compiled application. If you want to build something such as a web application or an Enterprise Java Bean, it's trivial to create a new project and have it compiling in a few minutes.

## Criticism

The criticism includes the following:

- **Eclipse is too complex to use:** Many developers push back on using Eclipse because of its perceived complexity. They feel that there are too many buttons and menus to learn, and too many dialog boxes to configure. They'd rather continue using `vi` or `emacs` to edit their code. Unless the entire development team uses the Eclipse IDE, it's not possible to rely solely on the JDT build tool.

- **Eclipse requires a lot of CPU power and memory:** This is certainly true for large projects that contain thousands of source files. The problem is most noticeable when Eclipse scans the entire source code base to build up the symbol cross-referencing database. If a new user chooses to evaluate Eclipse by loading a large software project, that user is quite justified in feeling that Eclipse is slow.

- **The build process is limited:** As you've seen, the Java build tool is limited in capability and can't do much more than create class files for each of the Java source files. If you have more complex requirements, use a different build tool.

- **You can't create a repeatable build process:** Eclipse JDT uses an incremental build system in which files are recompiled whenever they're saved. This ties the build process to the developer's workflow instead of providing a clean end-to-end build process. (Although forcing a clean build can somewhat achieve this goal.)

- **You can't see what's happening in the build process:** For people who like to see every compilation command being executed, Eclipse is not an appropriate build tool.

## Evaluation

Let's evaluate the Eclipse JDT builder against the quality measurements discussed in Chapter 1, "Build System Overview."

- **Convenience:** *Good*: Creating a build system in the Eclipse JDT environment is so simple that most people don't even think about. On the downside, it has a limited set of features in this area, forcing the use of external build tools (such as Ant) for nontrivial builds.

- **Correctness:** *Excellent*: Eclipse JDT is intimately familiar with the structure of your Java code and knows exactly which parts of the code have changed. Eclipse is unlikely to miss a file dependency or recompile a file that wasn't impacted by a change.

- **Performance:** *Good*: Eclipse uses a "compile on save" approach in which a Java file (and dependent files) is recompiled whenever the file is saved. In this respect, the program is immediately available for execution, providing a fast build system. The downside is that performing a fresh build of a large program doesn't offer the same performance.

- **Scalability:** *Poor*: Eclipse JDT wasn't designed to support large build systems, especially those with complex requirements. It's standard practice to delegate to other build tools to support larger build systems.

The Eclipse environment is far more than a build tool and is the ideal environment for a wide range of code-development tasks. The build tool within Eclipse

JDT is suitable for interactive development but is not suitable for large-scale deployments in which other build tools excel.

# Similar Build Tools

Many software development IDEs are available, and developers choose their favorite based on usability, supported programming languages, or brand loyalty. Some of the simpler IDEs defer to an underlying tool, such as GNU Make or Ant, for their build system support. On the other hand, the more advanced IDEs are tightly coupled with their compilers and provide integrated build support.

This section looks at the Eclipse C/C++ Development Tooling (CDT) [33] plug-in, which is fairly different from the Eclipse JDT plug-in already discussed.

## CDT for Eclipse, C/C++ Development Tooling

This section won't go into exhaustive detail on how Eclipse CDT compiles C and C++ code, but let's look briefly at some of the key differences between CDT and JDT, the Java plug-in already discussed.

Perhaps the most noticeable difference is that CDT delegates the work to external tools. Unlike Java, which uses byte codes, C and C++ programs are usually compiled into machine code, with developers relying on their target platform's native compiler. For example, the CDT compiler in a Linux/x86 environment defaults to using the GNU C Compiler (GCC) for an Intel x86 CPU. In addition, CDT defaults to using GNU Make to implement the build system.

The next section discusses the important steps to create and manage a C or C++ project.

### Creating a New C/C++ Project

The CDT plug-in enables you to create either a C project or a C++ project, depending on what type of tool support you need. In both cases, you select a project name, specify the type of build artifact you want to create, and choose a compiler toolchain to be used by the build system. Finally, you can select one or more build configurations.

When selecting the artifact type, you have a choice of several different variants. You can choose the `Executable` option, which produces an executable program by linking all the object files. Alternatively, you can choose the `Static Library` or `Shared Library` option to produce a library archive. As you saw with Java-based projects, you can combine a number of these smaller projects into a single larger program.

The capability to select a compiler toolchain offers a lot of flexibility in compiling code. By default, the project uses the standard compiler for the current build machine, such as GCC on Linux. However, if you have cross-compilers installed, you can elect to generate object code for a different CPU. Even though you're encouraged to select the toolchain when the project is first created, there's nothing stopping you from changing it later.

### Managed Makefiles

For the `Executable`, `Static Library`, and `Shared Library` project types, CDT creates and manages an underlying makefile system, just as you saw with CMake. Whenever a developer adds a new source file to the project and selects the `Build Project` menu item, CDT autogenerates a corresponding GNU Make build system. The exact rules and targets added to the makefile depend on whether you're building an executable program or a library.

If you're editing a program that already has its own build infrastructure (using GNU Make or any other tool), you should instead select the `Makefile project` type. In this case, CDT won't autogenerate the build system; instead, it calls upon whichever external build tool you've configured for the project (by default, this is the `make` command).

As with JDT, for large and complex projects, you'll almost certainly resort to creating your own build system instead of using whatever Eclipse generates for you.

### Build Configurations

In a C or C++ project with default settings, all generated files are written into the `Debug` subdirectory. This includes object files, libraries, executable programs, and all the autogenerated build system files.

In addition to the `Debug` configuration, a project supports a `Release` configuration. As you'd expect, `Debug` generates object files with debugging information enabled, whereas `Release` stores the customer-ready version of programs and libraries. The generated files for each configuration are placed within their own subdirectory, keeping the two variants completely separate.

Aside from `Debug` and `Release`, a developer can create new configurations and are free to customize the behavior. This allows the selection of a different compiler toolchain (for different target CPUs), the use of preprocessing symbols to modify the software's behavior, and the use of different compiler flags for tighter control over the generated object code.

Developers can switch between configurations as often as they like, making it possible to develop multivariant software.

### Reporting Errors

Unlike JDT, the compiler isn't built into the CDT plug-in, so Eclipse relies on the output log of the external compiler to identify errors. By using a special-purpose parser to extract the compiler's error messages, the source code editor can underline the invalid code with a red line for errors or a yellow line for warnings. In addition, any error or warning messages are shown in the `Problems` window.

In most cases, the error and warning messages are updated only when the software is compiled, since the external compilation tools must first be invoked. On the other hand, CDT performs a limited amount of syntax checking while the user is typing. Unfortunately, anything more than basic syntax problems can only be caught be a real compiler, and won't be reported until the build system is next invoked.

### Content Assistance

Finally, it's worth noting that CDT can provide content assistance while a developer edits the source code. Instead of using an external compiler, CDT uses a built-in indexer tool to scan each of the source files and learn what they define. When developers press the `Ctrl-Space` key combination, they're presented with a list of possible variable and function names that are defined in the same source file, in a header file, or in one of the related source files.

---

## Summary

An integrated development environment (IDE) such as Eclipse provides a range of features such as code editing, compilation, version control, unit testing, and tracking of tasks. The build tool is just one portion of the IDE, although having everything integrated into a single environment can enhance the normal edit–compile–run cycle. In particular, an IDE provides faster feedback to the developer when errors appear in the source code.

Each project has an associated type. Among other things, this controls how the various source files in the project are compiled and linked into a program. If a new source file is added to a Java project, it's automatically included in the build system. Whenever that source file is saved, it's automatically compiled into a class file.

In the Eclipse JDT system, a program can be divided into a number of smaller projects, each compiling independently. One project can make use of the output from other projects, making it possible to generate large programs. All projects contain one or more source code directories, each with an associated output directory for Java class files.

When a project is executed, the developer must first select a suitable runtime environment. For example, a Java project can run on a standalone virtual machine, as an application inside a Tomcat server, or as a JUnit test case.

The Eclipse JDT system contains a fully featured Java compiler and maintains an internal model of each project. It has the capability to report compilation errors within a few seconds of the user typing the invalid code. It can also provide content assistance, symbol cross-referencing, and refactoring support.

Although Eclipse makes it easy to create a Java project and compiles the software automatically, the build system is rather limited. For larger projects, you'll likely end up writing your own build system using an external build tool such as Ant.

# PART III

## Advanced Topics

Part III focuses on some of the more advanced topics of developing a build system. Now that you've seen the basic concepts (in Part I) and some of the available build tools (in Part II), you can dive deeper into these advanced topics.

The upcoming chapters emphasize the experiences you'd have gained if you worked with build systems for many years. Instead of inventing your own solution to common problems, you can learn from the experience of others. Developers have made many mistakes in the past, and it's pointless for you to make them again.

Some of these chapters introduce additional build and compilation tools that Parts I and II don't discuss. They're introduced now because they illustrate a way to solve some of these more advanced problems.

The chapter layout for Part III is as follows:

- **Chapter 11, "Dependencies":** You'll explore the many ways a build tool can determine which files need to be recompiled and in which order the compilation tools should be invoked.

- **Chapter 12, "Building with Metadata":** You'll examine some additional build variants that add metadata to the output of the standard build process. You consider topics such as debugging and profiling support, code documentation, and unit testing.

- **Chapter 13, "Software Packaging and Installation":** The final step of a build system is to package the software ready for installation on the target machine. You've already explored this at a high level, but a release package can be generated in many ways.

- **Chapter 14, "Version Management":** Most software products are managed with a version-control tool, to handle multiple code streams and reproduce older versions of the software. Version control impacts many aspects of a build system.

- **Chapter 15, "Build Machines":** The machine on which you build the software plays a critical role in the accuracy of the build process. All changes to the build machine must be made in a controlled way.

- **Chapter 16, "Tool Management":** Likewise, all compilation tools must be managed in a controlled way to ensure that older versions of software can be reproduced. It's vital that all developers build with a consistent set of tools.

When you finish reading these chapters, you'll have a much better appreciation of creating and maintaining a reliable build system.

# Chapter 11

# Dependencies

Parts I, "The Basics," and II, "The Build Tools," discussed the basic concepts of a build system and then explored a number of common build tools. You also learned about the idea of **dependencies**, which are fundamentally important in any build system. This chapter digs much deeper into how dependency analysis works, how a build tool constructs a dependency graph, and how it invokes compilation tools in the correct order.

Even though developers in a small software project can afford to rebuild their entire source tree frequently, this is unrealistic with larger projects. If a source tree takes longer than 30 seconds to compile, developers expect **incremental compilation** to be used. That is, they expect the build system to recompile only files that have changed since last time the build tool was invoked. Any files that haven't been modified or don't make reference to such files, shouldn't be recompiled at all.

A key concept in incremental compilation is that of the **dependency**. That is, you must identify which files in the build tree are dependent on which other files. For example, if the content of file A is somehow derived from the content of file B, you say that A has a dependency on B. If a developer modified file B, the build system must take into account that file A might need to be regenerated. On the other hand, if there's no dependency, file A can't be any different from the last time it was compiled.

The big-picture diagram in Figure 11.1 now focuses on how the relationship between different files in the build tree can be determined. It's also important to determine whether the files are **up-to-date** with respect to each other.

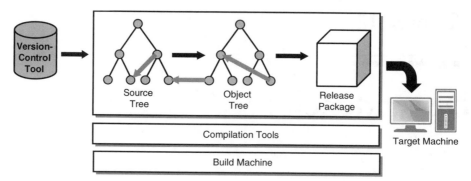

**Figure 11.1** *The focus for this chapter, the dependency between source and object files.*

In any real project, the dependency relationship among all the files in the source tree can be extremely complex. Determining the relationships involves prescanning source code, inferring dependencies based on the compilation tool's options, and specifying a bunch of hard-coded dependencies. All this work is vital to keep end-to-end build times small yet always ensure that you construct a valid software image.

From a high-level perspective, a build tool must follow three main steps:

1. Determine all the interfile dependency relationships. The tool creates a **dependency graph** of the entire program to show which files depend on which other files.

2. Using the dependency graph, determine the set of files that have been modified since the last time the tree was built, and therefore determine which files need to be recompiled.

3. Rebuild the tree by performing the individual compilation steps in a logical order, possibly using parallel processing.

This chapter looks at several topics, including these:

• The basic theory behind dependency graphs

• The practical problems you'll experience if your dependency graph is incorrect

• The process by which the dependency graph is constructed

• The methods you can use to determine which files are out-of-date with respect to their dependencies

• How to schedule the compilation to bring the tree up-to-date

# The Dependency Graph

A dependency graph is a structure that defines the relationships between various things. In this case, those "things" represent files in the source and object trees, and the arrows between them indicate that the content of one file depends on the content of the other. To clarify, an object file (with .o or .obj suffix) can have a dependency on a C source file (with .c suffix). Likewise, a Java .class file has a dependency on the corresponding .java file.

Figure 11.2 shows the relationship among four source files and their corresponding object files, a dynamically linked library, and an executable program.

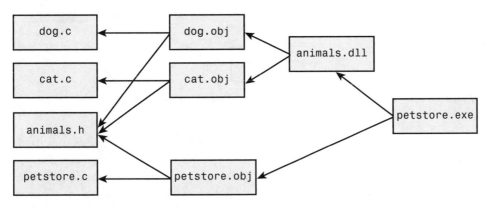

**Figure 11.2** *A pet store application, showing the dependencies among various files.*

Anyone who has used a build system should find few surprises in this diagram. The only unusual concept is that animals.h is listed as a dependency for each of the object files, not a dependency for the C source files. Although the C files use #include to incorporate the content of animals.h, they don't need to be regenerated if animals.h changes. Instead, the object files would be considered out-of-date.

The source files (on the left) do not depend on any other files. That is, they're hand-written by the developer, not generated by a compilation tool. Additionally, the final program, petstore.exe, isn't the target of any dependencies, so it is thus the final ending point of the build process.

## Incremental Compilation

What's interesting from a build system perspective is thinking about how an incremental compilation would work. If you assume that all object files are up-to-date and that the developer proceeds to modify cat.c, the build tool's task is to determine which object files are impacted. The build tool must invoke the correct compilation tools to bring things back to a consistent (fully built) state.

Figure 11.3 focuses on the parts of the dependency graph that require some action.

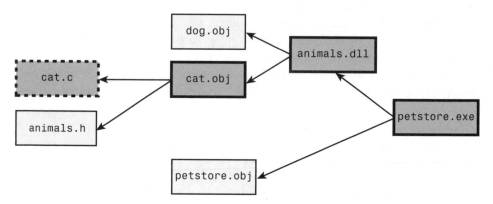

**Figure 11.3** *The pet store example, showing the impact of modifying cat.c.*

The dashed box indicates the file (cat.c) that the developer has modified. The bolded boxes (cat.obj, animals.dll, and petstore.exe) are directly or indirectly dependent on cat.c and, therefore, require recompilation. The remaining boxes (animals.h, dog.obj, and petstore.obj) are also required to successfully build the software, even though they haven't been modified in any way and don't need to be regenerated.

When recompiling this tree, the build tool executes the necessary compilation commands to bring everything up-to-date. The commands must be executed in a particular order (left to right in this diagram) so that any file that uses another file as input can be sure that it's using updated information. For example, you must ensure that cat.obj has been regenerated before animals.dll is regenerated; otherwise, the changes that were made to cat.c won't be propagated through to the final executable program.

Another important observation is that the dependency graph must be **acyclic** (with no cycles). That is, there's no way in which a file can depend (directly or indirectly) on itself. This type of arrangement would make it impossible to bring the build tree to a consistent state, with all the object files being up-to-date with respect to the source files.

## Full, Incremental, and Subtarget Builds

Before moving on to examine how the dependency graph is created, and the type of problems you'll see if it's done incorrectly, a couple of important concepts need to be reiterated. First, there's a distinction between two types of build process:

1. **Full builds:** This scenario assumes that the developer has never compiled the build tree. The tree consists of only source files, and none has been compiled into an object file. The first time the developer builds the tree (known as a **fresh** or **virgin** tree), all the compilation commands must be executed to bring the tree up-to-date.

2. **Incremental builds:** In this case, the tree has previously gone through a full build and contains all the required object files. However, the developer has more recently made changes to one or more source files, and the object files are no longer consistent. A subset of the object files needs to be rebuilt to make them consistent again.In large-scale incremental builds, the build tool might spend several minutes analyzing the build tree to determine what needs to be done. When the recompilation starts, it can be orders of magnitude shorter than a full build (such as 30 seconds versus 30 minutes for a full build).

The second important concept is the **subtarget build**. That is, instead of always generating the final executable program (in this example, `petstore. exe`), the developer might choose to build only a portion of the tree. Developers typically do this as an optimization to their build process. In some large software projects, this approach could save an hour of unnecessary compilation time.

For example, developers might decide that they need to recompile only the `animals.dll` file instead of the full application. Given that dynamically linked libraries can be recompiled and upgraded without changing the final executable program, this is a common way to save compilation time. Developers install the new library on their system and proceed to test their code. Figure 11.4 shows the portion of the dependency graph that requires action. The `petstore.obj` and `petstore.exe` files are no longer part of the recompilation.

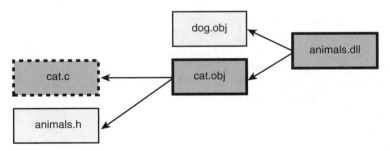

**Figure 11.4** *The pet store example, building only the animals.dll target.*

Selectively limiting the dependency graph in this way is a highly desirable feature of any build tool. Let's now look at the benefits of making sure your dependency graph is correct.

## The Problem with Bad Dependencies

As the preface of this book touched upon, a badly constructed build system can be expensive, accounting for more than 10% of your development costs. Many of these problems are attributed to a poorly constructed dependency graph. Let's now look at some practical case studies in which incorrect dependencies cause the build process to fail, generate bad software images, or take much longer than necessary.

Experienced programmers likely can relate to most, if not all, of these problems. You might have discovered them after hours of retrying failed builds. You probably studied the output of your build log to see which compilation commands were executed (or not) and then examined a number of files to see if they'd changed. In the end, the root cause of the problem was likely related to missing or incorrect dependencies.

### Problem: Missing Dependencies Causing a Runtime Error

The first and perhaps most common problem you'll see occurs when dependencies are completely missed. In this case, a file that should have been recompiled is left unchanged instead of being updated to match the most recent source code. If the code in this file was meant to exchange information with code from other files that were updated correctly, the result could be a confusing set of runtime problems.

In Figure 11.5, if `dog.c` and `cat.c` both made use of a data structure (`struct food`) defined in `animals.h`, they must both include that header file. However, if the dependency between `dog.obj` and `animals.h` is missing, `dog.obj` won't be recompiled when the header file changes.

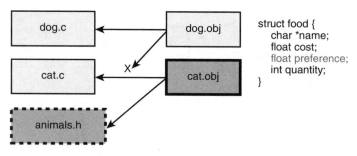

**Figure 11.5** *A missing dependency between dog.obj and animals.h.*

This problem manifests itself when `dog.obj` and `cat.obj` exchange data that uses `struct food`. Because of the newly added field (`preference`), any structure exchanged between the two parts of the program will be mismatched. Not only is the structure of a different size, but the memory location that `cat.obj` uses for the `preference` field is the same location that `dog.obj` uses for the `quantity` field.

This problem could cause a sequence of runtime bugs that can be hard to detect, potentially wasting hours of development time. The issue will be resolved only when `dog.c` is changed (and, hence, `dog.obj` is recompiled) or when the build tree is cleaned. With a better set of dependencies, this error would never have occurred in the first place.

## Problem: Missing Dependencies Causing a Compile Error

A similar situation occurs when an automatically generated file isn't updated correctly. Developers might add a new symbol definition to their program, but when the software is compiled, they receive a number of `undefined symbol` errors. Again, this is the result of invalid or missing dependencies.

In Figure 11.6, the developer has added a new `Bison` entry in the `food.list` file and has also modified the `cat.c` file to use that new definition. Given that `food.list` is a plain text file, it must first be translated into an equivalent header file (`food_gen.h`) before the C file can use the definition.

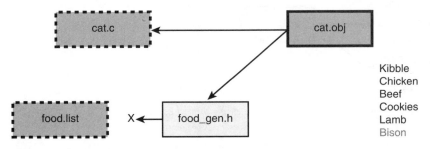

**Figure 11.6** *A missing dependency between food_gen.h and food.list.*

Because of the missing dependency information, the build tool doesn't realize that `food_gen.h` needs to be updated whenever `food.list` is modified. As a result, the compilation of the C code causes errors such as `Bison is not defined`. From the developers' perspective, they've changed all the necessary files and thus are left to wonder why the C compiler isn't finding the correct definition.

This scenario is common when multiple developers share a code base. Developers can update their existing source tree by obtaining the latest code from the version-control system. In doing so, they receive updated copies of cat.c and food.list, but the food_gen.h file doesn't get regenerated when they attempt to rebuild the tree. This is especially confusing for them, given that some other developer made the offending code change.

In a real-world development project, you'll likely find a number of developers who hesitate to update their source tree from the version-control system, just in case it takes a day or two to resolve this type of problem.

## Problem: Unwanted Dependencies Causing Excess Rebuilding

Although it's not as critical as a missing dependency, an extra unwanted dependency can also cause problems. In particular, a file might be recompiled even when it doesn't depend on anything that was changed. This doesn't cause any compile-time or runtime problems, but it does force the developer to wait longer for their compilation to complete. For large build systems, there may be 10–20 minutes of excessive compilation.

In Figure 11.7, an incorrect dependency exists between dog.obj and cat.h.

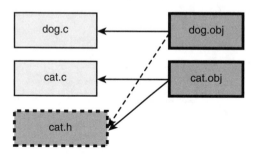

**Figure 11.7** *Incorrect dependency between dog.obj and cat.h.*

Perhaps at one point in time, developers were including cat.h into dog.c, but they've since removed it. However, the build system still contains that dependency, thereby causing dog.obj to recompile when it doesn't need to.

## Problem: Unwanted Dependencies Causing Failed Dependency Analysis

Even before the software compilation starts, it's possible for dependencies to cause problems. While the build tool attempts to construct the dependency graph, it might get to a point at which it cannot proceed. This usually results in a don't know how to make error message.

In Figure 11.8, developers have decided that penguins should no longer be sold in the pet store. They've removed both the `penguin.c` and `penguin.obj` files and recompiled the program. However, the build system still contains the old dependency information and complains that it doesn't know how to make `penguin.obj`.

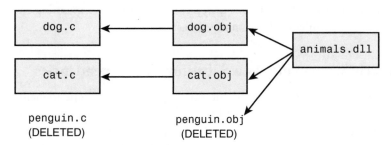

**Figure 11.8** *Stale dependency information, causing the build to break.*

If the `penguin.c` file had not been deleted, the build system could still rebuild `penguin.obj` from source code. In this case, though, it searched for all the possible ways to regenerate `penguin.obj` but didn't find a way of doing so.

A similar situation can occur when developers relocate their build tree to a new disk location (such as from `C:\Work` to `D:\Work`). Even though all the files have changed, the dependency information still refers to the old location. Naturally, the build tool won't find the files in their old location and has no way of rebuilding them. The only remedy is to remove all the stale dependency information and start again.

## Problem: Circular Dependencies

One of the basic rules of constructing dependency graphs is that they shouldn't contain any cycles. However, that doesn't stop developers from accidentally creating a dependency graph that can never finish its job. One real-life example arises when the developer wants to compress a large data file but then reuses the original data file's name. Figure 11.9 is an example using Make syntax.

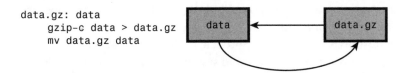

**Figure 11.9** *A makefile rule that generates its own input files, causing a cycle.*

In this case, the data.gz file depends on the data file. If data is newer than data.gz, you would execute the gzip command to compress the file, followed by the mv (move) command to rename it.

The problem is that data (the input to the dependency) ends up being modified, and data.gz (the target of the dependency) is never actually created. No matter how many times you rerun the build tool, it'll always execute these commands. The end result is wasted compilation steps and a completely meaningless data file because it was compressed too many times.

## Problem: Implicit Sequencing As a Substitute for Dependencies

When developers don't want to spend the effort getting their dependencies correct, they often resort to using the build tool's implicit sequencing of commands. This sequence gets the job done but almost never results in an optimal build system. You saw this situation in Chapter 6, "Make," in discussing the recursive Make technique.

The following makefile fragment uses sequencing to guide the order in which commands are executed:

```
.PHONY: program lib1 lib2

program: lib1 lib2
    @echo Linking my program

lib1:
    @echo Building library 1

lib2:
    @echo Building library 2
```

The program, lib1, and lib2 targets are labeled as being **phony**, informing Make that the target name is for human use only instead of having a real disk file with that name. The dependency relationship of program: lib1 lib2 thus doesn't correspond to real disk files, but instead describes the sequence of rules to be triggered. In this case, lib1 is built first, then lib2, followed by the creation of program.

Although this isn't an optimal method, it's perhaps one of the common methods of constructing a build system, especially for small software. It's often much safer to follow an explicit sequence of commands than risk the chance of obscure compilation or runtime errors caused by invalid dependencies.

The unfortunate downside of this approach is that too much compilation takes place. Also, the more complex the build system, the more careful the developer must be to get the sequence of commands correct. Another downside is that parallel build systems rarely work correctly if they don't have access to a correct dependency graph.

## Problem: The Clean Target Doesn't Clean Everything

One unfortunate outcome of the dependency problems discussed so far is that developers lose faith in the build system. If they can't identify and resolve a build problem within an acceptable period of time, they simply choose to clean their build tree and start again. They're then required to perform a full build of their tree, but that could be faster than trying to diagnose and fix the broken dependencies.

The first step is to execute the build system's "clean" operation. This should remove all object files, autogenerated files, and stored dependency information, leaving only the developer's source files. These source files will likely have a developer's local changes, which must be preserved at all costs. (After all, the developer spent days or weeks making those changes.)

As you might expect, the clean operation can also suffer from problems. If it doesn't fully clean the tree, you're left with stale object files or dependency information that doesn't get removed. When the tree is rebuilt, the same dependency problems exist, which frustrates developers. Their only option at this point is to take a backup of their local changes and then completely "blow away" their whole build tree, including source code. This ensures that no stale information can possibly remain. This whole operation is clearly a waste of development time.

## Step 1: Computing the Dependency Graph

Now that you understand the problems that arise if the dependency graph isn't accurate, think about the methods used to create the graph. This is one of the most complex challenges build systems must address, and if it's not handled correctly, it will be the root of many problems. The basic approach is to learn how each compilation tool accesses files and find some way to predict which files the tool will access in the future. In some cases, this ends up being a guessing game.

But what actually is a dependency? If there's some way in which file A depends on file B, there must be a compilation tool (such as compiler or linker) that somehow uses the content of file B when it generates file A. If it's a direct dependency, that compilation tool must directly read file B. For indirect dependencies, the dependency graph could have any number of hops between A and B, although there must still be a way in which B's content can potentially impact the generation of A.

The first step in determining the dependency graph is therefore to understand which input and output files each compilation tool uses. This can be done in a variety of ways. Specifically, a compilation tool can be asked to access a file in three general approaches:

- **Command-line arguments:** The compilation tool can be told to read or write a file by explicitly mentioning the file on the tool's command line. For example, the C compilation command `gcc -c test.c -o program` explicitly asks the compiler to read the `test.c` file as input and write to the `program` file as output. Some tools enable the use of environment variables to specify the input and output files; although, these tend not to be common.

- **Source code directives:** Most programming languages have a mechanism for importing/including other source files. In this respect, the compilation tool must parse the source code to determine which other files it depends on. Common examples include C's `#include` directive and Java's `import` directive.

- **Convention:** Some tools have input or output files they use by default. For example, the UNIX Lex tool writes its output to the `lex.yy.c` file, unless explicitly asked to use a different filename.

With these three approaches, you can determine the set of files a compilation tool is accessing, at least for any well-behaved tool. The next question is how the build tool (such as Make, SCons, or Ant) can determine this information and build the full end-to-end dependency graph for the program.

## Gathering Exact Dependencies

In most cases, the build tool and compilation tools are completely separate programs, and they don't share a lot of information. For the build tool to operate effectively, it must predict which files a compilation tool will read and/or write. This is done before the compilation tool is actually executed, instead of learning the dependencies as the compilation progresses. If this weren't the case, you can end up with compilation commands executing in the wrong order.

In Figure 11.10, the build tool determines that both `cat.c` and `food.list` have changed. However, until `cat.obj` is regenerated from `cat.c`, the build system might not be aware of the dependency that it has on `food_gen.h` (the dashed line). In this scenario, you must somehow determine the dependency in advance, therefore making sure that `food_gen.h` is regenerated from the latest copy of `food.list` before `cat.obj` is regenerated.

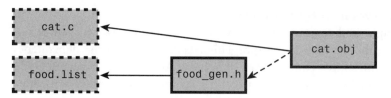

**Figure 11.10** *A scenario in which rebuilding files in the wrong order can cause problems.*

A build tool can predict a compilation tool's dependency information in several common ways.

### Hard-Coded Dependencies

By having the dependencies hard-coded into the build description file (such as the `Makefile` or `SConstruct` file), the build system uses the developer's knowledge of the dependencies. The build tool has little work to do, other than parse the build description file and update the dependency graph. For example, using the Make tool, you can explicitly state the dependencies that an object file has on source files:

```
cat.obj: cat.c animals.h
```

This is the simplest way to specify dependencies, but it doesn't work well for large programs. The constant maintenance and the chance of introducing errors makes this impractical. Regardless, this method is often used when the more automated methods (see below) are too hard to implement.

### Dependencies Derived from Command Lines

Given that the build tool is responsible for constructing the compilation tool's command line, the build tool already has some amount of advance knowledge. This information won't always be complete, but some information is better than none. For example, the following SCons directives are used to build the pet store example:

```
lib = SharedLibrary("animals", ["dog.c", "cat.c"])
Program("petstore", [lib, "petstore.c"])
```

Not only are the `SharedLibrary` and `Program` builder methods used to state which files should be compiled, but they also participate in the construction of the dependency graph. For example, there's an implicit knowledge in the SCons tool that object files are created from source files and that shared libraries are created from object files. Almost the entire dependency graph can thus be created from these two SCons commands.

### Dependencies Provided by Scanners

The last example had no automatic way for the build tool to incorporate `animals.h` into the dependency graph. This is solely because the dependency is embedded in the source code instead of being stated in the `SConstruct` file. To resolve this issue, you instead use a **scanner** tool to examine the source files. By searching for the `#include` or `import` directives in a source file, the scanner infers which other files are required.

Chapter 6 briefly mentioned the `makedepend` scanner, used in the UNIX environment. This isn't a full-blown compiler, but it knows enough to detect the header files included within a source file. For example:

```
$ makedepend -f - cat.c
# DO NOT DELETE

cat.o: animals.h
```

The output from this command would normally be appended to a makefile, hence the DO NOT DELETE comment. Because Make already knows that `cat.o` depends on `cat.c`, there's no need to list that dependency.

Scanners are often fast and efficient at locating dependencies, but their inability to understand the full semantics of the language can provide bad information. For example, when a scanner examines a C source file, it must be aware of preprocessor semantics.

```
#ifdef _USE_GOOD_FOOD_
#include "store_food/berries.h"
#else
#include "wild_food/berries.h"
#endif
```

In this example, a naive scanner could determine that both `store_food/berries.h` and `wild_food/berries.h` are dependencies, whereas only one of them will ever be included at one time. This isn't a fatal error, but it can result in unnecessary recompilation.

### Dependencies Provided by Compilation Tools

Perhaps the most accurate way to determine which files a compilation tool will access is to ask that tool itself. However, as discussed earlier, we need to have this information before the tool actually performs its work. As shown in Chapter 6 (which discussed GNU Make), one such tool providing this capability is the GNU C Compiler. By providing the `-M` option, the compiler scans the source files and determines the dependencies, but doesn't actually compile the code.

```
C:\work> gcc -M dog.c
dog.obj: dog.c animals.h
```

After the full dependency graph has been computed, the build tool ensures that any files that dog.obj depends on are up-to-date. It then calls upon GCC for a second time, but this time without the –M option.

### Dependencies Determined by File System Monitoring

Modern build tools, such ElectricAccelerator [48] and clearmake [5], can go one step further by monitoring which files a compilation tool accesses while it's running. This is done by observing any interaction the compilation tool has with the computer's file system, accurately determining the inputs and outputs.

The advantage of these systems is that they're guaranteed to find the exact set of dependencies. Assuming that the compilation tool accesses the same set of files in the future that it has in the past, you'll never suffer from missing or excessive dependency information. This feature is a benefit for compilations with a large number of dependencies that could be hard to predict, such as a release packaging script. (Chapter 13, "Software Packaging and Installation," discusses these in more detail.)

The downside of using monitoring tools is that an additional file system plug-in must be added to the computer's operating system, which not everyone feels comfortable doing. Also, the monitoring software will record absolutely every file access (unless you tell it otherwise), and many files don't make sense to have as dependencies. For example, /usr/include/stdio.h can be accessed, but because it'll never change (unless the operating system is upgraded), there's no point in recording it in the dependency graph.

Finally, you might be asking how these monitoring systems can determine dependency information before the compilation command is executed (per our requirement). This is answered later in the chapter.

## Caching the Dependency Graph

Using the previous techniques, the build tool will have built up a complete dependency graph. As much as possible, you want to store what you've learned in a cache so that you don't need to recompute the full graph each time the build tool is invoked. Some developers build their software as often as every few minutes, so it's important to reduce the amount of time spent computing the dependencies, thereby providing a much faster build experience.

Each build tool has its own mechanism for caching dependencies. For example, a typical Make-based system uses a separate file (with a .d suffix) to store dependency information for each of the object files. In contrast, SCons uses a single database file to cache dependencies for all files in the build tree.

When dependencies are hard-coded into the build description files (such as a makefile), or when they're derived from compilation tool command lines, you'd see only a small benefit in storing the information in a cache. The next time the build tool is started, it still would need to reread that same description file anyway, so a cache wouldn't save much time.

On the other hand, you can save a significant amount of time by not recomputing dependencies that were found by running a compilation tool or a scanner. Executing these additional programs takes a lot of time, so you should use precached copies of the graph if possible.

This idea of caching dependencies isn't a difficult problem to solve, but it's tricky to know when the cached information becomes stale. Now think about how to update the cached dependency graph if the software itself is modified.

## Updating the Cached Dependency Graph

In a real-world development project, your dependencies change over time. Any dependency information that was previously computed and cached could be out-of-date and needs to be replaced. Failure to delete old dependency information either causes the build system to do too much work or causes it to fail if the old source files no longer exist.

Probably the most common reason for a change in dependencies is developers modifying their source code to add new #include or import directives, thereby adding new dependency relationships to the graph. A second scenario occurs when a compilation tool's include path flags are modified by editing the build description file. Regardless of the change, the build system must compute the new dependency graph and regenerate the object files accordingly.

Based on the three ways in which a compilation tool is asked to access a file (via command-line arguments, via source code directives, or by convention), let's now examine how each change impacts the dependency graph. Keep in mind that you're now operating in a build tree that's already fully built or perhaps has a small number of modified source files. You no longer need to be concerned with building a completely fresh tree.

### Updating Cached Command-Line Arguments

Given the variety of compilation tools and command-line options, no single solution addresses the problem of argument changes. Here are three different scenarios:

1. For command-line options that change the name of the input or output files (for example, -o prog), the dependency graph must be modified to include the new name of that file, and the old name must be discarded. Assuming that the build tool didn't cache this part of the dependency

graph, but instead created it while reading the build description files, no additional work is required. Simply invoking the build tool again ensures that the correct dependencies will be used.

2. For compilation tool options that impact the content of the object files (instead of their name), you might need to completely rebuild all the existing object files in the build tree. For example, if the developer added the −g option to request that debugging information be generated, all previous object files would need to be discarded and recompiled. A similar rule would apply if the compilation tool was upgraded to a newer version and could generate different code than the older tool.From the perspective of the dependency graph, you must add a dependency from each object file to the set of flags it was compiled with (see Figure 11.11). In this case, there's nothing special about the bear.flags file, but if the command-line flags are modified, this file must be "touched" to make it appear newer. As a result, bear.obj will be regenerated.

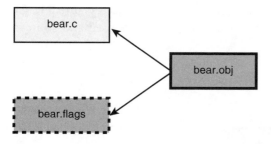

**Figure 11.11** *An object file that depends on its own compilation flags.*

3. If you modify a command-line argument that changes the tool's search path, you need to recompute each object file's dependencies. For example, if you change the include search path (-I) or library search path (-L), it's possible that a different set of files will be included. In the following example, bear.c includes a different berries.h header file, depending on the order of the -I directives.

   If bear.c contained the following directive

```
#include "berries.h"
```

then the following two command lines result in different dependencies:

```
gcc -Iwild_food -Istore_food -c bear.c
    => includes wild_food/berries.h

gcc -Istore_food -Iwild_food -c bear.c
    => includes store_food/berries.h
```

This scenario might seem a little obscure (and it probably is), but failing to determine the correct dependencies could waste a lot of development time.

### Updating Cached Source Code Directives

If a source code file changes, it's possible for the set of other files it depends on (via #include or import) to now be different. Assuming that you precached the file's dependency information (using a compiler or a scanner), this information could now be out-of-date and must be regenerated.

In the most common situation, a source file (such as bear.c) is modified to include a new header file (such as honey.h). In this case, the build system detects that bear.c was modified and that bear.obj is outdated (see Figure 11.12). By virtue of this recompilation, all the correct input files are used and you can recache the new set of dependencies.

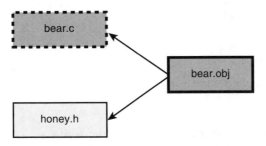

**Figure 11.12** *A new #include directive is added to bear.c.*

The situation becomes a lot more complex when you consider what happens if the included header file is itself an autogenerated file. Somehow the build system must determine whether that newly included header file is up-to-date. It would be a problem if you accidentally included an out-of-date header file in bear.obj.

In Figure 11.13, the developer has modified bear.c, so it now includes the food_gen.h header file, whereas it didn't before. The developer has also modified the food.list source file. For the compilation to succeed, the build system must already be aware that food_gen.h is autogenerated from food.list, and this step must be undertaken before bear.obj is regenerated.

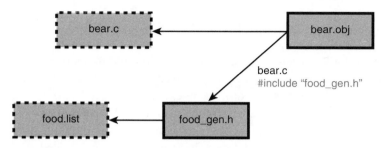

**Figure 11.13** *bear.c and food.list are both modified, but the autogenerated header file must be recompiled before the source file.*

To reiterate, here are the steps for a successful build:

1. Determine that `bear.obj` has a new dependency on `food_gen.h`. (This information could be determined by a scanner.)

2. Regenerate `food_gen.h`.

3. Regenerate `bear.obj` from `bear.c` and the new version of `food_gen.h`.

Finally, imagine an even more complex scenario. What would happen if `food_gen.h` included yet another header file (say, `meats_gen.h`) that was also autogenerated? You might not detect this new dependency until `food_gen.h` is regenerated. Therefore, you must regenerate `meats_gen.h` before compiling `bear.obj`, but only after `food_gen.h`.

### Updating Cached "By Convention" Rules

A compilation tool won't suddenly start using a different set of "by convention" rules. If it accesses a specific file by default, it'll continue to always access that same file (such as the `lex.yy.c` case). One possible exception is when a shell script is used as a tool and has recently been modified. In this case, the developer also needs to modify the build description file so that it hard-codes the new dependency relationship. For build tools that use file system monitoring, the tool automatically detects the change in dependencies, with no human intervention.

At this point, you've finished looking at all the approaches to building up the dependency graph. Getting the exact list of dependencies correct can be a challenging problem, especially when parts of the cached dependency information must be marked as invalid because dependencies are introduced or removed.

# Step 2: Determining Which Files Are Out-of-Date

You're now ready to look at the second of the three main build tool steps identified earlier in the chapter. As a reminder, the first step was to create a complete dependency graph, possibly with some of it being cached since the last time you invoked the build tool. The second step is to figure out exactly which files were modified since the last build took place. Files that haven't changed and that don't depend on other files that have changed don't need to be recompiled.

This part of the build process isn't too complex to understand or implement. When compared to creating a dependency graph, significantly fewer opportunities exist for errors to creep in and cause invalid builds. However, a build can take longer than necessary for several reasons, causing some amount of wasted development time.

This section examines different ways to detect whether a file has changed, including time stamp comparison, checksum comparison, and flag comparison. You'll also consider some advanced techniques for detecting change.

## Time Stamp-Based Methods

The classic method of determining whether a file has changed is to examine the file's time stamp. All modern operating systems keep track of when a file was last written to, and the build tool can easily query the file system for this information. Although it seems simple in theory, consider a few implementation methods:

1. In traditional Make-based systems, a file is considered to have been modified if it has a more recent time stamp than any of its derived files. For example, if `dog.obj` depends on `dog.c`, you should assume that `dog.c` has been modified recently if it has a more recent time stamp than `dog.obj`. This method doesn't particularly care about files having absolute time stamps, as long as it can detect a relative ordering of file changes. An interesting feature is that a file can be "touched" to modify its time stamp, without actually making any real changes to the file. This is useful when forcing a file to be recompiled for some reason (such as recovering from bad dependencies). It's also important to delete the output file if the compilation fails for any reason. Failure to do this causes the half-created output file to appear as if it's newer than the source file. Future invocations of the build tool will incorrectly decide that no recompilation is necessary, and the broken object file will remain in the object tree. GNU Make and Ant commonly use this technique, as do a number of the decider functions in the SCons tool.

2. In another approach, the build tool has some way of caching each file's time stamp. In this case, you no longer need to compare different files; instead, you can detect whether a file has changed by comparing its current time stamp against its previous time stamp. This method clearly involves the extra overhead of storing time stamps in a cache. An advantage of this mechanism, when compared to using relative time stamps, is that it can detect changes in source files that have occurred in the past. It's an incorrect assumption that any change made to the content of a file will result in using the current time stamp. For example, if a source file has been restored from a filesystem backup, the time stamp of that file probably reflects the last point in time the file was modified, which was sometime before the backup was taken. This may be a much older time stamp than when the object file was last compiled. If you incorrectly assumed that the source file hadn't been modified because it's older than the object file, the build tree wouldn't end up in a consistent state.

```
$ ls -l foo.c
-rw-r--r-- psmith 3500 2009-05-17 19:13 foo.c

$ ls -l foo.o
-rw-r--r— psmith 73923 2009-05-17 19:17 foo.o

$ rm foo.c        # OOOPS!
```

Now restore the file from a backup. You'll restore a version of foo.c from 2 days ago.

```
$ ls -l foo.c
-rw-r--r-- psmith 3223 2009-05-15 12:22 foo.c

$ ls -l foo.o
-rw-r--r— psmith 73923 2009-05-17 19:17 foo.o
```

Unfortunately, foo.o no longer matches foo.c, but it won't rebuild because the object file is newer than the source file. If you instead compared the source file's current time stamp against the time stamp it had when the last build was performed, you'd notice that the file was different and the object file would correctly be recompiled. This second time stamp approach is used by the SCons build tool, but not by GNU Make or Ant. Only SCons keeps a database of file time stamps, whereas other tools don't maintain the necessary persistent state.

3. The third time stamp method is often used when it is too hard to compute the correct dependencies in a build tree. Instead, the final step of the build is to create a .stamp file that specifically marks the point in time when the

last successful build completed. When a developer requests a new build, the tool examines all the time stamps on all the files in the build tree, without even considering the dependency graph. If any newer files exist, the entire tree is cleaned and then rebuilt.Although this method uses a brute-force approach to recompilation, it's still commonly used in build systems, especially those that use GNU Make. It trades off recompilation time for the extra effort of ensuring correct dependencies. This is a reasonable approach only for small build systems or those that don't change often.

For all three of these time stamp methods, the build tool spends a lot of time querying the file system to determine each file's current time stamp. As you'll see in Part IV, "Scaling Up," this operation can become expensive, especially for large build trees.

It's also important for the build tool and the file system to have synchronized clocks; otherwise, their ability to compare time stamps will fail. This isn't usually a problem on a standalone machine where all files are stored on the same disk, but problems can occur in a network file system environment.

For example, if dog.c is stored on a remote file system that has a slow clock, and dog.obj is stored on a local file system, it's possible that dog.obj will have a newer time stamp, even though dog.c was modified more recently. Here's the sequence of steps:

1. dog.c was modified and saved to a network file system. (The time on the file server is 10:01am.)

2. dog.c was compiled and dog.obj was saved to a local disk. (The time on the local machine is 10:03am.)

3. dog.c was modified again and saved to the network file system. (The time on the file server is 10:02am.)

4. The build tool won't regenerate dog.obj because it's newer than dog.c.

## Checksum-Based Methods

After observing the problems with time stamp-based detection of whether a file has been modified, it seems that a more accurate method might be useful. Using **checksum** (or **hashing**) techniques such as MD5 or SHA, it's possible to obtain a numeric fingerprint (such as a 128-bit number) that summarizes the content of the entire file. These checksum methods are not guaranteed to uniquely summarize the content of a file, but if two files have the same checksum value, it's extremely likely that the files have the same content.

Any build tool that uses a checksum method must have the capability to compute and store each file's checksum whenever the build tool is invoked. Computing checksums isn't a trivial operation, so the build tool's performance can suffer. In large projects with thousands of source files, the time required to compute all the checksums might be unacceptable.

One interesting outcome of using a checksum-based system is that simply touching the file won't make it appear to have changed. If the content is the same, the checksum will be the same, and no recompilation takes place. This approach leads to a few interesting scenarios:

- Changes to code comments don't cause the program to be relinked. Even though the C compiler is called into action, a change in a code comment won't cause the output of the C compiler to be any different than last time (assuming that no time or date stamps are embedded in the output file). Therefore, the build tool deduces that the linking phase can be skipped (see Figure 11.14).

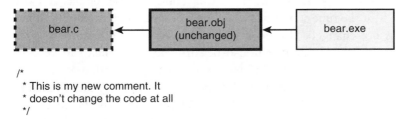

**Figure 11.14** *Adding a source code comment doesn't impact the object file. No linking step is required.*

- Autogenerated source files don't necessarily cause object files to recompile. Build systems that use a large number of autogenerated files might end up touching too many files, causing the entire tree to rebuild. With the checksum method, only files that actually ended up being different will trigger recompilation of other files.

  In Figure 11.15, you can see that `animals.list` is used as the main source code file for autogenerating many C files. Given the way the compilation tool works, any change in `animals.list` causes all the C files to regenerate from scratch, thus changing their time stamps. Using a checksum-based method, only the files that have actually changed (in this case, `cat_gen.c`) cause object files to rebuild. Other object files remain untouched.

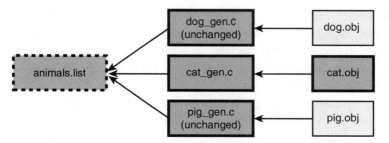

**Figure 11.15** *With checksum-based checks, you compile only the autogenerated files that have actually changed.*

This technique avoids a large amount of unnecessarily recompilation, thus making the developer more productive.

As a reminder, Chapter 8, "SCons," discussed the MD5-timestamp decider function that optimizes this checksum approach. You can ask the build tool to perform the checksum operation only if the time stamp on the file has actually changed. That is, if the time stamp has not changed, you know for sure that the file content has not changed. However, if the time stamp is different, there's a good possibility that the content will also be different. This then can be confirmed or disproved by computing the checksum. This optimization works well because reading a file's time stamp is much faster than computing the checksum.

Although SCons is the only build tool that natively supports the checksum approach, it's possible to implement this same feature in other build tools. Using the GNU move-if-change script, it's possible to update the target file's time stamp only if the file content is different from the last build invocation. The trick is to generate the new content into a temporary file, but copy that temporary file into the target location only if the content has changed. If not, the file isn't copied and the time stamp isn't updated.

## Flag Comparison

One concept touched on in an earlier section is that an object file should have a dependency on the tool's command-line options. If the options changed (such as by adding a debug flag), the object file would need to be rebuilt with the new options enabled. Therefore, you need a third method of determining whether a file is up-to-date, but this time the method is not based on the file's content.

A build tool that supports this feature must have some mechanism for storing each object file's command-line options. With SCons, this feature is built into the basic tool, and the SCons database maintains a list of compilation flags used. Any change to these flags causes all object files to be rebuilt.

In the case of GNU Make, this feature isn't a standard part of the tool, but by adding a supplementary file (for example, with the `.flags` suffix), a comparison between old and new `.flag` files is sufficient to detect a change.

## Advanced Methods

The three change-detection methods discussed so far (time stamps, checksums, and flags) are currently used in a number of common build tools. However, if you carefully think about how files are actually changed, you have other clever ways to optimize this process. After all, the time stamp and checksum methods are fairly brute-force approaches that require looking at each file in turn. For large build systems, this can take several minutes to complete.

The following are some advanced methods of solving the file change problem:

- **Ask the version-control tool:** One of the main ways the files in a build tree are modified is by the version-control tool (such as CVS or Subversion). When these tools update the files in your source tree, they can provide the build tool with a list of files that have changed. With this list in hand, you shouldn't need to query each file's time stamp or checksum.

  The ClearCase version-control system [5] is a great example of how this works. The clearmake build tool is tightly integrated with the version-control tool and knows exactly which version of each input file was used to generate an object file. It then queries the version-control system to determine whether any of those input files have been modified.

- **Ask the integrated development environment (IDE):** Users of IDEs, such as Eclipse or Visual Studio, can assume that the only way a source file can change is if the IDE saved a new version of that file. By asking the IDE for a list of files that have changed (since the time of the last build), the build tool avoids querying each file to see if it's different. Clearly, this solution assumes that the developer doesn't change source files using any other tool or directly from the operating system's command line.

- **Ask the file system:** Regardless of which development tools are used, the file system itself is the ultimate authority on whether a file has changed. Using a log-based tracking system, you can ask the file system for the list of files that have changed since the last build. Although this would be significantly faster than querying each file one by one, most file systems don't support this functionality. In any case, it might not work well in a networked environment where files can be modified from many different computers.

Hopefully, future generations of build tools will use these types of optimization more often.

## Step 3: Sequencing the Compilation Steps

Finally, you've come to the third step in the build tool's high-level workflow. As a reminder, the first step was to construct the dependency graph, and the second was to identify which files have changed since the build tool was last invoked. This section discusses the third step, in which the compilation tools are actually put into action. For many people, this is where the build tool starts doing useful work.

Ironically, the process of creating a dependency graph and then determining which files are out-of-date can take longer than executing the compilation steps themselves. This is certainly true in large software projects in which only one source file has changed. The net effect is that developers perceive that the build system is doing nothing, until they start to see the commands being executed.

The remaining problem is how to invoke each of the compilation tools in the correct order so that the final software image is brought completely up-to-date. As a general rule, a particular file that is currently out-of-date must be regenerated after each of its dependencies has been regenerated (see Figure 11.16). From a simplistic perspective, the compilations must occur from left to right in the diagrams. That is, the object files are compiled first, followed by the libraries and then the executable program.

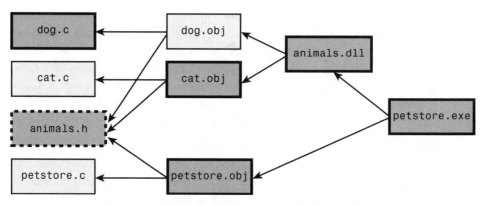

**Figure 11.16** *A change to animals.h causes the files to be recompiled from left to right.*

For a build tool that executes compilation jobs one at a time, the simplistic approach is probably the best. However, you have more choice on computers that have enough processing power to execute multiple jobs in parallel. These computers include single-CPU systems that have excess capacity, multicore systems, and distributed clusters of computers that share access to the same build tree.

For simplicity, assume in this discussion that each compilation job takes exactly the same amount of time. If you execute one compilation after another, the following sequence is likely:

| Time | CPU 1 |
|------|-------|
| 1 | dog.obj |
| 2 | cat.obj |
| 3 | animals.dll |
| 4 | petstore.obj |
| 5 | petstore.exe |

Note that because all three of the .obj files depend only on source files instead of anything that needs to be regenerated, they could be compiled in any order. However, the build tool will likely handle them in the order in which they're specified in the build description file. This also explains why animals.dll is built before petstore.obj.

If two jobs are built in parallel, you may see the following sequence of events:

| Time | CPU 1 | CPU 2 |
|------|-------|-------|
| 1 | dog.obj | cat.obj |
| 2 | animals.dll | petstore.obj |
| 3 | petstore.exe | |

The build process now takes three time units instead of five units, yet you still end up with the same results. Because dog.obj and cat.obj don't have dependencies on each other, they can compile in parallel. The same is true for animals.dll and petstore.obj.

Now examine a scenario with three jobs executing at once:

| Time | CPU 1 | CPU 2 | CPU 3 |
|------|-------|-------|-------|
| 1 | dog.obj | cat.obj | petstore.obj |
| 2 | animals.dll | | |
| 3 | petstore.exe | | |

Unfortunately, you've now reached the maximum parallelism level for this build process. Because `animals.dll` must wait until `dog.obj` and `cat.obj` are complete, and because `petstore.exe` can't start building until `animals.dll` is complete, you don't see any further speed-up. In this particular example, there's no benefit to adding the third parallel job.

What would happen if your build tool lacked sufficient information in the dependency graph? After all, this is a fairly common problem, especially when building in parallel. Now examine the situation in which the dependency that `animals.dll` has on `cat.obj` was missing:

| Time | Job 1 | Job 2 |
| --- | --- | --- |
| 1 | `dog.obj` | `petstore.obj` |
| 2 | `cat.obj` | `animals.dll` |
| 3 | `petstore.exe` | |

In this case, `animals.dll` is incorrectly scheduled at the same time as `cat.obj`, which definitely causes a problem. Most likely, `animals.dll` will observe `cat.obj` changing as it's being read, resulting in a build failure.

Oddly enough, this missing dependency wouldn't cause problems if only one job was executed at a time. The two files would always be executed in the correct order, and nobody would notice anything wrong. This is simply a side effect of the build tool always sequencing the jobs in the same order, regardless of dependencies. When building many jobs in parallel, the problems start to show up.

As a final example, it's interesting to understand how the ElectricAccelerator tool can build on massively parallel clusters (with potentially hundreds of CPUs). The strength of this tool is that it can still produce a correct software image, even if critical dependencies are missing. The key to ElectricAccelerator's success is that it uses the file system monitoring technique to determine each compilation tool's exact set of dependencies.

In Figure 11.17, each box represents a single compilation job. You have four different CPUs executing jobs, with each job taking one time unit (again, a simplification). Everything compiles smoothly until Job B is executed on CPU 2 at time 5. At this time, ElectricAccelerator notices that the job has just written to a file that was already used by a previous job (Job A). Although no rules explicitly informed the tool of this dependency, it discovered this on its own.

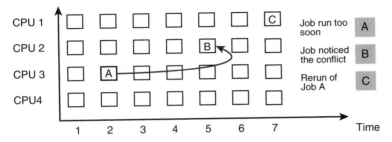

**Figure 11.17** *The ElectricAccelerator conflict-resolution system.*

The next step is for ElectricAccelerator to rerun the job that was performed in the wrong order. In the example, Job C is identical to Job A, except that it now has access to the necessary output from Job B. ElectricAccelerator also takes note of this situation (known as a **conflict**) and ensures that future invocations of the build tool are properly aware of this dependency.

## Summary

A build tool must follow a three-step process. First, it builds up the dependency graph to determine which files are derived from which other files. Next, it checks the file system to determine which of those files have been modified since you last invoked the build tool. Finally, it calls upon the individual compilation tools to bring all the object files, libraries, and executable programs up-to-date.

Constructing the dependency graph is perhaps the most challenging part of creating a build system because you have various ways of gathering the required information. The goal is to predict which files a compilation tool will access and make sure that all prerequisite files are first brought up-to-date. Although it's possible to cache some of this information, you need to make sure the cache is kept up-to-date with ongoing changes to build description files, source files, and compilation flags.

When determining whether files need to be recompiled, you can query each file's time stamps, compute its checksum, or use one of several more advanced methods.

Finally, having an accurate dependency graph is important to ensure that compilation commands are executed in the correct order, especially when the workload is executed in parallel across multiple CPUs.

# Chapter 12

## Building with Metadata

Although the primary goal of a build system is to create an executable program to deliver to a customer, many build variants are intended only for software developers. As you saw in Chapter 5, "Subtargets and Build Variants," build variants enable you to generate a range of release packages, such as for different CPU types or different software editions. This chapter discusses another group of variants, with the focus on producing metadata.

The simple definition of **metadata** is data that describes the structure or attributes of data. In the context of a build system, metadata is additional information about the structure of an executable program. A developer can use that information to study or monitor the program in various ways.

This chapter discusses the following types of metadata:

- **Debugging support:** Enables source-code level debugging of a running program, which helps a developer identify the location of bugs.

- **Profiling support:** Determines how a program spends its execution time, enabling a developer to optimize the most time-critical portions of the code.

- **Coverage support:** Determines which lines of code are being executed. This gives developers a better understanding of whether their code has been fully tested.

- **Source code documentation:** Provides formatted documentation of code APIs, in a format such as HTML. Developers can understand the code's main entry points without diving into the detailed code itself.

- **Unit testing:** Validates whether the individual units (modules or functions) of a program are performing correctly instead of testing the release package as a whole.

- **Static analysis:** Identifies common programming errors at compilation time, in contrast to finding bugs when the program is executing.

Each of these build variants requires support from the build system, either by invoking a special-purpose compilation tool or by passing additional flags to the standard compiler. Although these features are optional, a well-maintained build system should support them all.

Now let's take a brief look at each type of metadata listed to see how it can improve software quality. Although this chapter discusses only one way of generating each type of metadata, you'll likely find that your own development tools provide similar features.

## Debugging Support

Debugging support is one of the most common compiler options. Developers must have the ability to monitor the progress of their code as it executes. They should examine which lines of code are executed and which values are assigned to their program variables. Lack of good debugging support makes finding and fixing software bugs much harder.

Even though a program executes as a sequence of machine code (or byte code) instructions, developers prefer to think about the lines of source code they wrote and the variables they declared. The compiler must generate extra information so that a debugger tool can reverse-engineer the execution of the program. It can then display the program's runtime state in developer-centric terms.

For example, the compiler must record the following:

- The memory address and data type of each variable in the program

- The start address of each function within the machine code, along with its list of parameters

- The memory address of each individual line of source code

Using this information, a debugger can fetch the necessary values from memory (and the CPU registers) and display the source code relating the current line of code being executed. It can also read the value of variables and display them in the appropriate data format, such as a character, number, string, or pointer.

All modern compilers offer debugging support, which is enabled by adding a command-line option (such as -g). Because of its importance, many build systems generate debug information by default. The following example shows how the GNU debugger [67] traces the execution of a program. Entering the `list` command shows the first ten lines of the program's source code.

```
$ gcc -g -o prog prog.c
$ gdb prog
...
(gdb) list
1       #include <stdio.h>
2
3       int main(int argc, char *argv[])
4       {
5         int i;
6
7         for (i = 0; i != 100; i++) {
8           printf("The next number is %d\n", i);
9         }
10      return 0;
```

Next, a breakpoint is set at line 7 of the code (at the start of the `for` loop) by invoking the `break` command. The compiler-generated metadata informs the debugger that line 7 is at machine code address `0x8048435`.

```
(gdb) break 7
Breakpoint 1 at 0x8048435: file prog.c, line 7.
```

When you run the program, execution stops at line 7, and you continue on a line-by-line basis (as requested by the `next` command).

```
(gdb) run
Starting program: /home/psmith/Book/examples/debugging-
➥ session/prog

Breakpoint 1, main (argc=<value optimized out>,
    argv=<value optimized out>) at prog.c:7
7           for (i = 0; i != 100; i++) {
(gdb) next
8               printf("The next number is %d\n", i);
(gdb) next
The next number is 0
7           for (i = 0; i != 100; i++) {
(gdb) next
8               printf("The next number is %d\n", i);
```

You also have the option to display the value of each program variable. The compiler provided enough metadata for the debugger to learn the variable's memory address and data type.

```
(gdb) print i
$1 = 1
```

Although this debugging session is entirely text based, many environments also support graphical debugging. Developers can set breakpoints directly from their editor and see which line of code is currently executing. Some debuggers provide a graphical display of data structures, showing each structure or class as a box, with references between these structures represented by arrows.

If you're using the GNU C compiler, you should investigate the GDB debugger used in our example. Additionally, consider using the DDD [68] front end, which provides a more graphical view of the program.

Passing the -g option to GCC generates debug information, encoded in a format such as DWARF [69]. When an executable program is created, GCC inserts the metadata into a special section within the executable file. GDB extracts this information to debug the program.

For Java development, you might want to look at the jdb command-line tool (part of the JDK [30]), although most IDEs provide Java debugging as a built-in feature. The same is true for C# and the Microsoft Visual Studio tools.

## Profiling Support

The act of profiling a program means that you can determine how long the CPU spends executing each part of the code, or how much memory is used to store each type of data. The goal is to give the developer a view of how the program spends its resources and, therefore, how it can be optimized. If you focus your optimizations on the most time-consuming portions of the program, you'll see the most dramatic performance improvements.

For example, the following output shows the CPU profile of the CVS source code–management tool at the point it was downloading source code from an Internet site. The GNU Profiler tool [70] generated the output; it requires all C source files to be compiled with the special -pg flag. In this case, the CVS tool's standard build system was modified to include this additional flag.

```
Each sample counts as 0.01 seconds.
  %    cumulative   self              self     total
 time   seconds    seconds    calls  ms/call  ms/call  name
 33.33     0.01       0.01     2541     0.00     0.00  buf_
 read_line
 33.33     0.02       0.01     2171     0.00     0.00  getstr
 33.33     0.03       0.01                              find_
 rcs
  0.00     0.03       0.00    76003     0.00     0.00  stdio_
 buffer_input
  0.00     0.03       0.00    16072     0.00     0.00  xmalloc
  0.00     0.03       0.00    15226     0.00     0.00  xstrdup
  0.00     0.03       0.00     3396     0.00     0.00  hashp
  0.00     0.03       0.00     3280     0.00     0.00  getnode
```

| | | | | | | |
|---|---|---|---|---|---|---|
| 0.00 | 0.03 | 0.00 | 2542 | 0.00 | 0.00 | buf_ |
| flush | | | | | | |
| 0.00 | 0.03 | 0.00 | 2542 | 0.00 | 0.00 | buf_ |
| send_output | | | | | | |
| 0.00 | 0.03 | 0.00 | 2542 | 0.00 | 0.00 | stdio_ |
| buffer_flush | | | | | | |
| 0.00 | 0.03 | 0.00 | 2541 | 0.00 | 0.00 | read_ |
| line | | | | | | |
| 0.00 | 0.03 | 0.00 | 2367 | 0.00 | 0.00 | freen- |
| ode_mem | | | | | | |
| 0.00 | 0.03 | 0.00 | 2171 | 0.00 | 0.00 | getline |
| 0.00 | 0.03 | 0.00 | 1950 | 0.00 | 0.00 | get- |
| date_yylex | | | | | | |
| 0.00 | 0.03 | 0.00 | 1864 | 0.00 | 0.01 | fgeten- |
| tent | | | | | | |
| 0.00 | 0.03 | 0.00 | 1762 | 0.00 | 0.00 | fputen- |
| tent | | | | | | |
| 0.00 | 0.03 | 0.00 | 1753 | 0.00 | 0.00 | Entn- |
| ode_Create | | | | | | |

[ output truncated ]

In this example, you can see the list of functions executed (in the name column), as well as how many times each was invoked (in the calls column). The main observation is that roughly one-third of the CPU time (according to the % time column) was spent in each of the buf_read_line, getstr, and find_rcs functions.

Interestingly, only 0.03 seconds (see the self seconds column) was spent executing these three functions, whereas the program itself ran for a total of 15 seconds. This indicates that the program is I/O bound instead of limited by the performance of any functions in the code. Given that the CVS tool was downloading code from the Internet, this should hardly be surprising.

Code profiling can be implemented in several ways. For the previous example, the computer's operating system took periodic snapshots to determine which function was executing at each point in time. Only 100 snapshots were taken each second, so the measurement isn't very fine-grained. In the example, most of the functions appear not to have been called at all, simply because they weren't executing during any of these snapshots.

Another implementation method is for the compiler to add machine code to count how many times each function is called. This metric (see the calls column in the example) is guaranteed to be accurate because it's based on reliable counters instead of periodic snapshots. When profiling each function's use of memory (not shown in the example), the same method is used to count the number of times memory chunks are allocated or freed.

## Coverage Support

Code coverage is similar in nature to profiling, although the focus is more on determining which lines of code, or paths within the code, are actually being executed. The goal is to help developers understand which parts of the code might need more testing and, therefore, may still contain unfound bugs.

As an example, the following output shows the annotated source code of a simple program. This output was produced by running the GNU gcov tool [25] over a program that was compiled with the GCC -fprofile-arcs and -ftest-coverage command-line options.

The number in the first column indicates how many times the line of code was executed, with ##### indicating that it was never executed.

```
      -:    1:#include <stdio.h>
      -:    2:
      -:    3:void divide(int number)
    100:    4:{
    100:    5:  if (number % 3 == 0){
     34:    6:    printf("This number is divisible by 3\n");
     66:    7:  } else if (number % 200 == 0){
  #####:    8:    printf("This number is divisible by 200\n");
      -:    9:  } else {
     66:   10:    printf("Not an interesting number\n");
      -:   11:  }
    100:   12:}
      -:   13:
      -:   14:int main(int argc, char *argv[])
      1:   15:{
      -:   16:  int i;
      -:   17:
    101:   18:  for (i = 0; i != 100; i++){
    100:   19:    divide(i);
      -:   20:  }
      1:   21:  return 0;
      -:   22:}
```

As you can see, line 8 is never reached, which offers a clue that additional test cases are required to test that branch of code.

Counting the number of times each code block is executed offers code coverage information. With some coverage tools, it's also possible to count the number of times a decision is made within the program, even down to the level of individual Boolean tests. For example, the following simple expression has four possible outcomes:

```
if (a < 10 && b < 5) {
  ...
} else {
```

```
    . . .
}
```

Although clearly just two code paths can be followed, you can consider each part of the Boolean expression individually and, therefore, use four different counters. This is especially important if you care about why the code path was taken.

| Counter Number | a < 10 | b < 5 | a < 10 && b < 5 |
|---|---|---|---|
| 1 | False | False | False |
| 2 | False | True | False |
| 3 | True | False | False |
| 4 | True | True | True |

As with profiling, additional "counting" instructions are inserted into each object file, assuming that the necessary command-line options are passed to the C compiler. Naturally, this makes the object code slightly larger and slower than a program compiled without the coverage instrumentation.

## Source Code Documentation

Although the primary goal of a build system is to produce an executable program, it can also generate web-based API documentation. This includes the high-level detail of functions, methods, classes, variables, and constant definitions, but without going into any of the low-level implementation detail. Having this documentation available is a great way for new developers to understand a library's external API. It makes it possible to learn the available definitions without studying the fine detail of source code that might be thousands of lines long.

Clearly, expecting developers to update an API web page on their own would be too time-consuming and error prone. Given that developers are supposed to focus on writing code, updating web pages becomes a secondary task that ends up being neglected. Instead, you can use automated tools to extract the information directly from the source code and then generate the corresponding web page.

To illustrate, let's consider a short Java class and the resulting output of running the Javadoc tool (part of the Java Development Kit). This particular tool is widely used in the industry to describe the APIs provided by Java classes. In fact, the entire set of standard Java libraries is described in this format. From the build system's perspective, Javadoc is simply a compiler that generates web pages instead of .class files.

This Java source code exports a public API. The purpose of this code isn't important, but take careful note of the method names and parameters, as well as the code comments.

```java
/**
 * Manage a time using the 24-hour clock system.
 *
 * @author Peter Smith
 */
public class ClockNumber {

    /** The hour number, from 0 to 23 */
    int time;

    /**
     * Construct a new ClockNumber object, using
     * the provided parameter as the initial value.
     * @param hour The initial value for the hour, from 0 to
23.
     */
    public ClockNumber(int hour){
        time = hour;
    }

    /**
     * Construct a new ClockNumber, using midnight as
     * the default time.
     */
    public ClockNumber() {
        time = 0;
    }

    /**
     * Add the specified number of hours to the current time.
     * @param hours The number of hours to add to the current
       time.
     * @return The new hour value.
     */
    public int add(int hours) {
        time = (time + hours) % 24;
        return time;
    }
}
```

Figure 12.1 shows the web-based output generated by running Javadoc. This can be done via the standard `javadoc` command-line tool or from an IDE that supports Javadoc (such as Eclipse).

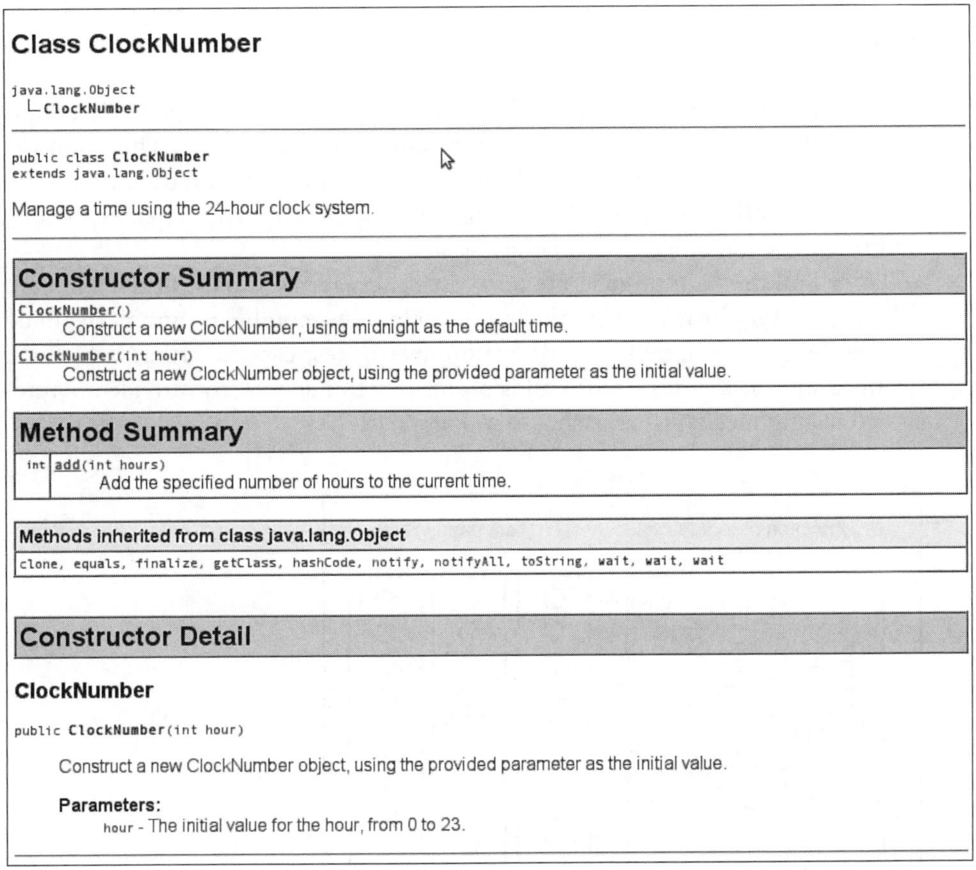

## Class ClockNumber

```
java.lang.Object
  └ClockNumber
```

```
public class ClockNumber
extends java.lang.Object
```

Manage a time using the 24-hour clock system.

### Constructor Summary

| |
|---|
| `ClockNumber()` |
| Construct a new ClockNumber, using midnight as the default time. |
| `ClockNumber(int hour)` |
| Construct a new ClockNumber object, using the provided parameter as the initial value. |

### Method Summary

| | |
|---|---|
| `int` | `add(int hours)` |
| | Add the specified number of hours to the current time. |

### Methods inherited from class java.lang.Object

`clone, equals, finalize, getClass, hashCode, notify, notifyAll, toString, wait, wait, wait`

### Constructor Detail

**ClockNumber**

`public ClockNumber(int hour)`

Construct a new ClockNumber object, using the provided parameter as the initial value.

**Parameters:**
hour - The initial value for the hour, from 0 to 23.

**Figure 12.1** *Output from the Javadoc tool.*

As you can see, this page contains only the high-level information from the class, not the actual lines of code. The class constructors are listed first, followed by each of the public methods. Note that Javadoc extracts text from the code comments and applies special meaning to Javadoc tags such as @param and @ return.

Although Javadoc is specifically designed for Java code, other tools support other languages. These include Doxygen [71] and DOC++ [72] for C/C++, and Sandcastle [73] for C#.

## Unit Testing

Adding a unit test variant to a build system enables a developer to determine exactly which unit of code (module or function) contains a bug. This contrasts with the more traditional approach of testing the complete program to see if it behaves correctly. Experience shows that a unit-testing approach makes locating and fixing a wide range of bugs much easier.

For a build system to generate unit tests, it creates a variant of the standard release package. Instead of producing the default executable program, the build system links the program code with a number of test case functions, which are grouped into test suites. It also adds a unit-test framework to provide an automated testing mechanism, as shown in Figure 12.2.

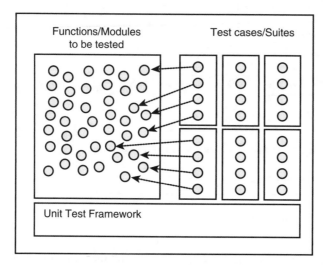

**Figure 12.2** *A set of functions or modules tested within a unit test framework. Everything is linked into a unit-test executable program.*

When the program executes, the unit test framework invokes each of the test cases in turn. Each test case calls a particular function or module from the main program's code, to ensure that it works correctly. This is done by invoking each function with a predetermined set of input parameters and then checking the return value to ensure that it matches what was expected. If a test case fails, an error report is provided on the program's output, producing the metadata you need to debug the problem.

Now look at a simple unit-testing example, using the JUnit test framework [74]. It starts with a simple Java class representing a rectangle:

```
1   public class Rectangle {
2
3     private int width;
4     private int height;
5
6     public Rectangle(int w, int h) throws InvalidSizeExcep-
      tion {
7         if ((w <= 0) || (h <= 0)) {
8             throw new InvalidSizeException();
9         }
10        width = w;
11        height = h;
12    }
13
14    public int getWidth() {
15        return width;
16    }
17
18    public int getHeight() {
19        return height;
20    }
21
22    public int getArea() {
23        return width / height;
24    }
25  }
```

The `Rectangle` class defines a constructor (in line 6) that requires both a width and height value to be provided. These values are recorded within the new object's `width` and `height` fields (lines 10–11). However, if either of these values would cause the creation of a zero-sized or negative-sized rectangle, an `InvalidSizeException` is thrown (line 8).

This class also provides accessor methods for retrieving the width (line 14), the height (line 18), and the area of the rectangle (line 22). Note that the area calculation on line 23 is incorrect, resulting in bad values produced by the `getArea()` method.

Now examine a second class, `TestRectangle`, used to test the functionality provided by `Rectangle`. The `TestRectangle` class is linked into the program only for testing purposes and won't be copied into the default release package.

```
1   import static org.junit.Assert.*;
2   import org.junit.Test;
3
4   public class TestRectangle {
5
6     @Test
7     public void testRectangleValid()
8             throws InvalidSizeException {
9         Rectangle r1 = new Rectangle(1, 2);
10        assertEquals(1, r1.getWidth());
```

```
11              assertEquals(2, r1.getHeight());
12
13          Rectangle r2 = new Rectangle(50, 23);
14              assertEquals(50, r2.getWidth());
15              assertEquals(23, r2.getHeight());
16      }
17
18      @Test(expected= InvalidSizeException.class)
19      public void testRectangleInvalidSize()
20              throws InvalidSizeException {
21          Rectangle r3 = new Rectangle(-1, 10);
22      }
23
24      @Test
25      public void testArea() throws InvalidSizeException {
26          Rectangle r4 = new Rectangle(10, 15);
27              assertEquals(150, r4.getArea());
28      }
29
30  }
```

The TestRectangle class is an example of a JUnit test suite. It contains three different test case methods (testRectangleValid, testRectangleInvalid-Size, and testArea), each of which verifies a feature of the Rectangle class. Each test can pass or fail independently from the other tests.

The testRectangleValid method (lines 6–16) validates the basic creation of Rectangle objects. It creates two objects (stored in r1 and r2), each with a specific width and height. It then invokes the getWidth() and getHeight() methods to ensure that both the constructor and the accessor methods work as expected.

The assertEquals() method is defined within the JUnit framework. If the expected value (the first parameter to assertEquals()) differs from the actual value seen by calling getWidth() or getHeight(), the test case is marked as having failed.

The testRectangleInvalidSize method (lines 18–22) ensures that creating a zero- or negative-sized rectangle isn't possible. The directive in line 18 specifies that the method is expected to throw an InvalidSizeException when a new Rectangle is created. If no exception is thrown, the test case fails.

Finally, the testArea() method confirms that the getArea() method works as expected. However, there's a bug in getArea() (the calculation used / instead of *). Figure 12.3 shows the output from the Eclipse JUnit view when this particular test case fails.

**Figure 12.3** *The JUnit view from Eclipse, showing results from the TestRectangle class.*

Although creating a good set of test suites involves significant work, the benefits can be enormous. Running through all the tests might take a few minutes, but having a detailed report of exactly where the problem lies is so much easier than debugging a full executable program. As an analogy, it's like being told exactly where the needle is within a haystack, instead of trying to find it for yourself.

In many development environments, it's standard practice to consider the software build broken if the unit tests don't pass at 100%. It's not just a matter of whether all the code compiles correctly; the software must pass all the test cases. If any failures occur, the code isn't ready to be shared with other developers.

This simple JUnit example doesn't show the full power of unit testing and doesn't even start to uncover the numerous techniques involved in writing good tests. For a more complete view of unit testing best practices, refer to [75]. To learn how to retrofit legacy software with new unit tests, refer to [76].

## Static Analysis

The final type of metadata discussed in this chapter provides the capability to identify software bugs, or at least suggest where potential bugs might turn up if you're not careful. Studying the program's source code, a static-analysis tool can pinpoint lines of source code where a bug might be lurking. The developer reviews this information and decides whether there's a true problem to fix.

The following example shows a small Java class that contains a few programming errors.

```
1 import java.util.List;
2
3 public class Buggy {
4     int myField;
5
6     public void buggyMethod(List list, int number, String
      str) {
7         int count;
8
9         if (list == null) {
10             list.add(Integer.valueOf(number));
11         }
12         myField = number;
13
14         if (str == "Hello"){
15             System.out.println("Hi");
16         }
17     }
18 }
```

Running this source code through the FindBugs tool [8], you can automatically identify three different problems. Although the output from FindBugs is slightly cryptic, any Java or C# programmer should be able to determine the errors.

```
$ findbugs Buggy.class
H C NP: Null pointer dereference of ? in Buggy.
buggyMethod(List, int,
        String) Dereferenced at Buggy.java:[line 10]
H B ES: Comparison of String parameter using == or != in
        Buggy.buggyMethod(List, int, String)   At Buggy.
java:[line 14]
M P UrF: Unread field: Buggy.myField  At Buggy.java:[line 12]
Warnings generated: 3
```

Ironically, these issues often escape the attention of developers, who tend to focus more on their program's logic than mistakes of this nature. A static-analysis tool is good at finding commonly recurring patterns, identified by a brute-force approach. Humans simply aren't good at brute-force analysis.

In addition to FindBugs, consider using tools such as Lint, Coverity Prevent [6], or Klocwork Insight [7].

## Adding Metadata to a Build System

As you saw in Chapter 5, you can add variants into a build system in several ways. In Part II, "The Build Tools," you also saw how each build tool (GNU Make, Ant, SCons, CMake, and Eclipse) facilitates the addition of variants. Creating metadata in the build process is handled the same way.

From a developer's perspective, several approaches exist for requesting the additional metadata. The first approach is to build the standard software release package but provide an extra command-line flag to request that metadata be added. For example:

- `gmake DEBUG=1 all`: Builds the standard release package, but with additional debugging information

- `ant -Dcoverage=yes`: Builds the standard software, with added instrumentation for collecting coverage data

- `scons profiling=on`: Builds the standard software, but with code instrumented for profiling the program's execution

In each of these examples, you build the standard release package, but with additional metadata included. As you saw in Part II, the build system can either select which compilation tool is used (the GNU Make `CC` variable) or modify the flags passed to the standard compiler (the GNU Make `CFLAGS` variable).

For the remaining types of metadata, which produce a different type of build output, it's common to make use of a completely different build target:

- `gmake tests`: Builds and executes the unit test suites

- `ant doc`: Generates the API documentation using Javadoc

- `scons analyze`: Analyzes the code using a static-analysis tool and produces a bug report

In these three cases, you would add a completely new section in the build description file stating which commands, tasks, or builder methods were used to generate the metadata. This contrasts with simply modifying the existing build steps.

Finally, the Eclipse IDE has built-in support for these types of metadata—or at least the capability to interconnect with third-party tools. Enabling these features is a simple matter of opening the correct Eclipse view or selecting a configuration check box.

## Summary

In addition to building a customer-ready release package, a build system should enable the creation of metadata. This data isn't visible to the end user; it instead offers developer-facing techniques for improving software quality or enabling more efficient development.

A program's metadata includes debugging support, coverage support, and profiling support, which enable developers to view their program's runtime behavior. A document-generation tool summarizes the program's main functions or methods, making it easier to visualize the program's structure. Finally, unit testing and static analysis provide details on a program's actual or suspected bugs.

Adding metadata to a build system is simply a matter of adding build flags, alternate compilation tools, or new build targets. The exact technique depends on how the particular type of metadata is generated.

# Chapter 13

## Software Packaging and Installation

The final step in the build process is to create a **release package** (see Figure 13.1). This package contains the complete set of files to be installed on the target machine. Anyone who has added software to a computer, which is almost anyone who owns a computer, will be familiar with the installation process.

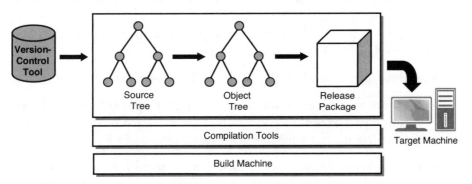

**Figure 13.1** *The big picture, with focus on creating a release package.*

Assume here that the end user isn't a developer and won't know how to compile the program directly from source code. It's more likely that users will download the software from the Internet and double-click on the Setup icon. On the other hand, users might insert a CD-ROM and wait until the software is automatically installed. This is clearly a place where the Windows and Mac OS X operating systems excel, partially explaining their popularity. As you'll see later, UNIX-like systems are also starting to support the same user-friendly ways of installing packages.

351

The **packaging** process consists of a number of steps. The main goal is to copy the required executable programs, dynamic libraries, and data files out of the object tree and place them in a release package. This is also the point at which a version number is added.

Unlike the object tree, the release package contains only files that are required to execute the program. It doesn't contain any of the intermediate object files generated by the build process. Also, the layout of the files within the release package must match the desired layout on the target machine. This can be quite different from how the files are stored in the source or object trees.

When installing software on the target machine, some systems have all their files placed in a single file system directory, whereas other software is spread across multiple directories. As an example, Microsoft Windows device drivers might need to be copied into the `C:\Windows\system32` folder, whereas the program itself would go into `C:\Program Files`.

You may also need to customize some of the target machine's system configuration, such as adding new user accounts or access groups, all of which could be based on input the user provides during the installation process. For software that uses interpreted byte-codes, such as Java or C#, the correct version of the virtual machine must also be installed.

This chapter examines three different approaches to packaging a release image. Each method has its own set of benefits.

- **Archive files:** A simple approach in which the user manually extracts files

- **Package-management tools:** A more complex approach in which prerequisite packages are identified, files are extracted to specific parts of the file system, and a post-installation script can be run.

- **Custom-built GUI installation tools:** An advanced approach in which a GUI interface enables the end user to customize the way the software is installed.

The chapter now discusses each of these approaches in more detail and gives an example of each case.

## Archive Files

The most basic approach to packaging a software release is to store the files inside an **archive**. A common tool in the Microsoft Windows world is the `zip` utility, which compresses each of the input files and joins them into a single large file. It also takes note of whether the input files were inside subdirectories so that it can reproduce that same hierarchy on the target machine. In the UNIX world, the same effect is achieved by using the `tar` tool to create an archive and using the `gzip` or `bzip2` tools to compress the archive file.

To implement a packaging system using this approach, you first copy the necessary files out of the object tree and place them in a temporary holding directory (see Figure 13.2). The files should be arranged in this directory using the same layout they'll have on the target machine.

When the temporary holding directory is fully populated, you invoke the archiving tool to package everything into a single file. This file is delivered to the end user, who then runs the same archiving tool, but in the reverse mode, to extract the files onto the target machine. At that point, the software is ready to be executed.

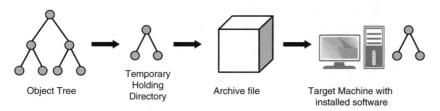

Object Tree          Temporary Holding Directory          Archive file          Target Machine with installed software

**Figure 13.2** *Creation of a release package, using a temporary holding directory in the creation of a file archive.*

## Packaging Scripts

The temporary holding directory can be created with a simple script that copies the required files from the object tree. The following is a small Windows batch script (named `packager.bat`) that creates a `.zip` file. This example uses the 7-zip utility [77] to compress the files into an archive.

```
1   @echo off
2   REM Packaging script for a simple application.
3   REM This batch script is executed after the full object
    tree has
4   REM been created. It copies files into a temporary direc-
    tory and
5   REM then creates a zip file of the content. The user must
    provide
6   REM a version number.
7
8   REM Version number of this package (supplied by the user)
9   set VERSION=%1%
10
11  REM Name of the final software package
12  set APPNAME=myapp
13
```

```
14   REM Path to the fully built object tree.
15   set OBJDIR=obj
16
17   REM Name of the temporary directory (that we'll zip up)
18   set PKGDIR=myapp.%VERSION%
19
20   REM Create the temporary directory
21   mkdir %PKGDIR%
22
23   REM Now, copy files from the object tree to the package
     directory
24   copy %OBJDIR%\calc.exe                    %PKGDIR%
25   copy %OBJDIR%\libs\libmath.dll            %PKGDIR%
26   copy %OBJDIR%\libs\libgraphics.dll        %PKGDIR%
27   copy %OBJDIR%\images\splash_screen.jpg    %PKGDIR%
28   copy %OBJDIR%\languages\errors.en         %PKGDIR%
29   copy %OBJDIR%\languages\errors.fr         %PKGDIR%
30   copy %OBJDIR%\languages\errors.de         %PKGDIR%
31
32   REM Finally, zip up the temporary directory to produce
     the final
33   REM archive file (called myapp.<version>.zip).
34   7z -tzip a myapp.%VERSION%.zip %PKGDIR%
```

By executing this packager.bat script and providing the software's version number as a parameter, you end up with a complete file archive ready to be installed on the target machine. In a typical build system, the build tool invokes this packaging script, just as if it were an ordinary compilation tool.

```
c:\work> packager.bat 3.0.1
        1 file(s) copied.
        1 file(s) copied.
        1 file(s) copied.
        1 file(s) copied.
        1 file(s) copied.
        1 file(s) copied.
        1 file(s) copied.

7-Zip 4.65  Copyright (c) 1999-2009 Igor Pavlov  2009-02-03
Scanning

Creating archive myapp.3.0.1.zip

Compressing   myapp.3.0.1\splash_screen.jpg
Compressing   myapp.3.0.1\errors.de
Compressing   myapp.3.0.1\errors.en
Compressing   myapp.3.0.1\errors.fr
Compressing   myapp.3.0.1\calc.exe
Compressing   myapp.3.0.1\libgraphics.dll
Compressing   myapp.3.0.1\libmath.dll

Everything is Ok
c:\work>
```

Assuming that everything worked correctly, you end up with a single archive file named myapp.3.0.1.zip.

Now you're ready to ship the release package to the end users. They receive a copy of the file via the Internet or on a CD-ROM and install it on their personal machine. They first create a directory in which to install the software, and then they execute an **unarchive** command to retrieve the individual files. Unless the user performs some manual customization steps, the files will be in the exact state as when they were archived in the first place.

Although a typical Windows user extracts these files by right-clicking on the .zip file icon and selecting Extract All, it's also possible to extract the archive's files using the command line:

```
c:\work> cd C:\Program Files
c:\Program Files> 7z x myapp.3.0.1.zip

7-Zip 4.65  Copyright (c) 1999-2009 Igor Pavlov  2009-02-03

Processing archive: myapp.3.0.1.zip

Extracting  myapp.3.0.1\splash_screen.jpg
Extracting  myapp.3.0.1\errors.de
Extracting  myapp.3.0.1\errors.en
Extracting  myapp.3.0.1\errors.fr
Extracting  myapp.3.0.1\calc.exe
Extracting  myapp.3.0.1\libgraphics.dll
Extracting  myapp.3.0.1\libmath.dll
Extracting  myapp.3.0.1

Everything is Ok

Folders: 1
Files: 7
Size:        91
Compressed: 1069
```

Finally, to execute the program, you use Windows Explorer to browse to the C:\Program Files\myapp-3.0.1 directory and then you double-click on the calc.exe executable program.

This example assumes that files are packaged into the file archive in the same hierarchy in which they'll appear on the target machine. This technique is acceptable for simple software packages, but it doesn't allow files to be placed in arbitrary locations. It also doesn't enable files to be modified after they've been installed on the target machine.

To overcome this limitation, most archive files contain an installation script as one of their included files. The user extracts the archive in the usual way and then executes a custom-written installation script to complete the process. For example, you could add the install.bat script into the file archive and execute it within the myapp.3.0.1 directory:

```
c:\Program Files\myapp.3.0.1> install.bat
Installation Complete
```

This installation script can perform an arbitrary set of operations, including moving files to a different file system location, changing the ownership of files, adding data to the Windows Registry, or adding new user accounts. The installation script can also interact with the user, to customize the way the software is installed.

## Other Archive Formats

In addition to the basic zip archive format and the equivalent `tar/gzip` format in UNIX, several others are worth mentioning:

- **ISO 9660 images [89]:** This is the standard format in which CD/DVD-ROM images are produced. Instead of creating a zip file, the packaging script creates a raw disk image, ready to burn onto a CD or DVD. The disk image file is an exact replica of the CD/DVD file system that'll be mounted onto the target machine. The target machine's operating system loads and executes scripts or other programs when the CD/DVD is inserted or when the computer first boots.

- **Mac OS X `.dmg` images:** This is similar in nature to the ISO 9660 format, although it is used specifically for Mac OS X systems.

- **Self-extracting archives:** This type of archive is similar to a ZIP file, except that the archive is an executable program in its own right. When the archive file is executed, the embedded files are extracted onto the target machine and the installation script is run. This provides a single extract/install process instead of manual installation.

Let's now discuss some important improvements to the `packager.bat` script.

## Improvements

Keep in mind that a simple script (such as `packager.bat`), for a program of less than ten files, won't suffer from the same scalability problems as a much larger system. Here are some improvements to make the `packager.bat` script more scalable, reliable, and user friendly.

- **Validate input parameters:** The version number parameter should have been validated, at least to make sure it's not empty. In the script, if the user doesn't provide a command-line parameter, the script silently continues with an empty string in the `%VERSION%` variable. This isn't too much of a problem here, but in more complex situations, the lack of a suitable input value could cause a corrupt release package.

To solve this problem, the script should at least validate that the user has provided a version string. If not, it should display an informative message to let the user know what's expected. You might also want to validate that the version string has the correct format (such as 3.0.1).

- **Abort on error:** If any of the commands inside the script fail, the entire script should terminate and return a suitable exit code. Without this rule in place, parts of the packaging script might fail, yet the final release package would still be constructed. Unless you carefully watch the build log for subtle error messages, you might be misled into believing that the packaging step succeeded. The truth is discovered only when the software fails to pass sanity testing.

  As an example, if you created a release package from an object tree that hadn't been fully built, the packaging script wouldn't be able to copy all the required object files, yet a release package would still be created. Of course, you'd quite rightly expect that the packaging step should never have been invoked in the first place, especially if the earlier build steps had somehow failed.

- **Provide meaningful error messages:** When an error does occur, always provide a meaningful error message to let the developer know exactly what went wrong. In the simple batch script, missing files cause the copy command to produce the following cryptic output: The system cannot find the file specified. This doesn't provide any information about which file is missing or how the developer should resolve the problem. A more meaningful message is required.

- **Avoid unnecessary copying:** Support the capability to package files directly from the source tree instead of only from the object tree. Adding the %SRCDIR% definition enables you to copy configuration files, graphic images, and other data files that the build process doesn't modify. For example, given that errors.en, errors.fr, and errors.de are plain-text files that are never customized by the build process, there was no need to copy them into the object tree in the first place.

- **Consider future scalability:** The approach of duplicating files from the object tree into the temporary holding directory won't scale for large software projects. If the final release package ends up being 100MiB in size (after being compressed), it would take several minutes to copy all the files to the holding directory—and probably much longer to compress such a large amount of data. Also, you'd need substantially more than 100MiB to store the uncompressed temporary files in the holding directory.

One solution is to use a build tool to perform the copying instead of using a simple shell script. With dependency analysis, the build tool copies files to the holding directory only if they've been modified since the last time the packaging step was performed. In contrast, the simple script blindly copies the files each time, even if they're unchanged.

Another approach is to use a symbolic link from the file's location in the holding directory back to the file's location in the object directory instead of making a temporary copy of each file. The packaging script takes very little time to set up the links; the archiving tool must follow the links and retrieve the true content of the files. Of course, this method works only with archiving tools that can follow symbolic links to retrieve the original file. Unfortunately this approach doesn't allow you to package the symbolic link itself.

- **Beware of stale files:** You might want to delete the entire holding directory before you start to fill it with files. Although any existing files should be overwritten by a newer version of the same file, there's still a chance that a stale file could be included in the release package. That is, when a file that was originally listed in the packaging script is removed (the copy command is removed), the stale version of that file remains in the holding directory instead of being overwritten or deleted. Unless the copy command is replaced by a del command (to explicitly delete the file) or the developer removes the entire holding directory, the file is still packaged into the archive.

- **Avoid using a holding directory:** Finally, instead of using a packaging script to copy files, which doesn't scale well for large programs, you can design the build system to store files in their correct target machine location. That is, instead of storing each executable program, dynamic library, or data file in an arbitrary location within the object tree, you place them in the holding directory in the first place. With this approach, the packaging script performs only the final archiving operation instead of the time-consuming (and disk-consuming) copying step.

Unfortunately, this approach requires extra work because most build systems store object files in a location that suits them, not the target machine. Many systems store generated files in an object tree directory that maps directly to the source code's path within the source tree. This approach makes it difficult to arrange files into the locations required by the target machine.

In closing, the archiving method of creating a release package works well, but primarily for target machines that have a predictable file system layout. In fact, it works very well for embedded systems that don't have a lot of software running on them and don't require any end-user customization. On the other hand, software packages intended for installation on desktop computers tend to require a lot more intelligence from their packaging tools. Let's now look at package-management tools that can handle more complex scenarios.

## Package-Management Tools

Historically, most software developed for UNIX-like operating systems was provided in source code format, typically written in C or C++. The user extracted the source code from the file archive (usually with a `tar.z` or `tar.gz` extension) and then invoked the build system to produce executable programs. The main reason for this approach is there was never a standard version of UNIX or a standard type of CPU that UNIX programs executed on. Source code distribution was the only feasible approach.

If you try to build UNIX software from source code but you're not using a suitably matching version of the operating system, you'll most likely see a number of compilation errors. The build might fail because of a missing header file, a missing dynamic library, or perhaps some symbol definitions that aren't available on your system. Clearly, your operating system is too different or is lacking one of the optional packages the software's author had on his or her machine.

After you get some experience installing UNIX software, you can probably figure out which optional packages are missing. If you're lucky, the software's author placed special compile-time checks to determine whether the prerequisite packages were already installed. At the very least, the author should have provided written documentation on which third-party packages the software uses. Some of the prerequisite packages might have their own set of dependencies, so you can sometimes spend the better part of a day compiling and installing a program.

To get around these issues, the approach to distributing software in UNIX-like systems has changed for the better. One common example is that the Linux operating system has become more standardized than ever, and most Linux systems run on Intel x86–based hardware. Linux is nowhere near as prevalent as Microsoft Windows, but there's still enough standardization that providing binary distributions is common.

## The RPM Package Manager Format

One of the most widespread methods for distributing Linux-based software is the RPM Package Manager format [78]. Originally created for Red Hat Linux, it's now the standard way of packaging software in a range of Linux distributions. The name RPM is a self-referential acronym for RPM Package Manager.

RPM files can contain either source code or executable programs, but the latter **binary RPM** is the most common. Using binary RPMs as the primary means of distributing packages reduces the task of installing software, including any prerequisite packages, to just a few seconds. It's clearly a benefit to not require the end user to perform compilation steps or deal with the possibility of compile errors.

From a simplistic view, an RPM file is similar to a UNIX archive, in that it contains one or more files to be installed on the target machine. The big difference is that RPM files come with a great detail of added intelligence, making the installation process simpler and more powerful. For example, RPM files have the following features:

- **Consistent metainformation:** The package's metainformation is stored in a consistent manner. Among other things, each RPM file stores the package's name, the version number associated with this particular release of the package, the date it was created, the author's name and email address, the URL from which the package can be downloaded, and details of the software's license agreement. Although this information could always be stored in a README file (and packaged into the archive), having everything in a consistent format makes it possible for external programs to read and act upon the various fields.

- **Embedded scripts:** Unlike basic .zip or .tar files, an RPM file contains a number of embedded scripts. An arbitrary sequence of shell commands can be executed on the target machine, both before or after the files have been installed and before or after the files have been uninstalled. Of course, there's no reason you can't just package a separate post-install.sh script as one of the archive's files and ask the user to run that script manually. It's just easier to have the correct script execute at the correct time without the user worrying about it or forgetting the extra step.

- **Dependency checking:** Software packages might need to ensure that other packages are first installed on the target computer. This includes runtime environments, such as the Java or C# virtual machines. Instead of leaving this as a manual exercise for the person installing the software, the RPM format enables the author to explicitly list the required packages, as well as the minimum versions. If the required packages are missing or the version isn't acceptable, the system won't allow the new RPM file to be installed.

- **Validation of CPU types:** The RPM installation mechanism also validates the type of CPU required to execute the software. Typically, there's no point in installing software destined for a PowerPC architecture on a machine that has an x86 processor.

- **Automatic uninstallation:** RPM maintains a database to record which packages are currently installed on the target machine, so the RPM tool has the means for uninstalling the software, even if the original RPM file is no longer available. The only caveat is that RPM gives an error if you try to remove a package that's required by one or more other packages. For example, if you tried to remove the standard C library package, you'd find that every other package in the system depends on it.

- **Intelligent upgrades:** The RPM system enables you to have multiple versions of the same package installed and can act intelligently when configuration files have been locally modified. For example, the configuration file for the Apache web server might be installed as `/etc/apache2/default-server.conf`. If you upgrade to a newer version of the server, the RPM tool would warn you if you made local customizations and would refrain from overwriting it with a new version. It would instead leave both the old and new configuration files in the `/etc/apache2` directory and request that you manually resolve any conflicts or changes.

These are some of the key benefits of the RPM system, but plenty of other useful features make it an ideal system for installing software. To see the wide range of features, refer to the excellent documentation on the RPM web site [78].

Users of Debian Linux (and other variants, such as Ubuntu) are probably more familiar with the deb file format [90], which is similar to the RPM system. Deb files use the `dpkg` and `apt` commands for manipulating package files.

Let's now look at a practical example of using the RPM system.

## The `rpmbuild` Process

This example is limited to packaging only four different files, but that's enough to demonstrate many of the basic features of the RPM format. You'll also see how package versioning works, how prerequisite packages are listed, and how the post-install and preuninstall scripts are specified.

First, examine the high-level flow of creating and installing an RPM file (see Figure 13.3).

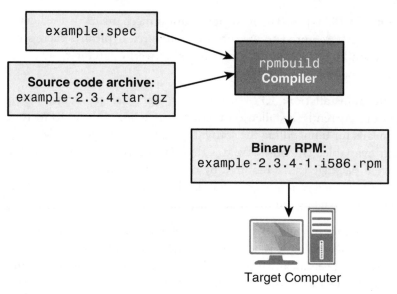

**Figure 13.3** *High-level flow of creating the example RPM file.*

The steps are as follows:

1. The build engineer responsible for maintaining the release package first constructs an RPM specification file (example.spec). This contains the list of files that should be packaged, as well as the package's metainformation and installation scripts. You'll examine one of these files in detail.

2. The second input to the RPM process is the original source code archive, often provided as a tar.gz file. The packaging process extracts the source files and uses the standard build and installation procedures to create the necessary executable files. There's nothing special about this step because you're simply using the same build instructions the end user would have used when manually installing from source code (for example, make all and make install). The major difference is that because you're the author of the code (not the consumer), you shouldn't have any trouble getting it to compile on your computer.

3. Next, the rpmbuild tool constructs the RPM file, ready for distribution to end users. It reads the directives within example.spec to configure the product source code and build the final executable programs. It also

embeds the necessary metainformation and installation scripts into the RPM file. The output of the build process is the `example-2.3.4-1.586.rpm` file, which, as you might expect, is in RPM file format.

4. The final step is for end users to obtain the RPM file (often downloaded from the Internet) and install it on their own computer. As you'll see shortly, the `rpm` tool is used to install and uninstall RPM packages, and it can also be used to query the set of packages currently installed.

## An Example RPM Spec File

Now examine `example.spec`, the RPM spec file that packages four different files. In the next section, you'll see how the `rpmbuild` tool parses this spec file and produces a binary RPM file. Let's start by looking at the entire content of `example.spec` so you can see how everything fits together. Then you can explore each section of the file.

```
 1   Name: example
 2   Version: 2.3.4
 3   Release: 1
 4   Group: Applications/Publishing
 5   Vendor: Arapiki Solutions, Inc.
 6   URL: http://www.arapiki.com
 7   Packager: Peter Smith <psmith@arapiki.com>
 8   Summary: This is an example program to show how RPMs
     work.
 9   License: Exampleware
10
11   # Sources come from /usr/src/packages/SOURCES/...
12   Source: %{name}-%{version}.tar.gz
13
14   # When installing the built software, use this as the
     root.
15   Buildroot: %{_tmppath}/%{name}-%{version}-buildroot
16   Requires: glibc > 2.8
17
18   %description
19   This is an example program that demonstrates how RPMs
     work.
20
21   We show a spec file that is passed into the "rpmbuild"
     program
22   in order to package up the files. In this example, we see
     how
23   to build from source code, how to run a post-installation
     script,
24   and how to ensure that prerequsite packages are already
     installed.
25
```

```
26   %prep
27   %setup -q
28
29   %build
30
31   # compile the source code, using the normal build
     procedure.
32   make
33
34   %install
35
36   # install the compiled software to our "fake" root.
37   make install PREFIX=$RPM_BUILD_ROOT
38
39   %files
40
41   # specify which files are to be installed, as well as
42   # their ownership and permission bits.
43   %attr(0750,root,root) /usr/bin/example
44   %attr(0755,root,root) /usr/lib/libexample.so.1
45   %attr(0755,root,root) /usr/lib/libhelper.so.4
46   %attr(0644,root,root) %doc /usr/share/doc/manual/example.
     pdf
47
48   %clean
49   rm -r $RPM_BUILD_ROOT
50
51   %post
52   groupadd exgroup
53   chgrp exgroup /usr/bin/example
54
55   %preun
56   groupdel exgroup
```

As a starting point for the discussion, consider the directory structure that the rpmbuild tool expects to use. If your Linux system is RPM based, you'll likely find a system-level directory dedicated to creating and publishing RPM files. You aren't required to use these directories (you can use your home directory, if you want to), but because the standard directories are already created, this example will use them. In this case, the Linux system already has the following world-writable directories inside /usr/src/packages.

```
$ ls -l /usr/src/packages/
total 20
drwxrwxrwt 4 root root 4096 2009-09-14 15:30 BUILD
drwxrwxrwt 9 root root 4096 2009-05-16 22:26 RPMS
drwxrwxrwt 2 root root 4096 2009-09-08 19:37 SOURCES
drwxrwxrwt 2 root root 4096 2008-12-02 17:41 SPECS
drwxrwxrwt 2 root root 4096 2008-12-02 17:41 SRPMS
```

Each of these directories has a specific purpose:

- BUILD: This directory is used by `rpmbuild` to store the source code and object trees it creates when compiling the original source code archive (in our case, `example-2.3.4.tar.gz`).

- RPMS: This is the output directory where the final `example-2.3.4-1.586.rpm` file will be placed.

- SOURCES: The original source code archive (`example-2.3.4.tar.gz`) must be stored here for `rpmbuild` to locate it.

- SPECS: The `example.spec` configuration file will be stored in this directory.

- SRPMS: This is similar to the RPMS directory but is used for storing source RPM files instead of binary RPM files. The example doesn't use this directory.

You now have enough background to start looking at the `example.spec` file. The first part of the file contains various metainformation fields that describe the software being packaged.

```
1   Name: example
2   Version: 2.3.4
3   Release: 1
4   Group: Applications/Publishing
5   Vendor: Arapiki Solutions, Inc.
6   URL: http://www.arapiki.com
7   Packager: Peter Smith psmith@arapiki.com
8   Summary: This is an example program to show how RPMs
    work.
9   License: Exampleware
```

Each of these fields has a specific meaning and is intended to be viewed directly by the end user, as well as by special tools that can process RPM files:

- Name: A short identifier that uniquely describes this package. The name is stored in the internal RPM database and is used to identify this package in future RPM operations. As an example, you would use this name if you later decided to query or uninstall the software.

- Version: The version number of this software release. Not only is it possible to have multiple versions of the same package installed, but the RPM system uses this version number when checking for prerequisite packages. Although it's unlikely, some other developer could create an RPM package that makes use of the functionality provided in the `example` package. In his own spec file, the user might state that version `2.0.0` or higher of `example` must first be installed before his own RPM can be installed.

- `Release`: Even though the `Version` field uniquely identifies the version of software being installed, you can end up producing two different RPM files that each contains the exact same version of software. This isn't common, but you might produce a Release 2 of the Version 2.3.4 software to replace the Release 1 RPM file that was incorrectly packaged. Ideally, this should never happen; the RPM build process should be fully automated and tested. Mistakes of this nature should never be made in production software.

- `Group`: When an end user installs software via a GUI tool, the software's group field provides information on which category of applications this software should be listed under. In this case, you're requesting that this RPM be categorized as a publishing application.

- `Vendor`, `URL`, `Packager`: These three fields provide detail on which organization created the package, where it can be downloaded, and which individual person did the packaging. This information is vital if you're looking for information about a package that's already installed on your system (or perhaps you stumbled across an uninstalled RPM file on your disk and wondered where it came from).

- `Summary`: This field provides a short description of the software in the package. This information is commonly used in GUI tools that display a short one-line synopsis of the software. If you need to provide further information, you also have the `%description` section (see later), which can hold multiple lines of text.

- `License`: This field describes the legal implications of installing this software. Many software products come with detailed license documents, but this field is designed for short license names, such as `BSD`, `GPL`, `LGPL`, or `Apache`.

Now that you've seen how to describe the high-level details of the package, you need to provide further information about how the source code is obtained and how it's to be compiled. The `Source` directive provides the location of the source code's tar-ball file, which must have been placed within the `SOURCES` directory.

```
12   Source: %{name}-%{version}.tar.gz
```

Note the use of variable substitution when forming the name of the tar-ball (in this case, it'll be expanded out to `example-2.3.4.tar.gz`).

The `Buildroot` directive informs `rpmbuild` where the program's executable files should be installed. This isn't the same as the `BUILD` directory you saw earlier, which is where the source code is extracted and compiled. Instead, the **build**

**root** is a temporary holding directory that mirrors the installation directory on the target machine.

```
15   Buildroot: %{_tmppath}/%{name}-%{version}-buildroot
```

Instead of installing the compiled program into /usr/bin on the build machine, it's placed in /tmp/example-2.3.4-buildroot/usr/bin. After all, you don't really want to install this software on the build host; instead, you want a convenient place to collect all the files that need to be archived, ready for installation on the target machine.

The next directive, Requires, states that the glibc package must already be present before the example package can be installed. In addition, the installed glibc package must be newer than version 2.8.

```
16   Requires: glibc > 2.8
```

If the package is missing or is too old, the rpm tool refuses to install the example RPM file. There can be any number of Requires directives, depending on how many prerequisite packages are needed.

Next, the %description area contains an arbitrary text-based description of the package. This provides more detail than the Summary directive you saw earlier.

```
18   %description
19   This is an example program that demonstrates how RPMs
     work.
20
21   We show a spec file that is passed into the "rpmbuild"
     program
22   in order to package up the files. In this example, we see
     how
23   to build from source code, how to run a post-installation
     script,
24   and how to ensure that prerequsite packages are already
     installed.
```

The %prep (prepare) section provides a list of commands for preparing the software's source code tree. Because you're using the standard behavior of extracting source files from a tar-ball and then building them in the BUILD subdirectory, you can use the built-in %setup -q command to extract the files.

```
26   %prep
27   %setup -q
```

On the other hand, if you'd rather obtain the source code from a version-control tool (such as CVS or Subversion), or simply make use of the developer's existing source tree, you'd place the necessary shell commands inside this section.

Next, the `%build` section provides shell commands to compile the source code into the resulting executable programs. Instead of cluttering the `example.spec` file with many build steps, this example uses the existing makefile. After all, it's pointless to have two different build systems, so having `rpmbuild` call upon your existing system is usually the best approach.

```
29   %build
32   make
```

Another approach is to let your developers execute the compilation commands by themselves instead of having it done for them. In this case, your build system must contain an explicit step to invoke `rpmbuild` after each of the object files is brought up-to-date. With this approach, the `%build` section is left empty because the compilation work is already complete.

It should be no surprise that the `%install` section provides commands for installing the software. However, instead of installing the executable programs onto the build machine, you install them into our temporary holding directory, referred to as `$RPM_BUILD_ROOT` (and previously specified by the `Buildroot` directive).

```
34   %install
37   make install PREFIX=$RPM_BUILD_ROOT
```

By reusing the software's existing `make install` build target, you end up placing the software in the exact directory structure that'll be required on the target machine. Again, any sequence of shell commands is allowed here, as long as they install the necessary output files.

Now for the part you've probably been waiting for. You must list all the files that'll be packaged into the RPM archive and consequently installed on the target machine.

```
39   %files
43   %attr(0750,root,root) /usr/bin/example
44   %attr(0755,root,root) /usr/lib/libexample.so.1
45   %attr(0755,root,root) /usr/lib/libhelper.so.4
46   %attr(0644,root,root) %doc /usr/share/doc/manual/example.
     pdf
```

You also specify the file's access-control information (permission bits, file owner, and file group), and the `rpm` tool sets these attributes when the package is installed. Also, you use the `%doc` directive to distinguish which of the installed files are just documentation (and can be optionally ignored).

To keep things tidy, the `example.spec` file provides information on cleaning up after the build process. In this case, you simply remove the content of the holding directory after the RPM file has been created.

```
48   %clean
49   rm -r $RPM_BUILD_ROOT
```

The last step in the `example.spec` file is to list the pre- and post-installation scripts. These sections provide a list of UNIX shell commands to be executed immediately before or after the software has been installed or uninstalled. You can therefore have four different sections, each run at a different point in time:

- `%pre`: Shell commands run before installation of the files

- `%post`: Shell commands run after installation of the files

- `%preun`: Shell commands run before the files are removed from the system (uninstalled)

- `%postun`: Shell commands run after the files are removed from the system

This example provides a post-install script that adds a new UNIX group (called `exgroup`) and ensures that only members of this group can run the `/usr/bin/example` program. Note that the permission bits have already been set to `0750` in the `%files` section.

```
51   %post
52   groupadd exgroup
53   chgrp exgroup /usr/bin/example
54
55   %preun
56   groupdel exgroup
```

Additionally, the preuninstall script removes the group, although, technically, you might want to uninstall the files before you delete the group; otherwise, the files could be group-less for a short period of time. In that case, you'd simply move the `groupdel` command to the `%postun` section.

That completes the RPM spec file example. To summarize, the added metadata states the name, version, and contact information for this package; information also indicates how to obtain and compile the source code, and the metadata includes a list of files to be packaged and a set of pre- and post-installation scripts. You can now use the `rpmbuild` tool to create the RPM file itself.

## Creating the RPM File from the Spec File

The following output shows the result of executing the `rpmbuild` command using `example.spec` as input. Although the listing doesn't show the entire output, you can see some of the basic operations discussed. Most notably, you can see the `gzip` command that extracts the source code into the BUILD directory.

Also, near the bottom of the listing, you'll see the `make` command that you told `rpmbuild` to use when compiling the source code.

```
$ rpmbuild -bb example.spec
Executing(%prep): /bin/sh -e /var/tmp/rpm-tmp.68587
+ umask 022
+ cd /usr/src/packages/BUILD
+ cd /usr/src/packages/BUILD
+ rm -rf example-2.3.4
+ /usr/bin/gzip -dc /usr/src/packages/SOURCES/example-
2.3.4.tar.gz
+ tar -xf -
+ STATUS=0
+ '[' 0 -ne 0 ']'
+ cd example-2.3.4
++ /usr/bin/id -u
+ '[' 1000 = 0 ']'
++ /usr/bin/id -u
+ '[' 1000 = 0 ']'
+ /bin/chmod -Rf a+rX,u+w,g-w,o-w .
+ exit 0
Executing(%build): /bin/sh -e /var/tmp/rpm-tmp.68587
+ umask 022
+ cd /usr/src/packages/BUILD
+ /bin/rm -rf /var/tmp/example-2.3.4-buildroot
++ dirname /var/tmp/example-2.3.4-buildroot
+ /bin/mkdir -p /var/tmp
+ /bin/mkdir /var/tmp/example-2.3.4-buildroot
+ cd example-2.3.4
+ make
Building all example code.
... Remaining output truncated ...
```

Just to double-check that everything worked correctly, you should find an RPM file in the RPMS subdirectory.

```
$ cd /usr/src/packages/RPMS/i586/
$ ls -l
total 4
-rw-r--r-- 1 psmith users 2706 2009-09-14 15:16 exam-
ple-2.3.4-1.i586.rpm
```

The naming of this file is important because it tells you the name of the package, the version number, the architecture on which it'll run (Intel i586 family), and, of course, the file extension to indicate that this is an RPM package file. All RPM files should follow the same naming format.

One additional feature of the `rpmbuild` tool is that you can detect whether files were installed into the build root directory (the temporary holding directory) that weren't explicitly listed in the `example.spec` file. By catching these errors, you avoid releasing software that's missing one or more important files.

These files might have been added by a developer who simply forgot to update the RPM spec file, even after making the necessary changes to the `make install` target.

The following example shows the error message.

```
$ rpmbuild -bb example.spec
... lots of output removed ...
Checking for unpackaged file(s): /usr/lib/rpm/check-files /
var/tmp/example-2.3.4-buildroot
error: Installed (but unpackaged) file(s) found:
   /usr/lib/libhelper.so.4

RPM build errors:
    Installed (but unpackaged) file(s) found:
   /usr/lib/libhelper.so.4
```

Now that you have a complete RPM file, let's look at how to install that file on the target machine.

## Installing the RPM Example

Installing an RPM file on the target machine takes relatively little effort, especially because the RPM file was destined for your specific operating system and CPU type, and you don't need to compile any source code. If all goes well, the installation is a silent operation; in the worst case, you might be asked to install some prerequisite packages.

Let's first explore the content of the RPM package. The `rpm` command with the `-q` option enables you to query the content of the RPM file. With the `-i` suboption, you can review all the metainformation:

```
$ rpm -q -p -i example-2.3.4-1.i586.rpm
Name         : example                Relocations: (not relocat-
                                       able)
Version      : 2.3.4                  Vendor: Arapiki Solutions,
Inc.
Release      : 1                      Build Date: Mon 14 Sep 2009
03:16:06 PM
Install Date: (not installed)         Build Host: linux
Group        : Applications/Publishing Source RPM: exam-
                                       ple-2.3.4-1.src.rpm
Size         : 12                     License: Exampleware
Signature    : (none)
Packager     : Peter Smith psmith@arapiki.com
URL          : http://www.arapiki.com
Summary      : This is an example program to show how RPMs
               work.
Description :
This is an example program that demonstrates how RPMs work.
```

We show a spec file that is passed into the "rpmbuild" program
in order to package up the files. In this example, we see how
to build from source code, how to run a post-installation
script, and how to ensure that prerequsite packages are already installed.
Distribution: (none)

With the -l suboption, you can review the list of files in the archive:

```
$ rpm -q -p -l example-2.3.4-1.i586.rpm
/usr/bin/example
/usr/lib/libexample.so.1
/usr/lib/libhelper.so.4
/usr/share/doc/manual/example.pdf
```

If you're convinced that this is the correct package, you can proceed with installation. You're installing files into system-level directories, so you must be logged
in as the root user. The rpm command with the -i option installs the package.

```
$ sudo -s
# rpm -i example-2.3.4-1.i586.rpm
```

There's no output from this command, so you should assume that everything
went smoothly. Just to be paranoid, use the -q option again to check that the
package was installed. The -a suboption lists all the packages currently installed
on the system, but you're interested in only the example package.

```
# rpm -qa | grep example
example-2.3.4-1
```

As a matter of interest, try running this command without the grep filter, and
you'll see all the packages currently installed on your system.

You can also double-check the installation by validating whether the necessary files are installed where they should be and whether they have the correct
file permissions. As you might expect, the /usr/bin/example file is group-
owned by exgroup and isn't accessible to other users.

```
# ls -l /usr/bin/example
-rwxr-x--- 1 root exgroup 3 2009-09-14 15:16 /usr/bin/example
# ls -l /usr/lib/libexample.so.1
-rwxr-xr-x 1 root root 3 2009-09-14 15:16 /usr/lib/libexam-
➡ple.so.1
```

Removing the package from the system is equally simple. Using the -e (erase)
option removes all the installed files from the system, and the uninstallation
script removes the exgroup UNIX group.

```
# rpm -e example-2.3.4
```

There's no output from this command, so you can safely assume that everything went smoothly.

If you're wondering what happens when things don't go well, consider this scenario. If you try to install the example package on an older Linux system, you might not have the necessary prerequisite packages installed. Here's the output you see if the target machine doesn't have a new enough version of the standard C library:

```
# rpm -i example-2.3.4-1
error: Failed dependencies:
        glibc > 2.8 is needed by example-2.3.4-1.i586
```

The end user must therefore decide whether to upgrade the C library (and potentially the entire operating system) or locate an older version of the example package that doesn't need such a new version of the C library.

As a second example, see what might happen if exgroup already existed on the target machine. This would be a common scenario when upgrading to a newer version of the package because the group was already created by the older version.

```
# rpm -i example-2.3.4-1
groupadd: Group 'exgroup' already exists.
```

Clearly, you need to add some intelligence to the post-installation script so that it knows how to behave correctly when upgrading to newer package versions.

In summary, that's all there is to creating a complete spec file and then installing the RPM file on the target machine. All this is done with minimal intervention from the end user, making it much easier than would be the case with source code distributions. As mentioned earlier, the example.spec file is designed to give you a taste of what the RPM tools are capable of. An RPM spec file includes many other directives and sections, and you're encouraged to learn about these on your own.

## Custom-Built GUI Installation Tools

The third and final type of installation system to look at is the **custom-built GUI installation tool**. As a reminder, the first solution was to package files in a file archive, and the second solution was to use a package-management tool. In contrast to these two solutions, the third approach allows a much richer user experience when installing the software on the target machine.

Upon running the installer, the user is guided through a set of screens that control how the software is installed. This process will be familiar to anyone who has installed software on a Microsoft Windows system. You'll typically see the following pages of information:

- A splash screen or welcome message to announce which software is being installed

- A license agreement that explains the software's terms of use and seeks the user's approval before installing

- A file browser for the user to select the software's destination directory

- A list of optional software components the user can elect to install

- Any number of custom pages that allow the user to configure installation parameters

- A progress bar to show how the installation is progressing

In addition to these common pages, the installer might generate an **uninstaller** application to remove the software from the target machine. Finally, the installer might initiate a system reboot.

Graphical installers can also run arbitrary code on the target machine, which is something that RPM files can do but not something that simpler archive tools can do. This enables the installer to modify system configuration files, update the Windows Registry, or run any type of external application. This level of freedom makes it possible to do practically anything during the install process.

A few tools are widely available for creating installer applications, and these generally focus on the Microsoft Windows environment. Perhaps the most famous is InstallShield [79], which can generate native code installers for Windows. The InstallAnywhere tool [79], from the same vendor as InstallShield, allows the creation of Java-based installers for a much wider range of target machines (including UNIX-like systems). Next, the Windows Installer [80] is now a standard part of the Microsoft Windows environment and is thus becoming more popular. Finally, the Nullsoft Scriptable Install System (NSIS) [81] is a freely available tool that can be downloaded from the Internet.

The rest of this chapter walks through a realistic example using the NSIS tool. This tool was chosen because of the simplicity of creating a basic installer, but the tool is also freely available and is actively developed and supported.

## The Nullsoft Scriptable Install System (NSIS)

As the name suggests, NSIS has its own scripting language to describe the full workings of the installation process. It contains built-in functions for configuring the installer pages, and users can create their own functions. It provides support for arithmetic operations and has advanced features for designing custom dialog pages. Finally, it facilitates the creation of third-party libraries (plug-ins) that can extend the basic language.

An NSIS script is stored in a source file that has the `.nsi` suffix. This file is passed into the NSIS compiler, which then creates an executable installer application (see Figure 13.4). As part of this process, all the program files (executable programs, dynamic libraries, or data files) are first compressed and packaged into the installer program.

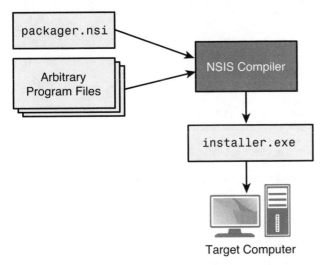

**Figure 13.4** *High-level flow of creating an NSIS-based installer.*

When `installer.exe` is executed, the program files are decompressed and copied to the appropriate place on the target machine.

To understand better how NSIS operates, let's look at a small installer application. This installer contains a number of standard concepts you're surely familiar with:

Software version number

License acceptance page

Page to choose the installation directory

List of optional language support choices (you must select at least one)

Addition of a Start menu item

Addition of a desktop shortcut (if desired by the user)

Creation of an uninstaller

To give you an idea of how simple NSIS can be to use, this example installer was constructed with only five hours of work, after the author read the NSIS documentation for the first time. It's not a difficult system to learn.

## The Installer Script

Although the installation script is discussed in multiple steps, the entire program actually resides in a single script file, called `packager.nsi`. Start by examining the full listing so that you can have an appreciation for what a complete program looks like.

```
 1  !define VERSION "3.0.1"
 2
 3  ; The Checkbox widget
 4  Var Checkbox
 5
 6  ; The state of the widget (selected or not)
 7  Var Checkbox_State
 8
 9  Name "NSIS Packaging Example - ${VERSION}"
10  OutFile "packager.exe"
11  InstallDir $PROGRAMFILES\Packaging-Example
12
13  ;--------------------------------
14  ; Page definitions
15
16  Page license
17  Page directory
18  Page components "" "" validateComponents
19  Page custom optionsPage optionsPageLeave
20  Page instfiles
21
22  ; Uninstaller pages
23  UninstPage uninstConfirm
24  UninstPage instfiles
25
26  ;--------------------------------
27  ; Handle the license page
28
29  LicenseData obj\license.txt
30  LicenseForceSelection radiobuttons "Yes, I agree" \
31          "No, I don't agree"
32
33  ;--------------------------------
34  ; Define the main component
35
36  Section "-Main Component"
37
38    SetOutPath $INSTDIR
39
40    ; install mandatory files
41    File obj\calc.exe
```

```
42    File obj\libs\libmath.dll
43    File obj\libs\libgraphics.dll
44    File obj\images\splash_screen.jpg
45
46    ; Create directory for optional files
47    CreateDirectory $INSTDIR\errors
48
49    ; Create the uninstaller application
50    WriteUninstaller $INSTDIR\uninstaller.exe
51
52    ; Create the start menu entries
53    CreateDirectory "$STARTMENU\My Calculator"
54    CreateShortCut "$STARTMENU\My Calculator\Calculator.
      lnk"
55            $INSTDIR\calc.exe
56    CreateShortCut "$STARTMENU\My Calculator\Uninstall.
      lnk"
57            $INSTDIR\uninstaller.exe
58
59    ; Possibly create the desktop short cut
60    ${If} $Checkbox_State == ${BST_CHECKED}
61      CreateShortCut "$DESKTOP\Calculator.lnk" $INSTDIR\
        calc.exe
62    ${EndIf}
63
64  SectionEnd
65
66  ;-------------------------------
67  ; Optional language support
68
69  Section "English Language Support" sec_english
70    SetOutPath $INSTDIR\errors
71    File obj\languages\errors.en
72  SectionEnd
73
74  Section /o "French Language Support" sec_french
75    SetOutPath $INSTDIR\errors
76    File obj\languages\errors.fr
77  SectionEnd
78
79  Section /o "German Language Support" sec_german
80    SetOutPath $INSTDIR\errors
81    File obj\languages\errors.de
82  SectionEnd
83
84  ;-------------------------------
85  ; Validation functions
86
87  Function validateComponents
88
89    ; determine which components are selected
90    SectionGetFlags ${sec_english} $0
91    SectionGetFlags ${sec_french} $1
92    SectionGetFlags ${sec_german} $2
93    IntOp $0 $0 & ${SF_SELECTED}
```

```
94     IntOp $1 $1 & ${SF_SELECTED}
95     IntOp $2 $2 & ${SF_SELECTED}
96
97     ; $0 = total number of components selected
98     IntOp $0 $0 + $1
99     IntOp $0 $0 + $2
100
101    ${If} $0 == 0
102      MessageBox MB_OK "At least one language must be se-
         lected"
103      Abort
104    ${EndIf}
105
106  FunctionEnd
107
108  ;-------------------------------
109  ; Custom options page - optionsPage
110
111  Function optionsPage
112
113    ; Create a new dialog page
114    nsDialogs::Create 1018
115    Pop $0
116    ${If} $0 == error
117      Abort
118    ${EndIf}
119
120    ; Create a check box
121    ${NSD_CreateCheckbox} 20% 20% 100% 10u "&Create a
       desktop shortcut"
122    Pop $Checkbox
123
124    ; Select the checkbox, by default
125    ${NSD_Check} $Checkbox
126
127    ; Display the page content
128    nsDialogs::Show
129
130  FunctionEnd
131
132  ;-------------------------------
133  ; Custom options page - optionsPageLeave
134
135  Function optionsPageLeave
136    ${NSD_GetState} $Checkbox $Checkbox_State
137  FunctionEnd
138
139  ;-------------------------------
140  ; Uninstaller information
141
142  Section "Uninstall"
143
144    ; Remove the mandatory and option files
145    Delete $INSTDIR\errors\*
146    RMDir $INSTDIR\errors
```

```
147      Delete $INSTDIR\*
148      RMDir $INSTDIR
149
150      ; Remove the start menu entry
151      Delete "$STARTMENU\My Calculator\*"
152      RMDir "$STARTMENU\My Calculator"
153
154      ; Remove the desktop shortcut
155      Delete "$DESKTOP\Calculator.lnk"
156
157    SectionEnd
158
159    ;------------------------------
```

This is a long program, but let's address each feature in detail. To start, the script contains a number of basic definitions that any installer requires.

```
 1    !define VERSION "3.0.1"

 9    Name "NSIS Packaging Example - ${VERSION}"
10    OutFile "packager.exe"
11    InstallDir $PROGRAMFILES\Packaging-Example
```

The version number (3.0.1) is defined using a compile-time definition (similar to C preprocessor definitions). In a real installation system, you would provide this version number on the NSIS compiler command line instead of hard-coding it into the script.

Next, you state the name of the installer, which appears in the title bar of any of the GUI pages. In the example, this is the only place the version number is used.

The OutFile directive tells NSIS the name of the executable program to create. In a real system, you would want to incorporate the version number here, too, avoiding conflicts with other versions of the installer.

Finally, the InstallDir directive provides the default installation path. The user can change this path on the installer GUI. Note the use of the $PROGRAM-FILES variable, which always contains the target machine's idea of where programs should be installed (this is typically C:\Program Files).

## Defining the Pages

The next part of the installer script specifies the list of pages you want the installer to present to the end user. Some of these pages are standard across all installers (such as the license, directory, and instfiles pages), but it's also possible to create custom pages.

```
16    Page license
17    Page directory
18    Page components "" "" validateComponents
```

```
19  Page custom optionsPage optionsPageLeave
20  Page instfiles
```

In this case, you start with the standard `license` and `directory` selection pages. After that, the user is asked to select which optional components to install.

For this `components` page, a callback function (`validateComponents`) triggers when the user presses the `Next` button. This enables you to validate the list of components that were selected and possibly reject the submission if the user didn't complete the page correctly. (In this case, at least one language must have been chosen.) You'll examine this callback function shortly.

Following the components page, you create a custom page that's specific to your application (instead of being a standard reusable page). In this case, the `optionsPage` callback renders the various parts of the page's content, whereas the `optionsPage-Leave` function validates what the user enters. You'll also look at these functions later.

Finally, the `instfiles` page does the actual work of installing the program's files. It shows a progress bar and enables the user to see a detailed listing of what has been installed.

## The License Page

Now look at the initial `license` page (see Figure 13.5). This installer uses the default NSIS look and feel, which makes the screens appear as if they're running on an older version of Windows. For the more recent versions of Windows, NSIS also supports a more modern window style.

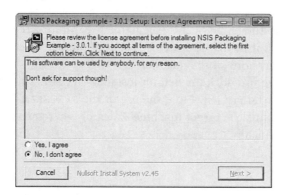

**Figure 13.5** *The installer's license page.*

The `license` page is fairly standard, but it's customized in a few simple ways.

```
29  LicenseData obj\license.txt
30  LicenseForceSelection radiobuttons "Yes, I agree" \
31              "No, I don't agree"
```

First, the `LicenseData` directive tells the installer where to find the license agreement text (a file somewhere on the build machine). Next, the `License-ForceSelection` directive forces the user to explicitly accept or decline the license agreement before continuing with the installation.

## Directory Selection

After agreeing to the license, the user is presented with the directory selection page (see Figure 13.6). The installer automatically calculates how much disk space is required, based on which additional files were packaged into the installer executable. It's also possible to tell the installer how much additional space is required, in case some of the installed content is downloaded or auto-generated during the installation process.

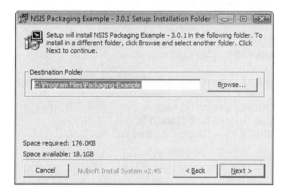

**Figure 13.6** *The installer's directory selection page.*

## The Main Component

To specify which content is to be packaged into the installer executable and, consequently, installed on the target machine, you must provide a mapping from the build machine's files to the target machine's files. The full set of files can be divided into multiple sections, which can be individually selected or deselected. In the example, one section must always be installed, but other sections are marked as optional and can be selectively ignored.

Start by examining the definition of the section called `Main Component`. This section contains all the files that are always installed. (The one exception is the desktop shortcut, as you'll see later.)

```
36   Section "-Main Component"
37
38     SetOutPath $INSTDIR
39
40     ; install mandatory files
41     File obj\calc.exe
42     File obj\libs\libmath.dll
43     File obj\libs\libgraphics.dll
44     File obj\images\splash_screen.jpg
45
46     ; Create directory for optional files
47     CreateDirectory $INSTDIR\errors
48
49     ; Create the uninstaller application
50     WriteUninstaller $INSTDIR\uninstaller.exe
51
52     ; Create the start menu entries
53     CreateDirectory "$STARTMENU\My Calculator"
54     CreateShortCut "$STARTMENU\My Calculator\Calculator.
       lnk"
55            $INSTDIR\calc.exe
56     CreateShortCut "$STARTMENU\My Calculator\Uninstall.
       lnk"
57            $INSTDIR\uninstaller.exe
58
59     ; Possibly create the desktop short cut
60     ${If} $Checkbox_State == ${BST_CHECKED}
61       CreateShortCut "$DESKTOP\Calculator.lnk" $INSTDIR\
         calc.exe
62     ${EndIf}
63
64   SectionEnd
```

This section has a number of interesting concepts. First, the SetOutPath directive on line 38 tells the installer which directory the files should be installed into. In this case, you want to install them in the $INSTDIR directory on the target machine, which is exactly what the user selected on the directory selection page. If you wanted to install files in some other directory, or even within a subdirectory of $INSTDIR, you would need to call SetOutPath again.

Lines 41–44 call the File command once for every file you want to install on the target machine. The File command takes a single argument that states where on the build machine (not the target machine) the file should be obtained. The NSIS compiler uses the File command to obtain all the input files and compress them into the installer executable. This information is later used to extract the files onto the target machine. In the extraction phase, the files are all written into the directory specified by the SetOutPath directive, and the original file's directory path from the build machine is discarded. Just to clarify, the command File obj\calc.exe obtains the file from the build machine at path obj\calc. exe and installs it on the target machine as $INSTDIR\calc.exe.

The `CreateDirectory` command on line 47 should be no surprise, in that it creates a directory on the target machine. The single argument informs the system of which directory should be created.

The `WriteInstaller` command on line 50 specifies the name of the uninstaller program to be created. You store the uninstaller in the same directory as the rest of the software so that it can be located easily when the user needs it.

The next step is to add both the `calc.exe` program and the `uninstaller. exe` as items in the Windows Start menu. This is a fairly straightforward process, on lines 53–57, that involves creating a new subdirectory within the `$START-MENU` directory (defined as appropriate for the target machine) and then creating two Windows shortcuts. These items automatically appear when the user next opens the start menu.

Finally, lines 60–62 create a shortcut from the user's desktop to `calc.exe`. As you'll see later, this step is optional and is configured from a custom installer page. The shortcut is created only if the user selected the necessary check box.

## The Optional Components

Now focus on the optional sections. In this application, you want the user to install one or more language support packages. To keep things simple, you install only a single file for each language and place it in `$INSTDIR\errors`. In a real system, these sections could be much larger and could contain multiple files.

```
69   Section "English Language Support" sec_english
70     SetOutPath $INSTDIR\errors
71     File obj\languages\errors.en
72   SectionEnd
73
74   Section /o "French Language Support" sec_french
75     SetOutPath $INSTDIR\errors
76     File obj\languages\errors.fr
77   SectionEnd
78
79   Section /o "German Language Support" sec_german
80     SetOutPath $INSTDIR\errors
81     File obj\languages\errors.de
82   SectionEnd
```

Two new concepts are shown here. First, the name of the section doesn't start with a dash (as the main component did), which means that the user can choose to optionally install the component (see Figure 13.7). By default, English language support is selected, and French and German are initially deselected (because of the `/o` option).

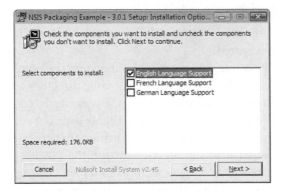

**Figure 13.7** *The installer's component selection page.*

The second interesting concept is that the sections have been labeled with `sec_english`, `sec_french`, and `sec_german`. These names enable you to refer to the sections from within any of the script functions. In this case, a callback function confirms that at least one of the languages has been selected. Earlier you saw how the `validateComponents` function was associated with the `components` page, but now look at the definition of that callback function.

```
87   Function validateComponents
88
89     ; determine which components are selected
90     SectionGetFlags ${sec_english} $0
91     SectionGetFlags ${sec_french} $1
92     SectionGetFlags ${sec_german} $2
93     IntOp $0 $0 & ${SF_SELECTED}
94     IntOp $1 $1 & ${SF_SELECTED}
95     IntOp $2 $2 & ${SF_SELECTED}
96
97     ; $0 = total number of components selected
98     IntOp $0 $0 + $1
99     IntOp $0 $0 + $2
100
101    ${If} $0 == 0
102    MessageBox MB_OK "At least one language must be
       selected"
103      Abort
104    ${EndIf}
105
106  FunctionEnd
```

This code looks rather awkward at first but demonstrates the way arithmetic is performed in an NSIS installer. Lines 90–95 retrieve the section flags for each of the English, French, and German sections. These flags are a binary bitmap of true/false values providing information about each section. If the `SF_SELECTED` flag is set, this indicates that the user selected the check box for that particular section. Recall that this function is invoked immediately after the user presses the `Next` button on the components page, and you're now evaluating whether the user provided reasonable input values.

The NSIS scripting language contains a number of built-in variables that don't need to be explicitly declared. You first read the section flags into the `$0`, `$1`, and `$2` variables; then you perform a bitwise `AND` operation against `SF_SELECTED` to ignore all the other bits in the value. The next part of the operation (lines 98–99) sums up `$0`, `$1`, and `$2` to obtain a zero value if none of the languages was selected, or nonzero if at least one of the check boxes was enabled.

On lines 101–104, if the result of this arithmetic is zero, the submission is rejected and the user is asked to select at least one type of language support. The `MessageBox` command pops up a dialog page with an `OK` button, and the `Abort` command tells the installer to stay on the components page instead of moving on to the next page of the installer's GUI.

## Defining a Custom Page

If all is successful, the installer moves ahead to the next page, which in the example is a custom page containing whatever content you decide to display (see Figure 13.8). As mentioned earlier, you install a desktop shortcut only if the user chooses to do so. The custom page has an added check box that users can disable if they don't want the shortcut.

**Figure 13.8** *A custom-designed installer page.*

This custom page makes use of two callback functions: `optionsPage` renders the page's content, and `optionsPageLeave` is executed when the user presses the `Next` button.

First, the `optionsPage` function:

```
  3   ; The Checkbox widget
  4   Var Checkbox
  5
  6   ; The state of the widget (selected or not)
  7   Var Checkbox_State

111   Function optionsPage
112
113     ; Create a new dialog page
114     nsDialogs::Create 1018
115     Pop $0
116     ${If} $0 == error
117       Abort
118     ${EndIf}
119
120     ; Create a check box
121     ${NSD_CreateCheckbox} 20% 20% 100% 10u "&Create a
        desktop shortcut"
122     Pop $Checkbox
123
124     ; Select the checkbox, by default
125     ${NSD_Check} $Checkbox
126
127     ; Display the page content
128     nsDialogs::Show
129
130   FunctionEnd
```

Creating this particular custom page involves four main steps. On lines 114–118, the nsDialogs::Create function creates a new page in the installer GUI. The return value from the Create function is implicitly pushed onto a stack and then explicitly popped off into variable $0. If an error code was returned, the function is aborted. This type of value manipulation will be familiar to users of stack-based programming languages.

The second step, lines 121–122, calls the NSD_CreateCheckbox function to add a check box widget onto the page. The numeric parameters provide positioning information, so the check box and its associated text label are positioned near the top of the page. A reference to the check box widget is popped off the stack and stored in the $Checkbox variable.

The third step, line 125, is for the NSD_Check function to enable the check box by default. Users explicitly uncheck the check box if they don't want the shortcut to be created.

The final step, on line 128, is to call the nsDialogs::Show function to render the content of the page.

To make sure you save the value of the check box (selected or unselected), an additional callback function executes when the Install button is pushed.

```
135  Function optionsPageLeave
136    ${NSD_GetState} $Checkbox $Checkbox_State
137  FunctionEnd
```

There's nothing on this page to be validated, so you don't need any logic to analyze the content. However, you must call the NSD_GetState function to save the check box's state into the $Checkbox_State variable. If you refer back to our original discussion of the installing the desktop shortcut, you'll see that $Checkbox_State was first examined to see whether it was set.

## The Installation Page and the Uninstaller

The final page of the installer provides a progress bar and a detailed list of the files that have been installed (see Figure 13.9). This page is automatically created and doesn't require additional configuration.

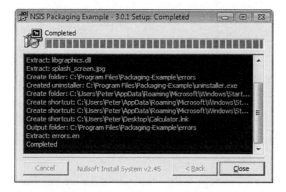

**Figure 13.9** *The installer's progress page.*

After the software has been installed, the uninstaller.exe program must also be saved to the installation directory. To configure this uninstaller, you simply create another section that deletes all the files and directories that you created during the install process.

```
22   ; Uninstaller pages
23   UninstPage uninstConfirm
24   UninstPage instfiles

142  Section "Uninstall"
143
144    ; Remove the mandatory and option files
145    Delete $INSTDIR\errors\*
146    RMDir $INSTDIR\errors
147    Delete $INSTDIR\*
```

```
148   RMDir $INSTDIR
149
150   ; Remove the start menu entry
151   Delete "$STARTMENU\My Calculator\*"
152   RMDir "$STARTMENU\My Calculator"
153
154   ; Remove the desktop shortcut
155   Delete "$DESKTOP\Calculator.lnk"
156
157   SectionEnd
```

The uninstaller doesn't require much information, other than confirming that you really want to remove the files (see Figure 13.10).

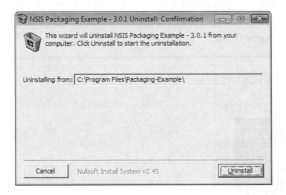

**Figure 13.10**  *The uninstaller page, asking the user for confirmation.*

And that's all there is to it. You can create a fully featured installer application in a matter of hours. Some of the language features are a little awkward to use at first, but NSIS creates a great user experience when installing your software release package. For more information on this tool, refer to the NSIS web site [81].

## Summary

Creating a software release package is usually the final step in the build process. An important goal is to make it easy for end users who are not technically minded to install the software on their target machine. This must be done without requiring them to compile the software from source code or perform lots of manual steps to get the software working.

To reduce wasted time, it's important for a packaging script to check for invalid user input, report all possible errors (instead of ignoring them), and spend as little time and disk space as possible while copying files. A poor-quality packaging script will likely create invalid release packages.

The first packaging solution is to compress all the target files into a ZIP or TAR archive, using a packaging script to store the files in the correct locations. This is a simple approach and requires an additional installation script to customize the files after they've been installed.

The second solution is to use a package-management tool to install the set of target files on the target machine. This approach enables the execution of arbitrary code before and after the installation process. By providing version dependency information in the release package, you ensure that all required prerequisite packages are already installed on the target machine.

Finally, a custom-built GUI tool facilitates the creation of a user-friendly experience, with separate pages for each of the main activities. These include selecting the installation directory, agreeing to license information, and selecting optional components to be installed. You can execute arbitrary scripts before and after the installation takes place.

# Chapter 14

# Version Management

A piece of computer software is unlikely to remain constant. One of the major benefits of software is that it can be updated frequently to fix bugs or introduce new features. To control these changes, any nontrivial software is managed using a **version-control system** (see Figure 14.1). This enables each of the project's developers to obtain a copy of the source code, make changes to that code, and then submit changes to the central repository to be shared with others.

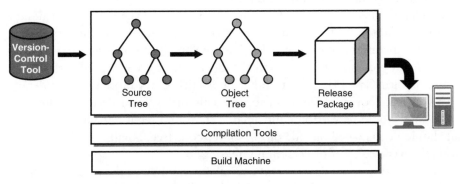

**Figure 14.1** *Big-picture diagram, with a focus on version control of the build system.*

A key feature of a version-control system is that a complete history of the source code can be reproduced. This means that different developers can be working on different versions of the software, while ensuring the necessary level of separation in their work (see Figure 14.2). If a customer reports a bug in an old version of code, a developer must reproduce the exact set of source files that were used to compile that older version. The developer then can fix the bug and release a new version of the software for the customer to use.

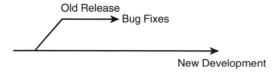

**Figure 14.2**  *Use version-control branches to separate code streams.*

This bug-fixing work is done in isolation from new-feature development. If this approach isn't followed, the customers are forced to receive new features when all they wanted was a bug fix. On the other hand, the bug fix must be forward-ported to the new development branches to ensure that the bug is fixed in future releases.

From the perspective of the build system, the version-control system manages all the build description files (such as a `Makefile` or a `SConstruct` file). At any point in time, the build description must match the current set of source files and must be changed in unison with the source code. The end goal is to build any earlier version of the software that needs to be reproduced. If the build system and source files don't match, this isn't possible.

This chapter focuses on how the version-control system can impact the design and implementation of the build system. However, it doesn't discuss any of the day-to-day operations, such as checking out or submitting code. For more information about common version-control tools (such as CVS [2], Subversion [3], Git [4], or ClearCase [5]), refer to other books that cover those topics in detail.

This chapter covers three main topics. This first section describes the type of files that should be version-controlled. The second section identifies the files that should be managed outside of the source code tree. Finally, the last section covers the basic concept of version numbering.

This discussion of version control covers only a subset of the traditional Software Configuration Management (SCM) discipline. SCM focuses on managing the change of software over time, which also includes tracking defects and new features. This chapter doesn't discuss those topics.

## What Should Be Version-Controlled

As a general rule, all human-created source files should be stored in the version-control system. In addition to source code, this includes the build description files that must exactly match the source code being compiled, even when multiple code streams (releases) are being maintained. In contrast, this doesn't include any files that are generated as part of the build process, such as object files or executable programs.

This section examines four different types of information that should be kept in the version-control system.

- **Build description files:** Describe the end-to-end process of compiling the source code.

- **References to tools:** Describe which compilation tools should be used.

- **Large binary files:** In the same way that small source files need to be version-controlled, large binaries files must be stored somewhere.

- **Source tree configurations:** Describe the way a full source tree is constructed.

In each case, keep in mind that a version-control system can contain multiple development streams, some of which contain the source code for software releases that have already been sent to customers. Other streams version-control new features that are being developed.

## Build Description Files

The idea that description files must be version-controlled shouldn't require further explanation. However, it's important to ensure that the automatic build process covers the complete set of instructions for building the product. Sometimes a build process can become fragmented into different steps, especially if nobody takes ownership of the full end-to-end process. If any of the steps are left for the developer to execute manually, the build process becomes error prone and is gradually forgotten over time. In the end, it'll be harder to reliably build older software.

To illustrate, it's not uncommon for a development organization to have a web page stating how to build the product. This information is modified over time as the build system grows and always contains the latest information needed to start a compilation. Developers add words of wisdom about the build process as they get more experience. The following is a typical excerpt:

```
Use the following steps to build the product:

To build the prerequisite libraries, do:
        cd src/libs
        make LIBARCH=i386
        make LIBARCH=mips

If you're using a code base newer than October 17th, or on
the Release_2.0
```

```
branch, execute "make LIBARCH=x86_64" instead of the i386
target.

To build a debug image, instead do "make LIBARCH=<arch>
DBG=1", but this
doesn't yet work properly for the MIPS target.

To link everything together, do:
        cd src/target
        make all
```

This build process might seem simple enough, but consider what happens when it grows over time. Given another year of development, the process might be two to three times longer and could contain a lot more references to dates and version-control branches. Trying to determine the correct set of build steps then becomes a major challenge.

Experienced developers might memorize the steps and perform them in their sleep, but newer developers will likely be overwhelmed by all the different options. As a result, you'll see an increase in the number of broken builds when important steps are accidentally missed. Also, developers become frustrated when they need to closely track the progress of their build and must be ready and waiting to enter the next command in the sequence.

To solve these problems, you should automate all (not just most) build instructions and keep them in the version-control system. This provides a standard way for developers to see the current set of build steps for the code they've checked out. These steps might vary across different code branches, but they'll always be accurate because they're version-controlled along with the source code.

For example, entering make help (or the equivalent command in another build tool) gives developers useful information on how to build their code:

```
$ make help
Help information:
  make help            - show this help page
  make libs            - build all the prerequisite libraries
  make libs LIBARCH={x86_64,mips}
                       - build the libraries for one architec-
                         ture
                         (i386 is no longer supported)
  make link            - perform the final linking phase
  make all             - build the entire program from scratch.

Options:
  Add DBG=1 to generate debugging information (mips not sup-
  ported)
```

There's no mention of dates or branches, given that the documentation is relevant to the source code tree currently checked out. If older code is checked out, the documentation would be different.

The `all` target is guaranteed to build the full product from beginning to end, without requiring the user to execute the steps independently. The detail of the build process can change over time, but developers can always rely on the `all` target. They still have access to the individual build steps (such as `libs` and `link`), but they aren't required to use them.

## References to Tools

Another key component of a reliable build system is the set of compilation tools used. The build tool invokes the compilation tools and passes in the necessary command-line parameters, such as source or object filenames. In the following makefile fragment, you can see that the GNU C compiler is defined as the compiler of choice.

```
CC := gcc
prog: main.o helper.o
    $(CC) -o $@ $^
```

The `$(CC)` variable is used by the explicit rule for `prog` and is also used by the built-in rule that knows how to compile the C source files (`main.c` and `helper.c`).

Unfortunately, this basic approach has several problems. It might work for simple projects with a small number of users, but a few problems arise when the development environment grows.

The first issue is that the `gcc` program is found by searching the user's shell path (the `$PATH` environment variable in UNIX-like systems). If `gcc` is installed in a well-known location such as `/usr/bin`, the correct version of the tool likely will be found. However, if `gcc` is stored in a nonstandard location (such as `/tools/bin`), or if the user has nonstandard directories in their `$PATH` environment variable, the wrong version of `gcc` could be used.

You might be wondering about the implication of using the wrong compiler. The exact problem depends entirely on how different the two compilers are and which language features you're expecting from them. For example, if one developer writes code that uses newer language features, a second developer who is accidentally using the older compiler will likely see build errors.

Consider some common examples:

- **Older compilers don't recognize newer commands:** For example, the Java language concept of **generics** was introduced with Java 1.5 compilers. Trying to compile a Java 1.5 program with a Java 1.2 compiler results in errors.

```
Generics.java:5 Identifier expected.
   public List<Integer> myList;
                 ^

1 error
```

- **Older programs cause problems with newer compilers:** For example, the assert variable is now a reserved word in Java 1.4, whereas older Java programs were free to use `assert` as a normal variable name. To compile this older code, either a Java 1.3 compiler must be used or the `-source` option must be provided to the Java compiler.

```
AssertTest.java:4: as of release 1.4, 'assert' is a keyword,
and may not be used as an identifier (use -source 1.3 or
lower to use assert' as an identifier)
int assert = 0;
      ^

1 error
```

- **Newer compilers report more warnings:** Newer versions of the GNU C Compiler report more warnings than older versions. For build systems that choose to halt if they encounter compiler warnings, using a newer compiler causes build failures.

```
#ifdef FOO
...
#endif FOO  /* error! */
program.c:27:8: warning: extra tokens at end of #endif direc-
tive
```

- **Bugs were worked around in an older tool:** Sometimes developers find a bug in a tool (or associated libraries) that requires a workaround in their source code. The logic of their program is now tied closely to the version of the tool they're using. Upgrading the tool to fix the bug makes the developer's workaround invalid, possibly causing other problems.

```
int get_stats(char *name, int size)
{
  int stats[size];
  int rc = process_stats(stats, size);

  /*
   * Because of compiler optimization bug,
   * the following adjustment is necessary.
   * It isn't supposed to be required.
   */
  if (rc == 1){
```

```
    size += 1;
  }
  send_stats(stats, name, size);
}
```

- **Deprecated command options are removed:** Over time, various compilation tools gain new command-line options and the older options are removed. Instead of completely disappearing, however, the old options are marked as **deprecated** for a period of time, which means that they're still accepted for now but will be removed in an upcoming release of the tool. As a result, old and new versions of the same compilation tool might not be interchangeable.

The standard way to avoid all these problems is to ensure that the required version of each compilation tool is hard-coded into the build description file, leaving no room for ambiguity. Even if a newer version of the software adopts a newer version of a tool, the version-control system still enables the older software to use the older tool.

A natural assumption is that multiple versions of a compilation tool can be installed on the same build machine. This might be true for most tools, but not if a new version of the tool overwrites the older version, essentially removing the older tool from existence.

Assuming that you're allowed multiple versions of the same tool, you can specify which tool is required in several ways.

## 1. Hard-Coding the Absolute Path

In this scenario, the build description file contains the full absolute pathname of the compilation tool. This path must include some type of version number.

```
CC := /tools/bin/gcc-3.3
prog: main.o helper.o
    $(CC) -o $@ $^
```

When using absolute pathnames, the user's search path ($PATH) isn't examined, which removes the chance of using the wrong compiler. Clearly, this method assumes that all build machines have an identical set of tools installed and that they're available in the same file system location. Chapter 15, "Build Machines," discusses the management of build machines in more detail.

Also notice that the compiler's version number has been appended to its filename, so you can version-control access to the tools. This is important if you ever want to upgrade the compiler, which is almost a certainty for projects that span many years. Imagine a scenario in which releases 1 and 2 of your software both used version GCC 3.3, but the next version is destined to use GCC 4.2. As you saw earlier, having the source code compiled with the wrong version of the compiler can be problematic.

Using the magic of the version-control tool, the code branches for software R1 and R2 would be hard-coded to use GCC 3.3, whereas the main trunk of development would use GCC 4.2 (see Figure 14.3). Therefore, each code branch would use the required version, without any problems.

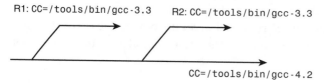

**Figure 14.3** *Hard-coding compilation tool pathnames so that each branch uses the correct version of the tool.*

Implement this pattern of versioning tools from the start of your project. If you made the mistake of using a nonversioned copy of GCC even for your first software release, you'd still find yourself in a predicament (see Figure 14.4).

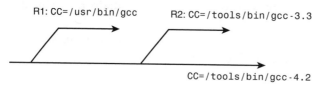

**Figure 14.4** *Problems occur if you fail to version-control the tool.*

In this scenario, the only way to be sure to reproduce the R1 source code is to ensure that /usr/bin/gcc is always set to version 3.3. Given that /usr/bin is part of the standard operating system image, you might not have much control over this version of the compiler. If you started compiling on a newer operating system, you'd need to downgrade /usr/bin/gcc to version 3.3. This might have unpredictable side effects for other programs running on the build machine.

You might be wondering why you can't change the tool reference in the R1 branch to /tools/bin/gcc-3.3. That would certainly work for any new bug fixes that you placed in the R1 branch, but it wouldn't help older versions of the software that you might need to reproduce. For example, if the current bug-fix release of R1 is software version 1.2.3, if you tried to reproduce version 1.2.2 or earlier, you'd still use the nonversioned compiler. For better or for worse, using a version-control system makes it impossible to "go back in time" and make changes to earlier releases.

A final observation is that you must be careful about removing old compilers from your system. As long as you need to reproduce older versions of software, you must keep the necessary compilers around. Some organizations support only a couple of old releases, so they might be able to remove old compilers after a year or so. Other organizations need to keep compilers for much longer periods of time because of their extended software support period.

### 2. Hard-Coding the $PATH Environment Variable

The second method for ensuring that the correct compilers are used is similar to the first method. However, in this case, you hard-code the value of the $PATH environment variable instead of relying on the user to have the correct search path already configured. Explicitly storing the path in the build description file also enables you to version-control and update the path over time.

```
PATH := /usr/bin:/tools/bin:/tools/java-1.5/bin
CC := gcc-3.3
JAVAC := javac
```

This example provides an exact sequence of directories in which to find compilation tools. When $(CC) and $(JAVAC) reference these tools, the path is searched in left-to-right order, starting with /usr/bin and finishing with /tools/java-1.5/bin. You end up using the first executable program that has the desired name.

This method works well, although the search path must be coordinated carefully. If the developer expected to use the javac program from the /tools/java-1.5/bin directory, but there was also a javac program in /usr/bin, the incorrect compilation tool would be used. This problem might take a while to resolve, but at least the incorrect behavior is consistent for all users (instead of only one or two developers suffering from the problem).

Another limitation of this method is that when the build tool is executing, the developer can't determine exactly which tool is being used.

```
$ make all
javac ...
```

Given this build log output, you know that javac is being executed, but you don't know which directory that program is from. If you had specified the full path to the tool, it would be displayed on the build output log:

```
$ make all
/tools/java-1.5/bin/javac ...
```

This distinction is important if developers want to manually cut and paste one of the lines from the build log. If they don't have their $PATH environment variable set the same way as in the makefile, a different tool could be used.

### 3. Store Tools in a Version Control System

A third method is to version-control compilation tools in the same way the source code is versioned. This provides the capability to associate a tool version with the source code that requires it. If you upgrade to a new compiler, you simply check in the new tool, and the build process starts using it. If you want to reproduce an old version of the source code, the correct (older) version of the tool is used.

The build description files must contain tree-relative paths for each tool, but you no longer need to have version numbers in the pathname:

```
CC := $(SRC_TREE)/tools/bin/gcc
JAVAC := $(SRC_TREE)/tools/bin/javac
```

For this system to work efficiently, you must be using a version-control tool that does a good job of storing large binary files. CVS is known for performing badly with large files, so it's not a good choice. In addition, if your version-control tool requires each developer to have an on-disk copy of every file, you might be overwhelmed by the extra disk space required. In contrast, tools such as IBM Rational's ClearCase enable developers to share a single copy of the tools.

## Large Binary Files

The concepts just discussed on version control of compilation tools also apply to other large files. Many programs use data files such as graphic images, sounds files, and third-party code libraries. If your version-control tool can handle large binary files, you could commit these files and have them checked out as part of each developer's source tree. However, if your version-control tool can't support large binary files or you simply want to save disk space, consider creating a shared repository of binary large objects (blobs).

Just as you did for compilation tools, each version of a blob would be stored in a file system path that contains a version number. Multiple versions of each blob can exist in parallel, with the build description files (stored under version control) referencing the correct version of each file. For example:

```
/usr/blobs/images/splash-screen/20100811/image.jpg
/usr/blobs/images/splash-screen/20100715/image.jpg
/usr/blobs/images/splash-screen/20100704/image.jpg
/usr/blobs/images/about-menu/20100728/about.jpg
/usr/blobs/images/about-menu/20100728/help.jpg
/usr/blobs/images/about-menu/20100713/about.jpg
/usr/blobs/images/about-menu/20100713/help.jpg
```

Each directory must be uniquely named to describe what the blob is used for and must contain a subdirectory for each version of the blob. Using a date stamp (such as `20100728`) makes it easier to determine when that version of the blob was created. In the build description file, you reference the appropriate version:

```
BLOBS := /usr/blobs/images
SPLASH_SCREEN := $(BLOBS)/splash-screen/20100811/image.jpg
ABOUT_MENU_DIR := $(BLOBS)/about-menu/20100728
ABOUT_IMAGE := $(ABOUT_MENU_DIR)/about.jpg
HELP_IMAGE := $(ABOUT_MENU_DIR)/help.jpg
```

Note that with the `about-menu` directory, two different files are stored (`about.jpg` and `help.jpg`) with each new version of the blob. From a logistics perspective, you might find it easier to version-control a large number of files in a single group instead of trying to manage a unique version number for each individual file.

## Source Tree Configurations

A final type of information to keep under version control is the source tree configuration. This is the set of source code directories that must be available in a developer's workspace for the software to build correctly. Depending on your version-control tool, you refer to this information as a **module**, a **configuration spec,** or a **view spec.**

For example, your developers might need to check out the following set of directories. These are mapped from version-control repository locations (on the left) to locations inside the developer's source tree (on the right).

```
/repo/trunk/libraries/graphic/       ->    libraries/graphic
/repo/trunk/libraries/math/          ->    libraries/math
/repo/trunk/programs/calc            ->    source
```

In this case, when a developer checks out a source code tree, the latest version of the `/repo/trunk/libraries/graphic` directory is retrieved from the repository. These files are stored in the `libraries/graphic` subdirectory of the developer's build tree. The remaining two lines of the specification file provide similar information. The number of entries in this file can be arbitrary, as can the mapping from repository to build tree.

Ironically, not many version-control systems allow this mapping to be version-controlled, therefore making it tricky to always reproduce older build trees. A developer must somehow know in advance which set of directories are required and must have external knowledge of how that mapping has changed over time. If developers want to obtain an older version of the source tree, they must use an older mapping.

One way to work around this limitation is to commit the mapping to a well-known location in the version-control system. For example, the file `/repo/trunk/view.dat` would first be checked out from the repository and used by the developer when accessing the remaining directories. If a new directory was required in the future, the additional configuration line could be added to `view.dat`. Unfortunately, it becomes a two-step process to check out source code, although the benefits of having this information under version control can be substantial.

## What Should *Not* Be in the Source Tree

In contrast to the previous section, you need to consider which files should not be stored under version-control. In addition, you need to know which files should not be stored in the same directories as the source code, even if they're not actually version-controlled.

This section looks at three categories of information:

1. Generated files in the source tree

2. Generated files under version control

3. Build-management scripts

Consider each of these categories in turn and understand why you need to be careful about storing them in the correct file system location.

### Generated Files in the Source Tree

By default, most compilation tools generate their output files in the same directory as their input files. In a build system, therefore, the default is to have the object files spread around the entire source code tree, intermingled with the source files. For example, you might see the following directory content:

```
$ ls
calc.c  calc.o  Makefile  math.c  math.o  numbers.c
numbers.o
```

Although it often takes extra work, large projects benefit from storing the object files in a separate output directory. If the source code is stored in the `sources` subdirectory, the object files should be stored in the `objects` subdirectory. These directories can contain a full hierarchy of subdirectories, so a source file such as `sources/a/b/file.c` would be compiled into an object file called `objects/a/b/file.o`.

If you decided to cut corners and not to take this approach, you'd likely end up with one or more of the following problems:

- **Autogenerated files look like source files:** Confusion might arise over whether a file is a source file or a generated file. This is not actually a problem for object files (with a `.o` suffix), but distinguishing autogenerated source files from true source files might be difficult. The usual practice is to prepend autogenerated files with a code comment of this form:

```
/* Warning - auto-generated file - do no edit */
```

Most version-control tools enable you to identify the files that should be committed but haven't yet been entered into the system. For example, many CVS operations provide a log of the files that have been modified, as well as a description of what will be done to them. Any files in a version-controlled directory that haven't been explicitly committed are marked with a ? symbol.

```
$ cvs update
? Data.java
U Main.java
U Database.java
U Data.list
```

The developer must figure out whether `Data.java` is a true source file that has yet to be committed to the repository or whether it's an autogenerated file that should never be committed. If it had been stored in an object directory in the first place, there'd be no question what type of file it is.

- **The clean target is harder to implement:** Supporting the `clean` build target is much harder if the generated files are interspersed with the source files. Whereas having everything in a single object directory makes it easy to clean the whole build tree (by simply deleting the directory), it's more difficult to delete the files if they're mixed in with the valuable source code.

In this case, either you do a lot of work to get the `clean` target working correctly (deleting the correct set of files) or you risk not cleaning out everything that was generated. This scenario can be painful for developers who resort to a clean build because of dependency problems. They could be stuck with a build tree in which files are not being rebuilt when they should be, but they also suffer from not being able to delete those files to start again with a fresh tree.

- **Object files for multiple CPU types get mixed together:** As discussed in Chapter 5, "Subtargets and Build Variants," some build systems can output code for more than one CPU type (such as i386 or MIPS). If you don't store the object files in two separate output directories, they get mixed together, making it difficult to distinguish one CPU's object files from the other.

- **Disk storage requirements are harder to meet:** Some computing environments have multiple tiers of disk storage, which are important to use correctly. Some disks are backed up on a regular basis, whereas others might not be backed up at all. If you care about keeping your source code safe and secure, you'll probably store it on the most reliable backed-up disk you have. In contrast, object files can easily be regenerated, so you'd instead use the cheaper disk. You clearly need to have source code and generated code in two different directories if you're using two different disks.

Hopefully, each of the previous examples has convinced you that generating object files (and autogenerated files) into a separate output directory is worth the effort, even if your build tool doesn't support this by default.

## Generated Files Under Version Control

If an object file or autogenerated source file has been committed to the version-control system, this is likely a mistake. A developer might have gotten confused and accidentally committed a generated file as if it was source code. As discussed earlier, this is an easy mistake to make if the generated files are incorrectly stored in the same directory as the source code.

One side effect of checking in generated files is that after they've been committed by the first developer, all other developers are likely to commit the same file by mistake. Because the generated file is automatically written to by the build system, the file in question will always be modified when somebody performs a build. The version-control system notices that the file has been modified and schedules it to be committed to the repository again. If developers aren't careful, they'll end up committing the same file over and over again.

To catch these situations more quickly, consider checking out files in read-only mode. (Some tools require this by default.) When the source tree is rebuilt, the build system fails when it tries to write to the generated file. The developer sees that the file was committed by mistake and removes it from the version control system before continuing the work.

Despite being a bad idea in general, in some cases, committing generated files actually makes sense. For example, you could speed up the build process by pre-compiling part of the build tree that doesn't change very often, such as a third-party library. By precompiling the library and committing the resultant files to the version-control system, developers can avoid compiling the library for themselves. A special build target must be used to build the library, so it won't be re-created by default and, therefore, won't be marked as "modified."

To extend this idea further, some version-control tools automatically cache generated files to save the developer from rebuilding them. Chapter 19, "Faster Builds," describes this mechanism.

## Build-Management Scripts

A final scenario in which code shouldn't be committed to the version-control system arises when a script or tool is more dependent on the external environment (such as build machines or disks) than it is related to the product's source code. Committing a tool of this nature only increases the amount of maintenance work required to fix bugs in the tool.

For example, a script that advises developers of which build machine is currently the fastest or which file system currently has the most disk space shouldn't be committed to the version-control system. It doesn't make any sense to have a different version of this tool for release 1 of the software versus release 2. In fact, fixing a bug in this script would require that every version-control branch of source code be modified. This is certainly not desirable.

Instead, the script should be kept in a regular disk file, such as /tools/bin/disk-advisor. Any changes to the script, such as adding the details of a new build machine or disk, can be done in a single place. The same script is used for all code branches and doesn't need to behave any differently for one branch of the source code versus another. Also, the script cares only about the build environment as it exists now, not how it was in the past.

If some of the script's behavior depends on a particular branch of code, it's still possible to store the script's configuration in version control but keep the main body of the script in the /tools/bin directory. For example, if the disk-advisor script needs to know which output directories are created by the build process, you could create a configuration file to list that information.

```
# list of output directories
obj
data
mips
powerpc
```

Each branch in the version-control system could have a different configuration file; thus, the script would behave differently in each case.

To be technically correct, the complete disk-advisor script must still be kept under version control, but not in the same place as the product's source code. The script has a life cycle of its own, and changes to that script must be version-controlled in a completely different version-control system. Changes to `disk-advisor` are therefore made independently of changes to the main product.

This completes the discussion of what you should—and shouldn't—keep under version control. Now let's take a quick look at version numbers and how they're used.

## Version Numbering

The final topic in the version control area is version numbering. Anyone who has downloaded and installed software has at least a passing awareness of the version number attached to it. Over time, the version number is incremented as new features and bug fixes are added to the software. The exact meaning of the version number is specific to each product, but it must somehow be attached to the software before it's sent to the customer.

This chapter doesn't spend a lot of time talking about version numbers, but it briefly covers the following build-related topics:

- What a version number looks like and what it means

- How the version number is managed and updated

- How the version number is stored inside the software and retrieved by the customer

### Version-Numbering Systems

Opinions differ on what a version number should look like, with no clear standards to follow. The basic rule is that numbers should increase whenever a new software release is made available. In some cases, numbers are not used at all, but are instead replaced by attractive marketing names. The following version sequences probably look familiar:

- R1, R2, R3

- 1.2.0, 1.2.1, 1.2.2, 1.3.0

- 3.1, 95, NT, 98, Me, 2000, XP, Vista, 7

- 737-300, 737-400, 737-500, 747-300, 747-400

The list of possibilities is endless, and it's up to the product managers to determine what makes sense for their product.

Perhaps the most common version system for software is the three-number approach. If in doubt, this is a tried-and-tested solution that won't get you in trouble with copyright lawyers. (Using `Vista` as a version name might land you in hot water). The three-number approach recognizes the difference in large feature changes, small feature changes, and bug fixes.

When using this approach, a version number should follow the format `X.Y.Z (Build B)`, where

- `X` increments when major feature changes are made to the software. This often means that configuration and data files that were used in previous versions of the software are no longer compatible (and must be upgraded).

- `Y` increments when minor feature changes are made. These changes add new capabilities to the software but don't significantly change the way the software is used or result in a disruptive upgrade.

- `Z` increments for every new bug fix (or set of bug fixes). No new functionality is added to the software, but the user can rest assured that the software now has better quality.

- `(Build B)` increments with every release build of the software. The customer need not be concerned with this number: It simply indicates how many times the test group has received a new package to test. It doesn't say anything about the new features or bug fixes that may be present in the package. This number is typically large and has no relation to the values of `X`, `Y`, or `Z`.

Individual customers use their own personal preference when evaluating version numbers. Cautious customers stay away from releases in which `Y` and `Z` are both 0, which indicates a totally new release of major features. They'll likely wait until `Z` has been incremented a few times to indicate that early product bugs have been resolved.

## Coordinating and Updating the Version Number

When implementing a release build system, some mechanism must exist for keeping track of the version number and updating it appropriately. Successive software releases use successive version numbers, incrementing the individual parts of the number as appropriate. The version number must therefore be recorded between release builds.

Between consecutive builds, the version number could be stored in one of the following ways:

- **In an external disk file:** The release engineer maintains a disk file containing the current version number, such as 1.2.3 (Build 832). After each successful build, a script increments the build number. Incrementing the number after a failed build is pointless, because a complete software package was never produced.

- **Inside the version-control system:** Instead of using an external disk file, the version number is committed to the version-control system (again, after each successful build). This has the advantage of permanently storing a version number alongside each build of the software. If developers went back to an earlier version of the software, the version-control system would show the matching version number.

- **Managed by the build-management tool:** One of the main goals of a build-management tool is to manage versions. The tool (such as Build Forge, ElectricCommander, CruiseControl, or Hudson) is responsible for storing the current version number in its own internal database and for incrementing the number after successful builds. If you're using a build-management tool, this is the easiest way to manage the version number.

Now that you've stored the version number somewhere, the remaining question is how to update the number. The build number B is automatically incremented after every successful build, but that is not true for the X, Y, and Z components. These should always be incremented manually after a conscious decision by the product managers.

The simplest approach for setting X, Y, and Z is for a manual decision to be made about the upcoming version number. For example, if the most recent software release was 2.3.0, the planned addition of a few bug fixes implies that the next release should be 2.3.1. On the other hand, if new features are added to the next release, the number would be 2.4.0.

As an example, the release engineering team might produce the follow sequence of release builds:

- 2.3.0 (Build 1623): Released to customers

- 2.3.1 (Build 1624): Internal only

- 2.3.1 (Build 1625): Internal only

- 2.3.1 (Build 1626): Internal only

- `2.3.1 (Build 1627)`: Internal only

- `2.3.1 (Build 1628)`: Released to customers

Customers will be unaware of all packages except the first and last in the list. You might want to hide the build number from the customer so that it's available only via a special command or menu option. They shouldn't care how many times the package has been built and sent to the test group. (Although a small increment might make them think the product hadn't been tested much!)

The test group refers to the packages by their build number, such as `1628`. When issuing bug reports, it relies heavily on build numbers to distinguish the different releases. After all, there are many different internal releases of `2.3.1`, and each could contain different bugs.

The release engineer tags the version-control system to indicate that build `1628` was the official release of version `2.3.1`. If developers wanted to reproduce the source code for this version, they'd reference the appropriate tag, such as `Release_2.3.1`. To reproduce internal releases, the tag would be `Release_2.3.1_Build_1626`.

Another common approach to versioning software is to add a release qualifier, such as `alpha`, `beta`, or `rc` (release candidate). These tags distinguish the pre-release versions of software from the final release. For example:

- `2.3.0 (Build 1623)`: Released to customers

- `2.3.1-alpha (Build 1624)`: Internal only

- `2.3.1-alpha (Build 1687)`: Internal only

- `2.3.1-beta (Build 1742)`: Internal only

- `2.3.1-beta (Build 1786)`: Internal only

- `2.3.1-rc1 (Build 1828)`: Release candidate; still internal

- `2.3.1-rc2 (Build 1829)`: Release candidate; still internal

- `2.3.1 (Build 1830)`: Released to customers

This approach keeps a clear separation between internal releases and those provided to a customer. The downside is that version `2.3.1-rc2` (in this example) must be recompiled to create version `2.3.1` and then retested to ensure that it still works perfectly. This extra effort is required even though no differences should exist between the two releases.

As mentioned earlier, you can implement a version-numbering system in many ways, with each product-development team choosing its own way of representing the change in software.

## Storing and Retrieving the Version Number

The last step in the version-numbering process is to store the number in the software package. Customers need a way to determine which version of software they're currently using or which version they're about to install. Additionally, a customer support engineer must determine which version a bug was reported against.

The version number should be stored in some obvious places, along with one that's not so obvious:

- **In the release package name:** The version string should always be embedded in the name of the software package the customer receives (for example, `package-2.3.1.zip`). For internal releases that aren't delivered to a customer, the name should also include the build number.

- **In the software's About menu:** When users select the `Help, About` menu on the GUI or enter some type of `version` command into a command-line tool, they should see the version string. This is an appropriate place to also display the build number.

- **In the installation directory name:** To support multiple versions of your software on the same target machine, always include the version number in the product's installation directory. For example, you could install it in `C:\Program Files\MySoftware-2.3.1`.

- **Inside the program's data segment:** This approach is a little less obvious, but storing the program's version string inside the data segment gives you access to the version number if the program crashes and creates a **core dump** (assuming your programming environment supports core dumps). This is particularly useful if the customer sent you a core dump for analysis without remembering which version number of the software caused the crash. (The customer may have upgraded recently.)

  Because operating systems don't include the program code (the **text segment**) inside a core dump, be careful to store the version string in a well-known data variable (in the **data segment**) instead of as a constant string.

Without going into too many details, it should now be obvious that some amount of work is required for your build system to insert the version number into the appropriate parts of the program. Start by adding a version flag to your standard software build command:

```
$ make all VERSION=2.3.1 BUILDNUM=1628
```

The build system inserts the value of VERSION and BUILDNUM into the pathnames, filenames, menu strings, or data segment, as appropriate for your product.

As a final note, you might be wondering what would happen if a developer did a private build without specifying a version string. In this case, the default might be to use the number 0.0.0, indicating to everybody that this isn't an official release build. You could also be more creative and mention the user's name, to indicate who actually built the software:

```
Private build by psmith@arapiki.com
Version 0.0.0 (Build private)
```

If you choose the approach of committing the release build number in the version-control system, you can create more specific version strings. For example, you can show which release build this private build was based on.

```
Private build by psmith@arapiki.com
Based on Version 2.3.1 (Build private)
```

The key point is to ensure that whoever uses the software package can determine who built the software and roughly what set of functionality to expect from it. It's also important to use version numbers as a means of reporting and tracking bug fixes.

---

## Summary

This chapter touched upon a wide range of topics related to version control of the build system. Failing to correctly version-control the build description or the compilation tools can result in broken builds or an inability to reproduce older versions of the software.

Various items should always be kept under version control. These include the build description files that record the complete end-to-end build process, references to each specific version of a compilation tool, large binary files, and the configuration of a source code tree that defines the directories to be checked out.

In contrast, you need to keep certain files out of the version-control system, such as generated source and object files, as well as build-management scripts that aren't directly tied to each version of the software.

Finally, version numbers are an important way for customers to measure the content and stability of the software releases available to them. These numbers are also used to track bug reports and corresponding bug fixes.

# Chapter 15

## Build Machines

In contrast to the last chapter's discussion on keeping the source code and build description under version control, this chapter focuses more on the underlying build machines (see Figure 15.1). A build machine may be upgraded on a regular basis as new versions of the operating system become available. Naturally, some amount of management is required to ensure that a change to a build machine doesn't break the build process.

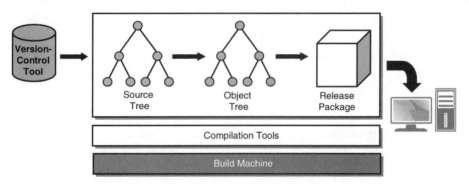

**Figure 15.1** *Big-picture diagram, focusing on the build machine.*

A typical build environment includes many compilation tools. Some are a standard part of the operating system, but others probably were acquired from third-party vendors (such as being downloaded from a web site). Some tools might even have been custom-written for the build environment and supported by your own organization. This chapter focuses on features and standard tools normally considered part of the basic operating system. Chapter 16, "Tool Management," focuses more on third-party and custom-built tools.

If you don't closely manage the build machine, plenty of opportunity for failed builds or corrupted software packages will arise. Even if problems are encountered only once or twice per week, the work required to diagnose and resolve compatibility issues can soon add up. A large development team of hundreds of people can require a full-time engineer to support and resolve build failures.

This chapter looks at the issues surrounding the version control of build machines. This includes centralized development in a closed and controlled environment, as well as in a typical open-source environment that has a wide range of end users.

This chapter also looks at a case study of using GNU Autoconf. This tool makes a developer's life easier when writing software for multiple platforms. Before moving to these topics, let's take a more in-depth look at the concepts of native and cross-compilation briefly discussed in Chapter 1, "Build System Overview."

## Native and Cross-Compilation

From a build system perspective, you often care about whether the target machine that *runs* the software is the same as the machine that *compiles* the software or whether it's a completely different type of machine. Each approach has its own set of benefits and challenges, and depending on your build environment, you might have some flexibility on the approach you choose. Let's briefly examine the two methods.

### Native Compilation

In a native compilation environment, the build system is free to use any files that reside on the build machine. On a UNIX-like system, any of the libraries in the /usr/lib directory and any of the header files in /usr/include can be incorporated into the build process. Given that the software executes on the build machine, or a similar machine, you need to use libraries and header files that match the build machine's operating system.

One advantage of native compilation is that it minimizes a developer's edit–compile–run cycle. The final program can be executed on the same machine it was compiled on, with no additional step to copy the program onto the target machine. This makes it easy to execute and debug the program from within the developer's editor or integrated development environment (IDE).

One point of concern when developing and testing code on a build machine is that you'll likely have additional libraries and tools that end users might not have installed. For example, if a Windows developer used Visual Studio to compile code, that developer must ensure that the software still works on a machine that doesn't have Visual Studio installed. Failure to test in a clean environment could result in `missing library` error messages when the end user runs the software. This is less of a problem in a cross-compilation environment where the developer has no choice but to test on a target machine that certainly won't have any development libraries installed.

## Cross-Compilation

In a cross-compilation environment, the program won't be executed on the same machine it was built on. It must not use any of the libraries or header files from the build machine because they won't be relevant to the target machine. Also, an additional step is involved to copy the executable program onto the target machine before it can be executed.

The main advantage of using cross-compilation is that not all target machines have sufficient processing power to run a full build system. Imagine the CPU inside a kitchen appliance: It isn't fast enough to execute a compiler and certainly doesn't have enough memory installed. Similarly, a device such as a gaming console has plenty of CPU power and memory, but it might not have the necessary user interface (keyboard and mouse) to develop software.

To successfully develop code in an embedded environment, you need two main things. The first is a set of cross-compilers that execute on the build machine but generate code for the target CPU. Some compilers, such as the GNU C Compiler, support a variety of target **back ends** and, therefore, are ideal for this environment. For example, a compiler for a gaming console would execute on a Linux machine with an Intel CPU but might generate code for an embedded MIPS processor.

The second requirement for an embedded system is a good communications link between the build and target machines (see Figure 15.2). The developer must download the software package to the target machine, start and stop the program remotely, and then use an interactive debugger to query the state of the target CPU.

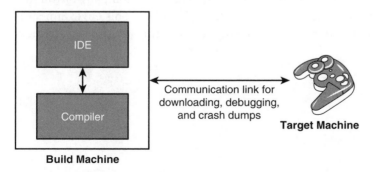

**Figure 15.2** *The separation between the development environment and the target machine, using a special-purpose communication link.*

If all these features are available, there's no reason developers can't continue to use their standard editor or IDE (on their build machine) to interact with the running program, as in native compilation.

## Hybrid Environments

During a product's development phase, before the customer uses the product, developers might choose a hybrid approach to developing software. They would compile their code for the target machine but still test the software on the build machine instead of downloading it to the real target hardware.

One way to achieve this goal is to develop in a language such as Java that uses a virtual machine. Because a Java program can run on any machine type, regardless of the target architecture, much of the software can be executed and tested on the build machine. Obviously, there are limitations when the software needs access to physical devices that are available only on the real target, but these can often be simulated on the build machine.

A second approach is to use a CPU emulator. In this case, the build machine creates an artificial environment that appears to be exactly the same as the target machine, at least from the software's perspective. When the CPU architecture differs from the build machine, the emulator interprets the machine instructions, giving the appearance the software is actually being executed.

In these types of hybrid solution, the developer gains a significant amount of productivity by reducing the awkwardness of working with real hardware.

---

# Centralized Development Environments

The next major topic related to build machines is centralized development environments. With centralized software development, you can use any number of build machines to compile the organization's range of software products. All the machines are managed by the same organization (such as a company or foundation) and are used for the same purpose (see Figure 15.3). This environment is distinct from the open-source development environment discussed in the next section.

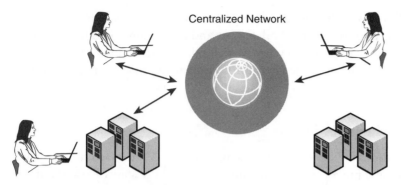

Centralized Network

**Figure 15.3** *A high-level view of a typical centralized environment with consistent toolsets and machine types.*

A centralized software environment might have anywhere from 10 to 10,000 build machines running a variety of operating systems. The machines could be spread across different countries and time zones and could be administrated by a range of different people. It's not uncommon to see build machines from 5 to 8 years old, even though, after 3 to 5 years, they're typically too slow to be useful.

In this type of environment, a lot of management is required to keep the build system running smoothly. The sheer number of developers and all their requirements can make it challenging to ensure that the build system produces the same result for everybody.

In an idealistic environment, all the build machines would be identical, at least from a software perspective. It doesn't matter whether the hardware is identical (in terms of CPU speed and memory capacity), but the operating system, CPU architecture, and set of tools must be the same on all machines. Any differences from one build machine to the next can cause build failures.

Imagine a scenario in which the same piece of software can be compiled on both Solaris and Linux systems. Although both operating systems are UNIX-compatible, they still have many differences in the location of the standard UNIX programs and in the command-line arguments accepted. Any special-purpose tools that the build system requires, such as compilers or code-generators, must be available on both platforms.

Anyone tasked with maintaining the build system faces an endless struggle to keep the build running on both types of machine. If developers prefer to compile their code on a Solaris machine, they need to double-check build system changes to ensure that they also work on a Linux machine. Most developers don't have the spare time to compile their software twice, so build breakages are more common than expected. Machine incompatibilities are a large contributor to broken builds.

The UNIX system administrators also have twice as much work to do. Not only do they need to be fluent in both Solaris and Linux administration, but they also end up doing twice as much work to maintain the operating system and tool patches for each of the machine types. Most system administrators prefer not to do everything twice.

## Why Build Machines Differ

Although it's desirable to have only a single type of build machine, for many reasons, this isn't practical. Keep in mind that build systems exist for many years, often longer than any particular build machine. Let's consider some reasons why a software organization might need to support more than one type of build machine:

- **Customers use different operating systems:** If you need to support one set of customers who use Solaris systems and another set who uses Linux systems, it might not be possible to support only one type of build machine. In contrast, you could manage with a single build platform if you could cross-compile your source code for each of the target machines. The only requirement is that cross-compilers and cross-libraries be available for each target platform.

  If you develop software for the home PC market, you have no choice but to upgrade to whatever the customers are using. At the time of writing, Microsoft has just released the Windows 7 operating system. At this point, you'd be foolish to support only Windows XP and Vista.

- **Development tools require specific operating systems:** A software developer might request a specific type of tool, such as a compiler for an unusual CPU type, or a custom code generator for a data-definition language. If problems with the tool arise, you can ask the vendor to provide the necessary information or software patches. The only caveat is that you must run the tool on an approved operating system. A vendor will support the latest version of Windows or something like Red Hat Enterprise Linux, but it won't likely support a 5-year-old version of FreeBSD.

  If you don't use a vendor-approved operating system, you'll be forced to switch to one that is, or perhaps reject the whole idea of using that tool in the first place. You might be able to use the tool on an older version of the operating system, such as an older version of Red Hat Linux, but you have no guarantees that it will work. The tool might fail because of missing operating system features or might give a `missing library` error if the required dynamic libraries can't be found.

If you have conflicting tool requirements, you could end up with a multimachine build process. To build the full software package, part of your build tree must be compiled with one tool (and, hence, one build machine), with another part of the tree compiled on a different machine. This clearly isn't desirable, but it might still be your best option if a special set of compilation tools is important for your product.

- **Newer OS versions are released:** When you started developing your software, you likely settled on a specific operating system as the basis for all your build machines. The build system will grow over time to take advantage of the operating system's features. Given enough time (normally 2 to 3 years), people will notice that newer versions of that same OS are now available and have additional features they'd like to use.

  Meanwhile, the version you're currently using is no longer supported. Most vendors support only the most recent two or three versions of their operating system and encourage users to upgrade to their latest release. They'll also stop providing bug fixes and security patches for their older versions.

  Unless you plan to support your build machine's operating system by yourself, it's best to upgrade. You'll need to make some changes to your build system, but upgrading is often the cheapest option in the long term.

- **Older operating systems don't support newer hardware:** Build machines tend to have a life span of 5–8 years. Even after 3 years, they'll be much slower than any new hardware you can buy. For a period of time, you'll probably purchase new hardware and install the same version of operating system you've used for many years—until you come across a nice new 64-bit quad-CPU system with 16GiB of RAM, which, unfortunately, won't be supported by a 5-year-old operating system. You'll be forced to upgrade.

- **Operating systems lose popularity:** You might have selected your build machine's OS many years ago and are obediently upgrading to the latest revision whenever updates are available. Over time, you might realize that the operating system is losing popularity in the market and that there's less support among tool vendors. A good example is the growth of Linux over the last 10 years and the corresponding decline of Solaris. If you've always used Solaris build machines, you might want to think about switching to a cheaper and faster Linux environment. In some cases, the vendor might even go out of business, forcing you to select a new platform.

- **Companies merge:** A common scenario in the world of high-tech companies is the familiar merger or acquisition. Two companies come together and find synergy by jointly developing their products or sharing development resources. In one case, two different product lines merge into a single product, requiring the two build systems to merge into one. In other cases, developers from one product line might be reassigned to work on the other product line, preferably using their existing build machines. Until the build machine platform can be standardized, there's good reason to be working with two different types of machine.

- **Developers have their personal favorites:** A final reason for having multiple build machines is that everybody has their favorite. Many people prefer to work with a certain operating system and sometimes go out of their way to make the build system work on their own platform. If the system administration group doesn't control the situation, you can end up with a wide array of build machines.

With all these motivations in mind, do not forget that your software releases might have a life span of several years. If you released a version of your product 2 years ago and are still providing customer support for that release, you need some way to compile the software. If your new build machines (with their newer operating system) cannot compile the old source code, your only option is to maintain two or more distinct types of build machine.

In Figure 15.4, Solaris versions 8, 9, and 10 have all been used to compile the product. The oldest release has reached its **end of life** (EOL), so you no longer need any Solaris 8 build machines. However, you must still maintain a small pool of Solaris 9 machines, in case someone needs to check out and recompile Release 2. Most developers would now use Solaris 10 as their default build machine.

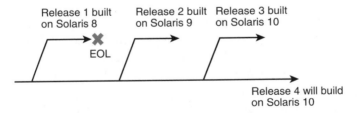

**Figure 15.4** *Each version-control branch might require a different type of build machine.*

As you might imagine, it often pays to proactively upgrade your build machines instead of waiting for an emergency. Anyone experienced in maintaining build systems has a horror story of how one build machine suddenly died of old age and had to be replaced in a hurry. Unfortunately, the necessary operating system version was no longer available, and none of the newer systems could compile the old software.

If you make a point of explicitly upgrading your build machines and modifying the build system accordingly, you'll be less likely to face these urgent situations. Being diligent about moving customers to newer software releases is also a good tactic to help with EOL releases.

## Managing Multiple Build Machines

Hopefully you now believe that having multiple build environments is almost a certainty, at least for short periods of time. Now consider what you can do to minimize the differences and, therefore, reduce the confusion when multiple build machines are used. Certainly no single solution to this problem exists, other than hard work by the system administrators and careful planning whenever changes are required.

- **Disallow special per-machine software:** Each user might have a preferred set of applications to install on their own machines, but consider disallowing this. If a software package is to be installed, it should be made available on all build machines, not just some. Have a group of reviewers evaluate each request for new software and then decide whether it should be installed on all machines, if at all.

  People might view custom installations as a superset of the standard build machine environment. However, installing extra programs into system directories (such as `C:\Windows` or `/usr`) can have nasty side effects that impact existing tools. For example, a program might decide to install a special version of a dynamic library, but the existence of that library could cause existing applications to act differently. The same is true for system configuration files that the new application decides to modify.

  One acceptable solution is for users to install their custom applications in their home directories. Because they don't have access to write to the system directories or configuration files, there's no way to modify the behavior of existing tools. This assumes that the build system rejects user-specific `$PATH` values, which it always should.

- **Disallow administrator access:** As much as possible, disallow users from having administrator/superuser access to build machines because this can add to the temptation for them to make custom modifications. If left unchecked, each machine can end up with a slightly different configuration, with the build system behaving differently in each case. Depending on the nature of the change, the problem might not be noticed for months or years, at which point tracking down what was changed is difficult.

- **Validate build machine changes on a test machine:** If you decide to make a significant change to your build machines, such as applying patches or upgrading the OS, first validate the change on a test machine. This involves rehearsing the installation steps and validating the build system to ensure that nothing is broken. Build both old and new code branches; in case there's a difference between them. The system administrators should work closely with the build maintainers to ensure that everything works correctly.

- **Use a single operating system image:** Instead of manually installing new software on each build machine, use some type of automation to do the job. Assuming that the installation process has been validated on a test machine, you shouldn't have any problems installing the same software on all other machines. Ignoring hardware differences, each machine should have started with the same set of software installed and, therefore, should end up with the same new set of software.

  If you purchase a completely new computer that doesn't yet contain any software, make sure you have an easy way to install the necessary operating system and tools. Using a **jump-start** or **kick-start** method can help with the deployment of cookie-cutter systems.

- **Say no to personal machines:** As mentioned earlier, many developers prefer to use the type of operating system they're most comfortable with or to work on their personal machines. Although it's a sacrifice for developers, disallowing personal choice is a great way to ensure uniformity. You might not want to disallow users from plugging their machines into the network, but you should at least refuse to support them if they have build problems.

- **Ask tool vendors to support your operating system:** Instead of changing your build machine's operating system to support a third-party development tool, you could ask whether the vendor can support your existing OS. The worst the vendor will do is decline your request, but if you happen to be lucky or have a great relationship with the vendor, you could avoid a lot of extra migration work.

- **Make sure your system administrator understands build systems:** It can't be stressed enough that you must keep the build machine's operating system and tools under tight control. If system administrators don't understand these issues, they might be tempted to apply patches and upgrades whenever they feel like it. In organizations that don't specialize in software development, the system administration group often has a lot more say in how the computers are managed and which versions of software are used. This freedom doesn't transfer well to build systems.

- **Watch closely for "magic" machines:** If you're not careful, you'll find that some part of your build system can be executed only on a custom-configured build machine. This is common when performing an obscure sequence of steps that use special file formats or one-off tools. In many cases, the magic machine sits in a dark corner of the server room or perhaps underneath a developer's desk. Few people might even be aware that the machine exists.

  Because of their obscurity, magic machines are unlikely to be involved in the main part of the build process; instead, they're confined to compiling a small or optional part of the software. For example, an embedded system might depend on a small bootloader that loads the full operating system from disk. The bootloader might be stored in flash memory (which stays intact when power is turned off) and doesn't change often; it might be modified only once or twice a year.

  You can now imagine the problem. Six months might pass before anybody notices that the magic machine has failed, leaving no way to recompile the bootloader software. It's important to keep track of magic machines and ensure that any tools are made available on the more common build machines.

- **Use virtual machines if you need to:** One way to avoid supporting magic machines is to instead use a virtual machine. This enables you to run an older operating system inside a newer operating system. The OS image is simply a large disk file that can be loaded into a virtual machine player at any point in time and that can be duplicated and distributed to any developer who needs access. The VM executes on any modern build machine, alleviating the concern about magic machines growing old and failing.

Managing a set of build machines isn't trivial; if it's not done properly, it can lead to build failures and inconsistencies between machines. It's worth creating solid and repeatable procedures for managing your build machines instead of leaving things to chance.

Now let's continue by looking at open-source environments, where there's much less consistency between the build machines.

## Open-Source Development Environments

The characteristics of an open-source project are different from centralized software development projects. Most projects have fewer than 20 active developers, but the software is downloaded and compiled by many thousands of consumers (see Figure 15.5). For common platforms such as Linux, the software might be available in precompiled form, but in other cases, consumers must compile the program for themselves. Each user has his or her own computer and is likely to be the administrator. (This is certainly true for home enthusiasts.) Sometimes the software is downloaded to corporate machines, but there's no standard type of build machine required.

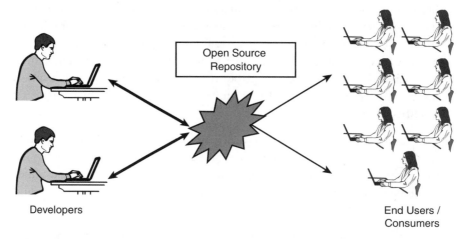

Open Source
Repository

Developers

End Users /
Consumers

**Figure 15.5** *A typical open-source environment with few developers and many consumers, each using their own version of build machine.*

Consider, for example, the Apache web server, which has a small number of experts who've contributed to the software. On the consumer side, many end users will compile the httpd program from source code. These novice end users have no idea how the tool works or how the software builds; they are interested only in the finished product. Luckily for most people, httpd comes precompiled for many operating systems, with no need to compile it from source code.

The key point here is that maintainers of open-source projects can't dictate exactly which operating system to use to compile the source code. No single company owns the build machines, so the build system must work correctly on any reasonable platform. New operating system versions are released frequently, and users expect their existing software to compile on each new build machine.

Anyone who has compiled open-source software, especially on less common versions of UNIX, has undoubtedly come across build failures. You're probably in luck if the maintainers of the software tested on the same OS version you're using. In general though, you should expect a few build errors if your operating system's features are slightly different than expected or if your system is missing any of the third-party packages this software depends upon.

Keep in mind that most open-source packages are designed to run on UNIX-like systems, although some of them support Microsoft Windows. Even then, plenty of UNIX-like systems exist, each having slightly different characteristics. Without thinking too hard, you've probably heard of most of the following: Mac OS X, Linux (Debian, SUSE, Ubuntu, Red Hat, and Gentoo, among many others), FreeBSD, NetBSD, OpenBSD, Solaris, HP-UX, AIX, Xenix, and Minix. Given the variety, your build system would need to be very versatile to work on all of them.

Now look at the common types of build failure you might encounter when compiling open-source software.

- **Availability of prerequisite packages:** In many cases, an open-source project depends on the target machine to already have the prerequisite packages installed. For example, if the software uses the MySQL database system, MySQL must have already been installed. Alternatively, the package might require that a Python or Perl interpreter be available.

  Most open-source projects come with detailed written instructions on which packages must be installed. The end user must download and install each of the packages, often requiring hours of extra work.

- **Version of tools and packages:** Although a prerequisite package might already be installed on the target machine, it might not be a recent enough version. You could expect the build system to validate the version of all required packages and fail with a meaningful error message. Unfortunately, developers don't always have the foresight to make that happen.

  In some cases, you're left staring at a confusing error message when the older package doesn't understand a newer command or file format. For this reason, some open-source maintainers deliberately avoid relying on newer versions of packages, just to ensure that their software still works correctly on older build machines.

- **Path to tools:** A big difference between UNIX variants is the location in which programs are installed. Most of the standard programs (such as `ls`, `cat`, and `more`) are installed in `/bin` or `/usr/bin`, but other nonstandard programs can be stored anywhere the OS maintainer chooses (such as `/opt`, `/usr/local/bin`, or `/usr/tools`). For a build system to find a required tool, it must depend on the user to have the `$PATH` set correctly or otherwise play a guessing game to figure out where each tool is installed. This can be a major source of build failures.

- **Availability of command-line options:** Even if a UNIX tool is successfully located, it might not accept the same command-line options or syntax as in other versions of UNIX. This is because each operating system packages a different version of the tool, sometimes up to a year or two old. In other cases, the operating system has its own unique implementation of the tool, which has a life of its own for many years. For example, BSD-based UNIX systems (NetBSD, FreeBSD, and OpenBSD) use the BSD version of the Make tool. This tool accepts a different style of makefile compared to GNU Make, which is the default on Linux systems.

- **Availability of preinstalled libraries:** You might find that a software package relies on a dynamic library that doesn't exist on your system. This happens when you attempt to execute a program that was compiled on either a much older or much newer version of your operating system. For example, the program might depend on `/usr/lib/libfoo.so.6`, whereas your system has only `/usr/lib/libfoo.so.5` installed. If you recompile the software from source code, there's a good chance that the problem will go away, because it now depends on a library that's available on your system. In the worst case, you might see a build error if the software uses a function that was recently added to `libfoo.so.6` but never existed in `libfoo.so.5`.

As you can see, compiling open-source software isn't always trivial. Some packages might work the first time, but others can take several days of tweaking before you get a successful build. Everything depends on your operating system, the features that the software uses, and how much effort the maintainers spent on making the software portable.

Thankfully, many OS maintainers bypass these problems by packaging software in precompiled form, while making source code available to those who really need it. Software packaging systems, such as the Red Hat Package Manager (see Chapter 13, "Software Packaging and Installation"), enable a user to install a precompiled software package in a matter of seconds, while also ensuring that all prerequisite packages are first downloaded and installed. In many cases, the OS maintainers ensure that their complete collection of packages work together in harmony and don't conflict with each other. Sadly, you don't have the luxury of using precompiled packages if you don't use a supported operating system or if you're trying to install less common software.

In closing, several tricks make software more portable between different operating systems:

- **Use platform-independent scripting languages:** Instead of writing software that depends on an operating system's native programs (such as those in /usr/bin), take advantage of scripting languages such as Perl or Python. These languages provide a platform-independent way of accessing the system's functionality. For example, instead of calling the operating system–specific function for creating a new directory, use the mkdir function in Perl that will work the same way on all platforms, including Windows.

```
if (mkdir("mydir", 755) == 0){
    print STDERR "Failed to create directory\n";
}
```

- **Use compatibility libraries:** These libraries are optionally added on top of the standard operating system libraries, to provide a level of compatibility and make it easier to compile open-source software. One of the most famous compatibility libraries is Cygwin [82], which provides a Linux-like environment on top of Microsoft Windows.

- **Use the GNU version of tools:** Instead of requiring a software package to work with every variant of every tool, rely on only GNU versions of the basic UNIX tools (ls, cat, sort, and so on). These are optional tools that replace the operating system's standard set, except that a Linux environment already uses GNU tools by default. A build system that relies on GNU tools is more likely to support multiple platforms. Some experts advocate never using tools in /bin or /usr/bin because compatibility across different systems is such a problem.

A final solution is to use the GNU Autoconf tool, allowing the use of operating system features that have actually been confirmed to exist on a build or target machine. This tool has played such an important role in the world of open-source software that it demands a section of its own.

# GNU Autoconf

The sheer number of UNIX-like operating systems demands a simple way to manage the differences. Although each system provides roughly the same functionality, some features will always be implemented differently. The difference might be in the set of C header files a program must include, differences in the C library functions, or differences in the file system path for standard programs. Accommodating these variations makes it challenging to write a single program that compiles and executes on all target platforms.

The GNU Autoconf tool [63] is the most popular way to manage these differences for the C and C++ languages, where low-level system programming is common. Autoconf inspects the build machine to determine which functions are available and how they're implemented. The software uses this information to customize the set of header files or functions used, thereby supporting a wide range of build machines. Autoconf comes from the same tool family as Automake, discussed in Chapter 9, "CMake."

If you've compiled software for a UNIX system in the past, you've probably used the Autoconf tool, even without realizing it. Most commonly, you'll see instructions to execute a `configure` script before typing `make`. Now let's look at an example of how this `configure` script is created and how it's used to customize the software you need to compile.

Languages such as Java don't require the services of Autoconf because they're designed to be platform neutral in the first place.

## The High-Level Workflow

Before diving into the detail of how Autoconf works, you need to understand the high-level flow of information. If you've ever used the Autotools system, perhaps as an end user running the `configure` script, you've seen a number of additional files created in your source tree. Many of these files start with the code comment `autogenerated - do not edit`, and the body of the file contains a lot of cryptic shell commands and directives.

The software's author cares mainly about the file `configure.ac`. This is the master file that describes the various operating system features the software needs. The author lists the compilation tools required to compile the software, the important C-language header files, and some of the library functions that the program uses. The upcoming example looks in detail at `configure.ac` to see how these requirements are stated.

As shown in Figure 15.6, the `configure.ac` file is used as input for two of the tools in the Autotools family:

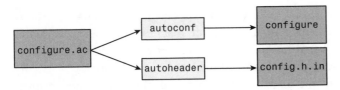

**Figure 15.6** *High-level flow of the Autoconf and Autoheader tools.*

- **Autoconf:** This tool reads the `configure.ac` file and generates a corresponding UNIX shell script, named `configure`. The purpose of this script is to detect the location of the required compilers and determine whether the necessary header files and library functions are available on the target machine. You can think of `configure` as an executable version of the rules that are specified in `configure.ac`.

- **Autoheader:** This tool is similar to Autoconf, in that it reads the `configure.ac` file. However, the main purpose is to create a template header file called `config.h.in`. As you'll see shortly, `config.h.in` is the basis for creating the `config.h` header file and lists all the system features the software intends to use. For example, if the build machine supports the `memcpy` function, this file defines the `HAVE_MEMCPY` symbol.

The Autotools family has several other programs, such as Automake and Autoscan, but this chapter doesn't discuss those in detail.

The second part of the Autoconf process takes place on the end user's build machine (see Figure 15.7). To make things easy for end users, the author probably prepackaged the `configure` script and the `config.h.in` file that were both autogenerated in the first step. Additionally, the author likely provided a template makefile, called `Makefile.in`.

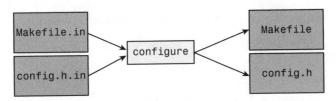

**Figure 15.7** *Using the configure script to generate a target-specific build system.*

As you might have learned from your own experience, the end user starts by executing the `configure` script on the local build machine. This script validates each of the requirements listed in the original `configure.ac` file, and an error message is provided if the machine isn't suitable. Although the software usually executes on the same machine on which it's compiled, the `configure` script is capable of handling cross-compilation of software.

In many cases, `configure` is run without specifying any command-line options, although end users can customize plenty of parameters if they don't like the defaults. They can enable or disable parts of the software, or even specify where compiled binaries and libraries should be stored (instead of the default `/usr/bin` and `/usr/lib`). This is another way Autoconf enables software installation on a wide range of machines.

After `configure` finishes, the end user is left with a fully functional `Makefile` and `config.h` (not just templates anymore). As you'll see in the example, these files have been customized based on the features the build machine does or doesn't have and take into account any of the command-line options the user provided to the `configure` script.

The only thing left to do is execute the standard Make tool. The software is compiled and configured to execute on the target machine, so end users needn't worry if their machines are different from that of the original author. The Autoconf tool should have already dealt with those problems.

Now let's look at an example of how the build and target machine requirements are stated.

## An Autoconf Example

This simple example demonstrates a few of the features of the Autoconf tool. Instead of putting together a fully functional build system, you'll examine only some of the basic features. From the software author's perspective, two files need to be constructed:

- `configure.ac`: Describes the build and target machine requirements

- `Makefile.in`: Acts as a template for the makefile that will build the software

Start by looking at `configure.ac`. For the sake of convenience, you'll see the full content first and then examine it section by section.

```
1   AC_INIT([Example], [1.0.0])
2   AC_CONFIG_HEADERS([config.h])
3   AC_CONFIG_FILES([Makefile])
```

```
 4
 5   AC_PROG_CC
 6   AC_PATH_PROG([JAVA], [java])
 7   if test "x$JAVA" = 'x'; then
 8     AC_MSG_ERROR(Cannot find a usable Java compiler)
 9   fi
10   AC_PROG_LN_S
11
12   AC_CHECK_HEADERS([errno.h fcntl.h limits.h],[],
13                    [AC_MSG_ERROR([Missing required header
                      file.])])
14   AC_CHECK_HEADERS([asm.h],[],[])
15
16   AC_CHECK_FUNCS([memcpy],[],
17                    [AC_MSG_ERROR([Missing required memcpy
                      function])])
18   AC_CHECK_FUNCS([strcpy],[],
19                    [AC_MSG_ERROR([Missing required strcpy
                      function])])
20   AC_REPLACE_FUNCS([megacpy])
21
22   AC_RUN_IFELSE(
23           [AC_LANG_PROGRAM([], [ return !(getpwent() !=
             0)])],
24           [AC_MSG_RESULT([getpwent() works correctly])],
25           [AC_MSG_FAILURE([getpwent() function non-func-
             tional])])
26
27   AC_OUTPUT
```

This file might appear to be written in a special-purpose language, but it's actually a combination of M4 macro instructions and UNIX Bourne shell commands. The Autoconf and Autoheader tools provide the necessary macro definitions to generate the `configure` and `config.h.in` files.

The first three directives provide the meta-information Autoconf uses to start.

```
1   AC_INIT([Example], [1.0.0])
2   AC_CONFIG_HEADERS([config.h])
3   AC_CONFIG_FILES([Makefile])
```

`AC_INIT` is a macro that takes the software package's name and version number as input. The `AC_CONFIG_HEADERS` macro states which header file should be used to record the available system features. That is, you want to create a customized `config.h` by using `config.h.in` as a template. Finally, the `AC_CONFIG_FILES` macro specifies that `Makefile` should be derived from `Makefile.in`, but with the template's parameters replaced by their actual values. You'll see the content of these files shortly.

The next portion of the file specifies which compilation tools are required when building the software.

```
 5   AC_PROG_CC
 6   AC_PATH_PROG([JAVA], [java])
 7   if test "x$JAVA" = 'x'; then
 8     AC_MSG_ERROR(Cannot find a usable Java compiler)
 9   fi
10   AC_PROG_LN_S
```

The AC_PROG_CC macro states that the configure script must locate a usable C compiler, and the variable $CC should be assigned the name of that compiler. The $CC variable can be referenced by other parts of the build system whenever a C compiler is required. If no compiler is available, the configure script fails with an error.

Because Java is a less common tool, you must use the general-purpose AC_PATH_PROG macro to locate a suitable executable program (that has the name java) within the user's shell path. If the tool is found, the $JAVA variable is assigned the absolute pathname of the java tool. If not, the $JAVA variable is left undefined and the additional Bourne shell code provides a suitable error message.

Finally, AC_PROG_LN_S is special-purpose macro that ensures that the target machine supports symbolic links on its file system. Autoconf provides a number of these special-purpose macros, covering many of the common operating system features that vary among UNIX platforms.

Next, similar checks look for the existence of C-language header files.

```
12   AC_CHECK_HEADERS([errno.h fcntl.h limits.h], [],
13                    [AC_MSG_ERROR([Missing required header
                      file.])])
14   AC_CHECK_HEADERS([asm.h], [], [])
```

The first AC_CHECK_HEADERS macro ensures that each of the errno.h, fcntl.h and limits.h header files are available for use on the build machine. If they exist, no further action is taken. (The second argument to this macro is an empty pair of [] .) However, if any of the files are missing, an error is reported to the end user and the configure script aborts.

The second AC_CHECK_HEADERS is more lenient, in that the program still executes correctly if the asm.h file doesn't exist. Instead of aborting the configure script, a C preprocessor symbol (HAVE_ASM_H) indicates whether the file is available. The C program can test for this symbol (using #ifdef HAVE_ASM_H) and modify its behavior accordingly.

In a similar way, you can check for the existence of required C functions. Depending on the version of UNIX being used, some of these functions might not be available.

```
16  AC_CHECK_FUNCS([memcpy],[],
17                    [AC_MSG_ERROR([Missing required memcpy
                      function])])
18  AC_CHECK_FUNCS([strcpy],[],
19                    [AC_MSG_ERROR([Missing required strcpy
                      function])])
20  AC_REPLACE_FUNCS([megacpy])
```

The first two uses of `AC_CHECK_FUNCS` look for the `memcpy` and `strcpy` functions, respectively. If the functions are defined, Autoconf defines the `HAVE_MEMCPY` and `HAVE_STRCPY` preprocessor symbols. If not, a suitable error message is provided and the `configure` script aborts.

In the case of `AC_REPLACE_FUNCS`, this example accepts the fact that `megacpy` might not exist on the target machine and instead provides an implementation of that function. If this can't be found in the available system libraries, the build process automatically adds the `megacpy.o` object file containing a custom implementation of the function.

The final test in the `configure.ac` file is to check whether a particular library function behaves the way you expect it to. This is useful when a function might have a buggy implementation.

```
22  AC_RUN_IFELSE(
23        [AC_LANG_PROGRAM([], [ return !(getpwent() !=
          0)])],
24        [AC_MSG_RESULT([getpwent() works correctly])],
25        [AC_MSG_FAILURE([getpwent() function non-func-
          tional])])
```

In this case, you test whether the `getpwent` function correctly returns a pointer value or whether it incorrectly returns a `NULL` pointer the first time you use it. The `AC_RUN_IFELSE` macro uses the `AC_LANG_PROGRAM` macro to generate, compile, and execute a small C program that calls the `getpwent` function. Depending on whether you see the desired result, the test passes or fails with an appropriate message.

Finally, the `AC_OUTPUT` macro sets everything into action and generates the two output files, `configure` and `config.h.in`.

```
27  AC_OUTPUT
```

At this point, you've completed the review of `configure.ac`, but the software's author still must provide another file. The `Makefile.in` file is simply a template for the real `Makefile`, but with a number of template variables (for example, `@CC@`) used in place of the real values. When the `configure` script is run, each of those variables is replaced by a machine-specific value, and the resulting makefile is created.

In the following example, @CC@ and @JAVA@ are defined because you used the AC_PROG_CC and AC_PATH_PROG macros, whereas the configure script implicitly created other template variables.

```
1   # @configure_input@
2
3   JAVA      = @JAVA@
4   CC        = @CC@
5   SRCDIR    = @srcdir@
6   BINDIR    = @bindir@
7   EXTRADEFS = @DEFS@
...  remainder of Makefile.in not shown ...
```

Later, this example looks at the resulting makefile that's automatically generated when the configure script is executed on the build machine.

## Running autoheader and autoconf

Now that you understand the content of configure.ac, let's look in detail to see what happens when you run Autoheader and Autoconf with this file as input. First, the Autoheader tool doesn't produce any output when it runs, but it does generate the config.h.in file.

```
$ autoheader
```

Given all the requirements specified in configure.ac, the Autoheader tool determines which features are present on the build machine. For each feature, a suitably named C preprocessor symbol indicates whether the feature exists. These symbols can be tested by the build system or the C source code.

In essence, config.h.in is just a template listing all the symbols that could potentially be defined. Only after you've run the configure script on the build machine will some of the symbols actually end up defined. These definitions are provided in the machine-specific config.h file, not the config.h.in template.

The following output shows a few lines of the config.h.in template file. Note that some of the symbols directly relate to the requirements specified in configure.ac, whereas Autoheader added a few more that it thought were necessary.

```
/* config.h.in.  Generated from configure.ac by autoheader.
*/

/* Define to 1 if you have the <asm.h> header file. */
   #undef HAVE_ASM_H

/* Define to 1 if you have the <errno.h> header file. */
   #undef HAVE_ERRNO_H
```

```
/* Define to 1 if you have the <fcntl.h> header file. */
#undef HAVE_FCNTL_H

/* Define to 1 if you have the <inttypes.h> header file. */
#undef HAVE_INTTYPES_H

/* Define to 1 if you have the <limits.h> header file. */
#undef HAVE_LIMITS_H

/* Define to 1 if you have the 'memcpy' function. */
#undef HAVE_MEMCPY

/* Define to 1 if you have the <memory.h> header file. */
#undef HAVE_MEMORY_H
```

In a similar way, the Autoconf tool doesn't produce any output (unless there's an error), but it does generate the configure script.

```
$ autoconf
```

Because of the complexity of the configure script, this book doesn't discuss the content. You're certainly welcome to download any GNU software package off the Internet and examine the resulting configure script for yourself. It's likely to be a complex script and not something you'd normally bother looking at.

The configure script is purposely written in a platform-neutral way. That is, the script should not use any nonstandard shell features, or there's a good chance it won't execute properly on the target machine.

## Running the configure Script on the Build Machine

Until now, the steps you've seen were executed by the original author of the software. To avoid complicating the installation, this author provides pregenerated copies of configure and config.h.in to the end users instead of requiring them to install Autoconf and Autoheader on their own machines.

After users have downloaded the software, they first execute the configure script on their own build machine. The script probes the machine to see whether it meets the requirements; then it autogenerates the Makefile and config.h files, as discussed earlier.

First, look at the output of the configure script. This will be familiar to anyone who has installed open-source software on a UNIX-like system. If you study the output carefully, you can relate many of the test cases back to the appropriate macro in the configure.ac file.

```
$ ./configure
checking for gcc... gcc
```

```
checking for C compiler default output file name... a.out
checking whether the C compiler works... yes
checking whether we are cross compiling... no
checking for suffix of executables...
checking for suffix of object files... o
checking whether we are using the GNU C compiler... yes
checking whether gcc accepts -g... yes
checking for gcc option to accept ISO C89... none needed
checking for java... /usr/java/latest/bin/java
checking whether ln -s works... yes
checking how to run the C preprocessor... gcc -E
checking for grep that handles long lines and -e... /usr/bin/grep
checking for egrep... /usr/bin/grep -E
checking for ANSI C header files... yes
checking for sys/types.h... yes
checking for sys/stat.h... yes
checking for stdlib.h... yes
checking for string.h... yes
checking for memory.h... yes
checking for strings.h... yes
checking for inttypes.h... yes
checking for stdint.h... yes
checking for unistd.h... yes
checking errno.h usability... yes
checking errno.h presence... yes
checking for errno.h... yes
checking fcntl.h usability... yes
checking fcntl.h presence... yes
checking for fcntl.h... yes
checking limits.h usability... yes
checking limits.h presence... yes
checking for limits.h... yes
checking asm.h usability... no
checking asm.h presence... no
checking for asm.h... no
checking for memcpy... yes
checking for strcpy... yes
checking for megacpy... no
getpwent() works correctly
configure: creating ./config.status
config.status: creating Makefile
config.status: creating config.h
```

Let's continue by examining the content of config.h and Makefile. At this point, configure now has solid information about the target machine, so it can fill in all the gaps in the template files.

In the case of config.h, you now know for certain which of the features are present, so the original #undef directives either have been commented out if the feature isn't present or have been properly defined to a value of 1 if the feature exists.

```
/* config.h.  Generated from config.h.in by configure.  */
/* config.h.in.  Generated from configure.ac by autoheader.
*/

/* Define to 1 if you have the <asm.h> header file. */
/* #undef HAVE_ASM_H */

/* Define to 1 if you have the <errno.h> header file. */
   #define HAVE_ERRNO_H 1

/* Define to 1 if you have the <fcntl.h> header file. */
   #define HAVE_FCNTL_H 1

/* Define to 1 if you have the <inttypes.h> header file. */
   #define HAVE_INTTYPES_H 1

/* Define to 1 if you have the <limits.h> header file. */
   #define HAVE_LIMITS_H 1

/* Define to 1 if you have the 'memcpy' function. */
   #define HAVE_MEMCPY 1

/* Define to 1 if you have the <memory.h> header file. */
   #define HAVE_MEMORY_H 1
```

In the case of `Makefile`, all the template variables from `Makefile.in` have been replaced by the machine-specific values. Most notably, `JAVA` and `CC` have been given the values that the `configure` script determined for you.

```
# Makefile.  Generated from Makefile.in by configure.
JAVA     = /usr/java/latest/bin/java
CC       = gcc
SRCDIR   = .
BINDIR   = ${exec_prefix}/bin
EXTRADEFS = -DHAVE_CONFIG_H

... remaining of Makefile.in not shown ...
```

Although only a small fragment of the overall makefile is shown, you can certainly imagine how a full makefile-based build system can be constructed. To help, Autoconf enables you to create a hierarchy of directories, each containing a customized makefile.

## Using the Configuration Information

The final step in the Autoconf process is to use the preprocessor definitions. Now examine a C-language source file that takes advantage of the configuration knowledge you've just acquired.

```
 1   #ifdef HAVE_CONFIG_H
 2   #include "config.h"
 3   #endif
 4
 5   #ifdef HAVE_ASM_H
 6   #include <asm.h>
 7   #endif
 8
 9   void example_func()
10   {
11       ...
12   #if HAVE_MEMCPY
13       mempcy(temp_buffer, source, sizeof(temp_buffer));
14   #endif
15       ...
16   }
```

The first thing to do is include the config.h file, which enables you to make decisions based on whether each feature is enabled. The #ifdef HAVE_CONFIG_H directive is required because you might have opted to not generate a config.h file but instead have all the preprocessor definitions passed in via the @DEFS@ makefile variable.

The next part of the file (lines 5–7) enables you to optionally include the asm.h header file, but only if it's known to exist on the system. Typically, you'd also provide a #else clause to make sure that the required definitions are made available in some other way.

Finally, inside the function body (lines 12–14), you test the HAVE_MEMCPY symbol to see whether it's safe to call upon the memcpy function. Again, a suitable #else clause should provide an alternate way to achieve the same result.

In summary, you can see how the Autoconf tool can avoid a lot of frustration from variations in the range of UNIX-like operating systems. No longer do end users need to face countless compilation errors because the software wasn't written for their particular machine type. Additionally, the software's author doesn't need to enumerate each possible operating system; instead, the author can focus on whether each specific feature is available.

## Summary

A build machine is a vital part of any software build system. Any changes to the machine must be carefully controlled, or you risk breaking the build and making it impossible to reproduce older versions of the software.

In a centralized development environment, it's desirable to have all build machines conform to a standard; otherwise, different developers see different build results. Variation will always exist among build machines, especially when customer requirements, compilation tool requirements, and hardware requirements force you to upgrade your operating system. In contrast, the need to support older versions of software encourages the continued use of older build machines.

In open-source development, the software's author has much less control over which build machines will eventually be used, because anybody can download the software and try to compile it. In this case, it's important for the build system to be more lenient and support a wider range of build machines. The Autoconf tool is a popular way of constructing a build system that functions on a wide range of UNIX-like build machines.

# Chapter 16

Tool Management

Chapter 15, "Build Machines," focused on build machines and the need to effectively control changes made to those machines. In a similar way, this chapter focuses on the management of compilation tools. The goal is to provide a reliable and repeatable build process, even when tools are upgraded or modified in some way.

Your build system might require that you install optional tools such as these:

- **Cross-compilers:** For example, you might need a MIPS compiler that executes on an Intel Linux platform.

- **Interface definition compilers:** This might include a CORBA compiler that reads high-level interface definitions and generates the appropriate client stubs in Java or C++.

- **Custom code generators:** You might install a tool that processes a domain-specific language and generates the corresponding Java code.

- **Build acceleration tools:** You might need a parallel-build tool or a build-avoidance tool, discussed in Chapter 19, "Faster Builds."

Assuming that these tools don't come as part of the standard operating system image, you'll need to install and manage them separately. Many tools are vendor supported, requiring payment before the tool is provided for installation. Other tools are free to use and are available in either binary or source code form. Of course, you can also design and construct your own development tools.

This chapter discusses some of the basic rules for developing, installing, and customizing compilation tools. It also touches briefly on what's involved in building your own tools.

# Rules for Managing Tools

No matter what the tool is or where it originally comes from, you need to follow some basic rules when managing them and installing them on your build machines. Now take a detailed look at each of the rules.

## Tool Rule #1: Take Notes

When compiling or installing a tool on your build machine, take notes. Take copious notes if the tool ends up being nontrivial to compile or requires unexpected steps to install. If you don't take notes, you'll likely need to rediscover the whole process in the future, and next time it could be an emergency (such as recovering from a disk crash). If the compile and installation process took you half a day of effort in the first place, you'll certainly be glad you took notes.

In your notes, record many types of information:

- From where did you download the software? If you found the tool by searching the Internet for an hour or so, make sure you quickly bookmark the URL of the web page and document it in your notes. If you don't, you might need an hour to find it next time as well.

- Write down the exact set of commands you used to compile the software. If you followed the software's README file and it worked the first time, you're lucky. In this case, make a note that you simply followed those instructions. If things didn't go smoothly and you had to perform extra steps, make a careful note of what you did.

- When the software is installed, take note of which file system directory it was installed into, as well as which installation options you selected. If somebody needs to maintain the software in the future, that person will need to know where the program is installed and how to reinstall it.

- What are the license restrictions for using this tool? Are there limits on the number of concurrent users or perhaps the number of machines it can be used on? For open-source software, just because the software is free to download and compile, doesn't mean you have unrestricted freedom to modify and redistribute the source code.

- Record all passwords, extra configuration details, and license keys. You'll almost certainly need this information when you next make a change to the tool. When it comes time to upgrade to a newer version, you might need to reconfigure the software.

- Document all license keys for all tools in a central location. It's easy to forget when your license is due to expire, and if the vendor doesn't remind you in time, the tool might refuse to work.

- If you stored the tool's source code somewhere, where did you put it? What are the commands for retrieving the source code?

All this information is important. If you don't believe this, imagine that one of your coworkers installs an important tool before going on vacation for three weeks. If an emergency patch needs to be applied, you'll be thankful your coworker took the extra time to write things down. A wiki page is a great place to document everything, especially because it's widely accessible and can be updated if information is missing.

Based on previous experience, some development tools (both commercial and open source) have taken several days of experimentation to get working correctly. This fact can't be repeated enough: Take notes!

## Tool Rule #2: Use Version Control for the Source Code

If you're managing a tool that you obtained in source code form, store the source code in a version-control system. Avoid the temptation of downloading the code, compiling and installing the tool, and then throwing away the source code. You might think that you can always download the source code again if you need to, but you have no guarantee that the same version will be available when you next go to look. The web site might be down or completely out of business, or the particular version you need might no longer be listed.

You might never plan to modify the tool, but when the developers are actively using it, they'll likely find bugs that you need to fix. If the tool becomes popular they might ask for custom features to be added. Always plan on this happening, even if the developers swear that it never will.

Often a software organization has a separate repository just for storing tool source code. Every time you make a local change to the tool (such as a bug fix or a new feature), you need to check in and document what you changed. If in the future you decide to upgrade to a newer version of the tool (downloading it from a web site), you'll need to reevaluate each of your local changes and determine whether it's still relevant. Reapplying local changes to a new version can involve significant effort, so avoid making modifications unless you really need to.

For open-source tools, consider submitting your local changes back to the mainstream distribution. If your bug fix or new feature is applicable to other users, the tool maintainer is quite likely to accept your changes in the public repository. The next time you download a new version, your local changes will already have been incorporated, with no extra work for you to do. In the spirit of open-source software, you'll also get to benefit from other people's bug fixes and new features.

Finally, in an ideal world, you'd be able to regenerate your entire set of compilation tools from source code simply by checking out all the source code from the version-control system and then typing `make all`. In reality, you should at least write a shell script that automates the compilation of each tool, making it possible to reinstall the tools whenever you make a change. As mentioned before, take copious notes. It's an extra benefit if these notes are in the form of an automated script.

## Tool Rule #3: Periodically Upgrade Tools

Keep track of all compilation tools your build system uses, and be sure to upgrade them from time to time. Although it's obviously not advisable to be upgrading tools just for the sake of it, you have many good reasons to be proactive about adopting newer versions:

- **To take advantage of bug fixes:** Clearly, this saves you time and frustration by fixing problems you're hitting in the current tool. In many cases, tool bugs manifest themselves as product bugs, and you can waste many days before you discover the true cause of the problem. Upgrading regularly minimizes this wasted time.

- **To take advantage of newer features in the tool:** Vendors spend a lot of time and effort researching which new features their customers need. If the product doesn't keep up with market requirements, customers may simply stop buying the product. You can expect those new features to be helpful when developing your own software.

- **To keep tools up-to-date with newer versions of your operating system:** If you try to use a five-year-old tool on the latest version of your operating system, it may no longer work as expected. Problems occur when the required dynamic libraries no longer exist or if an old tool no longer supports realistic memory or file sizes.

- **To continue receiving support for the tool:** Vendors would love to reduce support costs by having everybody use the latest version of their software. A common approach is to support only the most recent releases and refuse to support older versions of the tool. If you want to continue receiving support, you'll need to upgrade.

Naturally, upgrading tools involves some downsides. If the tool's behavior changes from one version to the next, or if the sets of commands or file formats are different, you can expect a nontrivial amount of work when upgrading. For example, when using the GNU C Compiler, you'll find that newer versions of the tool produce more compilation warnings than older versions. If you have a policy of removing all compiler warnings, you'll have a considerable amount of work to clean up your product's source code, all thanks to the new compiler.

Conduct major tool upgrades at an appropriate time in your development cycle. You don't want to treat a compiler upgrade as a minor feature or bug fix; instead, schedule it for the next major release of your software. For example, if the current release of your software is version 1.2.3, you should schedule the upgrade for 2.0.0 but continue using the older compiler for version 1.2.4.

It may be stating the obvious, but don't forget to test the new tool before rolling it out. The output of the tool might be subtly different from that of the previous version. Unless you fully verify that your software builds correctly and passes all regression tests, you might introduce product bugs. Before declaring the upgrade a success, plan on a significant amount of testing, and give all developers adequate warning.

You shouldn't necessarily upgrade to a new version of a tool as soon as it becomes available or as soon as the vendor suggests the idea. In practical terms, you might shy away from a new release that has a final version digit of .0, such as 4.0.0. Instead, you may wait until version 4.0.3 or 4.0.4, to be sure that the early customer bugs have been found and fixed. Of course, if you're interested in receiving the latest and greatest features, using the 4.0.0 release makes perfect sense.

## Tool Rule #4: Use Version Control for the Tool Binaries

As discussed in the previous rule, only newer branches of your product's source code should use an upgraded tool. This leaves the old branches to use the old tool, at least until that branch of code reaches the end of its life. Some mechanism for version control is necessary for each tool's executable program, not just for the source code.

As mentioned in the previous chapter, you should use version control for any references that a build system has to its tools. The build description file (such as a makefile) should contain the exact path of the tool, as well as the exact version number. Adding a suffix to each tool's name is one way of meeting this goal. For example, to maintain multiple versions of the python tool, you'd install them in /usr/local/bin as python2.5, python2.6, and python2.7.

Another outcome of this rule is that you should avoid using the standard operating system tools. If your build system depended on /usr/bin/java, you'd have no guarantee that a system administrator wouldn't update to a newer version of the Java language, possibly breaking your builds. This is particularly true for tools that automatically check for updates and upgrade themselves whenever a new version is available.

When storing development tools that aren't part of the basic operating system, always create a special file system location. Don't add any new programs into /bin or /usr/bin, which are reserved for built-in tools. Instead, create a totally new directory in a publicly readable place. For example, you could use /tools, /usr/tools, or /opt/devtools. No matter what directory you select, developers should be aware that these are custom-installed tools rather than part of the basic operating system.

Creating a tool-specific directory comes with important rules about how the directory is updated. Because of the importance of these rules, allow only tool experts to add new programs to the tools directory. You can do so by using a special file system group to limit who has write access to the files. If nonexperts were permitted to add new programs, they wouldn't necessarily follow the version-control rules, thereby making it difficult to rebuild old software releases.

The following file system layout is recommended:

```
/tools/pkg/gmake/3.79 /...
/tools/pkg/gmake/3.82/...
/tools/pkg/ant/1.7 /...
/tools/pkg/ant/1.8/...
/tools/pkg/python/2.5/...
/tools/pkg/python/2.6/...
/tools/pkg/python/2.7/...
/tools/pkg/perl/5.10/...
/tools/pkg/perl/5.12/...
/tools/pkg/gcc/i386-linux-gcc-3.4/...
/tools/pkg/gcc/i386-linux-gcc-4.5/...
```

In this example, each software package is neatly installed inside the /tools/pkg directory. A unique subdirectory is maintained for each version of each tool that's installed. When a new version is added, no changes are made to existing versions of the tool; instead, a totally new directory is created. You also shouldn't remove any old tools until all code branches that depend on them have reached the end of their life.

When referencing tools from the build system, always use the absolute pathname of the tool:

```
CC := /tools/pkg/gcc/i386-linux-gcc-3.4/bin/gcc
```

In addition, the /tools/bin is a directory that all developers should add to their $PATH variable. It contains programs that they'll execute from their command shell (such as gmake or ant) instead of those accessed by the build system.

```
/tools/bin/...
    gmake -> ../pkg/gmake/3.79/bin/gmake
    ant -> ../pkg/ant/1.7/bin/ant
    ...
```

The programs in this directory can be upgraded to a newer version at any time simply by changing the symbolic link to point to a newer version of the tool. Needless to say, the build system should access tools only via the relevant /tools/pkg directory; they shouldn't depend on the nonversioned tools in /tools/bin.

As a convenience for command-line users who need a specific version of the tool, it doesn't hurt to include versioned symbolic links in addition to the non-versioned links. For example:

```
/tools/bin/...
    gmake -> ../pkg/gmake/3.79/bin/gmake
    gmake-3.79 -> ../pkg/gmake/3.79/bin/gmake
    ant -> ../pkg/ant/1.7/bin/ant
    ant-1.7 -> ../pkg/ant/1.7/bin/ant
    ...
```

From a system administration perspective, you must ensure that the /tools directory is available on all build machines. Perhaps the easiest way is to use a network file system mount point for /tools so that the same copy of the files is available on all machines at the same time. Any additional tools that are added will instantly appear on all build machines, with no additional per-machine effort required.

In contrast, if you're aiming for a high-performance build system, you might want to have a local copy of all tools on each build machine. Accessing the tools from local disk can be much faster than accessing them across the network, especially at peak times of the day when the file servers are busy. You can install the same package across many machines in a number of ways, but it usually comes in the form of a software update mechanism (the same way software patches are automatically distributed). Unfortunately, this approach can be time-consuming if not fully automated, making it painful to push out small configuration changes to existing packages.

If your organization is distributed across multiple development sites, you also need to consider replication. A single network file system containing the /tools directory won't scale, so you need to replicate /tools across multiple sites (see Figure 16.1).

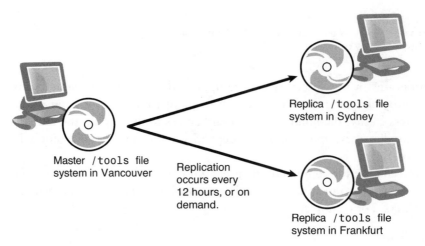

**Figure 16.1** *Replication of the compilation tools to multiple development sites.*

Be careful to replicate the files on a regular basis, or some development sites might not see the recently added tools. Before modifying the build system to use a new compilation tool, it pays to ensure that the tool has been successfully replicated to all sites.

As a final note, you have another way to ensure that each branch of the product's source code is using the correct version of a tool. In this case, you commit the tool's source code to the same version control repository as the software that uses the tool. As part of the product's build system, you first compile the tool from source code into an executable program. The build system then uses the tool that it just compiled.

This technique is useful, for example, when you've created a special-purpose language for use in your source code. The tool will change regularly as developers ask for new features to be added to the language, so versioning the tool alongside the source code makes a lot of sense. As you might expect, older code branches always use older versions of the compilation tool.

## Breaking the Rules

As with all rules, developers always have incentives to do the wrong thing. This is typically because it's inconvenient to spend the extra time doing what seems like unnecessary work. Don't forget that these rules are designed with the future in mind rather than being urgent requirements when the tools are first installed. Imagine yourself a year or two from now, needing to upgrade a tool, apply a bug fix, or restore a damaged file system. You'll wish you'd followed the rules in the first place.

Why are some people tempted to break the rules? Consider these common excuses:

- "I was just playing around with the tool, and I wasn't sure whether we were going to use it. Now that I've finally decided to officially start using the tool, it's a nuisance to go back and follow the rules."

- "It's fun to install new tools and play around with them, but documentation and formality aren't very interesting."

- "Another developer got the tool from somewhere and has been executing it from a personal directory for the last few months. We don't have the source code anymore, and they just gave me the executable program to install in /tools."

- "I'm too busy, and my manager is pressuring me to get this installed immediately. I don't have time for documentation, even though I know it's important."

Of course, whenever you decide that you don't want to pay the cost of something now, you often end up paying significantly higher costs in the future—usually with even more time pressure.

## Writing Your Own Compilation Tools

All software developers are familiar with hand-writing their program in a language such as C, C++, Java, or C#, because this is the standard way of developing software. In modern development environments, you also have the option of using automatic code generators that take a high-level language as input and generate source code as output. The obvious benefit is that writing the same functionality in a high-level language can be many times faster than writing in a general-purpose language.

Part II, "The Build Tools," discussed the `mathcomp` compiler as an example of a custom-built compilation tool. The tool itself is a Python script that takes a series of mathematical expressions as input and generates an equivalent C or Java file. The output files are then passed through a regular C or Java compiler to produce object files.

It's not uncommon in a large build system to use custom-built tools to simplify the construction of software. Writing the tool in a scripting language is common, especially for line-oriented input that's easy to scan and process. For more complex tools, with structured multiline input, it's more common to use a full-fledged scanner and parser.

Without diving into too much detail on how compilation tools do their job, let's discuss the basic theory and mechanism behind the scanning and parsing of input data. For more details on writing this type of tool, refer to a compiler textbook [83]. Be warned that compilers can be complex to understand, so writing your own is not an easy task.

## Custom-Written Tools with Lex and Yacc

The traditional approach to writing compilation tools is to use Lex and Yacc, or their more recent equivalents, Flex [91] and Bison [92]. These tools are specifically designed for creating compilers and have been used since the early days of the UNIX operating system. The Lex tool reads a sequence of characters from an input stream and converts them into meaningful language **tokens** or **keywords**, such as `if` or `then`, or the numeral `176`. The Yacc tool then ensures that these tokens are in a logical order, according to the specific rules of the programming language being defined.

The output of the Lex and Yacc tools is a set of autogenerated C-language files that implement part of your custom language's compiler. The following example demonstrates how patterns (also known as regular expressions) are used to match a sequence of input characters. When a complete input token is identified, some type of action (written in C code) is performed.

```
1   DIGIT [0-9]
2   NUMERAL {DIGIT}+
3   WORD  [a-z]+
4
5   %%
6   {NUMERAL}          { printf("The number %s\n" yytext); }
7   if|then|else|fi    { printf("You've selected a
                         keyword\n"); }
8   {WORD}             { printf("You've entered the word:
                         %s\n", yytext);
```

This code starts by defining the DIGIT class of characters (0 through 9), the NUMERAL class as a sequence of one or more digits, and the WORD class as a sequence of lowercase letters.

Next, you define three different rules, used to identify the following:

1. A whole number, as defined by the NUMERAL class

2. The name of a reserved word—in this case, `if`, `then`, `else`, or `fi`

3. An identifier, matching the characters described in the WORD class

In each case, when the appropriate pattern is matched against the sequence of input characters, the C code action on the right side is triggered.

From the build system perspective, the previous code should be stored in a file with the `.l` suffix. This source file is translated by the `lex` tool into a C output file named `lex.yy.c`. The output file contains all the user-specified action code, as well as the additional logic required to pattern-match the regular expressions against the input stream. Developers don't need to understand how the autogenerated C code performs its job; instead, they simply call the `yylex()` function whenever they want to receive the next token.

By executing the program that Lex generates, you can translate a series of input characters into a sequence of output messages. The input sequence

```
123
if then begin
hello
456
```

results in the following output being displayed:

```
The number 123
You've selected a keyword
You've selected a keyword
You've entered the word: begin
You've entered the word: hello
The number 456
```

The Yacc tool works in a similar way, but it ensures that the tokens (identified by Lex) appear in the correct order. A statement such as

```
if (a == 5) then hello();
```

makes perfect sense to most developers, but the statement

```
if (== 5) a then hello();
```

gives you a syntax error, simply because the tokens don't appear in a logical order. Although a developer can guess the intention of the code, the compiler would have no hope of guessing the true meaning. The code that Yacc generates can parse a sequence of input tokens and ensure that they arrive in a logical, meaningful order.

The following example (stored in a file with `.y` suffix) demonstrates how to parse simple arithmetic expressions, by ensuring that numbers, operators, and parentheses all match up.

```
expr: '(' expr ')'
    | expr '+' expr      { ... action ... }
    | expr '-' expr      { ... action ... }
    | expr '*' expr      { ... action ... }
    | expr '/' expr      { ... action ... }
    | INTEGER            { ... action ... }
    | FLOAT              { ... action ... }
    ;
```

In this case, you define an expression (`expr`) to be either another expression inside parentheses; the combination of two subexpressions using addition, subtraction, multiplication, or division; or simply a plain integer or floating-point number. Note, however, that this example was simplified for demonstration purposes and doesn't take into account the rules of associativity or precedence, such as multiplication taking priority over addition.

As with Lex, you use the Yacc tool to compile this high-level language into a lower-level C program that performs the actual work. The tool produces two main output files:

- `y.tab.c`: A C source file that contains the complete parser for the custom-defined language. It contains the C action code, as well as the necessary parsing logic required to ensure that the input is matched and the correct actions are triggered.

- `y.tab.h`: A C header file that defines the set of input tokens (such as INTEGER or FLOAT). Both Lex-generated and Yacc-generated programs include this file to ensure that they have a consistent view of which input tokens are expected in the input stream.

Figure 16.2 summarizes the process of creating a new compilation tool using Lex and Yacc. Although Lex and Yacc generate C code, other programming languages have their own version of these tools.

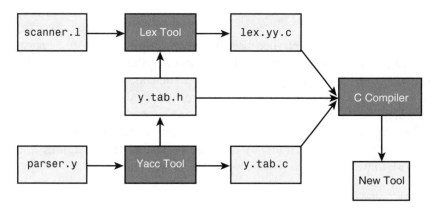

**Figure 16.2** *The use of Lex and Yacc to generate a small compiler.*

With this basic set of rules defined, you now have a simple scanner and parser that reads and processes input data. From the developer's perspective, invoking the autogenerated `yyparse()` function parses the input stream and triggers all the action code. Of course, this chapter hasn't discussed the action code, which can be complex in its own right. (Again, refer to a compiler text book for more detail.)

## Summary

To ensure that software builds are reliable and repeatable, it's important to manage the set of compilation tools used. This is especially true when new versions of a tool are introduced or a tool bug is fixed.

Several basic rules aid in the management of compilation tools. Noting how a tool was compiled or installed is vital for saving time with future tool changes. For tools maintained in source code form, be sure to keep that source code in a version-control system. This helps when you need to fix bugs or reapply local changes to an upgraded version. Periodically upgrade tools to take advantage of bug fixes and new features, as well as to avoid losing support from the vendor. Finally, make sure that the tool's executable programs are version-controlled, allowing different versions of the software to use different versions of the tool.

If you want to create your own compilation tool, consider using Lex and Yacc, or the equivalent tool for your programming language of choice. These tools enable you to generate scanners and parsers to deal with nontrivial input formats.

# PART IV

## Scaling Up

Part IV examines what happens when your build system becomes large—for example, when you deal with software that has more than ten million lines of code, with potentially hundreds of developers adding new features. You'll likely have one or more people maintaining the build system on a full-time basis. In this scenario, compiling the software becomes a major part of each developer's day.

It's an unfortunate reality, but the build system you first created when the software was small isn't likely to scale over time. In the same way that your development team grew and changed to more effectively write new code, your build system must change. The assumptions you made when the software was small no longer make sense with ten million lines of code. Part IV covers the following topics:

- **Chapter 17, "Reducing Complexity for End Users":** When a build system grows, it can become complex and confusing for software developers. You'll explore techniques for making build systems more usable for end users.

- **Chapter 18, "Managing Build Size":** When the code base grows over time, you start to reach the limits of your development tools and build machines. You'll learn how to subdivide a large software product into more manageable components.

- **Chapter 19, "Faster Builds":** More lines of code means more compilation work and a slower build process. You'll examine how you can measure the performance of a build system and find the location of your performance bottleneck. You also explore how you can avoid unnecessary compilation and use multiple build machines to quickly complete the work.

You might not currently manage a large build system, but it's still worth considering these topics. After all, a large software product starts as a small product, so foresight is useful. Some amount of upfront planning can extend the life of your build system, even when the source code becomes much larger than it is today.

# Chapter 17

# Reducing Complexity for End Users

For most software developers, a build system is purely a means to compile code. They don't care how the build process works, as long as their program is compiled in a reasonable amount of time. To produce a fully compiled software package, all they want is a single button to push or a single command to execute. In reality, though, a build system requires some amount of maintenance. At the least, developers must take the time to list the source files to be compiled and the compilation flags to be used. In the worst case, they can find themselves fighting against a faulty dependency system or simply waiting too long for their build to complete.

These problems become worse as the software grows in size, with more developers working on the code. The build system becomes cluttered with configuration variants, stale code that's no longer used, and a number of corner cases for handling peculiar source files or compilation tools. All this leads to a build system that's difficult for developers to use.

If you're an experienced software engineer, you understand that complexity can lead to unexplained failures and difficulties in maintaining the system. For example, if a dependency-analysis system is so complex that it takes a guru to comprehend, there's a good chance that errors will be introduced. The net result is that developers spend a lot of time blaming themselves for writing code that doesn't compile, at least until they realize that the build system is at fault.

In terms of support, a complex build system leads to an increased number of trouble reports. Developers report problems with missing dependencies, compilation tools that aren't doing the correct job, or even code that doesn't seem to compile for other people. Each time this happens, a build engineer must look into the problem to find out what the developer is doing wrong, or perhaps apply a patch to the build system to deal with a newfound corner case.

For a build system maintainer, a complex system can also be challenging to deal with. If the person who originally designed the build system is no long available, a new build engineer might struggle to understand everything. This is particularly true if a number of different people have modified the build system over the years, creating a patchwork solution.

This chapter focuses on techniques that reduce the complexity of a build system, making it simple for developers to use and possible for build engineers to maintain. In some respects, this can be conflict of interest: Making a build system easier for a developer could make it more complex for the build maintainer to work with. Keep in mind that complexity means different things to different people.

The chapter starts by discussing the concept of a build system framework and then considers the downside of supporting multiple build variants. Next it discusses a range of techniques for reducing a build system's complexity. Finally, it covers the importance of scheduling and adequately staffing build system changes.

## Build Frameworks

A large-scale build system will naturally have some amount of complexity. Software that uses a range of compilation tools or a number of file formats has more complex requirements than a smaller system. As discussed throughout this book, you're doomed to encounter many build failures unless you capture these requirements properly.

Most software developers are concerned with which source files will be compiled and which compilation flags will be used, but that's the extent of their involvement. They don't mind how the build system gets the job done, and it can be frustrating if they're forced to learn too much detail. As you learned in Chapter 2, "A Make-Based Build System," the concept of the build system **framework** is important. That is, you abstract out the build system's complexity and hide it away from the end users. Your build description therefore has two sections:

- **Developer-facing portion of the build description:** This part of the build description is highly visible to software developers. It lists all source files to be compiled and executable programs to be created. Software developers can also enable or disable optimization flags, debugging flags, and other compilation features.

- **Framework portion of the build description:** This part of the build description provides a number of extensions on top of the basic build tool. For example, the framework could support automatic dependency analysis, multidirectory compilation, and a number of new compilation tools.

Let's consider these two areas in more detail, emphasizing what they contain and how they relate to each other.

## Developer-Facing Portion of the Build Description

Developers want to see only the high-level detail of the build system. They need to add new source files, add new executable programs, and configure compiler flags, but they don't want to learn the syntax of the underlying build tool.

Here's an example of a GNU Make program that uses a framework:

```
1   EXE_NAME = myapp
2   C_SRCS := main.c data.c gui.c util.c
3   LINK_LIBS := z bfd
4   C_FLAGS := -O -g
5
6   include framework.mk
```

The first four lines define the name of the executable program, the list of C source files, the libraries to link into the executable program, and the compilation flags to use. The final line includes the framework file, which you know from experience will be complex. Luckily, the developers can get most of their work done without understanding what the framework does.

Tools such as Ant and SCons typically have less need for an additional framework because these tools already have many of the required features built into the language. For example, consider the equivalent program in SCons:

```
1   Program('myapp', ['main.c', 'data.c', 'gui.c', 'util.c'],
2                   LIBS = ['z', 'bfd'],
3                   CFLAGS = ['-O', '-g']);
```

You might suspect that this requires software developers to understand the basics of the SCons tool. This is true, but the SCons language is easier for novice users to understand, at least compared to a GNU Make solution.

Another benefit of abstracting out the high-level detail is that users can support themselves. They won't need to consult a build engineer every time they want to add a new source file or change a compiler flag. This is a productivity improvement for everyone.

On the other hand, you might find that some build system changes really do require that complex code be placed outside the framework. This is usually the case for special-purpose source files that don't fit cleanly into the model provided by the framework. As usual, make sure this code is adequately commented to explain to the end user what it does.

## Framework Portion of the Build Description

The goal of a framework is to hide the complexity from software developers. The software developer knows that a framework is used but shouldn't feel compelled to understand how it works. Only a qualified build engineer should care about the framework's build description.

For example, this is some functionality you'd normally hide inside a framework:

- With GNU Make, you're required to implement your own automatic dependency analysis, your own multidirectory build support, and custom rules for each new compilation tool. The user's makefile simply defines a number of high-level variables and then uses the `include` directive to invoke the underlying framework. It's vital to keep the framework in a completely separate makefile.

- With Ant, any custom tasks should be encapsulated inside the framework and then incorporated into the main `build.xml` file using the `taskdef` directive. You can also choose to create reusable helper targets, to be included via the `import` directive. The software developer can use these new tasks and targets as if they were built into the Ant language.

- With SCons, your framework contains builder methods and scanners for each new type of source file, as well as a number of helper functions to simplify the main build description. The `SConstruct` file imports these new functions to extend the basic SCons language.

You might think that because the framework is hidden from software developers, it can be as complex as you want. In reality, though, a few software developers will still poke around inside the framework and might even try to extend it for themselves. This is particularly true for engineers who already have experience maintaining build systems.

It's also good practice to make sure your framework is simple enough for an average developer to understand. You wouldn't encourage them to read the framework on a regular basis, but a complex build system is usually hard to maintain and often buggy. Keeping the framework as clear and concise as possible makes it less likely that you'll introduce bugs. Even build gurus sometimes have trouble understanding a complex framework.

In some cases, you have no choice but to have a complex framework. For example, the inclusive Make framework in Chapter 6, "Make," is by no means simple to understand. An average developer would have a hard time comprehending how it works, as would many build gurus. At the least, you should provide a detailed set of comments to explain how everything works.

As a final note, if your framework ends up being so complex that few people can understand it, perhaps you're using the wrong build tool. It's a bad business decision to have software that only one person can understand, and this rule applies equally to build systems. Make sure that developers cross-train each other on how the build system works.

## Convention over Configuration

One of the interesting design tradeoffs in choosing a build framework is simplicity versus flexibility. On one side, the developer wants to have a simple build system without putting in too much effort. On the other end of the scale, the developer may be willing to spend more time defining the build description, to gain more flexibility.

The concept of **convention over configuration** makes it easy to create a build system, as long as you're prepared to structure your software within the confines of a standard template. This doesn't mean that you can't customize the build system to suit your own peculiar needs, but you can get a long way before needing to do that.

As an example, the Eclipse build system is trivial to use, at least when compared to an Ant-based system. An Eclipse user selects the type of project needed and answers a few simple questions; then Eclipse generates the entire build environment. Admittedly, it's a limited build environment, but you can start your code development without much upfront work. If you need more power, you can switch to the more configurable Ant tool.

Build system conventions are everywhere. For example, the following conventions are fairly standard:

- For the C and C++ languages, source files end in `.c` and `.cc`, respectively. The filename tells the build system which compilation tool and compiler flags to use. Users don't need to provide this information unless they want to override the defaults.

- A default Eclipse project compiles all source code in the `src` directory and generates the corresponding object files into the `bin` directory. The build system automatically uses these paths, unless you decide to change the project settings.

- Most build systems have targets such as `compile`, `clean`, `package`, `test`, and `install`. Some build tools support these targets by default, but even if they don't, build system designers will probably create them. This makes it easy for developers to work with unfamiliar software.

Let's now spend some time looking at the Maven build tool, which follows the philosophy of convention over configuration. Maven makes creating a new build system extremely easy.

## Maven: An Example Build Tool

The Maven system [84] is a build tool for Java-based projects and is therefore an alternative to using Ant. Maven is a full-fledged build tool, and this book could have added a full chapter on it to Part II, "The Build Tools." Instead, the book simply focuses on the ease of creating a Maven-based build system, using the approach of convention over configuration.

To create a new Maven-based build system, the developer selects a project template, known as an **archetype**. This provides a default layout for the project's source and object files, as well as a number of standard build targets.

Creating a Maven build system is as simple as entering the following command:

```
mvn archetype:generate \
        -DarchetypeArtifactId=maven-archetype-quickstart \
        -DgroupId=com.arapiki.calc \
        -DartifactId=calculator \
        -DinteractiveMode=false
```

This command asks Maven to generate a new project (and build system) using the `quickstart` archetype. You request that the source code be stored in the `com.arapiki.calc` Java package and that the project name be `calculator`. You can customize other configuration parameters as well, but interactive mode has been turned off in this example to instead use the defaults.

After the project has been created, the default `quickstart` project tree is placed in the current working directory.

```
./calculator/pom.xml
./calculator/src/main/java/com/arapiki/calc/App.java
./calculator/src/test/java/com/arapiki/calc/AppTest.java
```

This might not look like much, but Maven has automatically generated the `pom.xml` file containing the build description. It doesn't hold a list of rules or tasks; instead, it provides high-level information about where things are stored within the project and which targets can be built.

You're also provided with the `App.java` file, which contains a simple main program, and the `AppTest.java` file, which contains a trivial JUnit test suite. Obviously, you'd replace these with your own source code, but it's nice that Maven started you off with a working project.

To compile this example application, run the unit tests, and create a JAR file, you issue the following command:

```
mvn package
```

Maven created this project from a template, so it already knows how to compile, test, and package the software, without any need for you to configure the build system. You can now execute your program:

```
$ java -cp target/calculator-1.0-SNAPSHOT.jar com.arapiki.
➥calc.App
Hello World!
```

The project also contains a number of other build targets, including `compile` (which performs only the compile step), `test`, `install`, and `clean`. The `quickstart` archetype was used, so everything that a simple Java project needs was created without any extra work.

For advanced users, it's possible to link multiple projects and set up dependencies among them. You can also ask Maven to download specific versions of third-party JAR files from the Internet and make them available for the program to use.

Finally, if the standard archetypes don't meet your needs, you can create your own. You can even distribute them to other people to create similar projects.

# Reasons to Avoid Supporting Multiple Variants

As you've seen throughout this book, a build system should support multiple variants for many important reasons. Whether it's for multiple CPU types, for multiple editions, or to add metadata for debugging or profiling, you might end up with a multitude of ways to build your software product.

On the downside, be aware of the problems of having too many choices. Each time you add a new way of building the product, you're taking on extra complexity that could end up costing you additional build time, development time, and testing time. It's clearly a business decision as to whether it's more important to support multiple variants or to reduce the cost of using the build system. A development organization wouldn't support the extra variants if it didn't have a good reason to do so.

This section demonstrates how this new complexity is introduced.

## You'll Have More Variants to Test

If you add another variant that's intended for your end customer, you now have an extra variant to test. Developers must validate that any code changes they wrote for one variant of the software also work for all other variants. First, they must build the software for all possible targets to ensure that there are no compilation errors. Next, the software must pass some basic sanity tests, again for all variants. Finally, before handing the software package to the customer, the test group must perform a complete test run of each variant.

In reality, though, developers don't have time to build and test all possible combinations. Often they compile for one target and then hope that it doesn't break for other targets. This is certainly a valid approach if the software is 99% the same in all cases. However, if developers are particularly suspicious that part of their code might not be portable (the remaining 1%), they'll need to double-check their work for all other variants. This is a common tactic for large software products that take many hours to build, and developers are left to use their best judgment.

To reduce the chance of somebody breaking the software when they don't have time to test for all targets, it pays to keep the variants as similar as possible. In particular, using the same compilation tool for all variants can reduce the differences that cause the build system to fail. Of course, this assumes that this doesn't defeat the purpose of having variants in the first place.

Keep the following guidelines in mind:

- **Use the same version of the same compiler for all target architectures.** For example, if you're using GCC version 4.2 for your Intel x86 target, you should use that same version for your PowerPC target. Doing this gives you more confidence that the two compilers accept the same programming language syntax and will issue the same warnings and errors. Unfortunately, a number of errors or warnings are architecture specific, so even though using the same compiler means fewer problems, you can't expect to eliminate all differences.

- **Don't write code that depends on the byte ordering of the CPU.** For example, code that depends on the CPU having little-endian byte ordering won't work on a big-endian machine. As much as possible, try to write code that's endian-neutral. In other cases, limit the endian-specific code to a small number of well-known places. No matter what you do, it's still important to build and test for all platforms.

- **Use consistent CPU word sizes.** Code that was written for a 32-bit CPU might not work cleanly on a 64-bit machine. Write code that doesn't make assumptions about the size of data types—or at least limit the places where you do.

If you're an experienced developer, you can probably think of many other differences that you typically try to avoid.

## Source Code Becomes Messy

A second reason to avoid having too many variants is that your source code can end up littered with conditional code. This is less of a problem when using per-file or per-directory variation (as you would with a Java program), but it can be extremely complex in C/C++ programs, where a single function can contain numerous #ifdef directives. For example, the following code is particularly hard to read, especially if you're unaware of what all the conditionals variables represent.

```
int init_database(char *db_ref)
{
    int data_index;
#ifdef SUPPORT_BACKUPS
    init_backups(db_ref);
#endif
#if (DB_VERS >= 4)
    db_fixup(db_ref, DB_VERS);
#endif
    data_index = get_index(db_ref, DB_MAX_SIZE);
#ifdef BIG_ENDIAN
    switch_endian(data_index, DB_MAX_SIZE);
#endif
    process_data(data_index, DB_MAX_SIZE);
#ifdef OLD_THREADS
    init_threads(0, 5);
#else
    init_threads(THREAD_START_PRIORITY);
#endif
}
```

This example illustrates a second problem of overusing conditional compilation. If the build system no longer uses the OLD_THREADS directive, all references to the symbol should have already been removed from the code base. However, because none of the current developers working on the project has any knowledge of what that directive means, the developers will be hesitant to remove the stale code. These unnecessary lines therefore continue to remain in the code base, cluttering the program.

## Build Times Can Increase

If you modify your build system to compile more than one variant by default, you might find your build times substantially increasing. Even though you'd normally build one variant at a time, there's no reason you can't build multiple variants in a single build command.

For example, imagine that you're building software for a target computer that contains both an x86 processor and a MIPS processor. If each processor ran similar software, you might be inclined to compile the same utility library for both CPU types. Originally, it might have taken 30 minutes to compile for the x86 processor, but after adding the MIPS variant, an additional 30 minutes would suddenly be added to the build time. Unfortunately, these increased build times are unavoidable, especially if a change to the x86 variant has a habit of breaking the MIPS variant.

### Higher Disk Space Requirements

If you choose to have a different object tree for each build variant, clearly your disk space requirements will increase. To counteract this problem, you can always limit yourself to using a single object tree, although you always face consequences for doing so. Either you'll spend more time recompiling each of the variants to ensure that they all still work correctly or you'll face an increase in the number of broken builds or failed test cases because of a lack of solid testing.

## Various Ways to Reduce Complexity

Now that you've seen how frameworks can make the build system easier to understand and how supporting multiple variants can cause problems, think about other approaches. Unfortunately, no single solution can eliminate the problem of complexity. Any build system feature that a build engineer can customize is a potential source of problems. What matters is how engineers use those features, and whether they follow the standard set of best practices.

This section examines a range of approaches to reducing complexity. *Complexity* is a subjective term, so some of these approaches reduce the complexity for end users, whereas others reduce the complexity of the underlying build system. These techniques aren't listed in any particular order, and they might apply to only certain build tools or programming languages. In each case, the sections talk about what could go wrong if you don't follow the guideline.

### Use a Modern Build Tool

Since the Make tool was created (in the 1970s), people have been looking for ways to improve its usability. Even GNU Make follows the same basic premise of defining dependency rules, with each rule providing shell commands to generate targets from prerequisites. Many users feel that it's nearly impossible to build large and reliable build systems using this approach.

In contrast, tools such as Ant, SCons, CMake, and Eclipse make every effort to reduce the amount of work required. Features such as automatic dependency analysis, multidirectory support, and cross-platform compilation are now standard features. In addition, these newer tools promote the task or builder model, in which developers specify what they want compiled instead of how it should be compiled.

In your own build system, think carefully about what you need. If you're a Java programmer, you'll most likely aim for an Ant- or Eclipse-based build system, or perhaps use a combination of both. For C/C++ developers, SCons or CMake is a better choice. Each tool emphasizes making the build description less complex, thereby reducing the chance of errors.

Use the GNU Make tool only if you're confident of your decision. Refrain from using it just because it's the most common tool. You'll likely find that you don't want to worry about the complexity of maintaining the dependency graph or adding framework support.

Finally, keep your eyes open for new build tools. Ant, SCons, CMake, and Eclipse have many limitations, and newer build tools are likely to supersede them in the future.

## Automatically Detect Dependencies

It should be obvious by now that incorrect dependency information is a leading source of build system problems. Relying on the developer to compute and document the interfile dependencies is simply asking for mistakes. If at all possible, use a dependency-analysis tool to do the work for you.

As you saw in Part II, when you studied each of the build tools, automatic dependency analysis comes in a number of forms. In some cases, you can ask the compilation tool which files it will depend upon. In other cases, the build tool uses a special-purpose scanner to identify a source file's dependencies. Finally, it's also possible to monitor the underlying file system to see exactly which files are being accessed.

Having accurate dependency information is an important way of reducing a build system's complexity and thus increasing a developer's overall productivity. If at all possible, use an automatic method for computing dependencies.

## Keep Generated Files out of the Source Tree

As discussed in Chapter 14, "Version Management," it's important to store all generated files in a separate directory from the source code. A clean separation makes it easier to distinguish valuable source files from those that can be regenerated. Failure to follow this rule increases the complexity of the build system.

For example, some code generators create files written in a high-level language, such as Java or C#. If these output files were incorrectly stored in the source tree, users could get confused and manually edit them by mistake. They might also submit the generated file to the version-control system, as if it truly was a source file.

Keeping the generated files in a separate location is therefore a good approach to reducing the number of user errors.

## Ensure That Cleaning a Build Tree Works Correctly

Although you'd like to believe that incremental builds always regenerate the correct set of object files, this isn't always the case. It can be useful to perform a clean build just to make sure that all object files are regenerated. In some cases, you no longer need the object files; you only want to preserve your source code.

It's important that your build system's `clean` target works as expected. If this target is invoked from the top level of the build tree, it should remove all generated files, leaving only the source code. If it's invoked from a lower-level directory, only the objects in that directory should be removed. Under no circumstances should any source code changes be lost.

If the `clean` target doesn't work correctly, developers might be stuck with a build tree they can't use. No matter how many times they perform the `clean` operation, they'll still have trouble compiling their source tree. The root cause is that generated files aren't being deleted and, therefore, aren't being regenerated correctly. Combining this with a poor-quality dependency system is just asking for a high-maintenance build system.

## Abort the Build After the First Error

It's generally a good idea for the build system to halt after encountering the first error. This provides immediate feedback to developers that something has gone wrong and lets them know they should pay attention. In most cases, the last 10–20 lines of the build log show the exact error message. However, if the build tool doesn't halt until later, or doesn't halt at all, identifying the root cause of a problem could take hours.

Luckily, the default behavior for build tools is to halt whenever one of the compilation tools returns a nonzero exit code. This is also the case for most (but not all) compilation tools when they encounter an error in the source code. Watch for rogue compilation tools that don't abort the build process after an error.

Perhaps the most common place where this rule is broken is in shell scripts. By default, most shells continue executing commands, even if one of the commands returns a nonzero exit code. After the shell script has run to completion, nothing indicates that the script failed, other than a few cryptic error messages on the screen. Many scripts still print a `Completed Successfully` message on their output, even if part of the script failed.

An even worse scenario arises when shell commands are intended to fail but developers are too lazy to suppress the error message. They might claim that the errors are harmless and can simply be ignored. However, these excessive error messages only cover up any real errors that might be reported. If the shell script is visible to end users, there's a good chance that each end user will report the same error message, only to be told that it's harmless.

To reduce the complexity of your build system, you can follow several approaches.

- Use only compilation tools that report nonzero exit codes when an error is found. If this isn't possible, consider wrapping the tool in a shell script that explicitly looks for error messages in the tool's output. For example, if any lines in the output log start with the keyword `Error`, the wrapper should return an appropriate error code.

- In all your scripts, configure the shell to abort if any commands return a nonzero exit code. Usually a command-line flag or shell variable controls this behavior.

- If a command is supposed to return a nonzero exit code as part of its normal behavior, be sure to write extra handler code to deal with that situation. For example, the UNIX `grep` command indicates whether it found any lines in a file that match a regular expression. The command's exit code can be used to state whether a match was found instead of reporting an error situation. In this case, the shell script shouldn't abort execution.

- To be extra safe, configure your compilation tools to return a nonzero exit code for warnings. This is a good practice because many tools provide a warning message that doesn't technically stop the program from compiling but instead indicates where your program could be improved.

Although the practice of halting on the first error is almost always the best approach, it's sometimes useful to override a tool's default behavior. For example, GNU Make supports the `-k` option to request that it continue invoking compilation tools until it completely runs out of work. Of course, use this feature only when you truly want to skip the error messages.

## Provide Meaningful Error Messages

Software developers are notorious for writing error messages from their own perspective instead of from the customer's point of view. For example, a developer might write the following error message:

```
Error: malloc failed for new data component.
```

This means a lot to the developer but isn't helpful for a novice end user. Instead, the developer should have written something like this:

```
Error: Your system is running low of memory, please close other
programs and try again.
```

In this case, end users can solve the problem on their own, without contacting the software's support team.

Although the end user of your build system is likely a developer, users still appreciate having meaningful error messages. They won't want to dig through your build description to find out why they're seeing an obscure `Missing File` error.

Of course, it might not be practical to surround every step in your build process with an error message, in anticipation of somebody hitting a problem. Instead, if you see a number of trouble reports in the same area of your build system, either fix the code so that it doesn't fail, or provide some meaningful error messages to explain the problem in more detail.

## Validate Input Parameters

If the build system's users have the opportunity to provide command-line input, there's a chance they could provide invalid data. To make sure everything runs smoothly, always validate command-line arguments before they're used. Even if there's no malicious intent, invalid data can cause confusion.

In the following UNIX shell script, the build engineer was lazy and didn't validate the input parameter.

```
1   #!/bin/sh
2
3   my_dir=$1
4
5   rm -rf $my_dir/
6   mkdir $my_dir
7   cp file.dat $my_dir/file.dat
8   ...
```

The purpose of this script is to package a number of files into a temporary holding location, after first removing and re-creating the directory. The problem with this script is that $1 (the first command-line argument) defaults to the empty string if the user doesn't provide any arguments. Here's what's actually executed in that situation:

```
rm -rf /
mkdir
cp file.dat /file.dat
```

The first line proceeds to recursively remove all files on your root file system, which might not be too bad unless you're logged in as root. The second line fails because it's an incomplete command, and the third line fails with a permissions error (unless you're logged in as root).

Most developers who are poking around your build system will invoke this script without any arguments, assuming that you've provided some meaningful help text. Little do they know that their file system is being deleted.

To reduce complexity for the end user, make sure you always validate user input. Check that the number of arguments is correct, and do your best to validate each input value before using it. If any of the user's values are incorrect, display a meaningful error message to explain why.

## Don't Overengineer Build Scripts

An age-old principle that so many developers choose to ignore is the concept of keeping things simple. Developers are creative people who like to predict the set of features their end users will need. They sometimes don't even ask end users what the software should do, because their plan is to make it do everything.

In the case of build systems, this results in a complex framework and set of support scripts. The downside is that it becomes too confusing to use and far too hard to maintain. Even the documentation is overwhelmed by all the possible corner cases. So much for a simple build system that developers can invoke with a single command.

A best practice is to start simple but be prepared for growth over time. Provide users with what they need now, but don't be too surprised if they ask for more in the future. Giving them a simple build system to play with after two weeks of work is better than surprising them with a full build system after six months. You might be surprised that the simple solution is all they need, at least for now.

## Avoid Using Cryptic Language Features

Over the lifetime of the product, several different build engineers could maintain a build system. If the original author is unavailable, a new build engineer will be asked to get involved. There's a good chance that the new engineer will know nothing about the build system and must learn on the job.

Unfortunately, many engineers take pride in knowing all the advanced features of their build tool and aren't afraid to use them. These can involve syntax tricks that are unfamiliar to novice users or that require undocumented behavior that's discovered only by trial and error. The engineer's end goal is to write the build description as concisely as possible, no matter how obscure the solution.

The obvious downside is that the learning curve to understand the build system becomes incredibly high. A novice build engineer might inherit a build system but might not comprehend how it works or why specific language features are used. Although the original author guaranteed his or her own job security, that person has since left the team with a confusing build system.

To reduce complexity, ensure that your build system uses only well-documented features that novice build engineers can understand. If you find yourself requiring advanced features, hide the complexity inside the framework and make sure all the code you write is well commented. A second pair of eyes should review all changes to the build system and reject them if they're too complex.

If you find it impossible to implement a build system using well-understood features, you're probably using the wrong build tool.

## Don't Use Environment Variables to Control the Build Process

All major operating systems support the concept of **environment variables,** allowing users to customize their login account. Among other things, these variables control the way command shells behave, identify the user's home directory, and store the search path for locating an executable program (the familiar PATH variable). It's even possible to define your own environment variables.

The operating system sets some of the variables when a login shell is first created, whereas the user's own start-up script (such as .cshrc or .bashrc in UNIX-like systems) sets others. The important point is that each user can customize the environment to suit his or her needs.

When it comes to writing a build system, relying on the user's environment is a bad idea. Doing so creates a build system that behaves differently for each user, requiring a lot of end user support. For example, if the build system relied on the user's PATH variable to locate an appropriate compiler, different users could end up with different compilers.

As a best practice, your build system should fully initialize any variables that it depends on instead of inheriting the value from the environment. This is particularly true for the PATH variable.

If you need to pass configuration parameters into your build system, you have two acceptable approaches:

- **Provide the variables on the command line:** For example, to inform the build system which CPU type to compile for, you could pass in the PLATFORM variable:

```
gmake PLATFORM=i386 build
```

- **Configure the build tree to store the variables:** To save typing, you can store the configuration parameters inside the build tree. Every time you invoke the build tool, it uses the saved parameters.

```
gmake configure PLATFORM=i386
gmake build
```

These PLATFORM definitions are explicit, so if two users execute the same commands, they'll see exactly the same results. You're not relying on the user's implicit environment to perform a build, because this can vary from one user to the next. In fact, it's a good practice for your build system to explicitly ignore environment variables that cause differences between two users.

Unfortunately, this problem isn't limited to environment variables. Most shells start by reading a sequence of commands from their start-up file. In addition to defining environment variables, these commands can perform an arbitrary sequence of operations, such as displaying onscreen messages. If your build system invokes a shell script, those commands also might be executed, causing no end of confusion.

The solution is to ensure that each compilation tool is invoked in such a way that per-user configuration files aren't read on start-up. If your tool doesn't have a suitable option, consider using a different tool.

## Ensure That Release and Debug Builds Are Similar

Many build systems enable developers to create either a debug release or a production release. In the debug case, extra information is added to the release package, making it possible to debug the software (either at runtime or via a post-mortem memory dump). On the other hand, production releases contain only the final software, without the extra information.

It's important for the debug and production images to be as similar as possible, except for the additional debug information. It's not acceptable for the customer to use different software from what the developer originally tested. If the customer reports a bug, a developer might have a hard time reproducing the problem.

As an example, it's common for developers to add special code that is available only in the debug image:

```
#ifdef DEBUG
display_record();
#endif /* DEBUG */
```

This adds extra support that the developer requires for testing, but it changes the program's behavior. In addition, this new code could mask bugs that still appear in the production release.

To get around these inconsistencies, consider two approaches:

- **Build the debug image, but strip the debug information:** Instead of compiling two different versions of the same software, consider building only the debug release. It's then a simple matter of stripping the excess debug information to create the production release. The executable code itself is guaranteed to be identical in both cases, making it possible to debug a memory dump from a production release, using the information from the debug release.

- **Add hidden commands to your production software:** Instead of adding special sections of code to your debug release, consider how you could enable these features in the production release without the customer knowing about them. This enables developers to use the features in their own environment, as well as typing a secret command or editing a configuration file to enable them at the customer's site. This feature makes it much easier to analyze the customer's bug reports.

  One example is an `assert()` function compiled into both the debug and production software. However, although the same code is present in both cases, only the debug version of software reports the errors. The production software silently ignores the runtime checks, unless it's explicitly enabled in some way.

## Display the Exact Command Being Executed

When it makes sense, your build system should echo the exact compilation command being invoked. This makes debugging problems easy because you can simply copy and paste a command from the build log and run it by hand. You can even modify the command-line options if that helps you solve a problem.

For example, you might see the following output on the build log:

```
gcc -o data.o -c -O -g data.c
gcc -o gui.o -c -O -g gui.c
gcc -o main.o -c -O -g main.c
gcc -o util.o -c -O -g util.c
gcc -o myapp main.o data.o gui.o util.o -lz -lbfd
```

If you noticed that `main.c` wasn't compiling properly, you might suspect that a C preprocessor symbol was missing. In this case, you can copy the line from the build log and replace `-o main.o -c` with the `-E` option:

```
gcc -E -O -g main.c
```

This command enables you to see exactly which lines of C code are compiled after the preprocessor has run. If the build system didn't display the command it was executing, you'd be left to guess how to invoke the compilation tool.

Although this is a nice feature, not all build tools support this technique. In particular, the Ant build tool doesn't display the underlying command line, and in many cases no command line is used. Instead, Ant directly invokes library functions or instantiates special-purpose Java classes to get the job done.

## Version-Control References to Tools

As discussed in Chapter 14, you need to version-control all references to compilation tools. This can be done by hard-coding the tool's path in the build description file and ensuring that each instance of the tool is labeled with a version number. Failure to follow these guidelines makes it challenging to upgrade to new compilers while still ensuring that older software releases continue to use the older tools.

## Version-Control the Build Instructions

Chapter 14 also introduced the idea that build descriptions should be version-controlled. As the software changes over time, the build system must also change. Failing to keep all the build steps in sync with the software makes it hard to reproduce older versions of the code.

At least make sure the build system's help text is under version control. If developers need to rebuild an old version of the source code, they can always read the help text to remind themselves of what needs to be done.

## Automatically Detect Changes in Compilation Flags

It's desirable for your build system to consider object files to be out-of-date whenever the compilation flags change. For example, if a developer originally compiled a program without optimization enabled, adding the new flag should cause all existing object files to be removed and regenerated.

Failure to clean up stale files causes mismatched object files to be linked into the same executable program. Whether this causes problems depends entirely on the nature of the compilation flags.

If possible, use a build tool that automatically supports this feature, such as SCons. For other build tools, it's still possible to implement this feature, although perhaps not in a straightforward way. Without any type of automation, developers must remember to perform a clean build every time they modify their flags.

## Don't Invoke the Version-Control Tool from the Build System

As a general rule, your build system shouldn't interact with the version-control tool, even though the program's source is stored within that tool. Unfortunately, some build engineers attempt to take advantage of this relationship.

A clear distinction is made here between a **build system** (using a tool such as Make, Ant, or SCons) and a **build-management tool** such as Build Forge, Hudson, or ElectricCommander (discussed in Chapter 1, "Build System Overview"). Build-management tools are supposed to invoke the version-control tool, whereas a build system isn't.

As a first example, it's not a good idea for your build system to update the source code tree with the latest content from the version-control system. When developers are working on a specific set of source files, the last thing they want is for the build system to download new versions of the code. Doing so creates an unstable environment that developers have no control over. It may also create source code conflicts that developers aren't ready to resolve.

A second example arises when the build system accesses the version-control tool to find out which revision of a file is being used. Good reasons might exist for acquiring a unique version number, but this ties the build system closely to the underlying version-control tool. If you change to another tool, you can no longer build older versions of the software.

As a final example, you might try to build your software on a standalone machine. Many version-control tools require direct access to a centralized server, making it impossible to work in a disconnected environment (such as on aircraft or at the beach).

## Use Continuous Integration as Often as Possible

Although this book hasn't spent much time on the topic of continuous integration, it's a good practice to follow when creating a build system. As in any other software, changes to a build system can be poorly implemented. You need to identify and resolve the problem as quickly as possible.

By compiling the source code on a regular basis (every hour, every day, or whenever the code changes), you also validate that your build system works. This is particularly true when incremental builds are used to compile the recent code changes. If your dependency system isn't high-enough quality, you'll likely see broken builds. To counteract these problems, make sure you regularly perform full builds, not just incremental builds.

## Standardize on a Single Type of Build Machine

As discussed in Chapter 15, "Build Machines," it's a good idea to have a single type of build machine on which the build system executes. If you support multiple machines, you'll see added complexity from platform differences. Minimizing these differences can help reduce support costs.

Unfortunately, you might still need to support multiple build machines. For example, you might be supporting multiple target machines (such as Windows, Linux, and Mac OS X), and your build can be executed only on the target machine itself (cross-compilation isn't always possible). You also might depend on compilation tools that are supported on only one type of build machine, but that machine doesn't support all your other tools.

## Standardize on a Single Compiler

Chapter 14 introduced the idea that different versions of a compilation tool might accept slightly different syntax. If your build process generates code for more than one target platform (CPU or operating system), ensure that the same compiler is used in all cases. You might have different instances of the compiler, but all of them should accept the same syntax and support the same features.

If it's not possible to use the same compiler or compiler family, you'll see an increase in complexity. If developers test their code for only one platform, the code might no longer compile on other platforms. To resolve this problem, you must test all code changes on all platforms.

## Avoid Littering Code with `#ifdefs`

As discussed in Chapter 5, "Subtargets and Build Variants," you can select the source code for each build variant in numerous ways. One of the most common techniques in C/C++ is to use the `#ifdef` directive. Unfortunately, overusing this approach leads to messy code.

If your source code starts to become unreadable, consider extracting the parts of the code that differ and maintain a copy for each variant. The main body of the code is the same for all variants, but the variant-specific code is extracted into a separate function. This type of extraction might seem like a lot of work, but if handling multiple variants in the same function creates a complex maze of `#ifdef` directives, extracting the differences to separate functions could be a better alternative.

## Use Meaningful Symbol Names

When your software compiles on a wide range of build machines, be careful to name your build system variables appropriately. For example, if your software is designed to use a threading model that first appeared in version 3.0 of your operating system, you might be tempted to implement the following code:

```
if OS_VERSION >= 3.0
    ... use the new threading model ...
endif
```

Unfortunately, you're making the assumption that all future versions of the operating system will also support this threading model. This might be true for several years, but eventually the code will fail to compile. Instead, try the following approach:

```
if HAS_THREADS
    ... use the new threading model ...
endif
```

In this case, your build system must somehow detect whether the operating system supports the threading model and must then define the HAS_THREADS symbol. As you've seen, a number of build tools support this type of autodetection, including Autoconf, SCons, and CMake

A similar example arises when the source code uses product marketing names. For example, if a company's marketing team declares the next release to be known as Aardvark, it's not advisable to implement the following code:

```
if AARDVARK
    ... use the new threading model ...
endif
```

Although this is a short-term name, future releases would also need to define the AARDVARK symbol, or the threading model won't be used. Again, you should instead use a feature name such as HAS_THREADS. In any case, the marketing team will probably change the product name several times during development, so you'll be glad you didn't include it in your code base.

Finally, try to avoid using the words NEW or OLD in any of your symbol names. If you define the HAS_NEW_THREADS symbol, the feature won't be new for long, and you'll be inclined to rename it to HAS_OLD_THREADS. Instead, use a version number, such as HAS_THREADS_V2.

## Remove Stale Code

When a piece of software grows large, the build system tends to be littered with support for build variants and compiler options. In some cases, the feature might no longer be required, but nobody bothered to remove the code. The simple fact that stale code is kept around increases your maintenance costs.

Don't forget that, over the years, many people will view and modify the build system. If you don't delete the stale code when it's no longer required, people will make the obvious assumption that it's still worth keeping. Nobody removes code unless they're confident it's no longer used.

Aside from cluttering up the build system, stale code causes the build engineers to waste their time. If they don't understand the purpose, they'll make every attempt to keep it working for each new build or target machine. In extreme cases, they might even port the functionality to a new build tool. If they knew the code was stale, they wouldn't have wasted their time.

If you're resisting the idea of removing stale code, remember that it's always available in the version-control history, so it's not lost forever. If you're hesitant, try commenting out the code and adding a note to explain that it's no longer used. Anything you can do to show that it's stale will benefit future maintainers.

## Don't Duplicate Source Files

Good developers understand that duplicating source code is a bad idea. However, many people still do it because of the limitations of their build system. It's unfortunate, but your build framework might limit the locations from which your program can obtain source files. You might be required to have all source code in the same directory as the build description file, which is often the case for recursive Make systems.

If developers want to save time by reusing an existing code function, they have a number of options for including it in their program:

- **Make a duplicate file:** In this absolute worst case, the developer makes an entirely new copy of the source file and places it in the desired directory. This creates a maintenance problem because source code must be updated in two locations.

- **Use a symbolic link:** On machines that support symbolic links, the build system can create a link from the source file's original location into the directory where it's needed. This eliminates the need to update the file in two locations, but because not all tools can handle symbolic links properly, this sometimes creates support issues.

- **Use a relative pathname:** If the build system allows it, you can use a relative pathname to access the source file from its original location. For example:

```
C_SRCS := main.c data.c gui.c ../../../dispatch/lib/util.c
```

This is a good solution, except that it starts to create a spaghetti-like source tree.

- **Create reusable libraries:** A final solution is to move the shared source files into a common location and create a library archive. Each part of the build system that needs access to the shared code can link against the common library instead of compiling the source code for itself.

Although this final solution of creating a library is the cleanest approach, it's often hard to implement. Unfortunately, many developers still resort to duplicating files or creating symbolic links.

## Use a Consistent Build System

A common way for software to grow quickly is by acquisition rather than by writing new code. Large amounts of new source code can be taken from open-source projects, written by third-party vendors, or added after a merger between two companies. It's not unheard of for software to double in size in a matter of days.

The fastest way to integrate new software is to use the source code's original build system. The downside is that your build system becomes a patchwork of different frameworks glued together. The support costs can be exceeding high if there's no consistent way of building the code.

If it's not too much work, consider using a common build system for all parts of your software. This involves throwing away the legacy build system, but that might be easier than trying to support many different frameworks with their own benefits and limitations.

Aside from the workload, the downside of replacing an existing build system is that it's harder to keep up-to-date with changes in the original code base. When you take advantage of open-source software or code from a third-party vendor, the original build system constantly changes. Each time you incorporate a new version of the software, you need to make corresponding changes to your new build system.

## Scheduling and Staffing Build System Changes

Now that you've seen how a build system becomes more complex, consider ways to solve the problem. The desired technical solution is usually clear, but in a real-world development environment, there's always too much work to do and never enough people to do it. Always consider the human resources aspect.

In a corporate environment, company leaders are often focused on pleasing customers to keep the company afloat. Their attention is on the development and release of new product features instead of the underlying infrastructure. It's certainly hard to imagine a customer getting excited about the quality of your build system, so managers tend to be equally uninvolved. In some cases, they see the build system as a necessary evil.

If you're taking care of a build system by yourself or are leading a group of build engineers, you must be an advocate for constantly monitoring and improving the build system. Even if you have tight schedules to deliver product features, keep in mind that complexity in the build system is extremely costly. Your leaders won't pay attention to the build process (other than complaining about it from time to time), so you'll end up carrying the torch in this area.

Consider some basic management rules when you're scheduling improvements to your build system.

- **Be realistic with the schedule:** Allocate enough time to do a good job with the work. Cutting corners on your build system can be disastrous because hacking together a quick solution introduces complexity. Choosing a good build tool or framework makes your job easier, but you might be confined to using a legacy system. Major build system changes can take weeks or months to complete.

- **Assign a build guru for new product development:** When creating a new product or making major changes to an existing product, involve a build guru as soon as possible. It should be obvious that you can't develop software without a good build system, but many projects assign one of their software developers to do the work. If that developer isn't experienced in this area, it won't be long before he or she runs into problems.

- **Don't wait until the build system fails before working on it:** For major software projects, it's important to preplan your build system changes. As with any other aspect of software design, it's a mistake to think about the work only when the problems show up. Waiting until there's an immediate need for change simply delays your project. After all, build gurus are usually busy people who might not be available the moment you need them.

- **Constantly monitor build system changes made by nongurus:** Software developers tend to make minor build system changes to suit their immediate needs. In their defense, they've often asked for a guru to do the work, but nobody was available at the time. When this happens, it's important to follow up later to ensure that the changes were reasonable. A build guru should review changes before they're committed to the version-control system.

- **Think about the target audience:** Just as you would for any software product, consider your target audience and its usage pattern. For a release engineer, the goal is to build and release fully versioned software packages. On the other hand, a software developer expects a quick turnaround time for incremental builds. Be sure to consider both of these audiences in the design of the build system. Failing to do so leads to either longer compile times for software developers (incremental builds would take too long) or an overly complex process for building customer releases.

Finally, you're likely to face pressure to make the build system changes immediately, especially if software developers didn't get you involved until the last minute. In this case, it's usually acceptable to give them a hacked-up solution to get them beyond their current problem. Making them wait for a final solution is unreasonable because that could take months.

In addition, never leave the hacked-up solution in place for too long. Make sure you complete the required changes properly, even if it takes a few months longer. This is the only way to ensure that complexity doesn't become a longer-term problem.

## Summary

Complexity in a build system is usually bad: It increases the chance of random build failure and forces developers to work around each pitfall. In many cases, the build system might work differently from one developer to the next, increasing the time taken to develop software. All these problems place an excessive load on the build system's support team.

Using a build system framework is a good way to hide some of the complexity from end users. In many cases, it's not possible to completely avoid problems, but at least you can limit the scope to specific build description files. This includes compilation rules, task definitions, macros, and builder methods, which are of interest only to build gurus. On the other hand, the list of files to be compiled, the set of compilation flags to use, and other high-level directives must be fully visible to software developers.

Complexity can arise in numerous ways, each with its own solution. For example, you could use a modern build tool, keep generated files out of the source tree, provide meaningful error messages, or remove stale code from the build description. Each of these techniques makes the build system easier to use and maintain.

Finally, scheduling build system changes can be challenging, especially in a team that doesn't proactively focus on that area. You might need to be an advocate for making improvements and ensuring that all future build changes are monitored closely.

# Chapter 18

---

# Managing Build Size

The second major topic in Part IV, "Scaling Up," is how to more effectively manage the size of a build system. Software products start with a single line of code but continuously grow as new developers join the project or when third-party libraries are added to the code base. What starts as a small and manageable piece of software eventually becomes a large and complex product.

A software build system is no exception to this rule. A program with 10 source files is trivial to manage with a single makefile or Ant script. With 1,000 files, you can still use the same build system, even if it now takes 15 minutes to compile the full product. The real problems start when the build takes 1.5 hours or even 15 hours to complete. Expecting each developer to build with `make all` is no longer reasonable.

As a general rule, scalability issues are much like the "frog in the boiling pot" problem. The end-to-end build process starts out simple and efficient, with everybody happy with the solution. Over a number of years, the build system slows and becomes more of a productivity drain, but nobody really notices. Just like the frog in the boiling pot, gradually getting hotter and hotter, the fact that change occurs slowly makes it less likely that people notice the ever-increasing problem. New members joining the team are far more likely to notice the inefficiencies.

This chapter focuses on the **component model** of constructing software, in contrast to the **monolithic model**. In the monolithic case, all source code is stored in the same tree and is compiled using a single build system. That build system might have multiple parts, but each developer first needs to compile the entire program before starting to work.

In the component model, you break the source code into multiple independent components, each with its own build system. Developers are required to obtain only the source code they're planning to modify and need to compile only that specific component. All other components are provided in binary form instead of compiled from source code.

This chapter covers the following aspects of component-based software:

- **The problem with monolithic builds:** The reasons monolithic builds aren't scalable and, therefore, why component-based builds can be attractive

- **Component-based software:** An overview of component-based software, including the internal structure of a component and the process for integrating them into a larger program

- **People and process management:** How managing and integrating component-based software is different from managing a single monolithic code base

- **Apache Ivy:** A brief study of a build tool that supports component-based development

Let's start by investigating why monolithic builds are troublesome and why you should instead use components. Other than the brief discussion of Ivy, this chapter is very conceptual. Each development environment must implement these features in their own unique way.

## The Problem with Monolithic Builds

Describing a build system as monolithic implies that the source code base is treated as a single entity. It can't be broken into smaller independent pieces, and different parts of the software can't be managed separately. From a build system perspective, you can extend this definition with more detail:

1. All code is stored in the same source tree, with each developer obtaining a complete copy of the source tree before starting to work. It isn't possible to compile the software if some of the files are excluded.

2. The whole product is built using a single build system. The different parts of that build system can be responsible for different parts of the source tree, but they can't operate in isolation.

3. Any source file can make use of definitions, functions, or classes from any other part of the source tree. A change to one source file could impact any part of the build system.

This monolithic approach is certainly common, and most software products start their life in this way. There's a lot of appeal to having all source code managed in a single source tree, with a unified build system to create the final release package. It's easy to understand, implement, and manage a monolithic piece of software.

The monolithic approach fails when the software becomes too large for developers to comprehend or too large for the build system to complete in a reasonable amount of time. Now consider some of the reasons monolithic software doesn't scale.

- **Boundaries are poorly defined.** When a software engineer is tasked with adding a new feature, it's often challenging to understand where that change should be made. Instead of having a clearly defined area for each subsystem, the new code could be added anywhere. This possibly duplicates effort and leads to a disorganized code base. In addition, the developer might not understand the political boundaries within the code and might accidentally change source files owned by a different team.

- **Changes have an unpredictable impact.** A developer might change a source file that could impact the compilation or functionality of other parts of the system. All changes should therefore be validated by compiling and testing the complete software product. It's a mistake to focus on only the area of code that was modified. Although senior developers understand the impact of a code change, a junior developer doesn't have that luxury and is more likely to break some other part of the system.

- **Build time increases.** With a monolithic code base, all developers must compile the entire source tree for themselves. Even if they're planning to modify only a small number of source files, they're still required to compile everything before they execute the program. Every developer must therefore invoke the entire build system, resulting in excessively long build times.

- **Build machine memory increases.** When a single build system compiles many source files, you end up with a large dependency graph. If the number of files in the source tree doubled over time, the dependency graph would be twice as large and thus would require additional memory on the build machine. If the interdependencies between files are complex, doubling the number of source files could easily quadruple the number of dependencies, requiring even more memory.

- **Disk usage increases.** Given that all developers are required to compile the entire monolithic source tree, they'll also have a monolithic object tree. Depending on the programming language, a 1GiB source code tree could easily result in a 10GiB object tree. This might not seem like a lot of disk, but the space is quickly consumed when hundreds of developers share the same file server.

- **Network utilization increases.** Many organizations prefer to use centralized file servers to ease their administrative overhead and to make file sharing between different users possible. High-performance file servers are generally fast, except when they're placed under too much load. If a large number of users compile the monolithic code base, any shared resources on the network will suffer. This results in build durations that are much slower than at off-peak times or when compared to using locally attached disk.

- **Security is more difficult.** For larger companies, it's desirable to outsource some of the product development to third-party vendors. For security purposes, you might not want to expose your entire code base to the vendor, but with a monolithic code base, you have no choice. It's simply not possible to compile a portion of the source code without having the whole source tree available.

You might wonder whether you can resolve some of these issues by simply purchasing faster build machines or file servers. Build servers are constantly increasing in performance, as is disk space, so you might find that upgrading your build machine every year keeps the end-to-end build time the same.

This approach might work for some software products, but a successful product could double in size each year, far surpassing any improvement in hardware. This is especially true if third-party or out-sourced code is added to the existing code base, giving an overnight increase in build time or disk usage. Adding a new build variant could also double the disk usage, such as when a UNIX-based product must also be compiled for Microsoft Windows, resulting in twice as much compilation time.

In summary, if you're not lucky enough to have a new build machine each year, or if your product simply grows too quickly, consider moving away from monolithic software. Even if build performance isn't your main concern, your developers will appreciate having smaller chunks of source code to deal with.

## Component-Based Software

The practice of breaking monolithic software into smaller components is a common way to improve scalability. In the same way that object-oriented programming divides software into classes and packages, you can break your software into high-level components. Developer productivity increases by allowing them to focus on the internals of their own components, without being forced to deal with the complexity in other components.

The source code for each component is independent from others, except where specific functions and symbols are exported. Each component defines a public API that other components can access, even though the majority of source code is kept private. From the perspective of the build process, each component has its own isolated build system.

To reduce compilation time, developers use prebuilt binaries for all components they aren't planning to modify. This concept should be familiar to Java and C# developers who frequently make use of third-party libraries. Although these are typically downloaded from the Internet, the mechanism is the same as if they were written locally by the developer's own team.

Figure 18.1 shows an example of an accounting program constructed by integrating multiple components.

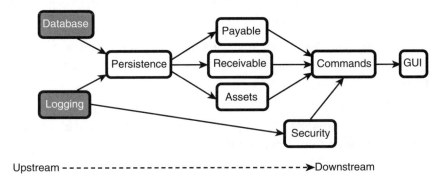

Upstream ‑ ‑ ‑ ‑ ‑ ‑ ‑ ‑ ‑ ‑ ‑ ‑ ‑ ‑ ‑ ‑ ‑ ‑ ‑ ‑ ‑ ‑ ‑ ‑ ‑ ‑ ‑ ‑►Downstream

**Figure 18.1** *An accounting program constructed from multiple components.*

Each component in this diagram can be thought of as a self-contained piece of software, possibly containing hundreds or thousands of source files. They each have a separate build system and can share code only via their public APIs. In the case of the `Database` and `Logging` components, the source code isn't even available because you obtained these components in binary form (such as downloading a Java JAR file).

To construct the final software product, this collection of components must be integrated together. The main program is in the `GUI` component, providing a graphical interface to the end user but delegating most of the work to the `Commands` component. In turn, the `Commands` component relies on `Payable`, `Receivable`, `Assets`, and `Security` to do much of the work. The output from each component's build system is linked to form an executable program.

To further explain how components are integrated, consider the relationship between the `Persistence` component and the `Payable`, `Receivable`, and `Assets` components. The `Persistence` component is upstream and exports a public interface to the downstream components. The build system for `Persistence` must therefore generate output files that can be linked into the downstream components.

For example, an output file could be in any of the following formats:

- `libpersistence.a`: For a component written in C or C++, the output is often a static or dynamic library that implements the component's functionality. Other components can link against this library without having access to the original source code.

- `persistence.h`: A library is usually associated with a header file, with each downstream component using `#include` to import the content. The function and type declarations contained within the header file provide enough compile-time information to use the library.

- `persistence.jar`: For Java-based software, each component is encapsulated inside a single JAR file. Downstream components are free to import any of the publicly visible classes.

- `persistence.dll`: Similarly, for Windows-based software a dynamic (shared) library provides a component's implementation, with downstream components importing that library.

The key fact is that downstream components aren't required to access the internal source code of an upstream component. All sharing is done via the public API, and components are joined by linking against libraries instead of compiling the upstream component's source code.

Another key observation is that `Payable`, `Receivable`, and `Assets` also need to produce libraries and header files of their own. The `Commands` component links against each of these components, in addition to linking against the `Security` library. The process repeats until the `GUI` component (the main program) is compiled.

As you'll see later in this chapter, coordinating changes to each component and integrating them into the final program is one of the many challenges in using a component-based build system.

## Advantages of Using Components

Now that you've seen an overview of component-based software, focus on some of the advantages. Many of these will be familiar because they were already provided as reasons for not using monolithic builds.

- **Developers find it easier to visualize the software:** From a developer's perspective, visualizing the component structure makes it easier to make changes. You should clearly document both the purpose of each component and the API between components. This makes it simpler to identify where a bug can be found or where a new feature should be added.

- **Developers can ignore the internal implementation of other components:** Figure 18.2 illustrates how a developer obtains the `Receivable` component's source code but uses prebuilt versions of `Payable`, `Assets`, and `Persistence`. The developer needs to understand the internal code within the `Receivable` component, as well as the `Persistence` component's public API. However, the rest of the code is considered a black box, with no requirement on the developer to understand how it works.

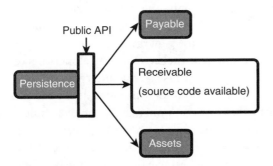

**Figure 18.2** *The relationship between components, with internal detail hidden.*

- **Internal code changes can't break other build systems:** Any changes made to a component's internal source code are limited in scope to that component. No matter which files are modified, there's no chance of disrupting the compilation of a second component. The build systems are distinct and simply can't share files. Note however, that modifying a component's public API could still cause other components to break, but these API-related files should be clearly identified as being public.

As you'll see later, changing an internal source file can potentially change a component's functionality, so other components might experience a difference in behavior. This however isn't a build-time concern, but is instead a difference in the way that components behave at runtime.

- **Each component has its own build system:** Having a self-contained build system for each component addresses many of the scalability issues with monolithic code. The build system is less complex; it requires a smaller dependency graph, uses less memory, requires less disk space, and places less strain on the file servers and network. In addition, the obvious advantage is that end-to-end build times are lower, particularly when prebuilt components are used.

- **Better source code security:** With a component-based system, it's trivial to share components with third-party vendors, without the need to share the entire code base. By providing prebuilt versions of all other components, the untrusted third-party can still produce a software release package.

This chapter has mentioned the use of prebuilt components a number of times, so let's now investigate the idea further. A key benefit of component-based builds is that developers need to compile only a component that they're actually modifying. To make this work, someone must have already compiled the other components and made them available for general use.

Figure 18.3 introduces the idea of a **component cache**. When developers make changes to a component, they compile, test, and release a new binary version for other developers to use. Later in this chapter, you'll look in more detail at how component caches are managed, particularly as components change over time.

In the example, a developer who modifies the `Receivable` component would need to compile and link against the `Persistence` libraries and header files. These would be imported directly from the cache instead of being generating from source code.

Prebuilt (binary) component cache

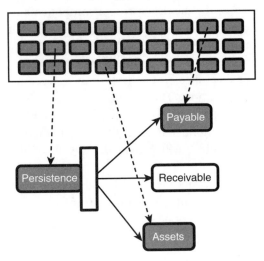

**Figure 18.3** *Using prebuilt (binary) components from the component cache.*

To be fair, component-based builds aren't the solution to every problem, and they certainly come with overhead. As you'll see later, extra layers of development process must be followed when adding components to the cache. No longer can code be added to an arbitrary part of the source code, with the change immediately appearing in the final executable program. Each component must instead be tested and approved before being released to the component cache. Only then is the code change available to other developers.

Before looking in more detail at these process changes, let's dig deeper into the exact structure of a component.

## What Exactly Is a Component?

The concept of component-based software is entrenched in the industry, although the exact definition depends on where it's used. The general theme is that components aren't considered programs in their own right, but must instead be integrated with other components. A number of third-party vendors design and develop components with the goal of reuse in mind.

Unlike executable programs, components don't always have a graphical user interface or even a command-line interface. The goal is to integrate them into a larger program, so the interface is often targeted at software developers. For a C/C++ component, the interface could be a static or shared library, with a header file describing the API functions. For a Java program, the interface could be a JAR file containing a number of publicly visible classes.

Some components are an interesting mix of graphical interface and API support. A web-based plug-in provides an API for the downstream components to invoke, although the main goal of the plug-in is to render graphic images. Of course, the GUI component in the accounting example has only a graphical interface, with the downstream consumer being the end users themselves.

In a build system, a component is considered to be a collection of source files that can be developed and compiled in isolation. This implies that the source code for other components doesn't need to be available on the build machine, and the developer clearly isn't required to compile that code. On the other hand, it's a requirement to have access to the public API provided by each of the upstream components.

Figure 18.4 shows a high-level view of a component. Although the content varies from one component to the next, each of the main sections must be considered.

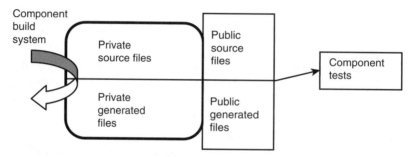

**Figure 18.4** *The constituent parts of a component.*

### Private Source Files

The **private source files** provide most of the component's functionality, hidden from the view of other components. To build the code, a developer must obtain a complete copy of the private source files. This essentially means that each component is monolithic in its own right.

It's possible to have any number of private source files within the component, written in any compiled language such as C, C++, Java, or C#. To make it worth structuring your code as a component, you'd need to start with a nontrivial number of source files. In contrast, it's also not practical to have too many source files because it negates the benefit of working with smaller components.

It's imperative that a component's private source files be visible only to other files within this same component. This again implies that other components must be able to compile independently. In addition, this component's build system can access each of the private source files, but the build system for other components must not be aware of their existence.

## Public Source Files

A component's **public source files** provide the external interface instead of providing the implementation. To minimize the interdependency between components, the public source files should contain only information that truly needs to be exported. For example, a C/C++ component should provide a header file containing a list of functions and types that other components are welcome to use. This file should not mention internal functions and data structures.

A component can contain any number of public source files, although typically a much smaller number than for private files. After all, a major goal of using components is to hide the implementation detail. It's important that as many source files as possible are hidden, instead of exposed in the public API.

Adistinction is also made between public source files and public generated files (the next category discussed). As the name suggests, public source files aren't generated by the build system. They're instead maintained directly by the component developer and presented as part of the component's API. A typical example is a C/C++ header file, but not something like a Java JAR file, which the build system must generate.

In extreme cases, a component might consist solely of public source files. It won't contain any private source files or require a build system. In this scenario, the component simply includes a number of header files, data files, or configuration files to be shared across all other components. For example, a C/C++–based program might have a common set of type and structure definitions to be used by all parts of the program. A change to one of these definitions could impact the compilation of any other component, so all definitions must be placed in the public API.

## Public Generated Files

The **public generated files** are created by the component's build system and exported as part of the public API. When developers think about importing a component, they normally refer to one of these generated files.

Public generated files come in a number of different forms, with each having requirements on how it's imported into the downstream components. Consider some common examples:

- **Static libraries:** Static libraries are a collection of object files merged into a single archive. A library exported by an upstream component can be linked into an executable program as part of a downstream component's build system. Static libraries are usually associated with a public header file that describes the functions and data types necessary to use the library.

- **Shared libraries:** Shared libraries are similar to static libraries, in that downstream components can link against them. However, instead of integrating the library into the executable program, a shared library's file (with `.so` or `.dll` suffix) must be packaged along with the final software product and then installed on the target machine.

- **Java JAR files:** In the Java world, JAR files (`.jar` suffix) are the universal approach to releasing components. An exported JAR file can be imported by a downstream component only if it's included in the Java compiler's class path. The same is true at runtime, when the JAR file is included in the virtual machine's class path. Unlike C/C++, there's no requirement to describe the component's interface in a separate header file.

- **Executable programs:** There's no reason a component can't generate an executable program. The assumption is that the final software release package contains a number of other programs and libraries, all packaged together into a single release. In addition, the component can export a compilation tool (in the form of an executable program) used to build downstream components.

- **Autogenerated header files:** Although C/C++ header files often are thought of as part of the source code, it's possible to autogenerate these files and make them part of the public API. For example, a component's build system might use a special-purpose interface-definition language to describe the internal functions. As a courtesy to downstream components, the interface definition is translated into C header files for inclusion with the `#include` directive.

- **Autogenerated source files:** Continuing the previous example, a component can autogenerate a number of source files, making them part of the public API. A downstream component would use those files as input into its own build process. For example, a remote procedure call (RPC) component might generate Java source files for accessing a remote RPC server. By compiling these source files for itself, a downstream component has all the functionality necessary to communicate with the server.

- **Frameworks or runtime systems:** It's increasingly common in modern software products to design and implement software that executes within a framework or runtime system. For example, most web-based applications operate within a web application server, avoiding the need to implement the features that all web applications have in common. If you include a framework as one of your components, the application developer can focus on the program's specific logic and presentation concerns, not on the common infrastructure.

In conjunction with public source files, each type of public generated file will be published to the component cache. From there, they'll be made available to other components and integrated into the program's final release package.

### Private Generated Files

A component's private generated files are simply the build system artifacts that aren't interesting to the end user. These include C/C++ object files (`.o` or `.obj`), Java class files (`.class`), or any autogenerated source files intended for internal use only. A developer who modifies a component needs to create these private files simply as a temporary step in creating the final build output.

A component's private generated files are never accessed by other components and aren't considered part of the public API. These files aren't published in the component cache.

### The Component Build System

The build system is a vital part of each component and is responsible for creating generated files. Some of these files (such as `.o` files) are for internal use only, whereas others are made part of the component's public API. The only case in which a build system isn't required arises when there aren't any private source files. In this case, the component contains only public source files.

A component's build system is like any other build system, except that it can't access the private source and generated files from any other component. However, it can access the public source and generate files from any upstream components, most likely via the component cache.

### Component-Level Tests

All pieces of software should be tested, no matter how large or small. The most common form of testing involves executing the program to see whether it behaves correctly. Testing GUI-based software involves triggering the widgets in a predetermined sequence to check that the correct response is provided. The same is true for command-line software, where different input values trigger different responses.

To more accurately locate test failures, the practice of **unit testing** (discussed in Chapter 12, "Building with Metadata") encourages the validation of small units of software, in isolation from others. Instead of trying to locate a test failure by executing the complete software product, you should explicitly trigger internal APIs to make sure they behave correctly. It's usually much easier to locate the source of a test failure when using a fine-grained approach.

Each component should have test cases to validate the component's functionality. The tests should be fully automated, making it easy to repeat the validation when changes are made. Only fully tested components should be added to the component cache, so that downstream components don't import buggy code.

A full discussion of unit testing is outside the scope of this book, but component developers should take the practice seriously. One of the main benefits of component-based software is the capability to improve quality, but that happens only if components are fully tested. Of course, it's still important to test the final product as a complete system.

## Integrating Components into a Single Product

Now that you've explored the internal structure of components, as well as the concept of a public API, it's time to focus on component integration. If a change is made to one component, you must ensure that all downstream components still compile. A careless change in one of the public APIs could easily break other components.

As an example, imagine that the Persistence component exports the save_database function, which is imported and invoked by the Payable component. The Persistence component exports a static library and an associated header file, named persistence.h.

```
1   /* persistence.h */
2
3   void save_database(char *name);
4   void load_database(char *name);
```

Within the Payable component, the payable.c file invokes the save_database function with a single argument.

```
1   #include "persistence.h"
2
...
56  void save_all()
57  {
58    save_database(my_db_name);
59  }
```

If a change is made to the Persistence component so that save_database now requires two parameters, the persistence.h header file is modified accordingly. Because of this change to the Persistence public API, the private source code in payable.c must also be fixed and the Payable component must be recompiled.

This problem is quite typical in component-based systems, but with a dependency graph in hand, it's not too hard to decide which other components must be recompiled. Now let's examine some common scenarios.

## Building All Components in a Single Build

The simplest approach to solving this problem is to always recompile the complete set of components from source code. This clearly takes a long time and defeats the goal of using prebuilt components. On the bright side, the build process is always correct, no matter which source files were modified. In many cases, there's a good chance that each downstream component's build system will complete within a few seconds, without the need to do any work.

Figure 18.5 shows the sequence in which components should be rebuilt. The leftmost components are available only in binary form and can't be recompiled from source.

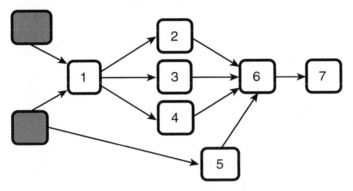

**Figure 18.5** *Building all components in a single build.*

This ordering follows the basic upstream/downstream relationship between components. The public files from an upstream component must be fully up-to-date before a downstream component can import them. Failure to follow the correct order simply leads to an invalid build.

You can definitely do better than this naive approach, especially because the developers should know which component they've changed and whether they modified the private or public source files. Now consider some more efficient solutions.

## Building the Final Application Using Prebuilt Components

If you make a code change to the rightmost component (in this example, the GUI component), there's no way to impact the compilation of any other parts of the software. As Figure 18.6 illustrates, no other components use the public API for the GUI component, so there's nothing left to compile.

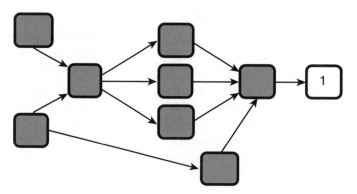

**Figure 18.6** *Using prebuilt components for everything except the final application.*

Even though all compilation is complete, you should still test the full system's behavior. There's a chance that your recent code change caused an upstream component to be invoked in a new way. For example, the GUI component might use a new function from the upstream API or use an existing function with different input parameters. Either of these cases could uncover a bug in an upstream component.

If you locate a new bug, be sure to add a test case for the upstream component. Future changes to that component shouldn't reintroduce the same bug.

### Modifying a Component's Private Source Files

If you modify a component's private source files, you cannot impact the compilation of downstream components, but you might change their functionality. As discussed before, a downstream component can import only the component's public API, so changes to the private source files won't have an impact. Figure 18.7 illustrates that only the component you've modified needs to be recompiled.

On the other hand, changing the private source files most likely change your component's behavior. Therefore, you must relink your component's public generate files into the downstream components or repackage them into the final release package. For example, if your component produces a static library, you need to relink downstream components for the library to be included. For shared libraries or JAR files, simply including the new file in the release package should be enough.

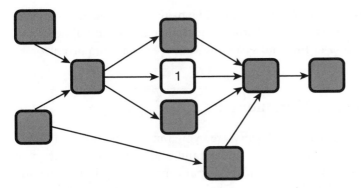

**Figure 18.7** *Modifying a component's private source files.*

Again, don't forget to unit-test your component changes and perform a full system test before declaring the product complete. Software that uses dynamic linking can easily break if a public function is removed from a shared library. It might have existed when the program was first compiled, but a change to the shared library can make it disappear. This mismatch is detected only at runtime.

### Modifying a Component's API

As a final case, consider what happens when a component's public API is changed. As shown in Figure 18.8, modifying a component forces you to recompile the downstream components. There's always a chance they'll make use of the API code you just changed and, therefore, could fail to recompile.

In this example, it's clear that the Commands component (number 2) directly depends on the Receivable component (number 1). However, there may not be a compile-time dependency between the final GUI component (number 3) and the public API of Receivable (number 1). In that case, it's sufficient to relink instead of recompile the GUI component.

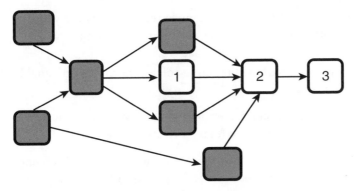

**Figure 18.8** *Modifying a component's public API.*

In this last scenario, you save compilation time by using the added knowledge of which component changed and whether that change impacted public or private files. Of course, unit testing and system testing are always important.

## People and Process Management

To benefit from component-based software, you must maintain component boundaries. Software developers must understand and follow the component model; otherwise, the software will quickly degrade into a monolithic collection of files. Although a good build system can help, most of the responsibility falls on developers.

A development team must have a strong set of processes to manage code change. This could involve a bug fix on a single line of code or perhaps a major change to a public API. In either case, rules must govern where and when the change can be made, how it must be tested, and when the code should be made available to other developers.

This extra management doesn't come for free, making component-based software challenging to implement in practice. If developers assume that each new version of an upstream component will fit seamlessly into their existing product, they'll be unpleasantly surprised when the integration effort starts. Integrating new component versions is a major challenge that isn't present when using monolithic software. That is, you trade off the benefits of separating the components with the cost of integrating them whenever they change.

To make life easier, plenty of rules cover the management of APIs. For example, ensuring that API functions are always backward compatible with previous versions results in fewer integration problems. Any new features added to the upstream component must involve adding a new API function that doesn't impact the existing functions. Although this discussion is important, it's out of the scope of this book.

This section discusses some of the process-centric requirements for working with component-based software and addresses the following topics:

- **Development team structure:** Dividing large software groups into smaller component-centric teams

- **Component line-up management:** Determining which version of each component should be integrated into the final software release

- **Managing the component cache:** Managing the cache of prebuilt components and expiring old versions that are no longer required

- **Coordinating new software features:** Ensuring that new software features are managed effectively, especially when they involve multiple components

Note that these topics aren't directly related to build systems, but they do give an idea of how an organization must rethink its development strategy.

## Development Team Structure

In any large software organization, it's common to divide the group into smaller subteams, with each team owning a portion of the code. Hundreds of developers may be working on the product, but each team has a single manager leading a small number of developers. Experience shows that the management of subteams is far more effective than placing all developers into a single team.

Although small teams are easier to manage, there's nothing to stop a developer from modifying another team's code, especially in a monolithic code base where internal APIs aren't defined. The boundaries between areas of responsibility can be unclear, making it difficult to change one team's code without impacting others. Even if the dividing line is initially well defined, a developer could mistakenly add new interdependencies. Some parts of the code might even be considered "common," giving everybody a free license to make changes.

This problem justifies your choice of component-based software. Each team of developers should be assigned one or more components, making it very clear where changes can be made and how those changes are allowed to impact other teams. Each team member obtains the source code for their component and then compiles, develops and tests that code. Luckily, the team members aren't required to know much about other components.

Figure 18.9 illustrates this division of responsibility for the example software product. Note that some teams own several different components, even though each component is managed only by a single team.

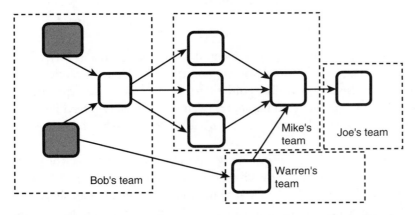

**Figure 18.9** *Component ownership, showing which team can modify the component.*

As a general rule, software usually ends up being structured in the same way your teams are structured [93]. If you already have a component-based system, you might already have this type of organization. In contrast, if you're just starting to divide a monolithic code base into components, a good starting point is to think carefully about your subteams.

Now let's summarize the benefits of having a single team responsible for each component:

- Only members of a component's subteam need to access the private files. This limits the number of developers who are required to compile the component. All other developers (in other subteams) use prebuilt and pretested versions of the component instead of compiling it for themselves.

- The team can focus its expertise on the internal implementation of its own component instead of worrying about other parts of the system. The team members still need to understand the public API of any upstream components, but these should be well documented and easy to understand. This type of focus allows them to be more efficient.

- Changes to a component are more easily managed, given that only one team of developers is permitted to make changes. The team's manager should be aware of all changes (at least at a high level), making it possible to control all new features and bug fixes.

- The team can be more agile in the way it works. All developers can meet in the same room and rapidly come to consensus on decisions. New features and bug fixes are small, making it possible to implement and test the code changes in a limited time frame.

- The team can specialize in testing its component in isolation from the rest of the system. This specialization improves the overall quality of the software.

On the downside, structuring teams around components creates territorial boundaries. No longer can developers make an arbitrary change in some other part of the system. Instead, they're required to negotiate changes with other teams, possibly involving the team manager. Even if a change is agreed upon, it may be a few weeks before the new code is published to the prebuilt component cache.

In reality, though, the clear division between teams is often violated for practical reasons. One subteam may allow changes made by another team, as long as there's enough collaboration. Developers from different subteams can share private source trees instead of waiting for an official component release. Luckily, these informal team structures still provide the benefits of using components, without too much management overhead.

## Component Line-Up Management

In a monolithic code base, each developer obtains a copy of the source code from a shared version-control system. A developer's code changes are then submitted back to the same shared repository. In this respect, a monolithic code base can be viewed as a single stream of code changes, with all changes being visible to all developers.

To release a monolithic software product to the end user, the full build system is invoked. The output is a software release package, ready to be installed on a target machine. The release package has a version number (such as 2.0.1) to distinguish different releases of the software.

When using component-based software, the same principles are followed, although at a different level of granularity. Each component is stored in its own source code repository, and changes are shared with other developers in the component team (but not with other teams). The component's build system creates the public generated files, which are packaged together and placed in the prebuilt component cache. A unique version number is required to distinguish one component release from the next.

Although they're similar, the most notable difference between monolithic and component-based software is how the components are integrated. Figure 18.10 illustrates that each component has its own release stream, with each release having a unique version number. In the final step, one release from each component stream is integrated into the full software release package.

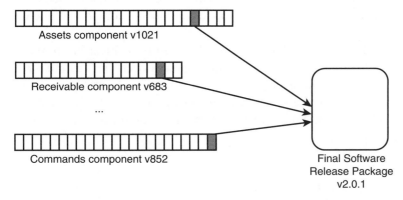

**Figure 18.10** *Each component has a stream of releases, with a version of each being integrated into the final product. Each component has a unique version number, as does the final software release package.*

For the build system to know which version of each component should be integrated, you need to understand the concept of a **component line-up**. The following listing shows an example line-up for the accounting program.

```
Database              5.1.12
Persistence           152
Logging               1.2.14
Payable               762
Receivable            683
Assets                1021
Security              53
Commands              852
GUI                   362
```

The exact version numbers are fairly arbitrary, with each component free to choose its own numbering scheme. For consistency, the components here use a single number that is incremented each time they're released to the component cache. In the case of `Database` and `Logging`, these components were obtained from a third-party vendor and simply follow the vendor's three-number version scheme.

Although Figure 18.10 shows integration as a final linking or packaging step, that's not how it usually works in practice. Instead when each downstream component is compiled or linked, it requires that upstream components already be compiled and published to the component cache. For example, to compile version 852 of the `Commands` component, the compiler or linker makes use of `Payable` version 762, `Receivable` version 683, `Assets` version 1021, and `Security` version 53.

As you'll see later, the exact line-up of version numbers is important to software quality. You can't simply use the latest version of a component from the cache, and you can't arbitrarily select different versions of a component. All changes must be carefully managed and validated before the component line-up is altered.

To allow reproducibility of older releases, the line-up file must be stored in the version-control system. As the source code changes over time, so must the component line-up. For example, if you add new features to the GUI component and fix some minor bugs in the `Payable` component, you would increase those component version numbers but leave everything else the same.

```
Database              5.1.12
Persistence           152
Logging               1.2.14
Payable               763
Receivable            683
Assets                1021
Security              53
Commands              852
GUI                   363
```

To reproduce older versions of the product, a developer obtains an earlier version of the source files, along with an earlier version of the line-up file.

One additional observation is that the final release package has a customer-facing version number that is separate from any of the component versions. Typically, a customer expects a version number to reflect the new content of the release. If the major version number has increased, the customer expects new features in the software. In contrast, a component's version number is internal to the software product, so simply increasing the number for each release is usually adequate.

In summary, a component-based build system requires a lot of extra work to manage each component's release stream. In monolithic software, submitting a change to the code base immediately causes the change to be integrated. On the other hand, to gain the stability and quality of a component-based product, an extra layer of management is required to control the line-up of components.

## Managing the Component Cache

You've already explored the concept of the component cache, used to store prebuilt versions of each component. You've also learned that multiple copies of a component can be placed in the cache, each with a unique version number. Finally, you learned that a line-up file specifies which version of each component should be integrated into the final release package.

At this point, two outstanding cache management questions remain to be answered. How often should new versions of the component be placed into the cache, and when should stale versions be purged? The solution to these questions depends a lot on your development process.

### Adding New Component Versions

As a general rule, you should store a component in the cache only when the quality is "good enough." This is a subjective measure that depends on what the downstream components expect. With this in mind, consider some guidelines on when to publish components into the cache.

- For a totally new component that's still under development, you could provide partial releases of the unfinished code. These won't ever appear in the component line-up and are solely used by downstream components for testing purposes. New versions of this component might be released every few months or whenever new functionality is ready to be tested.

- When the software is nearing its shipment date, the focus is on fixing bugs instead of adding new features. Bug fixes are made on a daily basis, with the component tested and published to the cache as often as possible. The component line-up is updated each day to incorporate new versions.

- When a component has reached a high-level of quality, the creation of new versions slows or even ceases. Unless new features or bug fixes are being added, a component can remain constant for months or years. In this case, no new versions are published to the cache.

- Some software products are built to support multiple variants, so each component must also support those variants. For example, a product that executes on an Intel platform as well as a MIPS platform must have two variants for each component version in the cache. To keep things simple, both variants should be published at the same time.

- In a final scenario, a component might have multiple streams of development, each published to the cache at different rates. For example, a component that is integrated into version 2.0 of the software might not change often, but a more recent version of the component, integrated in release 3.0, might receive frequent bug fixes. The source code for each component would therefore be managed on a different code branch within the version-control system.

As you can see, knowing when to publish a component to the cache is a management problem. Components should be published only when they're stable enough, but downstream components must have access to the code whenever possible. Now consider how often these component releases can be removed from the cache.

### Expiring Component Versions

In an ideal world, the component cache would have unlimited size. Developers would always have access to each version of a component, no matter when it was originally published or how infrequently it's used. In reality, though, the component cache uses a lot of disk space, which must be reclaimed when new versions are published.

Note that even if a component version is removed from the cache, it's still possible to rebuild it from source code. Version-control systems never purge old data, so given the component name and desired version number, it's always possible to re-create. The whole purpose of using the cache is to eliminate unnecessary build time, so it pays to remove only versions that you won't likely need again.

Without having the foresight of which component versions will be used in the future, a heuristic solution is the best approach. You can make decisions either based purely on the age of the component version (when it was published in the cache) or based on when the component version was last accessed.

For the first heuristic, you could choose to purge any versions that have been in the cache longer than three months (or whatever makes sense for the product). After this time period, all users of a component likely will have moved on to newer versions. For example, you could remove versions 1–856 of the Assets component because they were published more than three months ago. It's assumed that all users of the component are now on version 857 or higher.

Although this rule seems fairly simple, there are certainly a few corner cases. For example, if no new versions were published in the last three months (the component is considered stable), you'll need to keep the most recent version. This version is still referenced in the current line-up file, so it must be kept in the cache.

A second heuristic approach involves tracking which component versions are actively being used. When the build system is invoked and a prebuilt component is retrieved from the cache, a counter should be incremented. After a period of time, the cache mechanism has a good idea of which versions of each component are still being used and, therefore, which shouldn't be purged.

The advantage of this second approach is that when new versions are created in quick succession, such as once per day as bugs are being fixed, only the final version is kept. Other versions that were useful for only a single day will be purged quickly.

## Coordinating New Software Features

When new features are added to a software product, the starting point is a high-level natural language description of what the new feature should do and how it changes the behavior of the existing product. Later in the process, the software developers start to plan which lines of code will actually be modified. For large features, any number of developers could get involved, creating the need to coordinate their work.

With component-based software, there's a good chance that more than one component needs to change. New functionality must be added within each component, with the public API providing access to the new code. Figure 18.11 illustrates this concept.

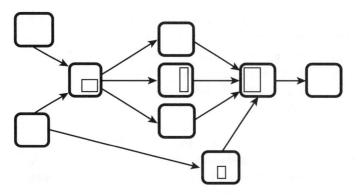

**Figure 18.11** *The introduction of a new product feature requires code changes in many components.*

From a management perspective, the addition of this feature requires that many different development teams get involved. They each have expert knowledge about their own component and know which lines of code should be modified. The challenging problem is to decide how each of the changes is to be shared with other component teams. In a simplistic world, the upstream team would complete its work and then publish it to the prebuilt component cache. Only then would the downstream teams start using the new APIs provided by the upstream component.

Obviously, this serial approach isn't very efficient because it lengthens the time required to implement features. In any realistic project, the different teams do their best to work in parallel, even if it involves extra management overhead to coordinate change.

### *Phased Releases*

One technique for working in parallel is to complete the upstream work in phases. After agreeing on the list of code changes required in the upstream component, the work is delivered in a sequence of steps instead of waiting until everything is complete and fully tested. Each version of the component is published in the cache, even though it's not fully functional.

The first release should contain the new public API changes, such as function prototypes or constant definitions. Even if the functions are simply stubbed out, the downstream component can compile and link against the API. This helps the downstream team move ahead with writing the code, preparing it for when the upstream component is finally complete.

Naturally, challenges arise with this approach. The team managers must agree on the public API changes, as well as the order in which features are to be implemented. It's frustrating to wait for a feature, only to learn that upstream teams have been working on some other task. In addition, the teams must not make changes to the public API that weren't agreed upon. The downstream team expects a certain API and won't be happy having to rewrite parts of their code.

### *Validating New Releases*

When a new component version is added to the component cache, it might not be ready to integrate into the final release package. Even though it was fully unit-tested in isolation from other components, the new version might not be compatible with its downstream neighbors. Until this problem is fixed, the line-up file shouldn't be updated to include the new version.

To solve this problem, a new component should be released to the component cache but used only for testing purposes. Downstream components should then be recompiled and tested against the new version, just to make sure they still function correctly. If not, a new version of the downstream component could be required. Figure 18.12 shows the creation of a new version of the `Persistence` component.

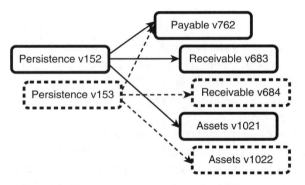

**Figure 18.12** *When a new component version is released, downstream components must be recompiled and tested again. New versions of those downstream components might need to be created.*

In this example, the new version of `Persistence` (version 153) is added to the cache. Each of the downstream components must then be recompiled and tested against this new version. In the case of the `Payable` component, no new version is required because version 762 continues to work perfectly. However, both the `Receivable` and `Assets` components require modification to work with the updated `Persistence` API. New versions must therefore be created and added to the component cache.

After all downstream components have been tested, the component line-up file can be updated. In this scenario, all three new components are added to the line-up file at the same time. If this change wasn't made in unison, an invalid release package would be created.

### *Obtaining All Source Code*

As a final approach, you can avoid the management overhead of coordinating releases by instead reverting to monolithic development. This simply requires all downstream developers to obtain their own copy of the upstream component's source code. Instead of waiting for the component to be released to the cache (which may take weeks), they have immediate access to all the latest code changes.

Naturally, developers must now face the same performance and quality problems they see with a monolithic build. They must also resist creating dependencies on the upstream component's private files. In reality, these risks are minimal compared to the added efficiency of working in parallel.

Let's now finish the discussion of component-based software by looking at a build tool that supports this approach.

## Apache Ivy

The concept of component-based software is rapidly becoming mainstream. This is certainly true in the Java world, where it's common to reuse third-party components that were downloaded from the Internet. These components provide a range of functionality, including database access, GUI management, and the implementation of network protocols.

The Apache Ivy tool [85] provides a mechanism for handling components in the form of Java JAR files. Components can be downloaded from Internet-based repositories or can be managed within private (company-wide) caches. In either case, the build system knows which version of each component is required and ensures that the correct version is downloaded. Although Ivy can be used as a standalone build tool, it's often used in conjunction with the more flexible Ant tool.

Ivy's build description captures the relationship between components and is essentially a text-based version of a component dependency graph. In addition, the version numbers listed in the line-up file must be provided. Ivy's main purpose is to download the correct version of each component and then include the downloaded `.jar` files into the Java class path. The Java compiler uses this class path when building downstream components.

The following Ant script shows the compilation of the `Persistence` component. Recall that `Persistence` depends on the `Logger` and `Database` components, which are both third-party products downloaded from the Internet. In this example, the Ivy build tool is invoked as an Ant task.

```
 1   <project name="Persistence" default="build"
 2             xmlns:ivy="antlib:org.apache.ivy.ant">
 3
 4     <import file="../template/build.xml"/>
 5
 6     <target name="build" depends="enable-ivy">
 7       <ivy:cachepath
 8           organisation="log4j"
 9           module="log4j"
10           revision="1.2.14"
11           pathid="logger.pathid"
12           inline="true" />
13       <ivy:cachepath
14           organisation="mysql"
15           module="mysql-connector-java"
16           revision="5.1.12"
17           pathid="database.pathid"
18           inline="true" />
19
20       <mkdir dir="${build.dir}"/>
21       <javac srcdir="${src.dir}" destdir="${build.dir}">
22         <classpath refid="logger.pathid"/>
23         <classpath refid="database.pathid"/>
24       </javac>
25     </target>
26
27   </project>
```

The interesting portions of this code are on lines 7–12 and 13–18. Although these are written in Ant syntax, the details are passed to the underlying Ivy tool. The first use of `ivy:cachepath` states that the build system (for `Persistence`) depends on version `1.2.14` of the `log4j` package, which is published by the `log4j` organization. The second instance states that version `5.1.12` of the `mysql-connector-java` is also required.

The rest of the code, lines 20–24, compiles the private source files for the `Persistence` component. The key observation is that compilation is done with the `log4j` and `mysql-connector-java` JAR files in the class path. The `Persistence` source code can now import the public API of these upstream components.

The Ivy tool does a lot of work to download the third-party components. By default, Ivy searches a public repository of prebuilt components, such as http://repo1.maven.org/maven2. This repository contains hundreds of freely available packages, each published by the component's vendor. The hierarchy of folders on this web site allows Ivy to single out a specific version of each component.

When a component is downloaded, Ivy also takes note of further required packages. It's common for third-party components to have their own dependencies on other packages, which they consider upstream components. Ivy ensures that the complete set of upstream components is downloaded and available to the local build system. The first time an Ivy-based build is invoked, it can take several minutes to download all the required JAR files.

In addition to third-party packages, Ivy enables the creation of local component caches. The locally written components (such as `Persistence`, `Payable`, and `Assets`) would be published to this cache (with a version number) and made available to downstream components.

Unfortunately, this brief description of Apache Ivy has barely covered the basic features. If you're interested in developing component-based software, you're encouraged to read more about this tool. The same is true for the Maven tool [84], discussed in Chapter 17, "Reducing Complexity for End Users," which has similar features for managing components.

## Summary

Large software products don't scale well when the software is managed as a monolithic set of source files. Instead, there are many benefits to breaking the software into smaller components and treating each as a separate product. The benefits of this approach include faster compile times, less disk usage, more control over the quality of the code, and less stress on the build machine infrastructure.

Each component consists of private source and generated files, as well as public source and generated files. Only the component's development team is aware of the private files; other developers are interested only in the component's public API.

Each component must also have its own build system and collection of unit tests. The build system compiles the component's private source files but can't access the internals of any other component. The unit tests must validate the component in isolation from other components by exercising the public API.

For a software team to develop component-based software, a number of process-centric issues must be considered. First, the developers should have a clear idea of which team owns each component. Next, the exact version of each component, to be integrated into the final release package, must be carefully coordinated. The cache of prebuilt components must also be managed with care, with versions being purged when no longer required. Finally, adding a new feature to the software requires careful interaction among the development teams.

The Apache Ivy build tool enables Java developers to specify the dependencies each component has on third-party or locally written packages. The appropriate version of each component is either downloaded from the Internet or obtained from a company-wide cache. When the component itself is compiled, the upstream JAR files are added to the compiler's class path.

# Chapter 19

---

# Faster Builds

This final chapter considers how a build system can get its job done faster. It should be no surprise that a large program takes a long time to compile. However, you have many ways to speed up the end-to-end build process and reduce the time spent on incremental rebuilds. Even if you break your software into multiple components, you want each component to compile as quickly as possible. Beyond simply suggesting that you buy a faster build machine (which is often a good idea), this chapter covers four main topics:

- **Measuring build system performance:** The first step in deciding how to speed up the build process is to analyze the various steps the build tool takes. When you've located the bottleneck, the approach to improving performance is often quite obvious.

- **Eliminating unnecessary rebuilds:** Invoking a compilation tool is time-intensive, so you need to recompile files only when they have changed.

- **Parallelism:** On a build machine with multiple CPUs, or in a cluster of build machines, you can invoke multiple compilation steps in parallel.

- **Reducing disk usage:** Reading and writing disk files takes time. If you reduce your dependency on disk access, the build process can take significantly less time.

In each of these cases, keep in mind that large build systems have hundreds of thousands of source files, can generate gigabytes' worth of output, and may even take a full day to complete. Even a minor improvement in performance can reduce the total build time by an hour or more.

# Measuring Build System Performance

The first step to improving a build system's performance is to understand how its time is spent. Your build system might spend an excessive amount of time checking file dependencies, or perhaps it spends too much time compiling source code. No matter what the situation, you need to quantify the cost of each part of the build process.

This discussion divides the build process into two main phases, analyzing each phase on its own. In the **start-up phase**, the build tool reads the build description files, creates a dependency graph, and determines which files have been modified. In the **compilation phase**, the build tool invokes each of the compilation tools, with the goal of bringing the object files up-to-date.

As you already know from previous chapters, the work done in each of these phases is quite distinct. The focus of the first phase is on the build tool itself, whereas the performance of the second phase is related to how efficiently each compilation tool does its job.

## Measuring Performance in the Start-Up Phase

When a build tool is first invoked, it does a considerable amount of upfront analysis. This work involves parsing the build description files, constructing a dependency graph, and scanning the source files to see which have changed. Reading build description files is I/O-intensive, whereas creating a dependency graph requires a lot of memory. Checking to see whether files have been modified also requires an extensive amount of disk I/O.

To developers, much of this work is considered overhead instead of productive work. Not until they see the compilation tools being invoked do they feel that the build is progressing. In practice, though, the more time is spent on upfront analysis, the more accurate the build tool is at invoking compilation tools. The build tool can actually save time by not rebuilding files it doesn't need to.

For the purpose of discussion, examine a hypothetical build system that most people would consider large:

- The source tree has 10,000 C/C++ source files, all compiled as a single component.

- The source files are spread evenly across a build tree hierarchy of 500 directories. Therefore, each directory has roughly 20 source files.

- The system includes 1,000 C/C++ header files that can each be included by any of the source files.

- Each source file includes an average of ten header files.

Instead of worrying too much about the actual time taken to perform each step in the build process, start by understanding how often each type of operation is performed—that is, how many files are read or written, how many dependency graphs are created, and how many time stamps are checked. The actual time depends on your build machine's CPU, the type of disk you have installed, how much memory is available, and whether the machine is busy doing other work.

With this software product in mind, let's consider four types of build system. Each system has a significantly different way of parsing the build description, building the dependency graph, and checking for out-of-date files. The scenarios are:

- **Recursive GNU Make with `makedepend`:** A separate instance of GNU Make is used for each source code directory. The `makedepend` tool provides the dependency information.

- **Inclusive GNU Make:** A single instance of GNU Make traverses the entire directory hierarchy. The GNU Make framework automatically computes dependencies.

- **SCons with default settings:** The SCons tool traverses the entire directory hierarchy. MD5 checksums are used to determine whether source files have been modified.

- **SCons with optimizations:** Instead of using the default SCons settings, you'll enable a couple basic optimizations.

This comparison isn't trying to prove which build tool is best. The intention is to understand where each tool spends most of its time and to learn about performance measurement.

### Example: Recursive GNU Make with `makedepend`

As discussed in Chapter 6, "Make," a recursive Make system invokes a new instance of the GNU Make tool for each source code directory. Our hypothetical build system invokes 500 separate instances of the GNU Make tool, each reading a single makefile and constructing the associated dependency graph.

If your build system also makes use of a separate framework file, with each makefile including that framework, this simply increases the number of files to be parsed. It's common to see the following at the end of a makefile:

```
include framework.mk
```

This example reads 1,000 files. Each of the 500 makefiles is parsed once, with each makefile including the single framework file. Additionally, if `framework.mk` were to include other files, you could end up with 1,500, 2,000, 2,500, or more file read operations.

Although framework files are usually considered an advantage, remember that each file requires separate disk access. File system caching makes future accesses faster, but there's still additional work to be done.

The next step in the build process is to find out which header files each source file includes. This scenario uses the `makedepend` tool instead of the automatic dependency system discussed in Chapter 6. Users explicitly invoke this tool before building their software, as well as whenever they happen to know the dependencies have changed.

This is the syntax for `makedepend`:

```
makedepend -f .depend -- $(CFLAGS) -- $(SRCS)
```

This tool acts like a C compiler, but instead of generating object files, it simply writes the dependency information to the `.depend` file. The makefile includes the `.depend` file to learn which header files each C or C++ source file uses. A typical `.depend` file might contain the following:

```
dog.o: header1.h header2.h header3.h
cat.o: header2.h
rat.o: header1.h header2.h
```

To create a `.depend` file for each directory in the source tree, you'll piggyback onto the recursive Make system. Computing the implicit dependencies requires GNU Make to be invoked 500 times (once per directory), with each invocation parsing a separate makefile and creating a separate dependency graph. In addition, the `makedepend` command is invoked 500 times, each creating a separate `.depend` file.

Because `makedepend` acts like a compiler, it scans each of the C/C++ source files to see which header files are included. Across the whole source tree there are 10,000 source files to read, each including an average of 10 header files. Each of these header files is also scanned to discover nested dependencies. Luckily, each instance of `makedepend` scans each header file only once, but because you have 500 different instances of `makedepend`, there'll be a lot of duplicated effort.

Now that you've computed all the `.depend` files, it's time to build the software using a second invocation of the recursive Make system. This involves 500 more invocations of GNU Make, each with its own dependency graph. Each directory contains approximately 20 source files and 20 corresponding object files. In addition, up to 200 header files could be included, assuming the worst case in which each source file includes its own unique set of 10 header files. Each instance of GNU Make therefore checks up to 240 time stamps to determine which object files are out-of-date.

This sounds like a lot of work, so let's now summarize what the recursive Make solution actually does. This analysis assumes that the user issued the following commands:

```
make depend
make all
```

This gives the statistics shown in Table 19.1.

**Table 19.1** *Solution Statistics*

| Operation | Count | Justification |
|---|---|---|
| Makefile reads/parses (including makefile fragments) | 1,500 | 500 for the make depend command, 500 for the make all command, and an additional 500 for reading all the .depend files. (This can be much higher if framework files are used.) |
| Dependency graphs created | 1,000 | 500 for the make depend command and 500 for the make all command. |
| Processes created | 1,500 | 1,000 GNU Make processes and 500 makedepend processes. |
| Source files read | 10,000 | 500 directories, with an average of 20 files each scanned by makedepend. |
| Header files read | Up to 100,000 | Assuming the worst case of 20 files per directory, each including 10 unique headers. |
| Files written | 500 | A single .depend file per directory. |
| Time stamps checked | Up to 120,000 | Assuming the worst case of 240 files for each of 500 directories. (Although this is highly unlikely to occur in a real system.) |

Of course, all this happens before any compilation work, but a later section looks at those numbers. Now consider a second way of using GNU Make, which uses only a single instance of the make command.

### Example: Inclusive GNU Make

In contrast to the previous example, an inclusive Make system uses only a single instance of the GNU Make tool. Each directory contains a `Files.mk` file, which is parsed by the same GNU Make process. Process start-up time is thus reduced, and you'll see all the benefits of having a single dependency graph instead of 500 fragments.

In this example, you also compute the implicit dependency information differently. Instead of performing the explicit `make depend` step before the build is performed, you automate the generation of `.d` files as part of the regular build process. If the `.d` file is out-of-date with respect to a `.c` file, it's autogenerated with the latest dependency information.

To create or update a `.d` file, you invoke two different processes. Here's a reminder of the GNU Make approach from Chapter 6.

```
%.d: %.c
        @$(CC) -MM $(CPPFLAGS) $< | sed 's#\(.*\)\.o: #\1.o
\1.d: #g' > $@
```

This solution passes the source file through the `gcc -MM` command which provides a list of source and header file dependencies. The `sed` command manipulates that output so that `.d` files also depend on those same source and header files. Refer back to Chapter 6 for a more detailed explanation.

The C compiler itself does the main work in this code, and the `sed` command modifies the compiler's output. The `sed` command is much more lightweight than the C compiler (which creates subprocesses behind the scenes) and is significantly more lightweight than when invoking the GNU Make tool again.

For each `.c` file, a separate C compiler process scans for dependencies, so different processes don't share dependency information. This results in 10,000 source files being read, each including an average of 10 header files. Unlike the `makedepend` situation, the worst case of 100,000 source file reads is also the average case because there's no way to share dependency information between files in the same directory. This is another way of saying that a `.d` file stores dependency information on a source file basis, whereas a `.depend` file works on a directory basis.

After the dependencies have been computed, GNU Make parses all the `.d` files, with the goal of creating a single dependency graph. This involves reading and parsing 500 `Files.mk` files and 10,000 smaller `.d` files. If framework files are used, they also need to be parsed, although only once for the entire build process instead of once per directory.

Clearly, it's important to optimize this part of the build process. Whenever a developer performs an incremental build, 10,500 files are parsed and the entire dependency graph is constructed. This can be extremely time-consuming if you have a slow file system to contend with. Of course, a GNU Make guru could optimize the inclusive algorithm to parse only the `.d` files that the current build target requires.

Finally, the single instance of GNU Make checks time stamps on all the source, header, and object files. Because you have only a single instance of GNU Make, each time stamp is only checked once. You therefore have 10,000 source files, 10,000 object files, and 1,000 header files to check to determine whether the object files are out-of-date.

Table 19.2 presents a summary of the operations in the inclusive GNU Make solution.

**Table 19.2** *Statistics for Inclusive GNU Make Solution*

| Operation | Count | Justification |
|---|---|---|
| `Makefile` reads/ parses (including makefile fragments) | 10,500 | There's a single `File.mk` file in each directory and a single `.d` file for each source file's dependencies. |
| Dependency graphs created | 1 | A single instance of GNU Make is used. |
| Processes created | 20,001 | To create each of the 10,000 `.d` files, two processes are created. Only one GNU Make process is created; although, it makes extensive use of CPU, memory, and I/O. |
| Source files read | 10,000 | Each source file is read once, as the dependencies are computed. |
| Header files read | 100,000 | To create a `.d` file, you invoke the C compiler 10,000 times, each reading 10 header files, on average (with no sharing of results between different C files). |
| Files written | 10,000 | A separate `.d` file is created for each source file. |
| Time stamps checked | 21,000 | Each source file, object file, and header file is checked once. |

Before leaving the topic of GNU Make performance, you need to realize that the first two scenarios differ in a couple ways. The first aspect is how you traverse the source tree to build up the dependency graph. The second aspect is how you determine a source file's implicit dependencies. There's actually no reason to tie these techniques together, but these examples do so for convenience.

By looking at the estimated number of I/O operations, you can see that having a single GNU Make instance reduces the number of processes created and time stamps checked. On the other hand, the use of automatic dependency generation could be more accurate but places a significant load on the underlying file system, at least when compared to the makedepend solution.

### Example: SCons with Default Settings

The third and fourth build system examples switch to using the SCons build tool. As discussed in Chapter 8, "SCons," SCons can build an entire source tree with a single instance of the tool, creating a single dependency graph. This makes it similar to the inclusive Make solution.

In a typical SCons-based build system, you aren't required to have a different SConscript file for each source code directory. It's often easier to have one file for each major portion of the software, regardless of how many directories it covers. For example, a single library within the software product could be spread across ten different directories. You'd use a single SConscript file at the top of the library's subtree instead of one file in each directory.

Of course, in a GNU Make–based system there's also no reason to have a single Files.mk file in each directory. To have a fair comparison, assume that you have 500 unique SConscript files. When the SCons tool starts up, it parses each of these files into a single dependency graph.

Implicit dependency analysis in SCons is similar to what you've seen with GNU Make, although it's built into the tool instead of being a user-supplied feature. SCons reads each of the 10,000 source files and each of the 1,000 header files, storing the dependency information in its internal database.

Instead of using a time stamp comparison check, SCons uses MD5 checksums to detect whether a file has been modified since the last invocation. MD5 calculations are by no means cheap to perform, especially in comparison to a simple time stamp check. In this example, SCons computes the MD5 checksum for 10,000 source files, 10,000 object files, and 1,000 header files. With these numbers in mind, it's not surprising that SCons has as reputation for being slow.

One place where SCons does well is in storing dependency information. Unlike GNU Make's solution of having a .depend file per directory or a .d file per source file, SCons uses a single database file to store all persistent state between builds. From an operating system perspective, reading and writing a single large file is far more efficient than accessing hundreds or thousands of small files.

Table 19.3 summarizes the I/O operations for the first SCons example.

**Table 19.3**  *Summary of I/O Operations*

| Operation | Count | Justification |
|---|---|---|
| SConscript reads/parses | 500 | One file per source code directory. If framework files are used, they're read once for the entire build process. |
| Dependency graphs created | 1 | A single instance of SCons is created. |
| Processes created | 1 | All dependency analysis work is done within the SCons tool. |
| Source files read | 20,000 | 10,000 reads for computing implicit dependencies, and 10,000 more reads for MD5 checksums. |
| Header files read | 2,000 | Same as for source files. |
| Object files read | 10,000 | Each object file's checksum is computed, to see if it changed since the last build. |
| Files written | 1 | A single database file is used. |
| Time stamps checked | 0 | By default, SCons doesn't check time stamps. |
| MD5 checksums | 21,000 | 10,000 source files, 10,000 object files, and 1,000 header files. |

At first glance, these numbers appear to be much lower than the corresponding GNU Make numbers. This is largely because SCons is performing all the tasks within a single process instead of invoking separate processes to compute dependencies. In contrast, the additional work of computing MD5 checksums can be excessive, making a SCons-based build unacceptably slow.

In addition to the numbers in the table, it's worth mentioning one more time-consuming activity. To locate your local machine's compilation tools, SCons searches a range of standard file system directories. When it locates a tool, SCons invokes it with the necessary flags to determine the tool's version number. For example, on a Linux system, SCons searches for the gcc program in /usr/local/bin, /opt/bin, /bin, and /usr/bin. After finding it, the gcc --version command is invoked to learn which version of the tool is available. This feature can be disabled by explicitly hard-coding the path to each tool.

Now consider a final build system example, in which you disable some of the default SCons features in an effort to gain more performance.

### Example: SCons with Optimizations

The previous SCons example used a total of 32,000 file system read operations. To make matters worse, the file content is used to compute both MD5 checksums and a list of implicit dependencies. This extra overhead might not be noticeable during a full build, but an incremental build takes excessively long. This is especially troublesome if none of the source files has actually been modified since the last build invocation. The designers of the SCons tool understood this bottleneck and created alternate solutions.

The first optimization requires you to add the following statement to your SConstruct file:

```
Decider('MD5-timestamp')
```

This directive requests that SCons perform an MD5 checksum only if the time stamp on a file has changed since the last build invocation. It's logical that if the time stamp hasn't changed, the file's content hasn't changed. On the other hand, if the time stamp is different from last time, SCons computes the MD5 checksum to see if there's now a difference in content.

The effect of using the MD5-timestamp decider technique can be dramatic. Instead of reading every source file in the whole build tree, SCons performs a time stamp check operation on each of them, which is significantly less work for both the CPU and the file system. This doesn't mean no checksums are computed, but the effort is focused on files that are more likely to have changed.

A second optimization involves caching the implicit dependencies instead of recomputing them each time the build tool is invoked. The following directive should be added to the SConstruct file.

```
SetOption('implicit_cache', 1)
```

This forces SCons to reuse the same set of dependencies that were computed in the last build invocation, which, in most cases, gives the same build results each time. When you add a new dependency and insert a new #include directive into a C/C++ file, SCons notices the change anyway. This modification (change to time stamp and MD5 checksum) causes the source file to be recompiled, so the new dependency information is discovered. There's certainly no need to rescan all the source files to find this one change.

However, using cached information is a problem in one scenario. Imagine that you're compiling source code with the following command line:

```
gcc -o calc/calc.o -IdirA -IdirB -c -O calc/calc.c
```

If the calc.c file contains the #include "config.h" directive, the C compiler searches for config.h in the dirA/ directory, followed by the dirB/ directory. If the file is found in dirB/, the path dirB/config.h is stored in the `calc.o` file's list of dependencies. With `implicit_cache` set to 1, SCons assumes that this fact continues to be true for successive builds.

Imagine now that you add a new file to the source tree, called `dirA/config.h`. When you invoke the C compiler, `config.h` is now found within the `dirA/` directory because `dirA/` was earlier in the compiler's search path. Unfortunately, SCons still believes that you depend on `dirB/config.h`. Clearly, there's an opportunity for changes to `dirA/config.h` to not trigger a new build, which is obviously a bad thing.

If this opportunity for error doesn't seem likely to cause problems, you can gain some extra performance by enabling the `implicit_cache` feature. Let's look at the summary of operations in Table 19.4.

**Table 19.4**  *Summary of Operations*

| Operation | Count | Justification |
|---|---|---|
| SConscript reads/parses | 500 | One file per source code directory. |
| Dependency graphs created | 1 | A single instance of SCons is created. |
| Processes created | 1 | All dependency analysis work is done within the SCons tool. |
| Source files read | A small number | Only files that have different time stamps will have their MD5 checksum computed. Implicit dependencies are taken from the cache. |
| Header files read | A small number | Same as for source files. |
| Object files read | A small number | Same as for source files. |
| Files written | 1 | A single database file is used. |
| Time stamps checked | 21,000 | Source files, object files, and header files all have their time stamps checked. |
| MD5 checksums | A small number | Only for files in which the time stamp changes. |

As a final note, you need to realize that these optimizations have an impact on only the second and successive builds. When the build tree is compiled for the first time, there's no content in the cache, so MD5 checksums and implicit dependencies must still be calculated.

Now let's move on to the second phase of the build process, where the compilation commands are actually invoked.

## Measuring Performance in the Compilation Phase

If the build tool has done its job properly, it now has a list of files to be recompiled. If no source file changes occurred, the build stops at this point without doing any compilation work. In reality, though, the developer wouldn't have invoked the build process if there weren't any changes, so you should still care that each compilation tool does its job as efficiently as possible. This section focuses on the performance of these tools.

Now consider three different aspects that can each be optimized. The first concern is how much time it takes to invoke the tool, which is partly related to how many times it's invoked. Next, consider whether the tool itself is highly optimized or whether it uses inefficient algorithms. Finally, the number of implicit dependencies hidden inside a source file plays a major role in the compilation time.

### Process Start-Up Time

Invoking a compilation tool takes time, even before it starts doing any meaningful work. Most tools are stored as separate executable programs, so you need to focus on how the underlying operating system creates a new process. You also need to care about how long the process takes to fully initialize its data structures. Think about the work required to start a compilation tool and how to reduce the start-up overhead.

The first step is for the operating system to locate the executable program on disk and read it into memory. If the tool uses shared libraries, it dynamically loads and links to those libraries before execution proceeds. Most operating systems cache disk files in memory, so loading the tool for the second or successive time is much faster. In addition, the whole purpose behind shared libraries is to reuse code that's already loaded into memory, making it much faster to get the tool up and running.

The next step is for the tool to read its configuration files and initialize internal data structures. The amount of time required depends on which tool is invoked. You might find that tools written in languages such as Perl, Python, or Java spend a lot of time reading configuration files, loading code libraries, and initializing data structures, even before the tool's own code is executed. On the other hand, a tool that is fully compiled into machine code can avoid much of that overhead.

When you take caching into account, a tool's start-up time is fairly consistent. A process that takes 0.2 seconds to load and initialize might not seem like a problem, at least until your build system grows in size. With 100 tool invocations, you're now adding a full 20 seconds onto the build time. With 1,000 invocations, you add more than 3 minutes. Thus, it's important to reduce the start-up time, if at all possible.

Consider some ideas on how to reduce the start-up time of your compilation tools.

- Always be aware of the number of unique processes your build tool invokes. For GNU Make, each command line in a rule is invoked using a separate shell. For example, consider the following fragment:

```
.depend:
    rm -f .depend
    touch .depend
    makedepend -f .depend -- $(CFLAGS) -- $(SRCS)
```

  In this case, GNU Make invokes a total of six processes. Each of the three command lines is passed into a shell (by default, /bin/sh), which, in turn, invokes either the rm, touch, or makedepend commands.

  In contrast, a build tool such as Ant implements many of the tasks internally, without invoking an external process. Where possible, an Ant task uses direct system calls to achieve the same effect.

- To take this start-up cost idea one step further, if you choose to implement your own compilation tools, it pays to avoid writing shell scripts. With the exception of shell built-in functions, each line of the shell script is guaranteed to invoke a separate process. In contrast, with a Perl or Python script, the program directly invokes system calls without the additional overhead of invoking a new process each time.

- Consider whether some of your tool's start-up initialization can be cached in a binary format. Instead of parsing a text-based configuration file each time the tool is invoked, it might be possible to cache the tool's internal data structures in a binary format and save them to disk. On successive invocations of the tool, the binary cache is loaded directly into memory without a parsing step. In the uncommon event that the original text-based configuration file changed, the tool must spend extra time regenerating the cached binary data.

- If your compilation tool supports the feature, pass as many source file names to the tool as possible, and have it compile all the files at once. This is in contrast to invoking a separate instance of the tool for each individual source file. For example, try to avoid compiling all source files with separate command lines:

```
cc -c aardvark.c
cc -c bear.c
cc -c camel.c
```

Instead, consider combining them into a single command:

```
cc -c aardvark.c bear.c camel.c
```

Depending on your compiler, you could end up reducing the process start-up time. If you're unlucky, your compiler could simply create a separate process for each source file anyway. In this case, the capability to list all files on a single line is purely a convenience for the developer.

Now move on and consider how a tool can be made to operate more efficiently when the start-up portion has finished and the real compilation starts.

### Compilation Tool Performance

As with any piece of software, it's usually possible to optimize the program so that it operates more quickly. In a large build system with thousands of source files, even a 10% improvement in performance saves a significant amount of time. Let's touch on a few methods for improving a compilation tool's performance, even after the tool has started executing.

If you wrote the tool yourself or have access to the tool's source code, consider the following optimizations:

- As already discussed, make sure your tool can process multiple source files in one invocation.

- When you have a choice, don't call upon an external program to perform a task; instead, use the equivalent system calls or library functions.

- Use file buffering wherever possible. Instead of reading or writing files on a byte-by-byte basis, consider whether it's faster to access the file in large chunks using internal buffers. Many operating systems and programming languages implement buffering on your behalf, but it doesn't hurt to check whether it's being done efficiently. You might be surprised that a small change to the way I/O is handled can drastically impact the tool's performance.

- Check all your tool's algorithms to see how they scale in a large build system. Tool developers often test their code in a small-scale environment (less than 100 source files) but never get the opportunity to test with many thousands of files. You might find that a small change to an internal algorithm helps the tool operate more efficiently.

- Use code-profiling techniques to see where your tool is spending its time. You'll often find that minor changes to your program can significantly improve the performance of your tool.

- When compiling open-source software from source code, enable as many optimizations as possible. Often people download, configure, compile, and install a new tool without thinking too much about what they're doing. Configuration options might make the tool more efficient, perhaps by disabling the optional features you never plan to use.

For closed-source tools, you won't have access to the source code, but you can still benefit from a couple of optimizations. Tool vendors often provide configuration options to control performance.

- Be careful to disable the tool's logging or debugging feature, unless you really need them. Log files are useful for troubleshooting problems, but the extra disk I/O might degrade performance.

- Take the time to learn about optional features, and disable them if they're not required. You can't stop them from being included in the tool (as you can with open-source tools), but the tool vendor might have provided a means to disable their use.

In summary, putting a small amount of effort into optimizing your tool algorithms and optional features can save you a lot of wasted build time. Now let's finish this section by considering how the content of the source code you're compiling impacts the performance of a compilation tool.

### Source Code Size and Implicit Dependencies

It should be no surprise that compiling a 10,000 line source file takes longer than compiling a 100 line file. The compilation tool reads and parses the source code, constructs internal data structures, and generates the corresponding object code. The larger the source file, the longer it takes.

To optimize this process, you must determine whether the tool is compiling more source code than it really needs to. Given that source code is usually the domain of software engineers instead of build engineers, you might find yourself offering the development team advice on how to optimize the source code structure.

For example, in the case of C or C++, each source file uses the #include directive to incorporate definitions from one or more header files. The compiler scans each of the header files to discover the type and structure definitions, preprocessor definitions, and function prototypes necessary to compile the main body of the source file. It's also common for a header file to include nested header files, forming a full hierarchy of file inclusion.

The question to ask is whether the program requires all these header files. Here are some cases to consider:

- The developer might have included them by mistake, even though they were never required in the first place.

- The program did require them at some point in time, but recent changes in the source code made the #include directives obsolete.

- A specific header file was included to make use of a symbol that was defined in that file. As a side effect, you also need to include a number of other header files, simply to avoid compilation errors.

This third case happens more often than you might realize. In many cases, the source code needs only a single definition from a header file, but that file contains hundreds of other definitions you're forced to include. Imagine that you have the following header file as part of an application program:

```
 1   #include <stdio.h>
 2
 3   /* graphics functions */
 4   extern void draw_line(int x1, int y1, int x2, int y2);
 5   extern void draw_circle(int x1, int y1, int radius);
 6   extern void draw_rectangle(int x1, int y1, int width, int
     height);
 7
 8   /* database functions */
 9   extern FILE *open_data(char *db_name);
10   extern void save_data(FILE *file_h);
11   extern void close_data(FILE *file_h);
```

This header file really has two separate purposes. It defines the prototypes for a number of graphics-related functions and it also defines a number of database-access functions. Notice that the stdio.h header file is included so that database functions can make use of the FILE data type.

At this point, you now have namespace pollution to deal with. A source file that performs graphics-related operations is probably not interested in using the database functions. However, because all the functions are declared in the same file, the developer doesn't really have a choice but to include everything, as well as the stdio.h file.

For a large piece of software, it's common for each source file to include literally hundreds of headers files, many of which aren't directly related to the source file being compiled. As a result, the compilation tool spends an excessive amount of time reading and parsing header files, making the build process longer than necessary.

An even worse situation occurs when the build system uses a long search path for locating header files. If the C compiler used the command-line options `-IdirA -IdirB -IdirC`, every one of the header files could potentially be found in any of the three directories, so each directory must be searched. Imagine what would happen with more than 100 directories in the search path. Discovering that a file isn't in a particular directory doesn't usually take long, but it's still unnecessary work.

Solving the header file inclusion problems takes time, especially when software developers are constantly creating new problems. Here are some approaches to consider:

- **Make use of precompiled header files if your compiler supports them.** These allow the compiler to load a binary-format version of the information in the header files instead of parsing the header files each time they're included. If the original text-format header files are modified, the precompiled header files must be regenerated.

- **From time to time, check how many header files you're actually including.** You might be surprised by the number of files, and many of them may no longer be required. Keep in mind that the common technique of placing an `#ifndef _HEADER_H_` directive at the top of a header file only stops it from being parsed multiple times; it doesn't stop the file from being read into memory each time.

- **Consider splitting your header files into a number of smaller files.** This can be a challenging task, but if it's successful, you can be more selective about which parts of the header file are included. As a result, you won't pull in directives you don't really need and won't be forced to include additional header files. Of course, there's also a performance tradeoff of including multiple small files instead of including a single large file. Use your best judgment on which situation is best.

Clearly, optimizing a build system by rearranging source files isn't always easy, but keep it in mind if you have a slow file system.

## Performance-Measurement Tools

So far, this chapter has taken an anecdotal approach to discussing performance and has avoided the question of how long each operation should actually take. Every build machine has its own unique set of timing parameters, so reading or writing a file on one machine could be dramatically faster than on a second machine. In addition, CPU, network, and disk performance constantly increase over time, so publishing numbers doesn't make much sense.

To make effective decisions on improving build performance, you need both an understanding of how the build tool works and some real timing numbers to back up your expectations. For example, you know that a default SCons build performs a large number of MD5 calculations, but you need a way to find out how long each operation actually takes. Likewise, a GNU Make system that uses .d files to store dependencies spends a lot of time reading and parsing those files. How long does each read take?

### Wall Clock Time

The first approach you should always take is to measure "wall clock" time. That is, measure how long the build process actually takes in seconds, minutes, or hours. For example, the UNIX time command provides the following output:

```
$ time make
. . .
[ build output will be shown here ]
. . .
2660.238u 279.513s 49:19.30 99.3%
```

In this example, the build system required 49 minutes and 19 seconds to complete, with 2,660 seconds (44 minutes) spent executing the compilation tools and 279 seconds (4.5 minutes) executing in the operating system kernel. The build system occupied the CPU for 99.3% of the time, indicating that I/O wasn't a bottleneck in this scenario.

This summary information isn't necessarily useful, but measuring the wall clock time for each portion of the build process enables you to narrow your search for the most time-intensive portion of the build. For example, it's useful to measure the following:

- The time required to read and parse the build description files

- The time required to determine which source files have been modified

- The time required to invoke each of the compilation tools

Depending on your build tool, you might need to insert special code into your build description to report the time at which each phase starts or completes. When you have the data, you'll have a fairly good idea of where the time is being spent.

*System Call Tracing*

Modern operating systems provide tools to monitor the interaction between a running process and the operating system kernel. In the following example, you can see how the Linux `strace` tool is used to monitor the execution of the GNU Make tool.

```
$ strace -tt -e trace=file make

9:20:28.867073 open("Makefile", O_RDONLY|O_LARGEFILE) = 3
9:20:28.867890 stat64("RCS", 0xbfa6d4d4) = -1 ENOENT
9:20:28.868048 stat64("SCCS", 0xbfa6d4d4) = -1 ENOENT
9:20:28.868104 stat64("Makefile", {st_mode=S_IFREG|0644, st_
➡size=98, ...}) = 0
9:20:28.869235 stat64("dog.o", {st_mode=S_IFREG|0644, st_
➡size=98, ...}) = 0
9:20:28.869339 stat64("dog.c", {st_mode=S_IFREG|0644, st_
➡size=43, ...}) = 0
9:20:28.869535 stat64("cat.o", {st_mode=S_IFREG|0644, st_
➡size=79, ...}) = 0
9:20:28.869636 stat64("cat.c", {st_mode=S_IFREG|0644, st_
➡size=21, ...}) = 0
9:20:28.869813 stat64("rat.o", {st_mode=S_IFREG|0644, st_
➡size=74, ...}) = 0
9:20:28.869914 stat64("rat.c", {st_mode=S_IFREG|0644, st_
➡size=21, ...}) = 0
```

In this case, you've asked the `strace` tool to report any system calls issued by the `make` program that take a filename as an argument. Additionally, you want to see the exact time (to microsecond accuracy) at which each system call was issued, to give you an idea of how long each call actually takes. Even though some of that time is spent executing the program itself (not in the kernel), this is all part of getting the task done.

Even though you might not know anything about Linux system calls, it should be possible to interpret why the `make` program is invoking those particular calls. Given your knowledge of the GNU Make tool, you can guess that the `open()` call is where `Makefile` is opened and parsed. Also, the `stat64()` calls are used to read the time stamp information of each of the source and object files.

It's not immediately obvious from this example, but disk I/O generally is a bottleneck for a build tool. (Although compilation tools are often CPU-intensive.) The fewer file accesses the build tool performs, the faster the system executes. Keep in mind that reading and writing files can take significantly longer than simply checking the time stamp on a file. In addition, although CPU operations are usually much faster than I/O operations, performing complex calculations such as an MD5 checksum can slow the build system.

The strace tool in the previous example was for the Linux operating system. Similar tools exist for Solaris, BSD, and other flavors of UNIX. Finally, several tracing programs are available for the Microsoft Windows environment.

## Fixing the Problem: Improving Performance

To finish the discussion of measuring build system performance, and to summarize the overall approach you can take to identify and resolve performance issues, you should follow three basic steps:

1. **Make sure you understand your build tool's flow of control.** Understand how the build description files are parsed, how the source files are checked to see if they're up-to-date, and how the build tool invokes compilation tools.

2. **Use wall clock time or system call traces to measure how long each phase of the build actually takes.** Also take note of the number of operations being performed. Studying these numbers will help you determine which part of the build takes the most time. Often the problem is quite dramatic, and you'll see a surprising number of files being accessed or processes being created.

3. **Revisit the design of your build system to eliminate the bottleneck.** This typically involves changing the build description files, but it could involve switching to a more efficient build tool. Making this type of change can be time-consuming, especially for a legacy build system that you don't fully understand.

This section also discussed some additional solutions:

- If you find that many small files are being created or accessed, try moving the same information into a single large file. It's usually more efficient to read large files if your build tool enables you to do so.

- If you see a large number of File not found errors when the compilation tools attempt to open header or library files, consider modifying the compiler search paths. Placing the most commonly used directories at the start of the search path reduces the number of file operations required.

- If your compilation tools include an excessive number of header files, ask your software developers to break them into smaller, more independent chunks. The goal is to reduce the total number of header files included, especially because many of them aren't actually required.

- If an excessive number of processes are being created, see if it's possible for each compilation tool to process multiple source files in one invocation instead of creating a separate process for each file.

- If a compilation tool appears to be generating files you don't need, check whether there's an option to disable the unwanted output.

- If a compilation tool takes too long to execute, check whether optional features can be disabled.

- If a compilation tool does a lot of work before it even opens the source file, consider ways to optimize the start-up process. It might be possible to disable the reading of start-up configuration files or to disable automatic tool discovery.

After you've tried all these options, you might end up deciding to completely rewrite the build system. For example, if your GNU Make–based build system is taking too long because of the thousands of small .d files being read from disk, it might be easier to move to a SCons-based build system and use a single database file to store the dependencies.

Let's now take a different approach to improving performance. In contrast to the analytical approach you've seen so far, you'll now see how the build tool can be more intelligent about avoiding work.

## Build Avoidance: Eliminating Unnecessary Rebuilds

It's a little-appreciated fact in life, but the fastest way to complete any job is to first decide whether it's worth doing. With some amount of upfront planning, you can avoid performing unnecessary tasks. The same is true for software build systems.

Every build tool discussed in this book follows the same approach of testing source files to see if they've changed. In addition, each build tool discovers the dependencies between different files to decide whether a change to one file may impact a second file. Without these features, each invocation of the build tool would result in a complete rebuild of the software.

Although most tools rely on a file's time stamp to see if it changed, some tools put more effort into making the decision. The default behavior for SCons is to compute an MD5 checksum on each file, giving a more accurate view on whether the content really is different from last time. The goal is to reduce the number of unnecessary rebuilds, at the cost of the extra upfront analysis.

This section examines a couple of advanced methods for more intelligently deciding whether recompilation is needed. This is above and beyond the simple checking of time stamps or checksums.

- **Object file caching:** When a number of software developers work on the same code base, there's a good chance that another developer has already compiled the same set of files. Object file caching creates a shared repository of object files for reuse by other developers.

- **Smart dependencies:** Most build tools assume that if file A depends on file B, then file A should be recompiled if file B changes. On the other hand, smart dependencies focus on whether the specific lines of code that changed in file B actually have an impact on file A.

This section also discusses a number of less sophisticated approaches to build avoidance, which can still save a lot of unnecessary build work.

## Object File Caching

The basic principle behind **object file caching** is that it's often faster to reuse another developer's object file than to compile it again. The obvious challenge is for the build tool to identify whether there's a cached version of the file that's exactly the same as the file you would generate.

The decision of whether an object file can be reused is challenging to implement, especially for languages such as C and C++. To ensure that an existing object file is compatible, the build tool must make sure that the same source file and header files were used and that the same command-line options were passed to the compiler. If one of the developers made local changes to a file, the object file in question shouldn't be reused.

Here's a more detailed process for determining whether an object file can be reused. The details vary from one tool to the next, but the basic process is the same.

1. Determine the exact set of source and header files that the compilation tool would read. The name of the source file is obvious, but some mechanism must exist to determine which header files are included.

2. For each source or header file, compute a checksum value. This is a substitute for reading and comparing the complete set of source files. If a developer made a local change to one of their files, the checksum would be different from that of other developers.

3. Determine exactly which compilation flags the compiler would use because these can impact the generated object code. For example, a -D definition on a C/C++ compiler's command line can impact which lines of code are compiled into the program. Also, the use of -O (optimize) or -g (debug) impacts the generated object file.

4. Search the object file cache to see if there's an existing copy of the object file compiled by another developer. An object file can be reused if it was generated from the same set of source and header files, each with the same checksum value and compiled with the same compiler options.

5. If a cached copy of the file exists, copy that file into the developer's own build tree. If not, invoke the compilation that would have originally taken place.

As you can see, a lot of upfront analysis is required before any reuse decisions are made. If a lot of files have been locally modified, the build tool does the upfront analysis yet is still required to build the object file for itself. This slows the build system.

A best practice is to allow software developers to reuse object files from the cache but not to contribute their own. For this to work, a release engineer must periodically build an untouched source tree, with the goal of populating the cache. Given that none of the files has been locally modified, there's a much higher chance that developers can reuse the cached files.

Several tools implement the object caching feature:

- **Ccache [86]:** The Ccache tool is an open-source product designed to work in conjunction with the GCC compiler. A developer uses Ccache by prefixing their gcc command line with the ccache command:

```
ccache gcc -g -c -o add.o add.c
```

Ccache is intimately familiar with the GCC command-line options and knows which options impact the object code. To identify which header files are used, Ccache passes the source file through the C preprocessor to effectively merge all source and header files. It uses this combined file to compute a hash value for the complete program.

If a matching object file is available in the shared cache, the file is copied into the developer's build tree. If the cache and the build tree are on the same file system, it's also possible to use a hard link to the cached file.

- **Clearmake:** The Clearmake tool is part of the ClearCase Source Code Management system [5]. To take advantage of Clearmake's "wink-in" feature, developers must compile their source code within a dynamic view, a special mode that enables the ClearCase server to act as a full-fledged file server. This unique feature means that ClearCase knows exactly which version of a source file you're using and whether you've made any local modifications to that file.

  Given that ClearCase is in full control of all source and object files, the developer needs to do little extra work. The ClearCase server acts as a file server, so there's no need to copy or link to the cached file. Instead, the file instantly appears at the correct location in the build tree.

  Although Clearmake uses a novel technique for sharing object files, the downside is that it's not fully compatible with GNU Make, and existing Make-base build systems might require modification. Additionally, other build tools, such as Ant and SCons, can't take advantage of the wink-in feature.

- **SCons** [56]: The SCons `Repository()` function informs the build tool where it can obtain source files or object files that don't exist in the current build tree. SCons already tracks the MD5 checksum for each file, so there's no extra work to compute checksums.

  The following example shows how the `calculator` program is built by reusing the object files from the repository. Instead of modifying the `SConstruct` file to include the `Repository()` method, you use the `-Y` flag to provide the location:

```
$ scons -Y /home/psmith/scons-repo
scons: done reading SConscript files.
scons: Building targets ...
gcc -o calculator /home/psmith/scons-repo/calc.o
     /home/psmith/scons-repo/add.o
     /home/psmith/scons-repo/mult.o
     /home/psmith/scons-repo/sub.o
scons: done building targets.
```

  In this case, SCons didn't find any object files in the local build directory, but it did find them in the repository. Instead of making a copy of the files, it simply refers to their repository location.

As a general rule, use object file caches with care. Although they often improve performance, developers can still see performance degradation, especially if too many changes are made in the local source tree. In addition, if the build tool doesn't provide you with an identical object file, you could waste hours debugging a confusing compilation error.

## Smart Dependencies

The second build-avoidance technique, **smart dependencies**, avoids an incremental compilation if a change to a file doesn't really impact other files. In most build tools, if one file depends on a second file, any change to that second file causes the first file to be recompiled. With smart dependencies, the build tool does more than simply check time stamps.

As an example, a change to a source code comment in a C header file doesn't impact the compilation of related files. Even if the header file is included into many different source files, the build output remains unchanged because comments are always thrown away. If the build tool can detect harmless code changes like this, it can avoid unnecessary work.

Note that smart dependencies have an impact only with incremental builds. There's no optimization to be gained for a completely fresh build because the object files don't yet exist and must always be compiled.

Chapter 10, "Eclipse," already touched on the idea that Eclipse uses smart dependencies, but now examine the concept in more detail. Let's look at a popular build tool for the Java language and consider how a C/C++ tool might implement this technique.

### jmake Example

The jmake tool [87] is specifically designed for compiling Java code. It's commonly used as a plug-in for Ant, introducing the `<jmake>` task as a replacement for the existing `<javac>` task. The jmake dependency system uses information from the Java `.class` files to determine whether a code change impacts other Java files.

If a developer changes any publicly visible parts of a class definition, the code change could impact the compilation of other classes. This includes any change to a public method's name, parameters, or return type. However, it doesn't include any changes to private methods or the lines of code within a method. By scanning the generated `.class` files, jmake determines the two cases.

Now illustrate this system with a Java code example. You start with two simple Java classes, A and B. Class A displays a short message and then calls the `hello()` method in class B.

A.java contains:

```
1 public class A {
2
3    public static void main(String args[]) {
```

```
4          System.out.println("Hello World");
5          B.hello();
6    }
7 }
```

`B.java` contains:

```
1 public class B {
2
3    public static void hello() {
4        System.out.println("Hello from class B");
5    }
6 }
```

When you first compile this program, `A.class` and `B.class` don't yet exist, so both source files are compiled for the first time. In addition, jmake stores information about class `A` and class `B` in a database file named `jmake.pdb`.

```
[jmake]  Jmake version 1.3.6
[jmake]  Compiling 2 source files
[jmake]  Writing project database...  Done.
```

Make a change to class `B` by adding a new code comment (see line 3).

```
1 public class B {
2
3    /* adding comments doesn't change a .class file */
4
5    public static void hello() {
6        System.out.println("Hello from class B");
7    }
8 }
```

After this change, the jmake output shows that one file (`B.java`) is being recompiled. As you might expect, the content of `B.class` won't have changed because comments don't affect the compiler output. Also, because you changed only a comment, `A.java` isn't considered for recompilation.

```
[jmake]  Jmake version 1.3.6
[jmake]  Opening project database...  Done.
[jmake]  Compiling 1 source file
[jmake]  Writing project database...  Done.
```

Now make a more significant change and add a new line of code to `B.java` (see line 7).

```
1 public class B {
2
3    /* adding comments doesn't change a .class file */
4
5    public static void hello() {
```

```
6         System.out.println("Hello from class B");
7         System.out.println("This line won't impact A's com-
          pilation");
8     }
9 }
```

Although this new line impacts the functionality of the `hello()` method—and, therefore, the behavior of class A's `main()` method—there's still no way for `A.class` to be any different from last time.

The output from jmake is now slightly different. Given that `B.class` has changed since the last time it was compiled, jmake inspects `B.class` to see if the change was publicly visible. It's not a public change, so the extra check doesn't result in any further compilation work.

```
[jmake] Jmake version 1.3.6
[jmake] Opening project database...  Done.
[jmake] Compiling 1 source file
[jmake] Checking B
[jmake] Writing project database...  Done.
```

Next, add a new method to class B (see lines 10–12).

```
 1 public class B {
 2
 3     /* adding comments doesn't change a .class file */
 4
 5     public static void hello() {
 6         System.out.println("Hello from class B");
 7         System.out.println("This line won't impact A's com-
          pilation");
 8     }
 9
10     public static void newMethod() {
11         System.out.println("newMethod won't cause A to re-
          build");
12     }
13 }
```

This might be surprising, but the output from jmake is the same as before.

```
[jmake] Jmake version 1.3.6
[jmake] Opening project database...  Done.
[jmake] Compiling 1 source file
[jmake] Checking B
[jmake] Writing project database...  Done.
```

Even when `B.class` is inspected, there's no publicly visible change. Given that `newMethod()` has been recently added, there's no way that `A.java` could have called `newMethod()` in the past, because it didn't exist. As a result, there's no way for the compilation of `A.java` to be impacted by this change.

Finally, make a change to B.java that definitely impacts the compilation of class A.java. In this case, you add a new parameter to the hello() method (see line 5).

```
 1 public class B {
 2
 3    /* adding comments doesn't change a .class file */
 4
 5    public static void hello(int i) {
 6        System.out.println("Hello from class B");
 7        System.out.println("This line won't impact A's com-
           pilation");
 8    }
 9
10    public static void newMethod() {
11        System.out.println("newMethod won't cause A to re-
           build");
12    }
13 }
```

As you might expect, jmake checks the content of B.class and detects a change to the hello() method's type signature.

```
[jmake] Jmake version 1.3.6
[jmake] Opening project database...   Done.
[jmake] Compiling 1 source file
[jmake] Checking B
[jmake] Compiling 1 source file
[jmake] /home/psmith/javamake/src/A.java:5:
        hello(int) in B cannot be applied to ()
[jmake]         B.hello();
[jmake]         ^
[jmake] 1 error
[jmake] Compilation invoked by jmake failed,
        messages should have been provided.
[jmake] Writing project database...   Done.
```

Given that A.java uses the hello() method, jmake recompiles the second source file. Unfortunately, A.java wasn't correctly updated to use the new method signature, so the compilation fails.

If you're an experienced Java programmer, you'll realize how much time this technique saves. Most code changes fall entirely within the private section of a class definition, so often there's no reason to compile anything other than the file you edited.

Smart dependencies decide only whether the compilation of related source files could be impacted. They make no decision about whether the functionality of the related classes will actually change. As a result, it's still useful to run unit tests on all classes that your code change might have impacted.

## Smart Dependencies in C/C++

The good thing about the Java language is that it's easy to distinguish the public sections of a class from the private sections. In a language such as C or C++, implementing smart dependencies is much harder. Let's briefly consider how a C/C++ build tool might solve this problem.

Dependencies in C/C++ are usually relationships between source files (.c, .C, or .cc suffix) and header files (.h suffix). When using smart dependencies, the build tool computes the list of symbols defined by each header file and then discovers where those symbols are referenced in other source and header files. If a symbol definition changes, only the source and header files that use that definition could be impacted.

Examine the following header file and associated source files. The first file, fruit.h, is a header file that defines a symbol and a new type.

```
1   /* fruit.h */
2   #define FRUIT_UNITS 10
3   typedef int ripeness;
```

The next file, apple.c, makes use of the FRUIT_UNITS symbols.

```
1   /* apple.c */
2   #include "fruit.h"
3   int get_apples_unit()
4   {
5     return FRUIT_UNITS;
6   }
```

Finally, the banana.c file uses the ripeness type definition.

```
1   /* banana.c */
2   #include "fruit.h"
3   ripeness get_banana_feel()
4   {
5     return 0;
6   }
```

In a normal dependency system, both apple.c and banana.c would depend on fruit.h. With a smart dependency system, apple.c depends only on the definition of FRUIT_UNITS, whereas banana.c depends only on the ripeness type. The build system must detect which of the symbols has changed and recompile the corresponding source file.

Nontrivial C/C++ programs could have a whole chain of dependencies. One header file could define a symbol used in the definition of a second symbol. The second symbol then could be referenced by a function defined in a source file. Any change to either of the symbol definitions could impact the source file.

Implementing a smart dependency system for C/C++ isn't impossible, but it's a lot more challenging than for a more recent language such as Java or C#. The C preprocessor enables you to define and redefine symbols to almost any value, enabling the possibility of changing the name of functions and variables without the user even knowing. For example, the following code shows how a function call can be renamed, depending on the type of the underlying OS.

The first file, os-header.h defines the WRITE symbol to refer to an operating system–specific function:

```
1   /* os-header.h */
2   #ifdef linux
3   #define WRITE write_it
4   #else
5   #define WRITE save_data
6   #endif
```

The second file, func.c, includes the header file and invokes the WRITE function. This code has a different effect, depending on the underlying operating system.

```
1   /* func.c */
2   #include "os-header.h"
3
4   int write_file(char *data)
5   {
6     WRITE(data);
7   }
```

This code isn't too hard to understand, but it would certainly make a smart dependency system a lot more complex.

## Other Build-Avoidance Techniques

To finish the discussion of build-avoidance techniques, you'll need to consider a few other ideas. These involve a lot more manual work than object file caching or smart dependencies, but they're still valid approaches.

- **Component-based builds:** As discussed in Chapter 18, "Managing Build Size," a component-based build system enables you to work with smaller source code components. Each component uses a well-defined interface to other components. As a result, you avoid the need to compile more code than necessary.

- **Plan for finer-grained build targets:** Even if you can't break your source code into components, make sure the various pieces of your software can be compiled with separate build targets. Developers are smart enough to decide which of the finer-grain targets need to be rebuilt, and doing so saves them a lot of time.

- **Manually remove files:** As build systems grow in size, there are likely to be source files that are no longer required. The build system might still compile those files on a regular basis, but the work is completely unnecessary. Performing a regular audit of the source files enables you to remove dead files or even a whole subtree that's no longer required.

- **Fine-tune recursive Make:** If you're using a recursive Make system in which the explicit sequencing of directories is hard-coded into the build system, you might find that certain directories are visited multiple times in the same build process. Fine-tuning the sequence of directories could reduce the total build time.

These methods aren't glamorous, but they reduce the time it takes to build your software, especially when performing incremental builds.

## Parallelism

Perhaps the most popular method for speeding up the build process is to use multiple CPUs to compile files in parallel. This is largely a result of the increasing popularity of multicore computers, as well as the ease at which you can cluster build machines on a local network. Up to a limit, doubling the CPU power can cut the build duration by almost half.

As discussed in Chapter 11, "Dependencies," the most important requirement for a parallel build system is to know the correct dependencies. If the build tool doesn't know that one file depends on a second, it might attempt to compile the two files at the same time or in the wrong order. This results in either a broken build or a corrupted software image.

Unfortunately, not all build systems can easily support parallel compilation. A poorly designed nonparallel build system might rely on jobs to always execute in the same order. It just happens that the compilation tools are invoked in a sequence that correctly builds the software. In reality, the dependency graph is incorrect, causing a parallel build to fail.

Parallel builds aren't too hard to understand, but let's look at a few interesting topics, including build clusters, parallel build tools, and the limitations of scalability.

## Build Clusters/Clouds

With some build tools, it's possible to invoke compilation jobs across different build machines, as long as each machine has access to the same set of files. Instead of starting a compilation tool locally, there must be a communication channel to invoke the tool on a remote machine, the capability to synchronize access to the same set of files, and the capability to send the compiler output back to the originating machine.

In a corporate environment, it's common to have a cluster dedicated for compiling code, often known as a cloud. Instead of each developer having his or her own local build machine, a central cluster is easier to manage and easier to upgrade to new equipment. As build machines fail or simply grow too old to be useful, the administrators can shut them down and replace them with new equipment. If there's a need for more CPU power, new machines can be added to the cluster.

Build clusters also provide support for queuing and monitoring of build jobs. Instead of forcing all jobs to run on the cluster at the same time, a queuing mechanism ensures that jobs receive sufficient CPU time to complete successfully. Excess jobs are simply queued until enough CPU power becomes available. The monitoring system alerts the administrator that capacity has been reached and that additional build machines might be required.

Unfortunately, fine-tuning a build cluster can be challenging. Access to files must be coordinated carefully, and if one machine writes a file, another machine might try to read that same file a few seconds later. Unless there's a guarantee that different build machines see a consistent view of the file system (challenging in a distributed system), endless reliability problems can result. A clever build tool takes care to schedule related jobs on the same machine or simply to wait until the new copy of the file is globally available.

## Parallel Build Tools

A few tools that support parallel builds, both on the same build machine and across a cluster of machines are briefly discussed.

- **GNU Make -j option:** The standard GNU Make tool can support parallel compilation, but only on the same build machine. By passing the -j *N* command-line option, GNU Make invokes up to *N* compilation tools at the same time. This is primarily useful for multicore build machines or machines with a lightly loaded CPU. The dependencies specified in each makefile must be accurate, or the build might fail.

- **The SCons -j option:** The SCons tool provides the same type of parallel functionality as GNU Make, allowing multiple compilation jobs on a single build machine. SCons does a good job of computing dependencies, so the likelihood of a successful build is quite high.

- **The distcc compiler [88]:** In contrast to GNU Make and SCons, distcc is not actually a build tool. Instead, it provides a front-end wrapper around the GCC compiler, making it possible to dispatch C compilation to remote machines. A standard build tool such as GNU Make or SCons must still be used, but instead of directly invoking the `gcc` executable program, it must invoke the `distcc` command.

  Each build machine in the cluster is required to run a special daemon process to receive and process compilation requests. The `distcc` program checks the `DISTCC_POTENTIAL_HOSTS` environment variable to discover which build machines it can dispatch jobs to.

  As usual, the same rules apply regarding the accuracy of build system dependencies.

- **ElectricAccelerator [48]:** ElectricAccelerator is a commercial product that focuses on high-performance compilation in a cluster environment. The Electric Make tool is a drop-in replacement for GNU Make and NMake, allowing existing build systems to execute seamlessly on the cluster. It also provides support for builds using Ant and SCons.

  In contrast to other build tools, ElectricAccelerator uses the file system–monitoring technique to discover implicit dependencies. It actively watches the files that each compilation tool reads or writes instead of relying only on the dependencies provided in the build description files. If it ends up executing two jobs in parallel (or in the wrong order) when they should have been sequential, ElectricAccelerator detects the conflict and reruns the first job. It also makes note of the mistake to ensure that future attempts to build the software use the correct set of dependencies.

Now let's finish the discussion by showing how the performance of a parallel build system eventually reaches a peak, no matter how many CPUs are available.

## Limitations of Scalability

Although a parallel build system is an excellent way to speed up the build process, it's not a perfect solution. Simply because you can add a new CPU to a cluster doesn't mean the build system can take advantage of that CPU.

To understand this problem, imagine a typical C/C++ build system in which a number of object files are compiled into a shared library or an executable program. For a large build system, this process repeats hundreds of times to produce all the shared libraries and executable programs required for the complete software package. In essence, the build system alternates between compiling object files and then linking those files into a library or executable program. For example:

```
gcc -g -c add.c
gcc -g -c calc.c
gcc -g -c mult.c
gcc -g -c sub.c
gcc -g -o calculator add.o calc.o mult.o sub.o
```

Although the object file–generation steps (for add.o, calc.o, mult.o and sub.o) can be executed in parallel, the linking phase is purely sequential and can be executed only on a single CPU. In this example, you'd be limited to performing four jobs in parallel, with the final job executing on its own. Adding a fifth CPU wouldn't speed up the build process.

With a large build system with multiple linking phases, each phase could be done in parallel, assuming that all the object files for each library or executable already existed. Of course, this assumes that the build tool has a global view of the dependency graph and can look ahead for future work.

A second limitation of build clusters is the result of the shared resources, such as network and file system bandwidth. Even if you add new CPUs into a cluster, the network link could reach its full capacity, slowing the build system. The same is true for the shared file system, which might not keep up with all the disk access requests.

These limitations aside, parallel builds are still an excellent way to speed up the build process.

---

## Reducing Disk Usage

As a final approach to speeding up the build process, it's important to consider how much data is written to disk. It's common knowledge that accessing data on a traditional hard disk takes several milliseconds, whereas writing the same data to main memory is thousands of times faster. By reducing the amount of data written into files, you can drastically reduce build times. This is especially true in a large build system that generates gigabytes' worth of output.

Disk access time isn't the only contributing factor to worry about. To write large amounts of data to disk, that data must first be generated by the CPU and stored in main memory. Each of these activities takes away from the build machine's capability to use that CPU power and memory space for other tasks. Simply reducing the amount of data you attempt to write saves on disk access time, CPU utilization, and main memory usage.

Consider a few simple approaches to reducing reliance on disk storage.

- **Limit the size of libraries or executable programs:** The larger your libraries or executable programs are, the more time it takes to create them from the constituent object files. If the linking process consumes too much CPU time or memory, the whole build machine slows down. This is especially noticeable when the linking process consumes most of the main memory and forces other processes to swap out to secondary storage. This swapping mechanism makes the build machine appear to freeze for the duration of the linking operation.

  Obviously, you shouldn't go to the other extreme and create too many small files, but limiting the size of each library or executable program enables the build machines to more effectively handle object file creation and linking.

- **Generate debug information only if you need it:** For any developer who wants to use a source-level debugging tool, it's mandatory to generate debugging information. When compiling the software, the compiler and linker annotate each object file with a mapping from machine code addresses back to the original lines of source code. Unfortunately, adding this debug information requires additional CPU time and disk usage.

  To reduce the size of your build output, ensure that your build system doesn't add debug information by default. Developers must still have the option to generate the information for specific parts of their code. This increases the build time and disk usage but only for the portion of the software the developer cares about, not the entire build tree.

  From a release engineering perspective, any software release intended for a customer must be built with debugging information. This information is never shipped to the customer but is kept available in case a bug is reported and a developer needs to diagnose the problem.

- **Be aware that small files require a lot of disk space:** Because of the block-structured nature of file systems, disk files tend to require more space than you often realize. For example, a 1-byte file is stored using an entire disk block, which, in many file systems, is 4 or 8KiB. If you have many small files in your build system, you might be surprised by the total usage for each build tree. This doesn't slow your build system, but it's useful to know if you're concerned about disk usage.

For example, the GNU Make build scenario that uses a separate .d file for each .c file's dependencies actually requires a full 4–8KiB for each file. From the developer's perspective, each file appears to be only 100–200 bytes long.

- **Avoid copying files to new locations:** If you analyze a build system in detail, you might find that it copies files from one part of the build tree to another without modifying the content. This seems like wasted effort, but it often results from developers trying to use that file within a different part of their build system. If the build framework can't access the file in its original location, copying the file is an attractive option.

  For example, if a software product was constructed by merging two different products, there's a good chance that two incompatible build systems were joined together. Copying the output from one of the products to the build tree for the second product could be the only way for them to conveniently share files. This is in contrast to fully rewriting the build system so that both products store files in the same build tree.

  If you decide that copying files is necessary, consider instead using symbolic links. This makes the original file appear in the new location without requiring the additional CPU time or disk space to make a completely new file. Symbolic links are messy if overused, so try to limit their use as much as possible.

- **Monitor the growth of your build tree:** It's quite reasonable to expect that as your development team writes more code, the size of your build tree increases. However, keep in mind that developers can make seemingly innocent changes to your build system that cause the build tree to grow in unexpected ways. By monitoring the size of your build tree on a regular basis, you'll keep these changes under control.

  For example, developers might download a third-party software package and add it to your source code base. They might not realize that adding this new software forces all developers to compile 10% more code than before. Try to preempt the situation and encourage developers to create a separate component that only a few people need to compile.

- **Periodically remove files you don't need:** In a mature software product, source and object files often are part of the build process but are no longer required in the final release package. To reduce build times, make an effort to identify these files and initiate a project to have them removed. At the least, remove them from the build process, even if you don't want to delete the source files.

- **Be cautious of network file systems:** Although storing source and object files on a network file server often is faster than using local disk, this isn't always true for a large build system. When a nontrivial number of developers access the same server, you'll start to see performance issues resulting from network and disk congestion. If this is the case, consider using a local disk to store build trees.

You can't ignore the fact that the worst build performance you'll ever experience is when you run out of disk space. The build process halts with an error, forcing you to remove unnecessary files before you continue. The situation is even worse if you're sharing a network file system with other users, because nobody can get work done until files are removed. Proactively watching your disk utilization is important in a healthy build environment.

## Summary

If you have concerns about the performance of your build system, try to understand how the system operates and then measure the time each phase takes. These phases include reading the build description files, creating one or more dependency graphs, computing and storing each source file's implicit dependencies, and invoking the compilation tools. By identifying the bottlenecks, it's often possible to rewrite small parts of the build system to gain an increase in performance.

Another approach to reducing build times is for the build tool to spend more time analyzing whether a file needs to be recompiled. In the case of object file caching, the build tool determines whether an object file has already been compiled by another developer, using the exact set of source files. If that's the case, the file can be copied to the local build tree instead of compiling it again.

A build system using smart dependencies spends time analyzing the impact of a source code change. The goal is to determine whether the code change is publicly visible and could impact other source files, or whether the change is limited in scope to the current file. Spending time on this upfront analysis avoids a lot of unnecessary recompilation.

Perhaps the most popular technique for speeding up the build process is to invoke multiple compilation tools in parallel. For this to work, the build system's dependency graph must be correct and the machines in the build cluster must have a globally consistent view of the source and object files. Unfortunately, theoretical and practical limits apply to the number of tasks that can be invoked in parallel.

Finally, reducing the amount of data written to disk files reduces the amount of CPU time and memory used to process the data, effectively speeding up the build process.

# References

[1]     Kumfert, Gary and Tom Epperly. 2002. *Software in the DOE: The Hidden Overhead of "The Build."* Livermore, CA: Lawrence Livermore National Laboratory.

[2]     Vesperman, Jennifer. 2006. *Essential CVS.* Second Edition. Sebastopol, CA: O'Reilly Media.

[3]     Collins-Sussman, Ben, Brian W. Fitzpatrick, and C. Michael Pilato. 2008. *Version Control with Subversion.* Second Edition. Sebastopol, CA: O'Reilly Media.

[4]     Loeliger, Jon. 2009. *Version Control with Git: Powerful Tools and Techniques for Collaborative Software Development.* Sebastopol, CA: O'Reilly Media.

[5]     Rational ClearCase. Product information available at http://www.ibm.com/software/awdtools/clearcase.

[6]     Coverity Prevent. Product information available at http://www.coverity.com.

[7]     Klocwork Insight. Product information available at http://www.klocwork.com.

[8]     FindBugs: Find Bugs in Java Programs. Project web site http://findbugs.sourceforge.net.

[9]     Google Earth. Available for download at http://www.google.com/earth.

[10]    Build Forge. Product information available at http://www.ibm.com/software/awdtools/buildforge.

[11]    ElectricCommander. Product information available at http://www.electric-cloud.com.

[12]    CruiseControl. Available for download at http://cruisecontrol.sourceforge.net.

[13]    Hudson. Available for download at https://hudson.dev.java.net.

[14]    Duvall, Paul M., Steve Matyas, and Andrew Glover. 2007. *Continuous Integration: Improving Software Quality and Reducing Risk.* Upper Saddle River, NJ: Addison-Wesley Professional.

[15]    Hähne, Ludwig. 2008. *Empirical Comparison of SCons and GNU Make*. Dresden, Germany: Technical University Dresden.

[16]    GNU Make. Software and documentation available at http://www.gnu.org/software/make/.

[17]    The Free Software Foundation. GCC, the GNU Compiler Collection. Project home http://gcc.gnu.org/.

[18]    Levine, John R. 2000. *Linkers and Loaders*. San Francisco, CA: Morgan Kaufmann.

[19]    Kernighan, Brian W. and Dennis M. Ritchie. 1988. *The C Programming Language*. Second Edition. Upper Saddle River, NJ: Prentice Hall.

[20]    ISO/IEC JTC1/SC22/WG14. 1999. The C99 Standard for the C Programming Language. Available at http://www.open-std.org/JTC1/SC22/WG14/.

[21]    Stroustrup, Bjarne. 2000. *The C++ Programming Language*. Third Edition. Upper Saddle River, NJ: Addison-Wesley Professional.

[22]    Microsoft Corporation. Visual C++ Developer Center. Documentation available at http://msdn.microsoft.com/visualc/default.aspx.

[23]    Green Hills Software. Green Hills Optimizing Compilers. Product details available at http://www.ghs.com/products/compiler.html.

[24]    Intel Corporation. Intel Compilers—Intel Software Network. Product details available at http://software.intel.com/en-us/intel-compilers/.

[25]    The Free Software Foundation. GCC online documentation. Tool documentation available at http://gcc.gnu.org/onlinedocs/.

[26]    von Hagen, William. 2006. *The Definitive Guide to GCC*. Second Edition. Berkeley, CA: Apress.

[27]    Tool Interface Standard Committee. 1995. Executable and Linking Format (ELF) Specification. http://refspecs.freestandards.org/elf/elf.pdf.

[28]    Objdump manual page. http://linux.die.net/man/1/objdump.

[29]    Lindholm, Tim and Frank Yellin. 1999. The Java Virtual Machine Specification. Second Edition. Upper Saddle River, NJ: Prentice Hall. Also available in HTML format at http://java.sun.com/docs/books/jvms.

[30]    Oracle Corporation. Software and documentation available at http://www.oracle.com/technetwork/java/index.html.

[31]    OpenJDK. Software and documentation available at http://openjdk.java.net.

[32]    The Free Software Foundation. The GNU Compiler for the Java Programming Language. http://gcc.gnu.org/java/.

[33]    Eclipse.org Home. Software and documentation available at http://www.
        eclipse.org.

[34]    Microsoft Corporation. .NET Framework Developer Center. http://
        msdn.microsoft.com/netframework.

[35]    ECMA International (2006). Standard ECMA-335. Common Language
        Infrastructure (Fourth Edition). Documentation available at http://www.
        ecma-international.org/publications/standards/Ecma-335.htm.

[36]    Microsoft Corporation. Microsoft/Express. Available for download at
        http://www.microsoft.com/express.

[37]    The Mono Project Page. http://mono-project.com.

[38]    Microsoft Corporation. Microsoft Portable Executable and Common
        Object File Format Specification. http://www.microsoft.com/whdc/
        system/platform/firmware/PECOFF.mspx.

[39]    Rumbaugh, James, Ivar Jacobson, and Grady Booch. 2004. *The Unified
        Modelling Language Reference Manual*. Second Edition. Upper Saddle
        River, NJ: Addison-Wesley Professional.

[40]    Feldman, S. 1979. *Make: A Program for Maintaining Computer
        Programs*. Murray Hill, New Jersey: Bell Laboratories.

[41]    Mecklenburg, Robert. 2005. *Managing Projects with GNU Make*. Sebas-
        topol, CA: O'Reilly.

[42]    Graham-Cumming, John. *Ask Mr. Make*. Series of articles archived at
        http://electric-cloud.com/resources/mrmake.php.

[43]    GNU Make Standard Library. Available for download at http://gmsl.
        sourceforge.net.

[44]    Miller, Peter. 1998. "Recursive Make Considered Harmful." *AUUGN
        Journal of AUUG Inc.*, 19(1).

[45]    Graham-Cumming, John. GNU Make Debugger. Software and docu-
        mentation available at http://gmd.sourceforge.net.

[46]    FreeBSD Man Pages: Make. Online manual page for the FreeBSD version
        of Make. http://www.freebsd.org/cgi/man.cgi?query=make.

[47]    Microsoft Corporation. NMAKE Reference. Documentation available at
        http://msdn.microsoft.com/en-us/library/dd9y37ha.aspx.

[48]    Electric Cloud, Inc., ElectricAccelerator: Software Build Acceleration.
        Product web site http://www.electric-cloud.com/products.

[49]    Electric Cloud, Inc., SparkBuild. Software and documentation available
        at http://www.sparkbuild.com.

[50]    The Apache Software Foundation. The Apache Ant Project. Software and documentation available at http://ant.apache.org.

[51]    Loughran, Steve, and Erik Hatcher. 2007. *Ant in Action*. Greenwich, CT: Manning Publications.

[52]    Ant-Contrib Tasks. Available at http://ant-contrib.sourceforge.net.

[53]    NAnt home page. Software and documentation available at http://nant. sourceforge.net/.

[54]    Microsoft Corporation. MSBuild Reference. Documentation available at http://msdn.microsoft.com/en-us/library/wea2sca5.aspx.

[55]    Hashimi, Sayed and William Bartholomew. 2009. *Inside the Microsoft Build Engine: Using MSBuild and Team Foundation Build*. Redmond, WA: Microsoft Press.

[56]    The SCons Foundation. SCons: A Software Construction Tool. Software and documentation available at http://www.scons.org.

[57]    Python Programming Language: Official Website. Software and documentation available at http://www.python.org/.

[58]    Beazley, David M. 2009. *Python Essential Reference*. Fourth Edition. Upper Saddle River, NJ: Addison-Wesley Professional.

[59]    Cons: A Make Replacement. Software and documentation available at http://www.gnu.org/software/cons.

[60]    Rake: Ruby Make. Software and documentation available at http://rake. rubyforge.org.

[61]    CMake: Cross Platform Make. Software and documentation available at http://www.cmake.org.

[62]    Martin, Ken, and Bill Hoffman. 2007. *Mastering CMake*. Clifton Park, NY: Kitware, Inc.

[63]    Vaughan, Gary, Ben Elliston, Tom Tromey, and Ian Lance Taylor. 2001. *GNU Autoconf, Automake and Libtool*. Berkeley, CA: New Riders.

[64]    Qt: Cross-platform Application and UI Framework. Software and documentation available at http://qt.nokia.com.

[65]    Carlson, David. 2005. *Eclipse Distilled*. Upper Saddle River, NJ: Addison-Wesley Professional.

[66]    Clayberg, Eric, and Dan Rubel. 2008. *Eclipse Plug-ins*. Third Edition. Upper Saddle River, NJ: Addison-Wesley Professional.

[67]    The Free Software Foundation. GDB: The GNU Project Debugger. Tool documentation available at http://www.gnu.org/software/gdb/ documentation/.

[68]    The Free Software Foundation. DDD: Data Display Debugger. Available at http://www.gnu.org/software/ddd.

[69]    DWARF Standards Committee. The DWARF Debugging Standard. Standards documentation available at http://dwarfstd.org.

[70]    GNU gprof. Documentation available at http://sourceware.org/binutils/docs/gprof/index.html.

[71]    Doxygen. Software and documentation available at http://www.doxygen.org.

[72]    DOC++. Software and documentation available at http://docpp.source-forge.net.

[73]    Sandcastle: Documentation Compiler for Managed Class Libraries. Software and documentation available at http://sandcastle.codeplex.com.

[74]    JUnit.org: Resources for Test Driven Development. Software and Documentation available at http://www.junit.org.

[75]    Meszaros, Gerard. 2007. *xUnit Test Patterns: Refactoring Test Code.* Upper Saddle River, NJ: Addison-Wesley.

[76]    Feathers, Michael. 2004. *Working Effectively with Legacy Code.* Upper Saddle River, NJ: Prentice Hall.

[77]    *The 7-Zip Archive Tool.* Available at http://www.7-zip.org.

[78]    The RPM Package Manager. Documentation available at http://www.rpm.org.

[79]    Flexera Software. Install Shield Product Page. http://www.flexerasoftware.com/products/installshield.htm.

[80]    Microsoft Corporation. Windows Installer. http://msdn.microsoft.com/en-us/library/cc185688%28VS.85%29.aspx.

[81]    The Nullsoft Scriptable Install System. Information at http://nsis.sourceforge.net/Main_Page.

[82]    Cygwin Installation and Information. Software and documentation available at http://www.cygwin.com.

[83]    Aho, Alfred V., Monica S. Lam, Ravi Sethi, and Jeffrey D. Ullman. *Compilers: Principles, Techniques, and Tools.* Second Edition. Upper Saddle River, NJ: Addison-Wesley.

[84]    The Apache Maven Project. Software and documentation available at http://maven.apache.org.

[85]    Ivy: The Agile Dependency Manager. Software and documentation available at http://ant.apache.org/ivy.

[86]    ccache: A Fast C/C++ Compiler Cache. Software and documentation available at http://ccache.samba.org.

[87]    The JMAKE Utility. Software and documentation available at http://kenai.com/projects/jmake.

[88]    distcc: A Fast, Free Distributed C/C++ Compiler. Software and documentation available at http://distcc.org.

[89]    Standard ECMA-119 Volume and File Structure of CD-ROM for Information Interchange. Specification available at http://www.ecma-international.org/publications/standards/Ecma-119.htm.

[90]    Basics of the Debian Package-Management System. Documentation available at http://www.debian.org/doc/FAQ/ch-pkg_basics.

[91]    Flex: The Fast Lexical Analyzer. Software and documentation available at http://flex.sourceforge.net.

[92]    Bison: GNU Parser Generator. Software and documentation available at http://www.gnu.org/software/bison.

[93]    Conway, Mel. 1968. How Do Committees Invent? http://www.melconway.com/Home/Conways_Law.html.

# Index

## A

aborting scripts, 469
About menu, 410
access
  administrator, disallowing, 422
  disks, 549
  files, 10
  source code, 528-529
Active Server Pages (ASP), 4, 7
add_executable command, 241
adding
  components, versions, 507
  custom commands, 242-243
hidden commands, 474
  machine code, 339
  metadata, 349-350
  targets, 242-243
  unit test variants, 344-347
add_library command, 241, 256
addprefix function, 117
add_subdirectory command, 256
administrator access, disallowing, 422
advantages of using components,
  491-493
algorithms, tasks, 165
Alias function, 212
analyzing
  Ant, 191-193
  brute-force analysis, 348
  CMake, 262-263
  dependencies, 156, 167, 210-212,
    277-278
  Eclipse, 298-299
  SCons, 231-232
  static analysis, 336, 348-349
  static tools, 4, 8-9, 29
Ant, 10, 98, 154
  analyzing, 191-193
  built-in tasks, 164-168
  conditions, 170-171

  directories, 168
  extending, 172-173
  flow of control, 161-162
  frameworks, 459
  Hello World, 157-158
  languages, 156-174
  out-of-date files, 324
  properties, defining, 162-164
  targets, defining, 158-160
  tools, 193-195
Apache
  Ivy, 512-514
  Tomcat, 284
APIs (application programming
    interfaces), 45, 491
  modifying, 501
applets, Java, 285
application programming interfaces
  (APIs), 45, 491, 501
applications
  Eclipse, 285
  installers, 374
     *See also installation*
  web-based, 6-7
applying
  build systems, 18-20
  frameworks, 31-33
  internal project models, 285-286
  multiple environments, 207-208
  relative pathnames, 479
  symbolic links, 479
  targets, 158-160
architectures, targets, 84, 94-98
archive files, 16
  formatting, 356
  JAR files, 281, 496, 514
  packaging, 352-359
arguments
  caches, updating, 320-322
  command-line, 316
ASP (Active Server Pages), 4, 7

**559**

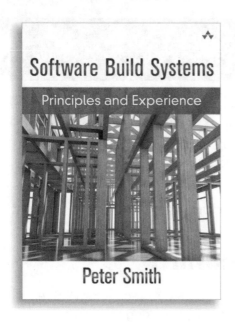

# FREE Online Edition

Your purchase of **Software Build Systems** includes access to a free online edition for 45 days through the Safari Books Online subscription service. Nearly every Addison-Wesley Professional book is available online through Safari Books Online, along with more than 5,000 other technical books and videos from publishers such as Cisco Press, Exam Cram, IBM Press, O'Reilly, Prentice Hall, Que, and Sams.

**SAFARI BOOKS ONLINE** allows you to search for a specific answer, cut and paste code, download chapters, and stay current with emerging technologies.

## Activate your FREE Online Edition at
## www.informit.com/safarifree

> **STEP 1:** Enter the coupon code: JLAWXFA.

> **STEP 2:** New Safari users, complete the brief registration form.
> Safari subscribers, just log in.

If you have difficulty registering on Safari or accessing the online edition, please e-mail customer-service@safaribooksonline.com

---